D1443363

The Lotus Quest

Also by Mark Griffiths

The New Royal Horticultural Society Dictionary of Gardening (editor)

The Royal Horticultural Society Index of Garden Plants

*The RHS Manuals—Climbers; Bulbs;
Orchids; Grasses* (series editor and author)

The RHS Shorter Dictionary of Gardening (with Michael Pollock)

A Century of Photographs: Gardening

Orchids: The Fine Art of Cultivation

The Lotus Quest

IN SEARCH OF THE SACRED FLOWER

Mark Griffiths

St. Martin's Press   New York

www.stmartins.com

Library of Congress Cataloging-in-Publication Data

Griffiths, Mark, 1963–
    The lotus quest : in search of the sacred flower / Mark Griffiths. — 1st U.S. ed.
        p. cm.
    ISBN 978-0-312-64148-1
    1. Lotus. 2. Lotus—History. I. Title.
QK495.L52G75 2010
583'.89—dc22

                                                    2010013035

First published in Great Britain by Chatto & Windus

First U.S. Edition: July 2010

10 9 8 7 6 5 4 3 2 1

For Yoko Otsuki
little leaf, big tree

Contents

III. Seeds of Eternity

IV. Tales of Genji

List of Illustrations

The Great Drum Bridge at Tsurugaoka Hachiman-gū, Kamakura, photograph by Yoshio Wada
Lady Masako's white Genji lotus, photograph by Yoshio Wada
The altar of Konjiki-dō. Temple authorities, Chūson-ji
Chūson-ji-hasu. Temple authorities, Chūson-ji

Section Two

Terracotta fertility goddess from Pakistan. Fayez Barakat, Barakat Gallery
Clay plaque of Astarte from Beth Shemesh. University of Pennsylvania Museum
Puabi's gold head-dress. University of Pennsylvania Museum
Coin from Croton. Classical Numismatic Group, www.cngcoins.com
Stone relief from the Apadana Palace, Persepolis. Bridgeman
Red figure ware drinking vessel. Fayez Barakat, Barakat Gallery
Stone relief of a winged genie. Private Collection/Giraudon/Bridgeman
Fragment of ivory lotus 'tree'. Ashmolean Museum, University of Oxford UK/ Bridgeman
Assyrian relief of Sargon II. Musée du Louvre. Author
Hexagonal stucco relief from Samarra. Iraq Museum, Baghdad
Darius the Great, from Persepolis. Giraudon/Bridgeman
Column base, photograph by Alireza Abkari
Silver lotus leaf phiale. Fayez Barakat, Barakat Gallery
Relief from the Great Stupa, Sanchi. J-E Berger Foundation, Lausanne
Detail from St Mary's, Iffley, by Edward Wilson. The Vicar and Churchwardens of Iffley
Nelum Pokuna, lotus bath. Polonnaruwa, Sri Lanka/Bridgeman
Jōmon lotus-lipped urn. Kyōdo no Mori Museum, Fuchu City. Author
Jōmon lotus receptacle toggle. Kyōdo no Mori Museum, Fuchu City
Jōmon model of a receptacle with seeds. Edo-Tokyo Open Air Architectural Museum, Fuchu City. Author
Jōmon ear-ring fragment depicting rhizome. Edo-Tokyo Open Air Architectural Museum, Fuchu City. Author
Kofun Period bronze mirror. Amagi Historical Museum, Asakura City, Fukuoka Prefecture
Earthenware roof tile. Kyōdo no Mori Museum, Fuchi City. Author
Semi-abstract lotus tiles at Zuigan-ji, Matsushima. Author
Jūichimen Kannon. Hokke-ji, Nara. University of Washington Libraries, Special Collections

Acknowledgements

My first thanks must go to Taeko Goto who not only inspired *The Lotus Quest* and shared her immense knowledge of *Nelumbo* with me but was also a perfect host in Japan. At Tokyo University's Experimental Station for Landscape Plants, Sadao Minami and Fumiko Ishizuna showed me the world's largest lotus collection, close to the site of Dr Ōga's famous find in Kemigawa. Minami-sensei also shared his recollections of the discovery of Ōga's lotus, and his expertise as President of the Japan Lotus Cultivation Society. Hisao Sakamoto gave me a wealth of material relating to Dr Ōga's career and that of his own father, the renowned lotus breeder and scholar, Yūji Sakamoto. The Mayor of Fuchu, Tadanao Noguchi, made me welcome in his city and placed its academic resources at my disposal. Staff at Fuchu's Edo-Tokyo Open Air Architectural Museum showed me the oldest surviving evidence of lotus culture, and the curator Hironori Asakawa painstakingly answered my questions. At the Fuchu City Museum I was shown relics of the same ancient culture, and the librarian Haruko Baba brought me closer to the present by unearthing a cache of Dr Ōga's papers.

In Tokyo the great potter and plantsman Shunji Mitsuhashi and his wife Noriko introduced me to the rites and arts of Traditional Japanese Horticulture. At the Tokyo National Museum, Masayuki Takanashi shed light on the lotus during the Tokugawa Shogunate. I am also grateful to Toyohiro Uchino of Shirakawa City Museum and to Atsushi Nishibayashi of Tenri University Library who helped paint a portrait of the plant's Edo

Period glory. I was made welcome in Kamakura by Professor Hideaki Ōba and Kunihiko Mōtō under the aegis of CULTA, Japan's institute for cultivated plant taxonomy. Their colleague Gen'ichi Mori was unstintingly helpful with my enquiries concerning Japanese fauna and other matters. I thank the resolutely anonymous priest at Tsurugaoka Hachiman-gū who brought the creation of Kamakura's greatest shrine and of Lady Masako's lotus ponds so vividly to life. The historian Masaaki Katō kindly furnished further information on this garden which was the birthplace of an entire society. To have met Yōzō In'nami in the midst of his hunt for the Utsunomiya Castle Lotus was great good fortune, and greater still now that his quest has borne fruit.

I am grateful to Yasuo Yatsui, Mayor of Ōjiya, for giving me the opportunity to experience rural life around his beautiful city, and to Kōichi Iwafuchi and Hiromitsu Yanagita for introducing me to the region's wild and cultivated flora. In Sendai, Toyo Ōtsuki shared her home and garden with a generosity rare even by Japanese standards. Her willingness to intimate the more personal and poignant aspects of lotus culture is typical of her warmth. Fumihiro Ōtsuki opened my eyes to the history and beauties of Sendai City and the mysterious lotus lakes of Miyagi Prefecture. Still further north, the Chief Priest Chōgen Haseki (Haseki-Jūshoku) was an inspiring guide to Chūson-ji and the lotuses that flourish there. Without the benefit of his enlightenment, there would have been no conclusion to quest and book.

From the start, my agent Michael Alcock has been encouragement personified. Having been slow to germinate, the book became rampant. Its eventual form and flowering are due to the brilliant cultivation skills of Jenny Uglow, Editorial Director of Chatto & Windus. My warm thanks go to her colleague Parisa Ebrahimi, who not only managed the book's progress but also placed the priceless lotuses of Persia within my grasp. Gina Douglas and staff at the Linnean Society of London revealed the botanical specimen that triggered the quest, and countless other resources. At Worcester College, Oxford, Edward Wilson fed me with clues, questions and texts in the great tutorial tradition. The chapters dealing with Japan's influence on Western culture especially would have been barren without him. Again in Oxford, Brian and Vicky Harrison provided support of every other kind – no author could wish for better friends.

That great collector of antiquities, Fayez Barakat, gave me the run of his treasures, yielding numerous lotuses from the Near East. Nearer home, the

Acknowledgements

Reverend Andrew McKearney allowed me to botanise amid the stone blooms of St Mary's, Iffley. I am also indebted to Oxford's Bodleian Library and Ashmolean Museum, the Lindley Library of the Royal Horticultural Society, the Royal Cornwall Museum, Truro, the British Museum, the Musée du Louvre, the National Museum of Iran, and the Iraq Museum, Baghdad, all rich lotus repositories. My last and largest thanks go to Yoko Otsuki who translated many of the key materials for *The Lotus Quest* and led the way to Japan's Deep North as guide and interpreter. Her steadfastness during the book's gestation has been second only to that of the lotus seed.

Extract from 'Canto IV' taken from *The Cantos* © The Ezra Pound Literary Property Trust and reproduced by permission of Faber and Faber Ltd. Extract from 'Burnt Norton' taken from *Four Quartets* © The Estate of T.S. Eliot and reproduced by permission of Faber and Faber Ltd. Haiku on p.259 from *The Narrow Road to the Deep North and Other Travel Sketches* by Matsuo Bashō translated with an introduction by Nobuyuki Yuasa (Penguin Classics, 1966). Copyright © Nobuyuki Yuasa, 1966. Reproduced by permission of Penguin Books Ltd. Haiku on p.259 from *The Narrow Road to Oku* by Matsuo Bashō, translated by Donald Keene. Published by Kodansha International Ltd., 1996. Reproduced by permission. All rights reserved. All other Bashō translations by Yoko Otsuki and Mark Griffiths. Quotation from *The Lotus Sutra*, translated by Burton Watson. Copyright 1993, Columbia University Press. Reprinted with permission of the publisher. Excerpt from *Mysticism: Christian and Buddhist* by D.T. Suzuki. Published by Routledge, Copyright © The Buddhist Society, London, 2002.

1

Prologue: In the Strong Room

A human skull is carved on the column beside the entrance. As we waited for our guest that morning, a flock of schoolchildren gathered around it. One of them began poking the eye sockets of this stone memento mori. A girl in the group told him to stop, that it was gross, possibly dangerous, and certainly not allowed. He knew better. This, he informed her, was how you found treasure. He was soon disappointed. No matter how vigorously he jabbed the death's head, there was no dull click, no grinding of megalithic mechanics, no slab that slid miraculously away to reveal a long-lost tomb.

What this treasure-hunter could not have known is that beneath him was a subterranean vault. Had he seen its contents, he would probably have found them just as disappointing as the unresponsive skull, but for biologists they are worth an entire unplundered Valley of the Kings. The vault is a room-sized safe, complete with bomb-proof door and combination lock. Its interior is more civilised than the *mise en scène* for the usual crime caper – softly lit, floored and shelved with polished hardwood, and atmospherically controlled. Once smelt, its odour is never forgotten, a blend of ancient vellum, beeswax polish and a potpourri of what, 250 years ago, was very nearly every known plant in the world. It is the odour of the library, archives and specimens amassed by the great Swedish botanist and father of modern biology Carl von Linné – Linnaeus – over a long and prolific lifetime.

The strongroom's contents form the nucleus of the Linnean Society of London. Founded in 1788, ten years after Linnaeus's death, it is the oldest society devoted to natural history, a fact manifest in its air of antique elegance. Along with other learned societies and the Royal Academy of Arts, the Linnean occupies Burlington House, Piccadilly's Palladian palazzo. Its rooms are lofty, colonnaded and galleried, dense with portraits and busts, papers and tomes, bell jars and brass scientific instruments. It is the archetype of the academic institution of yesteryear, a place from which one could imagine a defiant Professor Challenger embarking in search of the Lost World.

And yet these amber-frozen charms are deceptive. Beginning with its espousal of the work of Linnaeus himself, the society has always been the launch site of new and far-reaching departures in biology. This was where the world first heard of evolution by natural selection and where, in the following century, scientists shaped new disciplines such as ecology, heralded new techniques like DNA analysis, and predicted the new threats of mass extinction and climate change. The same innovative role is played by Linnaeus's herbarium specimens and library. They are not preserved in their underground safe like the relics of a patriarch; nor is their interest purely historical. They may have been dead for over two centuries, but in terms of their influence these pressed flowers, pinned beetles and flayed lizards are alive and active.

By international agreement, the scientific naming and classification of organisms begin with Linnaeus's work in the eighteenth century. Whenever biologists reassess known species or add new ones to their number, they must consider what has gone before, whether and how these organisms have been named already and where they have been placed on the map of life. More often than not, this process of diligence starts by consulting Linnaeus who gave a vast number of plants and animals their first formally accepted names. For each name he coined, the botanist also chose a specimen to exemplify his concept. Called the type, this specimen furnished the new species' evidential basis, its single and indisputable forensic reality. This has remained the basic method of taxonomists – biological namers, describers and classifiers – ever since. The strongroom of the Linnean Society is a collection of types which amounts to the world's first official registry of organisms. Enshrined in its herbarium sheets are the scientific identities of many of the plants we encounter day to day. Even taxonomists who work with wholly unfamiliar species take bearings from and make discoveries in this subterranean vault, this buried capsule of life on earth.

There were four of us in the strongroom – Gina Douglas, then the Linnean

Society's Librarian and Archivist; myself; Yoko Otsuki, my companion in life and botanical adventures; and our guest Taeko Goto, newly arrived from Japan. Taeko-san had come into our lives via an exchange of emails on the subject of the sacred lotus, a plant to which she consecrated her scholarly and spiritual devotions, her talents as a gardener, and even her skills as a cook. The thrust of these messages was that she knew Linnaeus had given the lotus its first accepted botanical name in 1753. She also knew he had pressed a live plant as the type of his newly named species and that this specimen now resided in the strongroom. She had proposed flying from Tokyo with a single mission – to see this desiccated bloom that had become the botanical standard by which all other lotuses were assessed. The least I could do was to arrange a viewing.

Beneath the pavements of Piccadilly, Gina Douglas produced a vellum-wrapped bundle of herbarium sheets. Wearing white cotton gloves, we sifted through the pile until we arrived at the object of Taeko-san's quest. Gummed across the bottom of the sheet, more or less intact, was a single leaf some 15 centimetres across. Above it was a flower, a crown of petals pressed flat soon after it opened in one North European dawn some 250 years ago. To either side of this bloom, a long-stalked bud and seed head were displayed like two sceptres. Below the leaf were two words written in Linnaeus's hand. One of them, *Taratti*, was a vernacular South-east Asian name for the lotus noted by the German botanist Georg Eberhard Rumphius in *Herbarium Amboinense*, his Indonesian flora published posthumously in 1741. The other was *Nelumbo*, the Sinhalese word for the same plant, recorded by the French botanist Joseph Pitton de Tournefort in 1700.

While perfectly legible, the botanist's ink had fared worse than the specimen. Linnaeus's lotus recalled tales of saintly sepulchres which, when opened, reveal their centuries-old incumbents in a state of miraculous preservation. Its foliage retained the blue-grey bloom of the plant in life. Although faded, the single flower held a hint of rose pink and had scarcely withered. The fruiting head rattled with seeds which, in the light of all that has happened since, I suspect might still be viable. Even more striking was the specimen's size. Until then, my own experience of the lotus was limited to the few plants I had encountered in gardens. But I knew enough to know it was a giant by nature, easily 1.5 metres tall and with leaves as much as a metre wide. By contrast, Linnaeus's plant fitted comfortably on an A3 sheet. I asked Taeko-san whether this was normal.

3

'No,' she replied, 'it's abnormally small. It may have been underfed or confined, which would have had a dwarfing effect. Or it might be something much more exciting – a miniature cultivar of the kind we call *chawan-basu*, "tea bowl lotuses", which have long been popular in China and Japan. The answer depends on how this plant was grown and where it came from, but I don't suppose we can really hope to know either now.'

Gina Douglas took a more sanguine view and pointed us in the direction of the paper trail that led to the parchment petals. In the autumn of 1735, the twenty-eight-year-old Linnaeus became curator of one of the finest private gardens ever made. It was created at De Hartekamp, the estate near Haarlem of George Clifford, an Anglo-Dutch banker, merchant and director of the Dutch East India Company. Clifford used his domination of Eastern trade routes to acquire an unprecedented range of plants, many of which were new to Western science and cultivation. His collection helped to make the Low Countries the clearing house and the powerhouse of modern botany. It also opened Linnaeus's eyes to a welter of biodiversity which he made it his life's work to render accessible. As he told his patron: 'I was astonished when I entered your hothouses, crammed with such profusion, such variety of plants as to enchant a son of the cold North, uncomprehending of the strange new world into which you had brought him.'

Among Clifford's 'treasures of Asia', as Linnaeus called them, was the lotus. In *Hortus Cliffortianus*, his catalogue of the De Hartekamp garden, Linnaeus styled this plant *Nymphaea foliis undique integris*, 'the waterlily with completely whole leaves'. When it appeared in 1738, this phrase was both a name and a description. As early eighteenth-century botanical names went, it was not that bad: it neatly differentiated the lotus from all other waterlilies whose leaves were cleft at the base; it was also only four words long. Compare it with another lotus name Linnaeus cites, the English botanist Leonard Plukenet's mouthful from 1696 – *Nymphaea glandifera indiae paludibus gaudens, foliis umbilicatis amplis, pediculis spinosis, flore roseo-purpureo* ('the marsh-loving nut-bearing Indian waterlily with large, navel-centred leaves, prickly stalks and rose-purple flowers'). This is the longest of eight scientific names, apart from Linnaeus's own invention, that were then in circulation for the same plant. The situation was a free-for-all. Any one of these labels was as good as the next. Which one prevailed was a matter of taste and who could shout loudest. This was no way to catalogue a garden, let alone run a science.

Having to deal with monsters like Plukenet's name for the lotus propelled

Linnaeus towards his simplest and greatest invention, binomial nomenclature. Within two decades of entering George Clifford's hothouses, he had separated the functions of naming and describing – how, after all, did *Carl Linné* describe him? He had decreed that any organism could have only one officially accepted name; that the name should be uniquely its own; and that it should consist of two essential parts – genus and species. In the case of the lotus, he went back to his days at De Hartekamp and to the earliest mention of this plant that he had found in Clifford's library – *Nelumbo*, the Sri Lankan name set down by de Tournefort in 1700. This became the specific epithet of Linnaeus's new species, *Nymphaea nelumbo*, published in 1753. It endures to this day in the currently accepted scientific binomial of the sacred lotus, *Nelumbo nucifera*.

But why was Linnaeus's lotus so small? The botanist's own description of its source – Clifford's garden – makes it clear that growing conditions were optimal. The plants were kept under glass in tanks; their boggy substrate was richly fertile. So we could exclude the possibility that the lotus was a starving dwarf which in happier circumstances would have been a giant. That left one other possibility – it was a horticultural variety that was dwarf by design, a miniature cultivar that had travelled from the Far East along the same trade routes that made George Clifford one of Europe's richest men. Taeko-san explained that chawan-basu, the lotuses so small they could be grown in tea bowls, had been popular pot plants in her country for around a century by the time Clifford's Haarlem paradise took root. Since his plant prospectors were active in Japan, that seemed the likely source of his and Linnaeus's lotus.

Having yielded a few more secrets, the specimen was wrapped again and consigned to its cupboard. We stepped from the strongroom into a different atmosphere and age. The massive door swung shut with an air-lock rush. Outside the Linnean Society, beneath the arch of Burlington House, we gathered ourselves beside the column with its stone skull. I ventured that it was a long way to have flown to see a plant that was probably Japanese.

'Not at all,' said Taeko-san. 'We can't be sure it's from Japan, and I'm not in the least disappointed. It was wonderful to see Linnaeus's lotus and his handwriting, and to think of it growing here in Europe all that time ago. I must find some way to thank you.'

A fortnight later, a matchbox-sized package arrived from Tokyo. Within were three seeds which resembled black acorns, wrapped in a sheet of minutely written instructions. Following these, I set about making a shallow nick in the outer coats of the seeds. Never before had I encountered such a diamond-hard substance in a plant. They brushed aside an entire *batterie de cuisine*, finally surrendering only when fixed in a vice and attacked with a file. Next I cast them adrift in a tank filled with tepid rainwater and peaty loam. Before the murk had cleared, the seeds began to swell, although how anything so obdurate and lifeless-seeming could double in size was a mystery. Whatever it was, the force within the shell was greater than any I had brought to bear on its exterior. A strange dance ensued in which the seeds shuddered, swayed and spiralled up and down from brim to bed before settling and pushing out a shoot, a comma of brilliant emerald. After just three days they produced their first leaves – the size and shape of an old penny, aquamarine, water-repellent and quilted with hair-fine veins. Within a fortnight the leaves had crossed the soupy surface like Lilliputian stepping stones.

As spring turned to summer, the lotus seedlings demanded new homes – three clay urns filled with water, peaty compost and rotted manure, which foul mixture they had a remarkable talent for turning clear and sweet. They prospered in a hot spot on the terrace. No longer floating but soaring, their leaves came to resemble parasols and were much the same size. Sea green and bloomy, their surfaces sent raindrops racing like mercury – a trick I never tired of watching even when it meant getting soaked to the skin. In autumn, as the leaves faded and collapsed, I reconciled myself to that having been that: nothing so exotic would survive a winter outside in Oxford and there was certainly no room for them indoors. Then a message arrived from Taeko-san telling me that if I cut the dead leaves back, drained the water and covered the urns, all would be well.

The following May, within days of my uncovering the urns and replenishing the water, the three seedlings were racing away, larger and stronger than ever. That summer, deep in the dog days, the first flowers appeared. Held on yard-high wands, the crimson buds opened in the dawn with the faintest of sounds, somewhere between a whisper and a kiss. As the sun peaked they expanded, becoming bowls of pale rose petals that brimmed with head-spinning perfume, an intoxicating blend of ylang-ylang, spices and sweet fermenting fruit. Each bloom lasted no longer than a day or two, but each was an event. No sooner had the last petals dropped than the seed pods began to develop, long-stalked spinning tops with honeycombed upper surfaces. As the season drew to a close, these reminders of the summer's rapture persisted, gauntly sculptural and still more striking than anything else in the garden.

The spring after they flowered, Taeko-san was in London again and we met for dinner.

'Those seeds I sent you. I'm so glad they made it. You see, they came from a very famous plant which germinated from a seed found in a dig near Tokyo.' I was about to thank her again for her gift, to attempt to convey the mesmeric effect of their shooting and blooming, when I began to wonder a little at that word *dig*.

'Yes,' she continued, 'the other relics found with it were carbon dated so we think we know the age of the lotus, or of the seed that it and so yours sprouted from.'

I dropped my fork. '*Carbon dated?* How old is it?'

She looked slightly embarrassed: 'Oh, three thousand years, give or take a few centuries.'

Inspired by the matchbox miracle, I had begun lotus-gathering even before this revelation. Yoko was pressed into translating my endless email enquiries to Taeko-san. In libraries where I was meant to be researching some aspect of garden history, perhaps an antique rose or a patrician folly, I found myself strangely drawn to shelves devoted to aquatic plants, theology and archaeology, and perplexed to find no English work on the world's most famous flower. Museums began to exert a greater pull on me than botanic gardens. In my own garden, the lotuses made me forgetful of all duties except watching and watering the three clay bowls. As autumn advanced and there was no longer anything to watch, I started assembling a biography of the lotus instead. Yoko had begun to worry that I was becoming a fanatic. Now I could offer her the news that my treasures were the offspring of a three-thousand-year-old seed as vindication of my zeal.

'You're obsessed,' she said.

'Yes,' I replied, 'but it's a rational obsession.'

Taeko-san's gift had become the seeds of a quest. Spent among those libraries and museums, its first phase took me to Ancient Egypt, Greece and Rome, to times and territories that I had thought familiar until I saw them in the light of the lotus. I soon discovered that *Nelumbo* soared above other plants that have been celebrated and turned into icons, the roses and lilies, orchids and tulips. This one flower had permeated the ancient world, touched the lives of the great, and sometimes changed the course of history. Next these explorations drew me further east – to Mesopotamia where I encountered lotus cultures replete with mysterious goddesses, all of them long-extinct, and to India where another such culture had given rise to two major religions that were very much alive.

Meanwhile, Oxford's dinner tables were growing rowdy with a debate I had thought done and dusted in that same university over a century before: Darwin versus God. In this climate, I trod cautiously at first in regions of spirituality where biologists are rarely seen. But I soon realised that any faithful portrait of the lotus would need to reconcile forces that were being described as foes – science and religion, nature and culture. Here was an organism that was also an artefact. Beyond a very early point, its tale was our tale and natural history became human history. The lotus-derived beliefs that a sceptic might disdain were based on observation of the plant's life cycle and ecology. At the start of my quest, these at least seemed intriguing examples of pre-scientific attempts to interpret the living world. By its end, they would become illuminating lessons in how anyone might relate to that world – even a botanist with no god in his life.

Travels among texts and artefacts could only take me so far. I had questions that fieldwork alone would answer. I wanted to study the plants in habitat, to be among a living lotus culture, and to see how far into prehistory I could trace our relationship with *Nelumbo*. My three seeds had come from an archaeological find that was three thousand years old. In their homeland, the lotus was still growing wild and still inextricable from society. Japan was the natural choice for the final phase of my quest. The greater part of this book describes my time there in search of the sacred flower.

In the Land of the Rising Sun, the dawn plant illuminates all. What began as a botanical field trip soon turned into a transect of a nation that has flourished alongside the lotus since its very beginnings. It took me from noodle bars to battlefields and from temples to tumuli, back and forth over twelve millennia until, on a mountain far to the north, I found a flower that encapsulated an entire civilisation and spoke equally to science and spirit.

I

A Celestial Plant

2

The Sacred Lotus

Before any of these wanderings could begin, there were some questions to be answered. Exactly what kind of plant was this marvel that had flown in from Tokyo? Was it related to anything else? How, in evolutionary terms, did it fit into the tree of life? Where was it found? What was known about its life cycle, its sex life and biochemistry? The whole world knew it as a spiritual symbol, but did this plant have any properties of material value? What natural gifts made the lotus the most famous flower of all?

Taeko-san's gift was *Nelumbo nucifera*, the sacred or Indian lotus. Because of its seeds, this plant also goes by the names Egyptian or Indian bean, although it is neither native to Egypt nor endemic to India. It is one of only two species that are currently accepted by botanists as comprising the genus *Nelumbo*, the other being *N. lutea*, the American or yellow lotus or water chinquapin. A chinquapin is a relation of the chestnut, so here is another reference to those bullet-like seeds. The American lotus is found as far north as Ontario and Maine and as far south as Honduras. The sacred lotus is a plant of the Old World, extending from Iran and Russia to Japan. It is found as far north as Kashmir and Tibet and as far south as Indonesia, the islands of the South-western Pacific and Northern Australia.

Populations at the western extreme of this range, around the delta of the Volga River and in the reedy fringes of the Caspian Sea, are sometimes treated as a species in their own right, named *Nelumbo caspica*. Meanwhile, at the other end of the Russian Federation, a second lotus has been considered

11

distinct. This is *Nelumbo komarovii*. Luxuriant and with large magenta-trimmed blooms that seem to bespeak the Tropics, it is confined to a region 100 miles north of Vladivostok where it endures winter lows of minus 42 degrees centigrade. Today botanists include both these Russian lotuses within *Nelumbo nucifera*. The two defunct names serve as reminders, however, of the range and adaptability of this single species.

The sacred lotus has become inseparable from humankind, not just as an object of worship but as a source of food, medicines, fibres, trinkets, artistic motifs, and, as with my own three plants, dazzling garden ornamentals. Wherever we have encountered the lotus, we have used it. In other places we have introduced it. This process, which has been continuing since prehistoric times, extended the range of the lotus and blurred the borders of its natural distribution.

The lotuses of the south-western Pacific islands and Australia may well have been carried there by early settlers. Those of Egypt, not to be confused with native Nile lotuses (the waterlilies *Nymphaea caerulea* and *Nymphaea lotus*), were introduced between the beginning and the middle of the first millennium BC. The rare pockets found in southern Europe, and in Italy especially, are thought to be relics of Roman horticulture, the garden escapes of antiquity. Long since lost, other lotus colonies around the Mediterranean and Aegean may have been founded by roving Phoenicians or travellers from further east. The greatest of these anthropogenic lotus diffusions follow the expansion of Hinduism and Buddhism. But these are not the only spiritual traditions that have nurtured the flower. Across vast areas, the crimson of the lotus runs like a tracer dye, tracking the spread, fusion and fission of cults and cultures.

Humankind should congratulate itself on having fostered the lotus diaspora. While the North American *Nelumbo lutea* still occupies or has reconquered a large part of its aboriginal domain, the same could scarcely be said of *Nelumbo nucifera*. It is a plant that appears to have been beaten back and in decline until we took up its cause.

The fossil record reveals that *Nelumbo* was once widespread across the land mass that would become Europe and Asia, even at northern latitudes. It first appears in the Lower Cretaceous Period and is abundant by the time of the Upper Cretaceous. In other words, its main natural expansion occurred between 145.5 and 65.5 million years ago. Until 2004, the primeval lotus-lands were believed to have been confined to the northern hemisphere. Then botanists reported the discovery of fossilised leaves and fruits in Patagonia which date from between 84 and 65 million years ago. The obvious deduction is that *Nelumbo* was once even more widespread than had been thought, and then dwindled as the earth grew cooler and drier.

The plight of *Nelumbo nucifera* worsened during the Pleistocene Epoch, between 1,800,000 and 10,000 years ago, as ice ages scoured two thirds of its territory. Many populations that were spared the glacial scythe succumbed to other climatic disasters. Near the ice shield formerly hospitable habitats became tundra or boreal desert. Later and further south, desertification began to affect the central band of the lotus's range, leaving only rare refugia like the Caspian region intact. Elsewhere, factors such as continental drift, rising sea levels and changes in ocean currents created conditions that offered the lotus no prospect of regaining its erstwhile sites. As the Siberian *Nelumbo komarovii* and the Canadian *Nelumbo lutea* show, the dormant lotus is impervious to winter cold. But it does demand soaring temperatures and high light values when in growth. An oceanic climate with so-so summers and mild winters is of no use. The lotuses that once inhabited the land that became Britain had no inducement to return there. In short, *Nelumbo nucifera* had attained the special, if not especially desirable, status of a living fossil until we coaxed it from its few last stands and spread it about the planet.

In the right place, however, the lotus tells a different story. *Nelumbo* species are large and rampant perennial herbs that inhabit the margins and shallows of ponds, lakes and slow-moving rivers, reed beds and marshes, sometimes forming vast colonies to the exclusion of most other plants. They advance rapidly by means of stout cylindrical rhizomes that are segmented like sausage links. When mature, the outer surface of these rhizomes is hard and glossy; their flesh is crisp and off-white. Running through them are long air chambers arranged like the bundled strands of some complex cable. Seen in cross section, these chambers present a pattern of holes which some have likened to Swiss cheese and others to a sheet of pastry from which tarts have been cut. Alongside the altar, the kitchen table is never far from lotus thoughts.

At each node of the rhizome are long feathery roots, two small sheathing bracts or cataphylls, and a leaf. Unspectacular though it may seem, this triadic arrangement of one leaf plus two cataphylls is unique and has long intrigued botanists who puzzle over phyllotaxy, the architecture of plants. There may also be branches which divaricate in a striking herringbone pattern. Exhumed whole and washed clean, the lotus infrastructure resembles an immense and simplified tree that has been felled and consigned to the mud. Its longevity is likewise more reminiscent of a tree than of most herbaceous perennials. Lotus colonies are known which consist of a single clone, a single plant in effect, that has survived unchanged and in the same location for over a thousand years. Had they known that they were clues, botanists might have used these features to solve a question that vexed them for two centuries and which has only just been answered: what exactly is the sacred lotus?

Within a decade of Linnaeus's publication of *Nymphaea nelumbo*, the French naturalist and explorer Michel Adanson concluded that the lotus was not nearly so closely related to waterlilies (*Nymphaea*) as the Swedish giant had assumed. In 1763, Adanson placed it in a genus of its own – *Nelumbo*. By the end of the eighteenth century, two species had been identified and had received the labels by which science knows them to this day. The sacred lotus of the Old World, Linnaeus's *Nymphaea nelumbo*, had become *Nelumbo nucifera* ('nut-bearing nelumbo'), a name published by Joseph Gaertner in 1788. Its North American cousin was named *Nelumbo lutea* ('yellow nelumbo') by Carl Ludwig von Willdenow in 1799. In the nineteenth century, the suspicion that *Nelumbo* was no waterlily grew among botanists. In 1829, the Belgian botanist and politician Barthélemy Charles Joseph Dumortier put the genus in its own family, Nelumbonaceae, where it remains.

Much as these developments testify to a growing sense of the lotus's singularity, in the broader picture it remained in the order Nymphaeales, side by side with waterlilies on the same branch of the tree of life. There were two reasons for this – first, taxonomists lacked the tools to judge whether or not lotuses were truly related to waterlilies; second, the lotus seemed to supply an important chapter in the narrative of evolution. Here, apparently, was a waterlily-like plant on the cusp of adaptation. Its feet dwelt in water or mud; its leaves, flowers and fruit were held in mid-air; its seeds, large, hard-coated and with rich reserves, were adapted to survive drought and other disasters that might befall its habitat and then to germinate on the water margin. The lotus seemed frozen in the very act of moving from aquatic life to terra firma, a snapshot of the greatest plant migration to transform the earth. It was an engaging story. It made scientific sense, accounted for the most obvious differences between lotus and waterlily, and was suffused with primeval romance. It was also more wrong than anyone could have imagined.

As the twenty-first century approached, botanists began to combine genetic fingerprinting with a deeper understanding of the fossil record and techniques for evaluating and contrasting plant characteristics that were more mathematical and less intuitive. The result was the latest and greatest shake-up of the plant kingdom since Linnaeus. The most surprising of many surprises that emerged from it involved the identity of *Nelumbo*. It turned out that the lotus was not remotely allied to the waterlily. Still more shocking, its closest living relations were not only woody but also denizens of dry land. They were the plane trees *Platanus*, and the shrubs that form the southern hemisphere family Proteaceae such as *Banksia, Embothrium* and *Protea* itself. The missing links between plane, protea and lotus may never be found, but the DNA does not lie: these disparate-seeming plants are more closely related to one another than to anything else. Rather than damage the evolutionary narrative, this discovery has energised it. Few proofs of adaptation could be more striking than the ancestral affinity between a drought-resistant shrub and an aquatic herbaceous perennial.

Throughout much of their range, both *Nelumbo* species are deciduous, producing foliage with startling rapidity from late spring onwards and collapsing with equal drama by mid-autumn. The leaf blades are circular and up to a metre across. In seedlings and adult plants at the beginning of the growing season, they float on the surface. By early summer, however, all new leaves are held clear of the water on slender and sometimes prickly stalks that stand as much as 2 metres tall. These are attached to the midpoint of the underside of the leaf blade, giving the whole the appearance of a plate spun on a stick. On the upper surface, the point of the stalk's attachment appears in the exact centre as a pale sunken spot, an omphalos. From this navel, the principal veins radiate like spokes and give rise to a faint and crazed network of subsidiary veins – picture the shatter pattern of a bullet hole in reinforced glass. Appearing bloomy or satiny and usually pale sea green or turquoise, the upper surface of the foliage is embossed with minute nipple-like protuberances, or papillae, and then covered in wax. This combination of features gives it remarkable water-repellent properties.

These properties allow the lotus to support some of the largest undivided leaves in the plant kingdom and in climates where foliage-battering downpours are common. But the trick is even cleverer than that. The lotus leaf is also adapted to conserve and to channel water. The navel-like centre is porous and the surface of the blade slightly dished. Falling upon the leaf, most raindrops scatter and are shaken off. Some, however, will run to the centre and gather on the omphalos where they are soon absorbed into the stalk.

Even when there is no rain, the leaf will catch and funnel dew. In this way the lotus supplements the massive water supply it requires when in growth, a requirement its underground hydraulics, though impressive, cannot meet alone. When not absorbing water, the navel of the lotus leaf acts as a vegetable flue or snorkel. Through this pale and permeable midpoint a vital gaseous exchange occurs, allowing the rhizomes beneath to flourish in conditions so stagnant that they would kill most other plants.

The flowers develop with such speed and force that their opening has become a spectator sport in some parts of the world. Long-stalked and ellipsoidal, the bud arises from the growing point of the rhizome, breaching the water as the summer temperatures begin to soar. By the time it is ready to open, the bud will resemble a spear standing clear of the surface by as much as 1.5 metres. Blooming happens in the dawn, always visibly and some-times audibly as the twenty or so infolded petals pop apart. By midday these will have reflexed in a ring to form a bowl some 20 centimetres across and encircling the plant's sexual organs.

In *Nelumbo nucifera*, the sacred lotus, the petals are typically rosy pink or white; in the American lotus, *N. lutea*, they are pale lemon yellow or cream. This is the principal difference between the two species, one echoed by *Magnolia*, another ancient and beetle-pollinated genus with a split Asian/American dis-tribution. At dusk the flowers close again, imprisoning a fragrance that has grown heavier as the day has grown longer. Known as volatilisation, this increase in scent is powered by the stamens which begin to generate heat as the afternoon draws on. By the time the flowers close, perfume is not their only prisoner. Trapped within are the small beetles and flies that pollinate the lotus and which have been attracted by the post-meridian spike in fragrance. To keep them alive and active during their night of captivity, the closed flower maintains its interior at a sultry 32 degrees centigrade – perhaps as much as 20 degrees higher than the ambient temperature. Encouraged by the warmth, the hostages feed and frolic on a litter of pollen shed by the golden anthers. The oubliette becomes the scene of an orgy.

On the morrow, the flower opens again to release its prisoners. Fit, fed, far from rested but ahead of the day and any rivals and predators, they fly or crawl into the chill dawn which, after their night of crimson-cushioned indulgence, feels like a false dusk. As they sense a drop in temperature, they seek a place to rest and hide. The obvious refuge is one of the many other lotus flowers that will have opened just as they were being released from their own gorgeous jail. Coated with pollen, the insects alight on them, unwittingly performing the work of cross-fertilisation. The flower repeats this routine on day two. By the third day, the bloom's brief tenure is drawing to an end and the petals fade and fall.

At the flower's centre is a smooth green structure shaped like an inverted cone. Once the petals have fallen away, this organ begins to enlarge, eventually becoming as much as 15 centimetres across at its flattened top and 20 centimetres deep. It is known as the receptacle, an apt term for something that resembles a cup and which carries the seeds. Around 2 centimetres long, the hard bean-like seeds form in pits which cover the receptacle's upper surface. At critical stages in their development, this vessel angles itself downwards to protect them from the weather and foraging animals. By winter, when the seeds are ripened and hard, the receptacle will have become dry and woody. It detaches from the stalk, striking the water like the splashdown of an Apollo command module. The cone then floats away with its flat upper surface lowermost. As its chambers rehydrate they dilate, releasing their contents.

With adamantine coats, imperishable food reserves, and embryos that make Rip Van Winkle look insomniac, lotus seeds are astonishing in their longevity. There are records of their germinating after centuries of storage either dry or buried in their native mud. My own three plants were the offspring of a lotus which sprouted from a seed believed to be some 3,000 years old. In time, I would encounter others reborn from seeds that had lain buried for at least 1,400 years. At the end of my quest, I would see the lotus which, to my eyes, was the most impressive of all these revenants. That specimen was a comparative stripling, however – grown from seeds that had been stored for a mere eight centuries.

Until recently, the process of radiocarbon dating a seed required its complete destruction. Understandably, few discoverers of ancient and possibly viable lotus seeds were prepared to submit to this trial by ordeal: germination was their objective, not combustion. Instead, they would deduce the age of their finds by radiocarbon dating other seeds or remains discovered with them, and from other sources of evidence – geological, archaeological and historical. Although there is often good reason to trust such datings, these days scientists take a tougher line. To spare the seed but test other materials found with it is no longer considered good enough; nor is deducing age from other types of evidence. At the same time, new techniques allow the radiocarbon dating of seed coat fragments after germination. In other words, one can now destroy and so date part of the seed while keeping the seedling itself alive.

In 1983, these stricter standards were applied to a lotus seed found in a peat deposit in north-eastern China. Aged 1,288, plus or minus 271 years, it was declared 'the oldest demonstrably viable and directly dated seed ever reported'. It held the record for two decades. Then, in 2005, the seed of a date palm (*Phoenix dactylifera*) discovered at the fortress of Masada in the early 1960s was finally sprouted and tested. At approximately 2,000 years old, the Dead Sea date beat the Manchurian lotus into second place. The Masada date is a fluke, however, that has survived by a rare convergence of conditions perfect for its preservation, whereas lotus seeds are built to last. These tungsten-tough beans have evolved as time machines. In order not to compete with their parents, they lie dormant in the muddy beds on which they fall. Freed from competition and given ideal conditions, they will spring into life; otherwise only a big sleep awaits them.

Sometimes it may last for just a few years. Around Lake Erie, for example, colonies of *Nelumbo lutea* attract beavers and muskrats which feed on the rhizomes and shoots so voraciously that the lotus is eradicated within a season or two. As the plant disappears, the rodents that have been feasting upon it leave in search of new lotus-lands. Once their fattened backs are turned, dormant seeds germinate apace, filling the shoes of their parents. So far as the lotus is concerned, this scorched earth, or uprooted swamp, policy is not as self-sacrificing as it sounds. The dam- and lodge-building of beavers and muskrats produces flooding and areas of still water; it also creates natural waterlily baskets, built of branches and leaf-litter, in water otherwise too deep for *Nelumbo*. Either way, the animals are husbanding their food plant's favoured habitat.

Few lotus colonies are such marvels of quick turnover ecology. Sometimes the seeds' sleep may last for centuries, until natural or man-made processes expose their deep and cradling strata, either placing them in the hands of some fortunate plant-prospector or restoring their surroundings to habitable wetland. Only then, long after their ancestors have vanished, do they germinate.

The lotus embryo is less like a fledgling nymph and more like Athena, capable of bursting forth from the acorn, its Jupiter's nut, fully armed for the trials of life. Although encased within the utter darkness of soil and seed shell, it remains full of chlorophyll, ready to seize the day in the midst of perpetual night. The moment light touches it, the lotus plumule is at work, photosynthesising, fully functioning and fast-moving. Within days of its emergence, this germ of brilliant green will have produced its first rhizome, roots and leaves. Unlike those of many seedlings, these features are not juvenile; they do not differ in any anatomically significant way from the mature *Nelumbo*; they are simply small, and do not remain so for long. Prior to that *fiat lux*, the embryo has been held tight between two pale cotyledons, seed leaves that are stocked with nutrients, fatty acids and water. So embraced, it has continued to respire, living in suspended animation as the seed's inner chamber has become hermetically sealed and its outer shell has grown harder and harder.

Although no light, air or water can reach it, the embryo may survive in this state for centuries and with undiminished viability. The reason for its survival is that not everything stops inside the impenetrable capsule. While the cotyledons are rich in food and water against the day of the seed's germination, the embryo itself is packed with something far more useful in the antenatal phase – compounds that maintain tissues and make good damaged protein. Even during its long dark dormancy, the embryonic lotus is capable of repairing itself, not so much embalmed as ceaselessly revitalised by a cocktail of chemicals. Some of these are familiar – ascorbic acid, for example, in which the embryo is exceptionally rich. Others are more mysterious, such as L-isoaspartyl methyltransferase or MT for short. This enzyme is common in plants as a protein structure repair agent, an inbuilt anti-ageing tonic. In seeds it plays a vital role in the maintenance of viability during storage, but only up to a point. In most species, its effectiveness decreases over time and they die as a result. But not in the case of *Nelumbo* – a thousand-year-old lotus seed will show MT activity comparable to that of a seed that has not long ago ripened and dropped from the receptacle. As a result, its tissues will betray no real sign of ageing.

Exactly why and how the lotus and no other plant should possess this talent to such a degree remains an enigma. So too does the trigger, the convergence of factors that finally informs the seed that its dormancy is over. The obvious candidates – water, warmth, light – play essential parts in this awakening, but they are not always incentive enough. All three factors are usually available to seeds that fall amid existing lotus colonies, and yet they may still enter prolonged dormancy. Quite how the message is sent and received, the information that now is the time to sprout, is another mystery. 'Just add water' is evidently not the lotus seed's sole motivation for breaking its slumber. Something else must happen to render an impermeable and rock-hard shell capable of breathing, imbibing, becoming twice its original size and softening to the point where a hatchling embryo can breach its hull.

While the nature of that trigger remains elusive, one thing is clear: chemistry is the secret of the lotus's power. We have sought to harness it. Soon after it was identified in *Nelumbo* seeds, cosmetics manufacturers began to take an interest in L-isoaspartyl methyltransferase: this miraculous enzyme which keeps polycentenarian lotus embryos as unwithered and unstaled as the Queen of the Nile, might it not be the perfect ingredient for putting crow's feet to flight? Around 1996, the patent applications started piling up. Anti-ageing lotions are not the only inventions to have been inspired by the lotus in recent years. No sooner was the intimate structure of its water-repellent leaves understood than it was biomimetically reproduced by makers of graffiti-resistant paint, the umbrella to end all umbrellas, and monsoon-defying mackintoshes. Other applications of *Nelumbo* technology have addressed graver issues than fending off wrinkles, rain and spray cans.

In the past two decades, extract of *Nelumbo nucifera* seeds has been found to have hypoglycaemic effects in laboratory animals, suggesting it might be useful in the control of diabetes. It has also been shown to inhibit the replication of the virus Herpes Simplex 1. Likewise derived from lotus seeds, the chemical (S)-Armepavine suppresses T cell proliferation, so curbing the ravages of the autoimmune disease systemic lupus erythematosus. Of the compounds derived from the plant's rhizome, one appears to improve memory and learning ability by promoting the growth of neural pathways in the hippocampus; some are antioxidants that have been found to outstrip vitamin C in potency; others again are antipyretic, reducing fevers. These are just a few of the lotus-inspired researches currently in progress. Many are still at the rat and rabbit stage and may go no further than laboratory and learned literature. Some of these applications, however, have already been tested on humans in an unscientific way, for they were suggested to modern clinical researchers by traditions of native medicine.

In India a team of researchers recently examined a *Nelumbo* seed extract which has long been used as an oral contraceptive by women in the Udaipur district of Rajasthan. In 2008 they published their findings. Tested under controlled conditions and on rats rather than humans, the lotus seed tincture suppressed oestrogen production, rendering the subjects temporarily infertile. It had no toxic effects and caused no long-term physiological alteration. Its short-term impacts on the body were a decrease in the mass of the reproductive organs and an increase in cholesterol which would otherwise have been spent in ovulation. All three phenomena – diminished uterine and ovarian weight, elevated cholesterol, and infertility – swiftly reverted to normal when the treatment stopped. In other words, the women of Udaipur knew what they were doing. In time, they may even be thanked for giving the world a new contraceptive, courtesy of the lotus.

Whether or not any of these investigations leads to a licensed product, they all illustrate a striking feature of *Nelumbo*: it is a natural chemical factory of prodigious inventiveness. In addition to lashings of vitamin C and the intriguing L-isoaspartyl methyltransferase, the seeds contain the antioxidant glutathione, oils comprising myristic, palmitic, oleic and linoleic acid, and the flavonoids isoquercitrin and quercetin. So far as humans are concerned, the last of these substances is anti-inflammatory and anti-tumour – yet more possible uses for a lotus seed. Alkaloids, the chemical compounds naturally produced by living organisms, are found in *Nelumbo* in profusion equalled by few other plants. Its tissues abound in neferine, lotusine, isoliensinine, roemerine, and anonaine to name but five. Another, one of the most powerful, is nuciferine, an alkaloid which in man produces much the same effects as Homer's famous lotos – depression of the central nervous system leading to sedation, somnolence and, if one is not careful, cataleptic trance and repetitive uncontrollable movements. Just as the lotus rhizome can stem forgetfulness, the lotus leaf can consign one to oblivion.

But people are careful, and have been for millennia. Taken as a tincture or powder of *Nelumbo nucifera*, they have used nuciferine (not that they called it that) as a nerve tonic, to calm palpitations, and to cure insomnia. And no sooner does one of the plant's elixirs anaesthetise than another arouses. According to recent studies, *Nelumbo* contains clinically significant quantities of apomorphine, a chemical that stimulates dopamine receptors in the central nervous system and which has been used in the treatment of Parkinson's disease and erectile dysfunction. The coexistence of these two compounds, nuciferine and apomorphine, in the same species may well explain the magical and apparently paradoxical powers – euphoric *and* sedative – that have been attributed to the lotus across history and its range.

With these powers in mind, some botanists have recently identified *Nelumbo nucifera* with Soma, the magical plant of Hindu scriptures. The scant descriptions of Soma that appear in Vedic texts, however, talk of a plant 'with jointed stems', 'yellow-green' in bloom, 'straw-like', and 'found in rocky mountainous places'. These details suggest not the lotus but *Ephedra*, a genus of wiry conifer allies that have been used as a stimulant in Asia since prehistoric times, and which gave modern medicine the adrenalin-like ephedrine and pseudephedrine.

Not that this is any loss to *Nelumbo*, a genus with more than enough to do. In almost every human population that has grown up alongside it, the lotus has been used for primitive or traditional medicines. In addition to contraceptives, tranquillisers and febrifuges, it has provided treatments for bleeding disorders, piles, skin inflammations, nausea, indigestion, obesity, loose stools and toadstool poisoning. Australian aboriginals and Native Americans gazed upon the lotus swamp and saw an al fresco pharmacy. In the great Asian traditions of Ayurvedic and Chinese medicine, *Nelumbo nucifera* was Panacea become vegetation goddess, infinitely bountiful, ministering to every ailment with every aspect of its anatomy, from roots to flower. Scientists in the developed West used to dismiss such uses as superstition. Now we are in the midst of a re-think: it seems the mumbo-jumbo may have had an empirical basis after all.

Food is medicine, as they say in the Far East. You do not need to be sick to be a lotus-eater. Most parts of *Nelumbo nucifera* feature in Oriental cuisine. Its seed kernels are eaten whole, fried or stewed, or pounded into a marron-like meal, its excised embryos as a vitality-restoring delicacy, its new shoots as a vegetable, stir-fried, pickled or steamed with rice, and its powdered leaves as a tisane so mind-erasingly relaxing that it would bar even the most inveterate madeleine dunker from Memory Lane. The plant provides the dinner service as well as food: its leaves are used as plates and its concave petals as exquisitely fragile spoons and saucers. Of all its parts, however, the rhizome is paramount, served cut into discs that are fried if young and simmered if older. Easily grown, harvested, stored and carried and rich in carbohydrates, vitamins and minerals, the lotus rhizome was a staple food throughout the domains of both *Nelumbo* species, domains which their transportation and cultivation by man first secured and then vastly extended. For many peoples unfamiliar with cereals and tuberous starch sources, these subaquatic stems were the staff of life. They were feeding populations in the Near East before the Fertile Crescent saw so much as a grain, sustaining South-east Asia and the Pacific while taro and yam were still objects of suspicion, and filling food bowls throughout much of Japan in her rice-free prehistory.

Their dietary importance went for the recent New as well as the remote Old World. The Comanche, Dakota, Huron, Meskwaki, Ojibwa, Omaha, Pawnee,

Ponca, Potawatomi, and Winnebago all depended in some degree on *Nelumbo lutea* and settled close to the creeks and swamps where it grew. They casseroled its rhizomes with meat or, at the start of summer, ate the new growth raw as a vitamin-rich salad. In winter the lotus became especially important as a carbohydrate source for these Native Americans. They would forage for it before the big freeze set in, cut the cylindrical rhizomes into lengths and hang them in their dwellings on twine threaded through their longitudinal perforations. I did say they resembled sausages. Some arranged these hanging *Nelumbo* in cool positions where they would remain succulent and retain much of their fresh nutritional value until spring. Others suspended them somewhere warm and smoky, either for want of space or because they liked their lotus kippered.

Plant medicines and foodstuffs fall in the province of economic botany as do a few other uses to which *Nelumbo* is put. It is a source of beads, toys and other decorations (the seeds and fruiting receptacles), of writing and wrapping materials (the leaf blades), and of textile fibres (the leaf and flower stalks). More recently, the lotus's rare capacity for growing in poorly oxygenated conditions and for translocating heavy metals and other pollutants has led to its being introduced to contaminated lakes and wetlands in the Far East and North America as a vegetable purge which will cleanse these failing ecosystems and prepare them to receive new life.

It is a small but critical step from husbanding a wild or semi-cultivated plant to identifying and maintaining superior forms of it. In the case of *Nelumbo nucifera* this process of selection appears to have begun early on. Lotuses that were moved around the Middle East, Asia and the Pacific may have been chosen and propagated on account of some special merit such as outsize rhizomes, prolific seed production or exceptional vigour. Plants so treated are termed cultivars, distinctive varieties selected by man and maintained through cultivation. The term applies equally to plants chosen for their beauty. In addition to the culinary forms, around four hundred named ornamental lotus cultivars survive today. Some of the most novel and successful of these arise from the hybridisation of *Nelumbo nucifera* and *N. lutea*, an east-meets-west marriage that took place as recently as the 1960s. But many of the extant cultivars are far older, having been selected between 800 and 1800, a period when China and Japan expended as much passion and ingenuity on lotus breeding as the West would lavish on the rose. In time I would meet these living antiquities face to face. For the moment, however, I was in search of even older plants. A new query had arrived from Taeko-san in Tokyo: 'What did the Greeks call the lotus?'

3

Metamorphoses Transformed

In the summer of 326 BC Alexander the Great arrived at the River Beas, or Hyphasis, the second easternmost of the Indus tributaries. After a decade of ceaseless campaigning, his army had reached the point of mutiny. They were being led, as one of Alexander's commanders bravely observed, into an India not even the Indians recognised, ever further beyond the limits of the known world, and all in the service of the king's *pothos*, his implacable, destiny-driven desire. They had conquered all and gained nothing. The time had come to go home. After a monumental sulk and some impassioned orating, the king acceded to their pleas.

He led them back to the Chenab, or the Acesines as he would have known it, another of the great rivers that rush from their mountainous head-waters before traversing the Punjab, joining the Indus and journeying south to the sea. There, on the river banks, Alexander noticed something that seemed the answer to his and his army's prayers – luxuriant colonies of *Nelumbo nucifera*. He was astonished to find the lotus so far east. He had thought it endemic to Egypt, a land he conquered in 332–331 BC. But the plant struck Alexander as more than a beautiful sight or a reminder of the comforts of the civilisations his army had left behind. It appeared to offer a solution to his immediate troubles. If the lotus's birthplace was Egypt, he reasoned, surely the River Chenab must lead to the Nile. The sacred flower was pointing the way home, and a way that was comparatively plain sailing – drifting downriver rather than battling overland.

The deduction could not have been better for Alexander, or better timed. It allowed him to give his army the answer they demanded and deserved, 'We're going home.' But it also appeased his pride. He had found the route, and by virtue of an observation only he among his entire army was qualified to make. He alone had discovered the object of numerous kingly quests, the source of the Nile. Moreover, the route home had no sense of retreat. It was, rather, a triumph designed by the gods and given the shape of destiny, a beautiful circle beginning and ending in Alexandria, the first great city he founded, the first to bear his name.

The way forward was clear: the lotus-fringed Chenab joined the crocodile-infested Jhelum; launching their boats in the latter, they would navigate back to Egypt. Alexander ordered a fleet to be built. Next, he wrote to his mother Olympias, informing her of her beloved son's deductive coup. Only then did he deign to speak to the locals and learn the truth. They knew nothing about the Nile, but they could assure him that the Chenab joined another river with great turbulence and that these in turn joined an even greater river. That vast flow, the Indus, finally disgorged not into Egypt's fertile flood plains but an ocean. Nothing but desert lay beyond it.

Alexander decided to sail downriver anyway. But he did issue one urgent command. The courier destined for Olympias was recalled and the passage in the letter concerning his lotus-inspired discovery of the source of the Nile was suppressed. His mother must not be given reason to believe that her son could make a mistake. Not that such an error was really possible. When Alexander was last in Egypt, he had gone to the trouble of having priests confirm that his real father was Zeus. His infallibility was god-given. Eventually he was indeed borne back to the banks of the Nile, but overland and in his sarcophagus.

Although tragically wrong about rivers, Alexander was well-placed to identify organisms like *Nelumbo*. As a youth he had been tutored by Aristotle. Also present at these tutelary sessions was another philosopher thirteen years or so younger than Aristotle and aged around thirty at the time of Alexander's schooling. Born on Lesbos, Tyrtamos had moved to Athens to pursue his philosophical career under Plato. When Plato died in 347 BC, he decided to follow Aristotle, his late master's most brilliant student. They grew close, so close in fact that he would become Aristotle's intellectual heir and legal executor, guardian of his children and keeper of his library and manuscripts. Aristotle also endowed Tyrtamos with the name by which the world has

known him ever since – Theophrastus, in recognition of his divine powers
of expression. Their collaboration had begun before Alexander's education,
as the two men roved across the Greek islands and the Near East. In
335 BC, the phenomena they noted and the methods they developed during
these wanderings bore fruit in Aristotle's founding of the Lyceum, his great
Athenian centre not just for the investigation of abstract moral questions
but for the study of the physical world in all its parts.

Following Alexander's death in 323 BC popular feeling in Athens turned
against those who had supported the Macedonian conquerors. Aristotle was
identified as one of them: his father had been physician to Alexander's grandfather; he himself had cultivated the young king's curiosity, equipped him,
as some saw it, to become the perfect tyrant. He decided to leave Athens,
a city, he observed, which had form as a killer of philosophers. Before going,
he appointed Theophrastus his successor as head of the Lyceum. It was a
role in which he flourished for thirty-five years until his death from natural
causes in his eighty-fifth year, around 285 BC.

True to his mentor, Theophrastus was an intellectual omnivore,
anatomising and taxonomising everything. The subject for which he is especially remembered, however, is botany. Given the running of the Lyceum, he
developed Aristotle's garden into the first known botanical institution in the
Western World. Its library was filled with reports of banyans and bananas,
mangroves and myrrh, cinnamon and cotton, pepper and papyrus, sent from
the furthest reaches of the empire Alexander had forged. Its borders were
stocked with exotics which, unlike the king, had survived the journey home.
If Linnaeus was the father of modern botany, Theophrastus was the father
of botany itself. He produced two major works on plants which shaped the
way we see the living world. Botanists ever since have referred to a passage
from one of these works as a turning point, perhaps *the* turning point, in the
history of natural history:

[Unlike the aforementioned Egyptian plants which grow in the River
Nile . . .] *the bean inhabits swamps and lakes. Up to four cubits long* [1.8
metres] *and as thick as a man's finger, its stalk is similar to a supple reed
but without joints. Right through the interior of the stalk run tubes which are
distinct from one another, resembling honeycomb. The head sits on top of this
stalk like a circular wasps' nest. It contains as many as thirty beans, one in
each of the cells and projecting slightly from it. Twice the size of a poppy's,*

the flower is a deep shade of rose and held clear of the water, as is the fruiting head. All around the plant grow leaves that are as large as a Thessalian hat, and on stems that are the same in appearance and dimensions as the flower stalks. Break open one of the beans and you will find bitter material curled within; this is the embryo. That is enough about the fruit.

Stouter than the sturdiest reed, the root is filled with distinct tubes, just like the stalk. It can be eaten raw, boiled or roasted and is a staple food of people living in the wetlands. Usually it grows spontaneously, but the people also sow its seeds in the mud after mixing them with chaff so that they will sink to the substrate and remain there without scattering. In this way, they create bean fields. Once they have taken hold, these bean fields become perennial. Their roots are as robust as a reed's, but prickly in places – a feature that causes crocodiles to shun this plant as they have poor vision and fear injuring their eyes on the prickles. Although it also grows in Syria and areas of Cilicia, its roots and fruit mature poorly in these countries. It is found too in a small lake around Torone in Chalcidice where its roots and fruits ripen to perfection.

Many have described the lotus, in a multitude of languages and genres, for reasons sacred and scientific. But this passage from Book Four of Theophrastus's *An Enquiry into Plants* is the most important lotus description of all, for the simple reason that it marked the beginning of all formal plant description. Never before had an account of a plant been so lovingly detailed for its own sake and in the name of pure enquiry. Many components of a modern botanical treatment are there – the habit and habitat, the progression through different organs, the obvious part played by dissection and close scrutiny, the effort to distinguish the bean (*Nelumbo nucifera*) from other plants. In the paragraphs that follow, Theophrastus deals with the Nile waterlilies *Nymphaea caerulea* and *N. lotus*. These, he says, are not the same thing at all as the bean *Nelumbo*, our sacred lotus. In saying so, he knew better than Linnaeus over two thousand years later. There is even a foreshadowing of ecology in the frightened crocodiles, and of ethnobotany in the cultivation and consumption of lotuses by the human marsh dwellers. Theophrastus was refining a precise botanical terminology. Nonetheless, his yearning for objectivity is sometimes beaten by the strangeness of his subject, as in his comparing the leaves to a Thessalian hat, a species of peculiarly broad-brimmed headgear worn by Alexander's cavalrymen.

Above all, this passage marks the triumph of method over myth. It was no longer good enough to inhabit a world of metamorphoses, to explain Nature in terms of the miraculous or of man's behaviour and beliefs. She had her own tale to tell and a new class of natural historians to tell it.

The name by which Alexander and Theophrastus knew *Nelumbo nucifera* was *kyamos*. This is widely assumed to be an imprecise generic term for a bean or any bean-bearing plant, and it is certainly applied by Classical authors to species such as *Vicia faba*, the broad bean. Seen in this light, naming the lotus appears to be one of several uses to which a Greek might have put this term. In the case of our lotus, it was sometimes qualified with the epithet *Aigyptios*, 'Egyptian' – Aigyptios kyamos was the Egyptian bean, *Nelumbo nucifera*. Often, however, kyamos, meaning sacred lotus, appears without any such qualification. In other words, to these Greek ears, kyamos meant *Nelumbo* in the sense of *The Bean*. This unadorned name is the one the lotus takes at the beginning of Theophrastus's famous description. Where the Greeks do qualify kyamos with Aigyptios, they are simply indicating that they are now talking of the lotus (kyamos) as it is found in Egypt – same plant, different place. Further evidence of this identification between kyamos and *Nelumbo* is provided by the word *kyamōn*, often translated as 'bean field'. Although it is only rarely used to signify an allotment-type planting of legumes, kyamōn appears frequently and unambiguously as the term for a colony of *Nelumbo nucifera*. A better translation of kyamōnes might be 'lotus-lands'. It would certainly help us to understand why the Greeks described them with such longing and affection. There is little romance in a row of beans.

Philologists are divided on the etymology of kyamos. Most put up their hands and resort to formulae like 'deriv. obsc.', or 'ambig.'. Some link kyamos to the verb *kyeō*, meaning to swell up or to be pregnant, a perfectly reasonable notion for either a bean pod or a lotus receptacle. Others maintain kyamos is a borrowing from some unknown language which happened so long ago that both its root meaning and origin are lost. Seen in the light of this second theory, kyamos is suggestive.

It broadly resembles names for lotus found in the ancient Near East. Perhaps its ancestors and far-flung kin can be glimpsed in the Sumerian of the third millennium BC (*khamala* or *khammu*), in the Semitic Akkadian that eclipsed it as a spoken language (*kimta*), in Iranian-Aryan (*haoma*, a word for a magic plant, later applied to *Ephedra* rather than *Nelumbo*), in Indo-Aryan Sanskrit (*kamala*), and Dravidian Telugu (*kalung*), and subsequently in Hindi (*kanwal, kamal*), Bengali (*kombol, komal*), and Nepali (*kamal*). If Greek kyamos is related to these words, it implies an eastern export of vast antiquity.

There were other Greek names for the lotus. Kyamos could signify the whole plant, but it could also just indicate the seed, the bean itself. Sometimes, however, authors named other parts of the lotus as if they were not only different organs but different plants. In addition to kyamos, we find the name *kibōrion* (later Latinised as *ciborium*) which could apply either to the fruiting receptacles of *Nelumbo* or to the plant in its entirety. Where the rhizomes were concerned, the lotus was named *kolokasion* (Latinised and feminised as *colocasia*). Again, this epithet might refer to one part only (the rootstock) or to the whole plant. It was not unknown for all three names, kyamos, kibōrion and kolokasion, to feature in the same text as if three different species were under discussion. Such are the perils and pleasures of ancient science.

Under the Roman Empire, kyamos, kibōrion, kolokasion continued to be used for *Nelumbo nucifera* and two further names were added to the list. *Melilōtos*, 'honey lotus', was a title bestowed on *Nelumbo* flowers when they were judged sufficiently beautiful and fragrant to be used in wreaths, garlands, household decorations and temple offerings. Along with colocasia, in the modern period the name melilotus was applied by botanists to plants that bore not the slightest relationship to *Nelumbo*. Finally, there was *Antinoeios*, a name which proliferated from 130 AD onwards. From it there depends a remarkable tale. But before that must come the one word the Greeks did not use for the lotus – *lōtos*.

In the first decade of the first century AD, Ovid gave a mythic explanation for the genesis of the lotus, name and plant. In Book Nine of *Metamorphoses*, the nymph Lotis is pursued by Priapus, that hardy perennial of gardens and groves. Taking pity on her in their characteristically back-handed way, the gods transform her into a tree to save her from rape. Lotis becomes Lotus. Ovid's tale, however, is a comparatively late invention. His transformed nymph has little connection with the root of the word.

Like kyamos, 'lōtos' is ancient and has forebears and cousins east of Greece. It is echoed in several Semitic languages, and is cognate with the Hebrew *lōt*, a name originally given to trees that produced aromatic oils. In the Greek world and as lōtos, it sometimes retained a shade of this early meaning, signifying valuable trees. Otherwise, it proved an astonishingly promiscuous, or perhaps one should say plastic, term, denoting a wide range of unrelated plants. What the lotuses in this loose bag do have in common is their value to man, be it economic or abstract.

In *An Enquiry into Plants*, Theophrastus identified six species as 'lōtos', and that was after a serious effort to clear matters up and weed out the field a little. In modern scientific parlance these lotuses are:

Celtis australis, a deciduous tree of the Mediterranean and Middle East which still goes by the name Lote, valued for its hard and smooth timber.

Nymphaea caerulea and *N. lotus*, two waterlilies that were revered as the original lotuses of the Nile and Ancient Egyptian culture prior to the introduction of *Nelumbo*. In addition to their ornamental and sacral value, their tubers were eaten and their seed heads were fermented and made into a boozy fudge-like cake or bread.

Trifolium fragiferum, a salt-tolerant perennial clover valued as a forage crop for livestock, for hay-making and as a source of nectar for bees.

Trigonella foenum-graecum, fenugreek, an annual herb in the pea family widely used in the Mediterranean and Near East as a forage crop for livestock, a vegetable, a spice (its aromatic seeds), lentil-like pulses (seeds again), a culinary herb (the dried leaves), and in many medicinal and ritual applications.

Ziziphus lotus, a deciduous spiny shrub or tree of arid regions in the Mediterranean and especially the African coast. Eaten dried or used to make wine, its sweet date-like fruits have soporific and euphoric properties.

In addition to these six, the name lōtos had been commonly applied since early times to a range of meadow plants in the pea family. Some of these pastoral peas would ultimately be gathered and formalised by Linnaeus in the genus *Lotus* which now includes familiar species like *Lotus corniculatus*, the bird's-foot trefoil, and *Lotus berthelotii*, a silver-leaved and scarlet-flowered native of the Canary Islands that is much in demand for hanging baskets. Yet another, and unrelated, species to which the Greeks attached this endlessly adaptable name was the deciduous tree we now call *Diospyros lotus*. Native to the Middle and Near East, this relation of ebony provided them with edible fruit (date plums) and highly prized timber. By the time we reach the Roman Empire and Pliny the Elder writing some 350 years after Theophrastus's death, still more 'lotuses' have been added to this improbable bouquet. Among them was *Syzygium aromaticum*, the clove tree whose product, Pliny complained, was costing Rome 50 million sesterces per annum, all thrown to an unconquerable India. Woe betide the Roman who simply told his gardeners to plant lotus – he might have ended up with anything, from an arable weed to a waterlily, from a spice to a source of hardwood. Anything, that is, except *Nelumbo nucifera*.

For Pliny this plant, our plant, was colocasia, or *Faba Aegyptiaca* ('Egyptian bean'), or just plain *faba* ('The bean'). He was perfectly well aware that this was not the same as lotus in the sense of the Egyptian waterlilies, *Nymphaea caerulea* and *N. lotus*. The native Egyptian waterlilies, he says, are useful in producing fruit which can be rotted down and turned into a cake that revives the spirits and fends off dysentery. The rhizomes of colocasia are likewise useful as a food source. Dioscorides, physician to Pliny's friend and patron Emperor Vespasian, goes further: colocasia (*Nelumbo*) was already identified in the first century AD as an important source of medicines. As an ornamental, says Pliny, this plant is 'nobilissima', 'spectabilis' – most celebrated, spectacular – and 'now being grown in Italy'.

Preserved by the same volcanic eruption that killed him, mosaics and wall paintings at Pompeii bear witness to Pliny's claim. Among them are images of the sacred lotus grown as the centrepiece of courtyard pools and on the fringes of informal ponds. Ducks are often present, splashing in the shelter of the parasol leaves. The association was obviously to the Romans' liking. Writing at around the same time as Pliny, in the 60s–70s AD, the soldier-turned-farmer Columella gives a charming account of the part *Nelumbo* plays in his dream of small-scale country living: 'When making a pond for your ducks, the banks need to be clean, smooth, plastered and kept free of vegetation. The centre of the pond, however, should be a bed of soil. This can be planted with colocasia and other aquatic vegetation which will provide shady haunts for the waterfowl.'

'The challenge,' said Pliny, 'is making old material new.' The sacred lotus – colocasia, *Nelumbo* – was evidently all the rage in Rome when he was compiling his *Natural History* and he describes this exotic novelty with appropriate gusto. Still more importantly, he clears up one very old matter by answering a question people had been asking since the eighth century BC: 'What was the lotus of the Lotus-Eaters?'

'In its native territory,' he says, 'the fruit is so deliciously sweet that it has even given its name to an entire race of people, and to a country which is too welcoming to foreigners who arrive there, causing them to lose all memory of their homeland.' He is speaking of a, or perhaps *the*, lotus of Classical antiquity. In this context it is the gaunt, spiny shrub of barren places, the unlovely but eminently palatable relation of the buckthorn which is now known as *Ziziphus lotus*. Not just sweet but psychoactive, its fruit are still consumed in the southern Mediterranean. People have searched long and hard for Homer's Lotus-Land, picturing some verdant haven. They should have looked instead to Djerba off Tunisia, or to places on the rocky coast of Libya, where *Ziziphus* is ingested to this day.

But they can hardly be blamed for expecting something less austere. In Book Nine of *The Odyssey*, Homer makes the land of the Lotophagoi, the lotus-eaters, sound like paradise, albeit one whose enchantments are better avoided. Like Alexander's army, Odysseus's men are in a desperate state. On top of their previous travails, they have just been storm-tossed at sea for nine days; they are starving, thirsty and frightened. No sooner do they land on the Lotus-Eaters' shores than they find an unexpected source of water. Better still, they are not killed by the natives, which fate they were certainly expecting. There is momentary disappointment when they find no bread, and then elation when they discover much more interesting fare. The lotus, the staple diet of this faraway shore, keeps the natives in a state of blissful stupefaction. Some of the crew members are only too happy to join them in this self-induced oblivion and find themselves losing any desire to complete the journey home, indeed losing all memory of home. Instead they idle away their time feasting on the honey-sweet fruit *and* flowers (says Homer) of the lotus. Odysseus knows better, says 'no' to the narcotic plant, makes his excuses and leaves. His comrades who have partaken have to be dragged back to the boats, weeping as they go.

While historians and naturalists from Herodotus to Pliny described the real-life Lotophagoi and their Libyan domain, the multitude seems to have found the truth hard to swallow. Where were the water and flowers, the languor and honeyed bliss that Homer had promised? As a result, the search for Lotus-Land continued, was still continuing in the 1830s when Tennyson wrote *The Lotos-Eaters*, and, some might say, continues even now. It was given a boost when Westerners began to encounter Hindus and Buddhists who strove for detachment and whose earthly and celestial paradises were filled with entrancing flowers that played the part better than sickly spiny *Ziziphus*. So, in the modern period, *Nelumbo* became identified with the lotus of Classical legend. But the Greeks and Romans had already identified it as their ideal lotus long before, and their ideal Lotus-Land with it. It was not some Libyan desert shoreline but a wet, fertile, nelumbiferous region a little to the east. Its name was Egypt.

4

Egyptian Mysteries

The first mystery, and there are many, is how and when did the non-Egyptian *Nelumbo nucifera* arrive in the country where it became so celebrated? Derived from archaeological and textual evidence, the usual answer to the question runs like this:

The iconography of the Egyptian lotus resembles its manifestations in other early Middle Eastern cultures, as a symbol of fertility, birth and ritual purity. In much of the Near East from the third millennium BC onwards, this lotus was *Nelumbo nucifera*. In Egypt, however, it was the native waterlilies of the Nile, *Nymphaea caerulea* and *Nymphaea lotus*, that were so important in life and death. These are the 'lotuses' that predominate in Ancient Egyptian myth and art. Only after the middle of the first millennium BC are these waterlilies demonstrably supplanted by *Nelumbo nucifera* in artefacts and documentary accounts. In the Near East, *Nelumbo*, the sacred lotus, had long been cherished as a food source, a garden ornamental, and a decorative and religious emblem. One of the most active *Nelumbo*-loving civilisations, the Achaemenid Dynasty of Persia, conquered Egypt in 525 BC. Therefore, the argument goes, *Nelumbo* arrived in Egypt with these Persian invaders.

A few commentators took issue, finding earlier *Nelumbo*-inspired paintings, inscriptions and objects some of which dated from early in the first millennium BC. Looking at these, I could not be sure that I was not seeing yet more depictions of *Nymphaea*, the Nile's native 'lotus', or of papyrus whose inflorescences are often simplified in Ancient Egyptian art as an inverted cone on a stalk, so causing them to resemble the receptacle of *Nelumbo*. At the same time, various peoples who interacted with Egypt in the second and first millennia BC not only knew *Nelumbo nucifera* but revered it. It seemed conceivable that the plant had infiltrated the Nile and its culture ahead of the Persian invasion in 525 BC. Before long Pythagoras no less would persuade me that was the case.

However it arrived, by the fifth century BC *Nelumbo* was so well-established in the Nile that it was believed to be native. In his *Histories*, Herodotus describes it as 'a type of lily [*krinon*] which grows in the river and resembles a rose'. He differentiates it from another 'lily', meaning the waterlily *Nymphaea*, which, he says, the people themselves call lōtos. This is the oldest surviving record of the term 'lotus' being associated with aquatic plants. Herodotus does not say how the Egyptians came to attach this old name used by the Greeks for peas and trees to their sacred flower.

The belief that *Nelumbo nucifera* was native, or even endemic, to Egypt is still more intriguing. It was this conviction that gave Alexander the Great his burst of ill-founded optimism on the banks of the Chenab. It was shared by Theophrastus and the Classical naturalists who followed him, even though Theophrastus himself had observed that *Nelumbo* could also be found in Syria and Cilicia (present-day South-eastern Anatolia) and around Torone in Greece's present-day Chalkidiki Prefecture. I suspect we should believe him. His master Aristotle was born not far from this Northern Aegean lotus colony and was a possible eyewitness to it. Aristotle's patrons, the grand-father and father of Alexander the Great, were also active there. The fourth- and early third-century tombs of Macedonia and Thrace are replete with *Nelumbo*-inspired artefacts, including silver bowls and stone carvings. Although these lotuses are usually attributed to a vogue for Persian and Egyptian designs, they do not always mirror them, nor do their dates always follow the overrunning of those lands by Macedonian forces. According to Theophrastus, the real-life inspiration for these objects was growing nearby all the time.

Other Classical sightings of the sacred lotus in Europe are even more mysterious. These might indicate the pathways of ancient travellers and traders like the Phoenicians who were expert in carrying edible commodi-ties west. They might reveal, but never explain, some wandering envoy of an Oriental power, or sporadic converts to some exotic faith. They might equally have been the remnants of shrinking wild populations. However it came there, *Nelumbo nucifera* was known on mainland Southern Italy in the fifth century BC and on Sicily a hundred years later. In the third century, the historian Phylarchus reported its miraculous appearance in Greece, in a swamp near the Thyamis or Kalamas River which flows into the Ionian Sea just south of Albania:

> *The Egyptian bean had either never been sown before or had refused to grow anywhere but in Egypt. And yet, in the reign of Alexander son of Pyrrhus [Alexander II, King of Epirus, succeeded 272 BC, died 242], it so happened that this plant sprang up in a swamp near the Thyamis River in Thesprotia, a region of Epirus. For two years or so afterwards it bore fruit and spread luxuriantly; but when Alexander stationed a guard to ensure that nobody would even dare come near this plant – let alone pick some of it – the swamp suddenly dried up. Not only did this place not produce the bean any longer, but whatever water it once possessed never reappeared.*

This might be the earliest record of the sacred lotus's extraordinary capacity for just-add-water rebirth. The seeds may have been lying in wait against the day when the river changed course or broke its banks, the water table rose, or the rains were heavier than usual. But the more I learnt about Alexander II, the more I found myself entertaining an alternative and stranger hypothesis. This King of Epirus is named in that remarkable lapidary record, the Edicts of Ashoka, as one of five Greek monarchs who received the Buddha's teachings. If so, his benefactor would have been Ashoka the Great (304–232 BC) who ruled India's Mauryan Empire and sent missionaries across the Hellenistic world. Ashoka's own dominions extended from Afghanistan to Assam, covering much of the Indian subcontinent. Throughout them, he recorded his activities as a Buddhist convert, proselytiser and law-maker, engraved sometimes on naked rock, sometimes on august pillars that were capped with lions and lotuses. In 1950, some 2,200 years after Ashoka commissioned it, one such capital, at Sarnath in Uttar Pradesh, became the emblem of India's nationhood. Alexander II of Epirus appears among fourteen edicts dating from 257 BC, carved on a boulder in the Girnar Hills in Gujarat. These inscriptions also describe Ashoka's policy of distributing medicinal and holy plants as part of his mission. Perhaps Thesprotia's miraculous lotus had something to do with an Indian visitor? That might at least explain the reverence Alexander II, a war-like king, displayed for the sacred flower.

The penetration of the Greek world by the Indian emperor's emissaries might also explain why, from the second century onwards, we find mention of a shrine dedicated to Athena Kolokasia, a head-spinningly syncretistic Our Lady of the Lotus, in Sicyon near Corinth. On the other hand, this cult may have been more to do with the Classical world's greatest source of numinous exports – Egypt which, as Phylarchus made plain in telling his tale, was believed to be the true home of the lotus. On the banks of the Chenab, Alexander the Great had insisted the plant was an Egyptian native even when the same species grew wild in his father's northern kingdom. By the time another of Ashoka's Buddhist embassies arrived at the Alexandrian court of Ptolemy II, *Nelumbo* had been hallowed on the Nile for at least 200 years. Never mind what happened in India or Persia, this was Lotus-Land proper. In Hellenistic Egypt there was nothing you could tell them about the sacred flower.

In 25 BC Cleopatra had been dead five years. Her former kingdom, the first and longest-surviving of the satrapies spawned by Alexander's conquests, had been annexed as Aegyptus. Her nemesis Octavian had taken the name Augustus two years earlier: Rome had acquired its first emperor and most productive province. These were good times to be a tourist in Egypt, especially if you had the protection of the prefect and a boundless relish for exotic customs. Strabo, a thirty-eight-year-old geographer and historian, had both.

Today Lake Maryut, just to the south of Alexandria, is smaller and shallower than it was in Graeco-Roman times, and seriously polluted, in places so nitrogen-bloomed that nothing but algae survives and elsewhere so salty that even algae spurns it. When Strabo visited it this lake was almost 100 kilometres wide from east to west, and fed by canals that connected it to the Nile. With fresh waters and fertile shores, Mareotis, as he would have known it, was an agricultural prodigy. The wine produced in the surrounding vineyards was so good that it was laid down and vintages declared – not the usual Roman practice where the grape was drunk almost as soon as it was squeezed. The lake itself was famed as a great aquatic pleasure garden, the lagoon of the good life.

Strabo was an elegant fellow, a lifelong scholar born to wealth. Nonetheless, when I read his account of Mareotis I could somehow hear the awe-struck baritone rasp of Enobarbus describing Cleopatra's barge. Of course Shakespeare's character was recounting an event that occurred in another lotus-land, the

River Cydnus in Cilicia; but Cleopatra's usual boating haunt was this lake which, like the queen herself, beggar'd all description. Here, says Strabo, kyamos (*Nelumbo nucifera*) grows as tall as papyrus. Its flowers and fruit are larger and more delectable than those of the kyamos he knows from home. From which we might conclude that Strabo's birthplace, Amasya in the Black Sea region of Turkey, was yet another ancient *Nelumbo* habitat. People flock to these beautiful Egyptian lotus colonies (kyamōnes) in cabin-boats and hold floating feasts and drinking parties deep inside the shade of their foliage. The leaves themselves are so large that they can be used as cups and bowls. Even when they have left the lake, the lotus-eaters can still avail themselves of their favourite plant, for Alexandria is full of artisans who fashion cups from the fruiting receptacles of *Nelumbo*. Meanwhile the lake-dwellers harvest the plant fresh and send it to the capital to boost their income.

Writing around the same time that Strabo was in Egypt, Horace describes the festivities that will attend the return of an old friend. Together, he promises, they will fill polished cups with oblivion-inducing wine. The poet's chosen word for 'cups' is *ciboria*, derived from kibōrion, the Greek term for the fruiting receptacles of *Nelumbo* and the very same term that Strabo uses for the beakers Alexandrians fashioned from the lotus. Ciborium, the lotus cup, was de rigueur for smart Romans at home and abroad. Writing some 85 years later, Pliny and Columella describe the plant's performance in domestic gardens. To their voices we can add mosaics and murals such as those at Pompeii. All indicate that *Nelumbo nucifera* was becoming a Roman favourite. It was beautiful and noble; it was useful, whether filling bellies, being filled with wine or simply keeping the ducks cool; above all, and despite abundant evidence to the contrary, it was Egyptian. And that mattered. Like many great empires, Rome yearned for an imaginary 'other place', a fantasy land filled with exotica ripe for export and capable of providing jaded appetites with an image, at least, of somewhere else to go. In the nineteenth century, the British looked to Japan; from the first century BC onwards, the Romans looked to Egypt: this was their Lotus-Land.

Its most glorious manifestation is in Central Italy at Palestrina, or Praeneste as it was in Roman times. A mosaic which extends over an area of 5.85 by 4.31 metres, it once covered the floor of the nymphaeum, the grotto-like sanctuary, of what may have been a temple dedicated to Isis, Rome's favourite non-Greek imported deity. During the temple's lifetime, this mosaic probably lay under a film of water, which would have been appropriate in view of its subject. It depicts the life of the Nile with detail, colour and energy of a kind that one would only have thought possible in painting. At the top (the background) the uppermost reaches of the river are shown, a mountainous region inhabited by creatures and peoples beyond even the imaginings of Herodotus. This section bears witness to an expedition to discover the source of the Nile mounted in 280 BC by Ptolemy II.

From this apex of untamed terra nova, the waters grow broader and calmer in an aquatic panorama filled with palm-covered promontories and reedy islets. Here and there a crocodile churns, a hippopotamus breaches or a boat's sail fills. Closer to the foreground, the islands grow larger, bearing temples and villas, and troglodyte gives place to toga-wearer. There is still a flourishing fauna – buffalos, hogs and ibises – but humble sloop becomes stately barge. As savage became angler and farmer so they in turn become merchants, priests and princes. We are now far into the Nile Delta, just below Alexandria, in Lake Mareotis perhaps where Strabo watched his lotus-eaters. And there they are, right in the foreground, unmistakable, unfaded, the roseate flowers of *Nelumbo nucifera*.

To the right, a group of figures, part-military, part-hieratical, is engaged in some ceremony or matter of state in what could be a temple or palace. To the left, the crocodiles and hippopotamuses reappear, joined now by an elephant, to warn us that today's cultivated paradise may be tomorrow's diluvial apocalypse, or that Isis the river goddess may withdraw her favours, causing famine rather than flood. In the centre, however, is a party or, if one is not too demanding about numbers, an orgy – two kingsize beds-cum-boats with a threesome on one and a foursome on the other. Linking them in an arc is a pergola of vines and *Nelumbo*, a lotus bower. All around, the same flowers emerge from the water. Cut, they even fill the prow of the papyrus canoe which plies the channel between the two groups.

Nobody is quite sure when the Praeneste mosaic was made. The dates proposed range from the second century BC to the second century AD. The current favourite is between 120 and 80 BC, which would place its creation at a time when Egypt was not yet in Rome's grasp. Nonetheless, the message of the mosaic's foreground seems clear: administrative order on the one hand, barbaric wilderness on the other, Dionysian delights in the middle. This may be an accurate depiction of life in Ptolemaic Egypt, but it is also a very Roman conception of Lotus-Land – a balanced paradise where oblivion is only temporary.

Nelumbo nucifera continued to be an object of delight and fascination for the Roman world, and almost always through its connection with Egypt, a country where it was no more native than the Romans themselves. In both Nature and culture, it had gradually been displacing the true lotuses of the Nile, *Nymphaea caerulea* and *N. lotus*, since the sixth century BC. It was an easy usurpation: not only was the plant more spectacular, vigorous and economically valuable than these waterlilies, but its looks and life cycle meant that it was better suited to ritual use, better able to express the mysteries of birth and rebirth, of spiritual purification and sensual celebration. Now, in the first century AD, the takeover process accelerated. Soon the moment arrived when *Nelumbo* finally became known as 'Lotus' to Egyptian, Greek and Roman alike.

At the end of the second century AD, Athenaeus, a Greek author based in the Egyptian city of Naucratis, produced his fifteen-book *Deipnosophistae*, 'The Philosophers at the Dinner Table'. Over the course of a fictional banquet, a cast of learned men covers a long menu of subjects, recalling long-dead authors who, in some cases, only survive thanks to this convivial compilation. It is here, for example, that we learn of Nicander, a poet of the late second century BC, who liked to plait wreaths from *Nelumbo* flowers and ply feasters with its boiled rhizomes and beans, and of Diphilas of Siphnos who complained that the rhizomes, though nutritious, were hard to digest, but easier than the beans, which were both laxative and bloating. As his dinner guests trade tales of lotus-eating past and thrash out the differences between kyamos, kibōrion and kolokasion, Athenaeus himself cuts across the conversation:

Nowadays this is the plant Egyptians call lōtos. But in my city Naucratis, we like to call it melilōtos [honey lotus], and from it we make the garlands we call honey lotus crowns which are very fragrant and cooling in summer.

There it was at last – after centuries of going by other names and competing with other plants for the title, *Nelumbo nucifera* was *the* lotus, even in Egypt, which had perfectly good lotuses of its own. More importantly, the plant's conquest of the Nile amidst a succession of invading armies had finally produced a Lotus-Land worthy of Homer's muse. But there was one more incarnation in store for *Nelumbo* in Egypt.

The Emperor Hadrian was forty-eight in 124 AD when he found the love of his life in the province of Bithynia in present-day Turkey. Antinous would have been in his mid-teens. Their affair scandalised Rome not because of its homosexuality or even the age difference, but because the emperor did the boy too much honour, treating him more like an official consort than an Oriental catamite. Like the beard Hadrian insisted on sporting, their relationship was seen as yet another symptom of the emperor's fondness for effete Greek ways. Out of imperial earshot, the mockery was merciless, greatly assisted by the boy's name. In Homer's *Odyssey*, Antinous was Penelope's most bumptious suitor, killed by Odysseus on his return home. Alternatively, it could be read as *anti-nous*, 'against or instead of intelligence, mindless'.

Untouched by the carping, Hadrian and Antinous roamed the empire surrounded by an entourage that was less like a court on royal progress than a fully functioning travelling administration. Cities were founded, temples dedicated, governors toppled or installed, new territories gained and permeable borders turned into impregnable walls. Hadrian oversaw all this and, when he had finished, gazed upon the boy. Five years into their relationship, the imperial itinerary took them to Egypt where, as was the custom during the Roman occupation, they devoted themselves to pleasure. Not that all was sybaritic: during a lion hunt, the emperor speared a man-eater that had been terrorising the outlying villages of Alexandria. Then, in October 130, Antinous drowned in the Nile during a boating party.

If Rome resented Antinous when he was alive, she had every reason to hate him in death. Hadrian devoted his vast resources and administrative talents to a single cause – expressing his grief. The Turkish twenty-year-old was promptly deified. At the scene of his death, on the east bank of the Nile near the village of Besa, the emperor founded a new city, Antinopolis, as the centre of the cult of his immortalised lover. He ensured that the cult would proliferate by sponsoring satellite temples throughout the eastern empire and commissioning hundreds – some say thousands – of portrait statues and medallions. Then Hadrian fell quiet. He does not surface again until the winter of 131/132 when we find him in Athens prior to putting down the Jewish uprising. The question is – what was the emperor up to in those missing months?

One answer is provided by Athenaeus, who was active in Egypt not long after Hadrian's own death in 138:

Now you come to mention Alexandria, I happen to know for a fact that in that fair city they make a special type of garland. It's called an Antinoeios because it's made from the flowers of a lotus that grows there and which bears the same name. Two plants flower in the marshes in summer, two different colours. One looks like a rose and it is this plant that they call Antinoeios and from which these garlands are woven; the other has blue flowers and is also known as 'lotus'. Pancrates, a poet I used to know from the region, showed Hadrian the rosy lotus when he visited Alexandria. He told the emperor that it was a wonder plant which ought to be called Antinoeios because it had sprung from the earth when the ground was soaked with the blood of the Mauritanian lion. This was a terrible beast that had been making parts of Libya near Alexandria uninhabitable and which Hadrian himself had killed while hunting with his friend. The emperor was so pleased with the ingenuity of this thought that he appointed the poet to a post in the temple of the Muses . . . So Pancrates wrote a poem which goes –

'The thyme with its downy sprigs, the pure white lily, the purple squill and gleaming celandine, and then the rose whose petals open to the zephyrs of spring – surely none of these can bloom until the earth has given us the flower that bears the name of Antinous.'

In the months after his lover's death Hadrian had endured a long winter of mourning and memorialising and then a summer of lotus-gazing and with it, perhaps, a coming to terms at last. Pancrates's conceit was bound to console him: not only was Antinous now a god, but he had achieved his new status by the oldest and most natural route possible – not a vote from the Senate but metamorphosis, Greek-style, into a flower. For the emperor other details must have seemed to confirm this transmutation. There was the plant itself, exotic, Eastern in origin, rosy pink and preternaturally beautiful. There was the lion hunt, the last and most valorous public episode that the two men had shared, and a traumatic catalyst of exactly the kind that figures in metamorphic myth. Finally, there was the habitat of the lotus: the waters of the Nile had taken Antinous from Hadrian, and now they were giving him back.

We cannot say whether the poet Pancrates was making Hadrian a gift of all *Nelumbo* in the Nile by naming them after Antinous, or whether he had some special form in mind, perhaps with extra dark or large or double flowers, something that looked as if it had sprung from the blood of a lion. Was Antinoeios *Nelumbo nucifera* in the broad sense or a cultivar, a unique selection with a commemorative name, like *Clematis* 'Princess Diana'? Roman mosaics of the Nile show lotuses in a range of flower shapes and colours, suggesting there was scope for a plantsman's connoisseurship; but these apparent variants might just be artistic licence. Whichever it was, the identification stuck. In texts dating from the period and long afterwards, *Nelumbo nucifera* is named as the flower of Antinous. In a second- or third-century papyrus discovered at the Egyptian site of Tebtunis, it is described in heroic terms, the ultimate immortal flower, nobler and lovelier than any other metamorphosed member of the plant pantheon, including Adonis and Narcissus. The lotus synonymous with the lamented lover appears on obelisks; it even materialises in an ode composed for the accession of the Emperor Diocletian in 284.

Meanwhile, despite initial Roman misgivings about its origins, Antinopolis flourished. So did the cult for which the city was founded. Wreathed with grape vines and ivy, some statues of Antinous clearly identify the new god with Bacchus, or Dionysus as the Greek-loving Hadrian would probably have preferred to call him. Other depictions, however, suggest the drowned youth became a posthumously naturalised Egyptian, a reincarnation of Osiris, the great god of the afterlife whose dominion over the Nile both gave life and took it away. The two deities, Dionysus and Osiris, had been converging since before Alexander's conquest of Egypt. Now they had finally fused at Antinopolis. As I looked deeper into this strange romance, I found a report of excavations of the city which had revealed sunken tanks around its sacred buildings. My bet was that they were designed for growing lotuses, but I could not be sure. As Plato chided, 'Socrates, how easily you make up stories about Egypt – or any country, come to that.'

5

What 'Beans' Means

Most lives of Pythagoras follow a pattern. He was born between 580 and 570 BC to a Phoenician father and a local mother on the island of Samos in the eastern Aegean. He travelled in Egypt and the Near East absorbing new learning and ancient doctrines. He may have been captured by the Persians during their conquest of Egypt and sent to Babylon. He may have journeyed as far as India. He settled eventually in Croton in Calabria, Southern Italy. There he established a school, part-academy, part-religious sect. Sometime between 500 and 480 BC, he died in circumstances unknown after a tyrant, jealous and suspicious of his powers, put the Pythagoreans to rout.

Then come his beliefs and practices. He fused the mystical Greek cult of Orphism with mythologies acquired on his travels. He believed in the transmigration of souls. All living creatures therefore had an equal claim to respect. This meant that women were not excluded from his sect; also that its members fought shy of slaughter anywhere – battlefield, altar or shambles. His followers believed in reincarnation, asceticism, vegetarianism, compassion, purity and contemplation. These principles were inculcated by means of riddle-like questions. This same teaching method, and a love of arcane symbolism, led to his society being described as a secret sect, so bringing about its downfall. Around the end of the sixth century BC, however, Pythagoreans played an open and active part in the life of Croton and its neighbouring settlements.

Next, the intellectual achievements. Pythagoras was the first man to call himself a philosopher. His philosophising was both sacred, spiritual as we would see it, and scientific, *mathematic* in its original sense. Numbers were everything and everywhere. Added up, the Tetraktys, the elemental series one to four, produced the perfect number, ten. From there he went on to formulate the theorem that bears his name, to discover heavenly harmonies, and ultimately to trace the pattern of the cosmos. Although no primary source survives for any of these endeavours, history has never hesitated to award Pythagoras the laurels as the wizard-like obstetrician, if not the actual father, of Western geometry, music theory, mathematics and astronomy.

All heroic stuff. After which the modern biographer stumbles and mumbles: Pythagoras's most cherished law was this – steer clear of beans.

How, after wandering the world, hearing the music of the spheres, and discovering the number that was the answer to everything, could this Olympian figure have entertained such a trivial taboo? How could a man who had taken the pulse of the universe be frightened by a bowl of pulses? The Greeks had a word for it – bathos. Commentators ever since Classical antiquity have offered helpful explanations for the great man's leguminous obsession. Too many beans lead to nocturnal indigestion and a disturbed dream life. The soul is an airy substance, composed of wind – one cannot risk farting one's spirit away. The bean is very obviously a seed and possibly the latent reincarnation of another creature, so to eat it is to stand indicted on at least two counts of illegal abortion. Best of all is a very elegant little body of work on Favism. Not uncommon in parts of the Mediterranean, this genetic disorder causes the breakdown of red blood cells in predisposed candidates. The trigger is believed to be eating broad beans (*Vicia faba*), or even just contact with the plant's pollen. Pythagoras, the argument goes, worked all this out 2,500 years ago and told his followers to give beans a wide berth.

Ensconced in Oxford's Bodleian Library, I started putting myself through these torments of vegetarianism, flatulence and anaemia for one reason. Soon after Pythagoras's time, the word that authors start using for his infamous bean is kyamos, and kyamos is also the most common Greek name for *Nelumbo nucifera*. The lexicon will tell you that it is merely a loose generic term – any old bean. It was certainly applied to the broad bean, *Vicia faba*, and in the modern period it is the repeated and unquestioning identification of this plant with the philosopher's bean that has caused champions of Pythagoras so much embarrassment. But my research was suggesting that kyamos was used with even greater frequency for the sacred lotus.

Did Pythagoras think the same? If he did, the entire bean taboo would make sense; it would be perfectly in tune with reincarnation-minded spiritual traditions that were already old by the time he travelled east and south to find them.

Post-Pythagorean texts are promising but inconclusive. Pliny, for example, states that the bean (faba or kyamos) was proscribed as a food by Pythagoreans because it was thought to contain the souls of the dead. Hard on this comment comes his description of *Nelumbo nucifera*, the sacred lotus, identified at first simply as 'the bean' and only later as 'the Egyptian bean'. Just before it, however, is a discussion of bean-bearing plants in general, the important crop *Vicia faba* among them. Writing between the second and third centuries AD, the philosopher Hippolytus observed that Pythagoras forbade men to eat the bean (kyamos) because:

> it arose at the very beginning of the genesis of all things when the earth was still a mass. His proof for this was that if one crushed a bean and exposed its germ to the sun even for a short while – for light soon changes it – it would emit an odour of human semen. He claims there is another, still clearer proof: take the flower of the bean, put it into a pitcher of water, bury it in the earth, and then, after a few days, dig it up again. You will see straight-away that it has become womb-like. On closer examination, you will discern a child's head developing within it.

Well, it could be either a lotus or a broad bean, although the embryo's sudden reaction to light and its seminal odour are suggestive of *Nelumbo*; likewise, the uterine 'flower' which might be the receptacle with its embedded seeds. Still not quite convinced, I decided to look instead at accounts of Pythagoras's followers. Compiled eight centuries after his death but on the basis of far earlier texts, one of these describes the persecution of Pythagoreans in Southern Italy by the ruler of Syracuse, Dionysius II (397–343 BC). Feeling threatened and excluded by this irenic but elite cult, the tyrant sent his cavalry after a group of its members, thirty soldiers against ten Pythagoreans. Despite the odds, the disciples were managing to escape. They lured the troops into a system of ravines; the valley floors were marshy; the soldiers were forced first to dismount and then to take off their armour rather than sink. Meanwhile, the Pythagoreans were fleeing when disaster befell them. They encountered a kyamōn, a 'bean field', a term often used for a colony of *Nelumbo nucifera*. Although only this vegetation stood between them and safety, they were powerless to cross it – the very faith for which they were being hunted would not allow them to step on the bean's roots or to damage its leaves. Before long the wading soldiers caught up with the fugitives and cut them down.

This was not enough for Dionysius II. He was after captives not corpses. What he really wanted to know, he said, was the secret of the bean. So he had two other Pythagoreans brought before him, Myllias and his nine-month-pregnant wife Timycha. 'Teach me one thing,' said Dionysius, 'and I'll set you free with a safe conduct. Why did your companions choose to die rather than tread on the bean?' Myllias replied that as his brothers would sooner have died than tell the tyrant the reason so he in turn would sooner tread on the bean than tell him why. In the end he neither spilled the beans nor trod on them, but die he duly did. Now it was Timycha's turn to be interrogated. Rather than reveal the secret of the bean, she bit out her tongue and followed her husband to the grave, taking their unborn child with her.

I found myself inclining to the view that these were all martyrs in the name of the lotus. First, who grows broad beans in a valley bottom so wet that soldiers have to dismount and disrobe? Second, what planting of broad beans is so tall, dense or wide that even the clumsiest or hastiest of fugitives cannot pick his way through it without damaging the crop? This, after all, was in the fourth century BC, long before a broad bean field would have been anything like its present-day counterpart in scale. A healthy lotus colony, on the other hand, is well-nigh impassable unless some violence is done to the plant.

No works by Pythagoras survive to put the identity of his bean beyond question, or indeed to certify the exact nature of any of his other beliefs. Although we know a great deal about him, it all comes to us thanks to later compilers and commentators. From them one can infer that the bean, kyamos, probably meant *Nelumbo nucifera* to Pythagoras as it did to Theophrastus and to Pliny 200 and 600 years later respectively. But I still had to admit there was room for doubt and that the fuss may have been about broad beans. Then I encountered an artefact that appeared to identify the Pythagorean plant once and for all.

It was a coin minted in Croton early in the fifth century BC, towards the end of the philosopher's life. Pictured in relief on one side was a device fairly common on Greek coins – a *lebes*, the tripod-mounted bowl used for burning sacrificed animals. Less common was the creature that stood beside this sacrificial bowl: it was a heron or an egret. We were entering mysterious waters. Less common still was what appeared on the reverse of the coin. At first sight it too looked like a lebes, but made by impression rather than relief. Read more carefully, however, it became clear that this was a sacred bowl with a difference.

It was a stalked hemispherical receptacle with a ribbed surface. Represented in relief halfway down the stalk was an ellipsoidal object no larger than a match-head. It was a bean shown falling from the cup. At the base of the stem other beans were arrayed in a zone figured with what I thought might be rippling water. I looked more closely: yes, it *was* water – the fourth bean from the left was very deliberately shown breaking the surface, sinking to join its nine companions. That made ten beans in a row. Ten, the Decad, was the sum of the numbers one to four which Pythagoras believed gave meaning to the entire universe, the mystical Tetraktys by which his followers affirmed their beliefs rather than swear on the usual gods. When I looked at the heron's side of the coin again, I realised that what I had taken for a casting blip, a foundry flaw, was in fact another bean. Seated solitary at the foot of the pedestal's middle leg, it was a clue to what was happening on the flip-side, a minute symbolic PTO.

The coin showed a cycle, a process of fructification, dissemination and germination embodied by the lotus receptacle and the ten seeds, the philosopher's seminal number. It seemed especially apt that Croton, the city that Pythagoras and his followers made their own, should have represented itself with a natural-born alternative to the lebes. What could be more eloquent than to replace this symbol of the established priesthood with the living vessel of the immortal bean? Other coins from Croton at its Pythagorean peak showed a similar suite of devices. The heron was often there, or perhaps a crab, an octopus or a dove, and always depicted with touching naturalism. The bean-dropping receptacle was frequently featured as the reverse of the more conventional lebes. Occasionally, the sacrificial cauldron itself had metamorphosed into the likeness of a lotus, its pedestal stalk-like or leafy, its cup marked with petaloid patterns. In some examples the periphery was pocked with sunken beans or edged with stylised petals and veins, so making a lotus receptacle, seen in plan, of the entire coin.

I would not see designs quite like them again until my quest took me to Japan. But those motifs were still part of a living faith, whereas the philosopher's coins told a different story. As one would expect, the lotus appears in

Croton's numismatic record during the Pythagorean ascendancy. Thereafter, it fades, its receptacle replaced by the conventional bowl, its beans consigned to eternal slumber. The lifelike native fauna, the herons and crabs that are such potent reminders that bean-counting was a cult of Nature, evolve into imperious eagles and stallions. Within a century of Pythagoras's death, the human face returns and we are back in the realm of familiar gods and self-promoting tyrants.

Plato failed to make a philosopher-prince of Dionysius II, persecutor of the Pythagoreans. In the first half of the fourth century BC, however, he succeeded in producing the tightest summary we have of Pythagorean cosmology – his philosophical dialogue *Timaeus*. In addition to nods to Ancient Egyptian mysticism and to the life-giving energy of the Nile, *Timaeus* strikes several beanish chords without mentioning the lotus by name. The Demiurge, the primal creator, mixes the elements to form a mass of undifferentiated universal soul. He does this in a bowl which is variously described as the mother, the nurse and the receptacle of all generation. He then divides this matter into portions which are described, and sown, as seeds. From these germinate the souls of men; their precise lineaments he leaves it to the gods (also born of the receptacle) to shape.

So we have a receptacle and seeds, and finally we have man himself, the ultimate product of this germination process. Man, says Plato, is 'a celestial plant', rooted in the base material of his generation but with his head held high as if suspended by divine power. Whether he was thinking of Pythagoras's beloved bean or not, this image of human transcendence and divine potential – roots in the mud, head in the heavens – is the second most important use to which our imagination has put *Nelumbo*, eclipsed only in age and significance by the lotus as a symbol of rebirth.

That idea, another Pythagorean tenet, also occurs in *Timaeus*. Reincarnation and transmigration are represented as a cycle of continuous birth and rebirth. There is a karma-like dimension to this wheel of being and becoming: those who slip from their state of native grace are reborn as lesser beings. Only by exercising divine-given reason can these demoted creatures transcend the tumultuous and irrational mass of creation and return to their original perfection. In other words, only something that sounds very like enlightenment will stop the turning of the wheel. Although I had no idea at the time, this concept would become a major theme of my lotus quest in the form of its Buddhist equivalent, the doctrine of Samsara.

In the first and second centuries AD, Plutarch devoted much effort to unpacking Plato's *Timaeus*, and travelled in Egypt in search of the source of Pythagoras's beliefs. It was there, he became convinced, that the first philosopher picked up the cult of the bean. In this view, Plutarch was echoing Herodotus who, in the fifth century BC, said Egyptians would not eat beans, and Pliny in the first century AD who claimed Egyptian priests used beans as offerings to the gods and the souls of the dead. By 'bean' (kyamos) here, we can assume that Herodotus and Pliny meant *Nelumbo*. *Vicia faba*, the other candidate for the title, was a day-to-day staple and subject to no such proscriptions. So it remains, as foules-mesdames.

In *Isis and Osiris*, Plutarch presents an Ancient Egyptian religion for the modern Roman. He does so using two arguments that might be described as essentially Pythagorean. Myths and fetishes do not require fundamentalist belief; they are, rather, to be read as cryptic allegories and symbols. Religion is not chauvinistically nationalist; it can be exported and resettled. He takes the example of the lotus to advance both arguments:

> Nor, again, do Egyptians really believe that the sun rises from a lotus flower as a newborn baby; rather, they portray the dawn allegorically in this way to symbolise the sun's rekindling amid the waters.
>
> There is nothing to fear so long as people hold these gods in common and do not insist that they belong to the Egyptians alone, to the Nile alone and to the land the Nile irrigates; nothing to fear so long as they do not claim that the marshes and the lotus are only achievements of Egyptian gods, and provided those same people do not refuse their great gods to the rest of us who have no Nile or Buto or Memphis.

While Plutarch was relegating belief to myth, myth was becoming a reality. People were participating in the cultivation *and* cult of the lotus, not just in Egypt but across the Roman Empire. A tradition was emerging, a strange, international and ecumenical hybrid of mysticism and philosophy whose proponents included both enlightened thinkers and tenebrous believers. Running through it, sometimes hidden, sometimes plain, was the lotus. It culminated in the fourth century in Chalcis, a city in Syria where *Nelumbo nucifera* had been a familiar sight since Theophrastus's time, so familiar in fact that some late Roman authors referred to the lotus as *Faba Syriaca*, the Syrian bean. Chalcis was also the birth- and workplace of Iamblichus (circa 245–325 AD), the Neoplatonist philosopher who turned this admixture of ancient and modern, science and supernature, familiar and foreign, into something resembling a new religion.

Iamblichus compiled ten volumes of commentary on Pythagoras, developing a system of his own with the first philosopher at its heart. In *Timaeus* Plato introduces the daimon, the essential and divine human spirit. Iamblichus transformed that idea into a master spirit, a helpful guide somewhere between a Christian angel and a Buddhist Bodhisattva, who acts as a bridge between the sacred and the secular, the eternal and the momentary. Pythagoras was just such a master, a great teacher who, like his contemporary the Buddha, could spawn avatars and reincarnations by his immortal example. Around the core Pythagorean teachings Iamblichus wove a rich fabric of rational philosophy from Greece and Rome, and of gods, arcana and ritual gathered from any race or religion that took his fancy. Theurgy was the term he gave to the ritual aspects of his practice, the summoning of strange gods. Others had different names for it – some called it sorcery, some an Oriental pollution of the pure stream of Greek thought. Not that Iamblichus recognised a distinction between the realms of reason and belief: 'the religions of the Chaldeans, Egyptians and Greeks,' he said, 'are no less scientific than sublime.'

One religion was conspicuously absent from this gorgeous brocade – Christianity which, under the patronage of the Emperor Constantine, had become the dominant faith in the Roman Empire, especially in the East where Iamblichus lived. It held his ideas in check until 361 when Julian was proclaimed Roman Emperor. Ten years earlier, at the age of twenty, Julian had secretly converted from Christianity to paganism. Now he could be as open as he liked about his polytheistic passion. Within a year of his accession, the new emperor had decreed an edict of religious tolerance; temples that had been taken over by the Christian Church were returned to their original cults or to new manifestations of theurgy; Neoplatonist and Pythagorean teachings were placed at the heart of academic curricula and a new priesthood groomed. Once more it became safe to speak of heavenly geometry and reincarnation, of receptacles and sacred beans.

Julian attributed his conversion to Iamblichus whose writings would be the key not to a new orthodoxy but to an old liberality and latitude. Not everybody rejoiced at this open-armed approach. In 363, the year after he proclaimed religious tolerance, the emperor was fatally wounded while campaigning against the Persians – perhaps by one of his ostensible adversaries, more probably by one of many disenfranchised Christians under cover of battle. His brief Neo-pagan revival died with him.

So what did Iamblichus and his followers like the Emperor Julian – Julian the Apostate as the Church likes to call him – actually believe? How did they integrate mystical cult with day-to-day morality? Here is a passage from Iamblichus's *Egyptian Mysteries*:

> God's being shown seated on a lotus signifies a superiority which rises above and excludes all contact with the mud of the world. It also points to the reign of the intellect in the heavens. For every feature of the lotus is circular, from the outline of its leaves to the shape of its fruit, and circularity alone is akin to the activity of the intellect as it invariably manifests itself in identity, ruled by one order and one reason. God himself is established in himself as being above power and activity of this kind, august and holy in his transcendent simplicity, abiding within himself – this is what his being seated on the lotus signifies.

Iamblichus's plant is not strictly Egyptian. This lotus which bloomed so briefly in the twilight of the pagan world is, rather, a complex hybrid with roots that extend not only to the Nile but also to the Indus and beyond by way of the Tigris and Euphrates. Iamblichus was offering a fissile empire a symbol which, in its ceaseless circularity and transcendence, borrowed from Hinduism and Buddhism and connected with the cults of Ancient Mesopotamia as well as Egypt. Meanwhile, his insistence on the primacy of the intellect looked west to the philosophers of Greece and Rome: as mystical emblems go, this was a very rational lotus. Like the rest of his thinking, his flower was denounced as decadent, retrograde, a creature of the dark that was doomed to perish in the light of Christian revelation. In a world of conflicting faiths, however, it seems a conciliatory invention, almost enlightened.

Over the next thousand years, *Nelumbo nucifera* declined in the West as plant, emblem and artefact. The occasional glimmer was really no more than an ember. Although Muslims, for example, carried lotuses from Sicily to their courtyard gardens in Spain, these living fragments of antiquity survived there no longer than their Caliphate guardians and admirers. In the Hebrew and Christian traditions, the lotus either disappeared or turned into a lily. Sometimes the transformation was deliberate: lilies were safe, untainted by paganism, and readily understood by believers in cooler or drier regions where

Lilium grew. Often, however, it was accidental. People who had never seen real *Nelumbo* could be forgiven for reading lotus motifs in architectural and other designs as lilies, and Classical authors from Herodotus onwards had described *Nelumbo* as a type of lily (krinon), so engendering confusion among later interpreters.

Translations of the *Song of Songs* illustrate this metamorphosis – 'My beloved is mine and I am his. He feedeth among the lilies.' King Solomon's lilies (Hebrew *shoshannim*) are valley-dwelling flowers to which a woman's lips and belly are favourably compared. These carnal plants sound unlike any *Lilium* species likely to have been known in Israel at the beginning of the first millennium BC. They are, rather, riparian blooms among which one feasts in an ecstatic state, and strangely reminiscent of the early Middle Eastern potentate's lotus world or of the Nile paradise beloved of Greeks and Romans. Unsurprisingly, some scholars detect similarities between the *Song of Songs* and Ancient Egyptian love poetry. Others draw comparisons between these rhapsodic verses and hymns to the Mesopotamian goddesses Inanna and Ishtar, both associated with the lotus. Meanwhile, many Hebrew authorities wisely interpret Solomon's shoshannim as 'lily-like plants' instead of identifying them strictly as *Lilium*.

But in Europe and the Middle East *Nelumbo nucifera* was facing graver challenges than being lost in translation. Ahead lay changes in climate and cultivation practices, the fall of the old cultures that protected it, and the rise of jealous new faiths that would exclude it. The fate of the word 'ciborium' exemplifies what happened next. Classical antiquity's name for the plant, its fruiting receptacles and the Bacchanalian lotus cup became Christianity's term for the vessel that contains sacramental bread. Any connection with *Nelumbo* was soon erased or forgotten, likewise the rites and festivities that once attended it. Before long, if the sacred lotus was known at all, it was as a relic of the pagan past and a property of the heathen East. By the Middle Ages it was falling extinct even in the Nile.

6

The Tree of Life

In terms of that pagan past, Egypt had no monopoly of the lotus. The plant's importance in Mesopotamia dates from at least the fifth millennium BC and the founding of Uruk. Like other Sumerian settlements in Southern Iraq, this city grew up close to abundant fresh water – the two great rivers that gave the region its name, of course, but also lakes and marshes. In time, these waters would support the earliest and largest agricultural expansion in the ancient world. At first, however, it was the wild larder they provided that made civilisation possible. Among Nature's provisions, it seems, was *Nelumbo nucifera*, a plant whose range may then have extended from Asia Minor and the Caspian to the Persian Gulf, following the flood plains of the Euphrates and Tigris.

The people of Uruk raised a ziggurat. On its summit was a temple dedicated to their patron deity, Inanna. This great fertility goddess would become the model for later mothers of earth and queens of heaven in the Near East, including the Akkadian Ishtar and the Phoenician Astarte. Inanna was also a lotus goddess. Plaques, pendants and seals dating from the fifth to the third millennium BC reveal the proliferation of her cult and the plant's role in it. They are the main evidence of the presence of *Nelumbo* in early Mesopotamia and of the reverence Sumerians accorded it.

Her lotus takes various forms. In the most minimalist icons, the goddess herself is reduced to nothing more than a cartoon *Nelumbo* receptacle seen sideways-on and atop a stalk. A seed pod is an obvious emblem of fertility;

but the simplification of its shape to an inverted triangle is also suggestive of the goddess's lower abdomen or perhaps even of her vulva which is so graphically apostrophised in Sumerian hymns. As if to underscore this receptacle/birth canal identification, in some fuller and more realistic sculptures of Inanna, Ishtar and Astarte, the pubic region is modelled to echo the delta-like outline of the lotus receptacle the goddess is holding.

In less abstract representations, she is shown holding two receptacles face-on to present their seed-pocked discs. At other times just one disc is shown, floating in space and haloed with petals as if it were the sun. These solar lotuses are often reduced to an astral form, the Star or Rosette of Ishtar as it would become known. Their points, or petals, are almost always eight – a number that predominates in the lotus iconography of the Middle and Far East both ancient and modern. We also find her dressed as if for battle, a winged figure with what appears to be a quiver of arrows on her back, like some avenging angel. These are strange arrows, however; their shafts terminate in fat buds. Far from firing them at an adversary, Inanna sometimes appears to have given one of them to a male attendant, perhaps a king or hierophant, perhaps a god who relies upon her afflatus.

Sometimes this sceptre-like lotus takes the form of a trident with three distinct petals, one erect, two recurved, like a turgid fleur-de-lis. As a decorative motif, this would percolate into the nearby cultures of European antiquity. In the Middle East, the lotus sceptre became a symbol of authority, adopted and reinvented by a succession of conquerors and cultures up to Darius III, the Persian ruler defeated by Alexander the Great in 330 BC. It was Inanna's, or Ishtar's, flower, symbolic not only of fertility and wealth, but also of her relationship with the sovereign deity: her gift to him of this bloom sparked the creation of the world. It was hardly surprising that temporal rulers wanted the same gift by analogy with the divine overlord. Each new ruler who seized control of Mesopotamia also embraced the goddess's flower, no matter where he came from or what beliefs he left behind. In 575 BC, for example, when Nebuchadnezzar II rebuilt Babylon as his glorious capital, he ordered that the Ishtar Gate, the city's newest and finest portal, be decorated with hundreds of stylised lotus rosettes.

Babylon had met the goddess and her flower long before. Hammurabi (circa 1795–1750 BC) was the city state's sixth king, the first Babylonian emperor and pioneer of written legal codes. In Akkadian, which by then had supplanted Sumerian as the spoken, if not the official written, language of Mesopotamia, his name means something like 'kinsman healer'. In Sumerian, however, the king's name may equally have been read as Khammu Rabi, meaning 'Great Lotus'. Another ancient rendering of Hammurabi, this time into Semitic, was Kimta Rapashti, again meaning 'Great Lotus'. Soon afterwards, a Middle Eastern monarch appears in India's Sanskrit tradition who may have been Hammurabi. This king is Pundarika, a name that once more signifies 'Great Lotus'. A particularly potent term, it would survive in Hinduism and Buddhism as the embodiment of divine order. Saddharma Pundarika, for example, is the Great Lotus of the Good Law.

In Mesopotamian artefacts from the third millennium BC onwards, *Nelumbo* begins to assume new guises. The tripartite bud acquires more petals, often obtusely tipped as opposed to sharp-pointed. The result is a semicircular motif that resembles a scallop shell. A similar design was derived from a lotus leaf that was cut in half so that the veins appeared to radiate from a basal midpoint (the transected omphalos) like a fully open fan. In time, and detached from the goddess, these emblems would evolve into the lotus-palmette or anthemion so abundant in Persian and Hellenistic decoration. In some cases the corona of petals was attached to a semicircular disc, a half-receptacle, giving a transected *Nelumbo* flower seen in plan. Here the lotus resembled the rising sun, an identification that became explicit when the Phoenicians took up this device as one of their most common emblems.

Whether trident, palmette, rosette or rising sun, these lotus buds, blooms and leaves might be given stalks and conjoined in a divaricate and often symmetrical arrangement, like the branches of a very simple tree. The intention was not to represent a tree, but a woven ceremonial display of lotuses or a whole plant including rampant rhizome. Sometimes the goddess Inanna or Ishtar stands in its fork clasping the two main branches. Sumerian and Babylonian inscriptions confirm the value attached to this device: the lotus is described as 'the plant of the deep', 'the plant of wells and pools', the 'lofty', 'priest's' and 'sovereign's plant'. Because this cartoon ramiform vegetation is evidently something elemental, priceless and holy, scholars have often interpreted this style of lotus icon as 'the tree of life'.

In Iraq's National Museum in Baghdad is an ivory throne-back. Neo-Assyrian, from the city of Nimrud, and dating from the eighth century BC, it is carved with a magnificent relief of five panels. The three innermost panels show two standing gryphons and, between them, a seated ruler. With his feet planted on a submissive lion, this king holds a cup to an opening

Nelumbo bud which towers above him on a sinuous stalk that ascends from a branching rhizome. The same 'tree' of life can be seen in a much later artefact from the same museum. This is a hexagonal slab, a fragment of a stucco relief found in Samarra and dating from the ninth century AD, in other words, from the early Islamic period. Here the lotus snakes and spirals its way through a symmetrical tableau of stylised grapes and fig or vine leaves, surrounding each in a life-giving embrace. Only at the top of the slab does it finally bear its own foliage and flower – two unfurling *Nelumbo* leaves carved with tender naturalism and, between them, a bloom complete with receptacle and embedded seeds. Greatly simplified or abstracted, in the Near East, botanical designs like this one would evolve into the rich decorative flora of the arabesque, of fretwork, tile and carpet. By then the *Nelumbo* element was often unidentifiable or mistaken for a rose. Detached from the lotus, this 'tree' of life would prove equally durable in the West, inspiring countless Romanesque and Gothic church decorations and refurbished with rose, oak and other familiar plants. Few such Christian ornaments could have been carved with any understanding that their roots lay in the Fertile Crescent and in the cult of the mother of all fertility goddesses.

The most sensational lotus 'tree' features in a pair of gilded wood and lapis lazuli sculptures which date from between 2600 and 2400 BC. These are the greatest of all the treasures to have been found in the royal cemetery of the ancient city of Ur in southern Iraq. Discovered by Sir Leonard Woolley between 1928 and 1929, they were swiftly required to share the unhappy name 'Ram in a Thicket'. A city called Ur, perhaps not this one, was where the patriarch Abraham was born. These sculptures, each of which shows a long-horned ungulate on its hind legs and seemingly caught in vegetation, brought Genesis 22:13, Isaac's mercifully aborted sacrifice, to Woolley's biblical mind. Since then, archaeologists have fought shy of this Old Testament association, but they have not done a great deal better. These splendid creatures, we are told, depict a typical Sumerian scene, not a ram but a goat browsing on a leafy shrub. They are meant as a testament to the importance of husbandry.

Gazing upon one of the pair in the British Museum, I found it hard to believe that even the richest Mesopotamian monarch would have invested so much in celebrating anything so prosaic. For a start, the beast is neither a ram nor a domesticated goat. It is a much more formidable creature, an ibex – possibly *Capra ibex* whose range once extended into these regions or more probably something akin to the wild subspecies of *Capra aegagrus* known as the Bezoar and Sindh ibexes. Horned beasts identifiable as ibex, urial, oryx and antelope appear with lotus symbols in artefacts found as far apart as Sumer, Denderah and the Indus Valley.

The same goes for the 'thicket'. Candelabriform and fashioned from wood so thickly gilded as to look like solid gold, it proliferates from a cylindrical trunk. The creature's forelegs perch on two main branches – not tethered, caught or scrambling, but with every appearance of commanding ease. Each of these branches fans out in four further divisions. These terminate in what might be either an unfurling leaf or a spear-shaped flower bud, except for the two outermost which are crowned with an open bloom. The flowers are identifiable as *Nelumbo nucifera*, anatomically accurate right down to the receptacle. As was often the case with religious depictions of the lotus from Mesopotamian and early Indian culture, these flowers have eight petals, a number that would retain its symbolic importance in Hinduism and Buddhism. This famous artefact may appear to be a ram in a thicket or a blue-chip celebration of agrarian life, but the iconography points to its being something more numinous – the union of ibex and lotus, Mesopotamia's two most richly symbolic organisms.

Not long after he discovered the rams in thickets, or ibexes with lotuses, in the royal cemetery of Ur, Woolley found the tomb of a woman who lived there sometime between 2550 and 2400 BC. She had been laid to rest with an immense cache of grave goods. Five soldiers and thirteen maidservants had either killed themselves or been killed in order to join their mistress in the afterlife. Seals and inscriptions revealed that her name was Puabi, perhaps a queen, more probably a high priestess. The most celebrated of all her possessions is the headdress described as 'Queen Puabi's Crown'. Fashioned in sheet gold, the leaves that form its shimmering veil are willow and poplar, indicating the all-important presence of water. The open crown is edged with small lotus flowers whose petals are inlaid with lapis and white paste. Standing behind this headdress, a large gold comb expands into a sharp-toothed flare with an eight-petalled lotus on each of its points. It is an image of the rising sun decked with the dawn flower, a sun that rose behind Puabi's head each time she wore this treasure.

Other city states and other peoples in the Middle East cleaved to the lotus. In some cases, their cults appear to have arisen spontaneously. Although overrun by Sumerians, Akkadians and Assyrians, the ancient

Elamite capital of Susa in south-western Iran produced an abundance of lotus artefacts. These differ from their Mesopotamian counterparts in favouring the open upturned flower of *Nelumbo*, its petals depicted with a lifelike flair reminiscent of early Indian representations. The resemblance may be more than coincidental: Elamite has been linked to Dravidian languages. Although these now predominate in southern India, before the second millennium BC they were spoken further north and west, around the Indus and its tributaries.

Susa's lotus style is beautifully illustrated by an object which dates from around 900 BC, now in Abu Dhabi's Barakat Gallery. Just 9.5 centimetres tall and 10.8 centimetres across, it is a silver flask with a gold-lined lip. The petals are sculpted in a bowl-like ring which extends a little beyond the flask's shoulders, as if collaring its neck. Susa lotus bowls would be copied by Persia's Achaemenid Dynasty after their conquest of the Elamite kingdom in 539 BC – usually in bronze and with far less skill, but still in ways close to the living *Nelumbo* flower. The same motif persisted in this region into the Islamic period, in the form of ceramic 'rose'-patterned bowls.

In other cases these lotus cults can be traced to contact with and conquest of the Sumerian domains, and the co-opting of Inanna. Although some of these invaders preferred to call her Ishtar, the great fertility goddess remained essentially the same. Sometimes, however, the goddess's or king's flower changed in the eyes and hands of its new owners – not in significance but in realism. This is of interest to a botanist because it suggests that the northern incomers were familiar with living *Nelumbo*, a plant which may already have been growing scarce in the ever-drier south.

In 713 BC, the Assyrian king Sargon II built himself a new palace at Dur-Sharrukin, present-day Khorsabad, near Mosul in Northern Iraq. It was decorated with sculptures of immense winged bulls and stone reliefs that told the tale of his ceaseless campaigning. By the time of his death in 705 BC, just after the palace's completion, the king had taken Babylon, Syria, Elam, Phrygia, Cyprus and the southern Caspian, and scored victories against the Philistines, Israelites, Medes and Egyptians. Several Dur-Sharrukin reliefs show the lotus in multiple guises, suggesting that the flower had remained an emblem of divine and kingly authority even for this rampaging ruler. Its importance may also have been conciliatory or unifying. It was a symbol familiar to many of Sargon's subjects, most of whom came from long-established lotus cultures, and some from regions where wild *Nelumbo* was still prolific.

Now in the Louvre, one relief depicts a towering kingly figure. His diadem and bracelets are ornamented with rosette-like lotus flowers. In one hand, held downwards, are two *Nelumbo* buds and an open flower, the ancient symbols of fertility and authority carved here with new verisimilitude. Gently supported by this figure's other hand is an ibex, alert but at ease, with its head held high to survey the same vista as the king's own fearsome gaze.

The most glittering examples of this new realism were feared lost until 2003 when they came to light in the flooded vault of a bombed-out bank. This was the Treasure of Nimrud, which had only been discovered in 1988, and then briefly exhibited in the National Museum in Baghdad before being salted away in the run-up to the first Iraq War. When these artefacts did not reappear after the war, some alleged that one of Saddam Hussein's sons had sold them. Those who hoped they were still in Iraq lost heart at the outbreak of the second conflict which unleashed the looting of countless Mesopotamian relics. But the Nimrud Treasure had been safe all along, banked in a rag-tag miscellany of soaking shoeboxes, Tupperware and other such improvised arks.

Consisting of over 600 items, the treasure was first discovered in three tombs beneath the women's quarters of the palace of the Assyrian king Ashurnasirpal II. He had moved his capital to Nimrud, or Kalhu as it was then known, near present-day Mosul in northern Iraq. The artefacts date from the period between 879 BC, when his new palace was completed, and 750 BC. Many incorporate the lotus in some form, often in association with the pomegranate. Several show craftsmen reconnecting the ancient symbol with its living inspiration, a reflection perhaps of the fact that the seat of power had shifted north towards *Nelumbo* habitats. The most impressive of all these treasures is a headdress even more elaborate than Puabi's. A pure gold cage, it swarms with scores of lotus blooms and pomegranates. The goddess appears in winged form, like a circle of angels, in an openwork band above the flowers and fruit. Above this in turn is a dome of golden vines, their fruit modelled in lapis lazuli. The crown has the appearance of some celestial arbour, which, it seems, is what it was – worn in death to shelter a royal child on the journey to a place where lotuses and pomegranates lasted even longer than gold.

Each of these civilisations disseminated its lotus cult through trade and conquest. As *Nelumbo* vectors, however, two later Middle Eastern cultures were even more energetic. Between 1550 and 300 BC the Phoenicians, or Canaanites as they are known in the Old Testament, peppered the Mediterranean seaboard with settlements. In some cases these were little more than trading posts; in others they were full-blown city states. Several of their settlements lay close to *Nelumbo* populations in the northern Aegean, Turkey, Syria and Sicily and may lie at the root of these far-flung lotus colonies.

One of the principal Phoenician deities was the goddess Astarte who, like Inanna, Ishtar and Isis, is associated with the lotus as a symbol of fertility and birth. In Astarte's case, this association is suggested in votive tablets such as those found at Carthage where the lotus appears in stylised sun-like forms and allied to the moon – the goddess's special plant contrasted with her special planet, as day with night. She also had a special beast, the bull, and this is often depicted crowned with a radiant arc of lotus petals, again linking this dawn-flowering plant with the rising sun. The most intriguing specimen of Astarte's nelumbiferous Taurus was discovered in 1832 by a labourer working on a stone wall at the vicarage of St Just in the Cornish parish of Penwith. For a few years this 5-centimetre-long bronze bull resided quietly on the workman's mantelpiece. Then, as the discovery became known, it set the antiquaries of Victorian England afire. It appeared to prove the ancient claim, made by Strabo among others, that Phoenicians reached metal-rich Cornwall in their endless quest for commodities. If that is so, the St Just bull is the westernmost evidence of the diffusion of eastern lotus culture.

The lotus-Astarte identification is made beautifully explicit in a series of plaques discovered at Beth Shemesh, 20 kilometres west of Jerusalem. Dating from between 1500 and 1200 BC, they show Astarte standing, naked and almost always holding lotuses. Her hair is often elaborately plaited and braided, a motif echoed in the rope-like border of the design. This may represent a serpent, recalling yet more mother goddesses, among them the Phrygian Cybele and snake-loving lotus deities from as far afield as India and Japan. Although crudely moulded in coarse clay, these simple figures are potently lifelike. In one plaque Astarte's head inclines ever so slightly to the left, an erotic note of naturalism. Equally naturalistic are the fruiting receptacles of *Nelumbo nucifera* which the goddess holds, one in each hand and perfectly in scale with her body.

As mariners and traders the Phoenicians made themselves useful to the last of these Near Eastern lotus cultures – that of Persia's Achaemenid Dynasty who, between 558 and 330 BC, forged the largest empire the world had seen. They hailed from a region that still contains wild populations of *Nelumbo nucifera*, or *Nelumbo caspica* as it should perhaps be called in this context. Already familiar with the plant in their homeland, the Persians consolidated the Sumerian, Assyrian, Babylonian and Elamite traditions that had held the lotus dear; then they moved west to absorb the Canaanite iconography of Astarte before sweeping south to the Nile. There they are commonly (if erroneously) supposed to have introduced *Nelumbo nucifera* soon after 525 BC. So numerous were the Persian lotus motifs that I found in museums in Oxford, London and Paris that I gave up keeping notes and making sketches. It seemed almost any object or surface could be nelumbified.

The extent of the Achaemenid lotus legacy has barely been measured even in the Persian heartland. In 2007 a new site came to light in the Fars province of southern Iran. Perfectly preserved beneath the mocha-brown soil was a constellation of smooth and pale stone blooms each a metre across and deep. These were column bases carved in the likeness of a downturned *Nelumbo* flower. As if the mason had not wished us to be in any doubt, in the sinus of each pair of mammoth petals is a smaller secondary lotus. These giant blooms may be all that survives of the long-lost city of Lidoma. They are far from isolated, however: ten other such sites have been found in the region in recent years.

Iranian archaeologists believe the model for these constructions was the Hall of the Hundred Columns in Persepolis, the ceremonial capital of the Persian kings, also in Fars. An immense colonnaded edifice that served first as a throne room, then as a place for honouring generals, and finally as the imperial museum, it was begun by Xerxes the Great and finished by his son Artaxerxes I towards the end of the fifth century BC. There, as elsewhere in Persepolis, *Nelumbo* was the theme of endless decorative variations. The city amounted to a hymn to the lotus in stone and faience, gold and ivory, ebony and cedar, all looted or vandalised by Alexander the Great in 330 BC. Still, the sacred flower would take its revenge on the Macedonian megalomaniac a few years later, on the banks of the River Chenab. Such designs had begun to penetrate the Greek world long before Alexander destroyed the Achaemenid Empire. After his conquests, their availability and cachet were only enhanced. From the hill forts of Macedonia to the villas of Athens, Persian-derived lotus-inspired objects became all the rage, even for those who, unlike Theophrastus, had not a clue what they meant.

Ornamental value notwithstanding, *Nelumbo* evidently meant something to the Persians. Stone friezes show enthroned rulers receiving lines of tribute-payers, probably from one or more of their many subject nations. In the ruler's hand a single lotus flower is held. As it had been for Sumerian and Babylonian kings, *Nelumbo* was a badge of office. In other contexts, the lotus signified divine as well as secular power, which, in the case of the Persians, meant solar power. Shown face-on, the radiant disc-like flowers are often associated with the sun and with the dawn-like ascent and expansion of rightful gods and rulers. Theirs was a macho and mighty lotus, a flowering that eclipsed the goddess – but only partially. A cylindrical seal from fifth-century-BC Susa shows two male figures, one reclining on a couch and the other bearing a trident, astride a giant fish and approaching the couch, it seems, with some alacrity. The reclining figure is in a state of languid bliss. Although alone, he might almost be in the clinch of some invisible lover. Look more closely and you see that he is drinking deep of the perfume of a lotus flower: the goddess is there in cryptic form.

7

The Birth of Lakshmi

Around 2600 BC, over two millennia before Alexander the Great saw *Nelumbo* on the River Chenab, the Indus and its tributaries supported a coherent, precocious and highly distinctive culture. Agriculture flourished and trade networks extended as far as the Gulf, the Mediterranean and the Far East. Alongside useful plants such as cotton and barley, animals were domesticated, including India's familiar hump-backed cow. The horse appears not to have featured in the lives of these people – an omission that cost them dear if, as is often assumed, they were eventually overrun by charioteering Aryans. Textiles were woven, gold, copper and bronze worked, stone engraved and pottery fashioned. Cities were systematically planned and built in astonishingly uniform fired brick. The largest of these settlements supported as many as 80,000 souls, a density made possible by hygiene and housing standards of a kind more usually associated with Rome. These were not only the first grid towns, they were also the first towns with drains, running water and under-floor heating. Vast granaries and warehouses housed communal commodities. Although it remains indecipherable, there was writing in the form of copious seals and inscriptions. There was mathematics, chiefly concerned with weights, measures and building dimensions, but sophisticated enough to have given Pythagoras food for thought. Above all there was art, manifest in numerous sacred objects embedded like pearls in the strange, almost modern-seeming monotony of these ancient cities.

This culture, which has only been yielding its secrets since the early 1920s, is called the Indus Valley or Harappan civilisation after the name of one of its most famous sites, Harappa in north-east Pakistan. It began as early as 6000 BC, flourished between 2600 and 1900 BC, and then went into decline – perhaps as a result of climatic change and alterations in the levels and courses of the rivers it depended on, perhaps in the face of equestrian northern invaders, probably because of both these factors and others unknown. Over a thousand sites have now been discovered, and more come to light all the time. So far the two largest and richest are Harappa itself in Punjab and Mohenjo-Daro further south on the Indus flood plain in Pakistan's Sindh Province.

Drains and hypocausts are not the only built features by which the Harappans anticipate the Romans. At Mohenjo-Daro, a public bath was discovered, 12 metres long and 2.4 metres deep, lined with brick and sealed with bitumen. Its purpose is thought to have been religious purification. For this reason, it has been described as the oldest surviving lotus bath – not a place for growing lotuses (although some were that too), but the forerunner of many thousands of tanks and pools created during the Hindu hegemony that followed the Harappan civilisation. In their waters, as in sacred rivers like the Ganges, the transcendent dirt-deflecting *Nelumbo* was imitated and body and soul were purified in a ritual rehearsal of rebirth.

Apart from the oldest known man-made lotus pool, sites like Mohenjo-Daro have yielded other clues that suggest the Indus Valley culture was a lotus culture. Models of lotus flowers, each with eight petals fashioned in bronze and gilt, have materialised among the excavations. The buds and fruiting receptacles of *Nelumbo* feature in numerous seals and plaques, some-times, it appears, as emblems of secular power, at other times in sacred roles. Among the latter is a representation of a horned goddess, perhaps Astarte's remote cousin, standing in the fork of what appears to be a simplified tree. Its candelabra-like branches are tipped with lotus flowers, just as in the Mesopotamian 'tree' of life. To one side of her is a splendid bull; before her stands a cohort of worshippers. So to the strange foreshadowing of the Vedic civilisation to come, we can add echoes of Middle Eastern civilisations that were flourishing not far away in the same period.

From the end of the third millennium BC onwards, this female figure evolves. Statuettes of her, some rudely sculpted in clay, others as smooth as soap in steatite, appear throughout the Harappan domains. Now she is a young woman with coiled hair, high breasts and a broad pelvis. Her arms are either flung wide in greeting or crossed in a pose that can only be described as come-hither. Her face combines nubile teasing and wisdom beyond her years. On either side, without fail, is a fruiting receptacle of *Nelumbo nucifera*, the stalks tucked into her hair, the embedded seeds facing the onlooker. Where petals are present, they are usually eight, again reminding us of Mesopotamian mysteries and looking ahead to the iconography of Hinduism and Buddhism. Impressed by her looks, one archaeologist opined that this girl represented a special class of sex worker, perhaps living and working beside the giant lotus bath and enabling men to alternate between sacred and profane. But this ignores the fact that she is not a courtesan but a goddess who has outlived the Indus Valley civilisation by millennia.

This figure is the precursor of Lakshmi, the Hindu goddess of prosperity, wishes granted, and goals attained. Lakshmi is the Vedic Venus, personifying beauty, fertility and good fortune, beloved of the principal male deities, loving them in turn, and born from an ocean of cosmic milk either with a lotus in her hand or seated upon a lotus. She is the *Nelumbo* goddess par excellence, wreathed with poetical epithets: *Padmapriya* (lotus-lover); *Padmini, Puskarnini* (abounding in lotuses); *Padmesthita* (standing on a lotus); *Padmamalini* or *Padmamaladhara devi* (lotus-garlanded); *Padmahasta* (lotus-holder); *Padmasundari* (she who is as lovely as a lotus); *Padmamukhi* (she whose face is as lovely as the lotus); *Padmasambhava* (lotus-born); *Padmakshi* (lotus-eyed); *Padma-uru* (lotus-thighed); *Padmavarna* (lotus-hued) and finally, just in case there were any lingering doubt, plain *Padma* or *Kamala*, meaning 'lotus one'.

In the entire Hindu pantheon and, indeed, in any other pantheon, Lakshmi's lotus credentials are outdone only by those of Vishnu, the supreme deity, to whom she is consort. Both are usually shown standing or seated upon open lotus blooms, with Vishnu carrying one or more lotus buds as living sceptres. These symbolise his authority and purity, his capacity for infinite rebirth and his dominion over Dharma, the rules of conduct that lead to spiritual awakening. In time, these rules would be symbolised in turn by the Dharmachakra, the eight-spoked wheel of the law, whose shape was inspired by the radiating petals or leaf veins of *Nelumbo* and which, through Hinduism and then Buddhism, would become the world's most common lotus motif.

Vishnu and Lakshmi star together in Vedic creation myth. They float in the void upon an immense multi-headed serpent whose concave body resembles the wall of a uterus and whose thousand mouths hold the planets. From Vishnu's navel issues a single flower of *Nelumbo* which opens to produce Brahma, the god who will set about the work of creation itself. This demi-urgic event earns Vishnu rather than Lakshmi the most important Indian lotus epithet of all, *Padmanabha*, lotus-naveled. Without it, there would be no world. At the same time the lotus, the primal generative organ, is Lakshmi's and hers alone. She is the female principle and principal, the essential earth in which Vishnu is rooted. Her catalytic energy is known as Shakti, a Sanskrit word for power. A similar symbiosis exists between other lotus goddesses and their male leads – between Isis and Osiris, between Inanna, Ishtar and their various spouses, between Astarte and Baal and El.

It used to be claimed that the Vedic beliefs which evolved into Hinduism arrived with Indo-Aryan invaders who displaced the Indus Valley Civilisation. First composed soon after their arrival, between 1500 and 900 BC, the *Rig Veda* makes no mention of Lakshmi. Her absence from these sacred hymns has been cited as evidence against the idea – now more popularly held and certainly more plausible – of cultural continuity between the Harappan and Vedic civilisations. The *Rig Veda* does, however, describe the birth of Agni the Brahminical Mercury, messenger god of fire and sacrifice. He was born, we are told, of a lotus. Soon afterwards, in the Khilas or later hymns that supplement the *Rig Veda*, this maternal lotus is identified as a goddess in her own right named Shri or Lakshmi. It is in one of these hymns that she begins to attract the cascade of padma-prefixed epithets. To these are added other titles associated with her role as a fertility goddess. Her sons are called Mud and Moisture. She herself is the Keeper of Dung, the Mother of Living Things, and, most simply and beautifully, Ksama, meaning 'Earth'.

All of which suggests a fairly rapid uptake of the native lotus cult by the incoming population. But would the lotus and its ritual role have been so unfamiliar to Indo-Aryans in any case? After all, they had moved south and east from the region of the lower Volga River, which even today is one of the most important *Nelumbo nucifera* habitats outside Asia. The artefacts excavated in their Southern Russian homelands are scant, primitive and hard to interpret. Among them, however, are ceremonial metal discs, crude examples of repoussé work patterned with pimples which may just be the tell-tale papillae of the lotus receptacle.

Among the next generation of India's sacred texts, the seventh- or sixth-century BC *Brhadaranyaka Upanishad* also makes no explicit reference to

Lakshmi. But it does invoke the lotus and in ways that recall the long-established symbolism of the flower and the goddess. It is, for example, identified with the sun: 'In the morning he worships the sun, praying – You are the sole lotus among the heavens. May I likewise become the sole lotus among men.' In a vivid paean to procreation and birth, the plant's habitat is compared to the gravid womb: 'As the wind moves the surface of a lotus pond, so may your unborn child quicken.' Dating from the same period, the *Chandogya Upanishad* contains something else that may or may not have been new to lotus symbolism but which is spelt out here for the first time.

Now flower and leaf become vehicles for values and, indeed, an entire philosophy. These are collectively named Brahman, a word that originally meant a vatic utterance but which had come by this time to describe god-given truths and laws, and the Vedic canon itself. Evil deeds and thoughts, says the *Chandogya Upanishad*, no sooner cling to the man who knows Brahman than water adheres to a lotus leaf. Brahman is visualised as a fortress. Within it is a lotus bud which, although small, contains the entire cosmos. The objective is to enter this bud, to dwell there, possessing it and possessed by it in turn. This is the nature of the spiritual quest. As a metaphor or a series of metaphors, *Nelumbo* is acquiring a moral dimension which it would retain throughout the development of Hinduism, something altogether more complex and abstract than its original connection with the goddess of sun, birth and fertility. The lotus is now the vehicle of the law. Its role as a vessel or an allegory of morality would become adopted and vastly elaborated by Buddhism whose expansion began around two centuries after these two Upanishads were composed.

And yet Lakshmi, the Hindu continuation of the Harappan lotus goddess, was not written out of the script. Far from it – she was allocated a leading role in the creation of the very cosmos that her flower was said to contain. The same goes for Buddhism, where avatars of the lotus goddess survive in their bodily simplicity to aid those who find the flower's abstract symbolism hard to comprehend. In both cases, the lotus and its patron goddess indicate a pattern of cultural continuity rather than extermination by invading forces. For millennia they did the same in Mesopotamia and the Levant despite wave after wave of conquests. But those Middle Eastern goddesses have long since departed, whereas Lakshmi is alive and well.

II

Western Dreamers

8

St Mary's Beehives

The River Isis may not sound like the answer for a man suffering from a surfeit of goddesses, but it leads to my favourite Oxford retreat, the Church of St Mary the Virgin in Iffley village. The baptistry of this twelfth-century Romanesque masterpiece contains a stained-glass window designed by John Piper and donated in 1995. A cartouche of brilliant azure, it shows a miscellany of animals proclaiming the Nativity around the (non-lotus) Tree of Life. Having strolled along the Isis to St Mary's, I was gazing at this swatch of heaven when I overheard a conversation.

She (slightly strident): No, I think they're beehives. But *burning* beehives – what would be the idea of that? I mean, I'm assuming all these decorations meant something to somebody, so what would a beehive on fire have meant?

He (very assured): Darling, take it from me – they're sunflowers. Look, I know a bit about these things. The Jerusalem artichoke's a kind of sunflower and this place was crawling with Templars and other crusader types.

Sunflowers, I reflected, hail from the New World and would be unlikely adornments for a church built in 1170. As for the Jerusalem artichoke, not only is it native to the United States, but the 'Jerusalem' in its name is a corruption of the Italian *girasole*, 'sunflower', which happened sometime after the 1600s. Sunflowers be damned, I thought, but decided not to spoil his moment. Instead I took a look at the object of their debate and found myself privately agreeing with her. And yet why set a beehive ablaze? Puff smoke at it maybe. There were fifteen of these controversial motifs arranged in an

71

arc. They surmounted a west-facing arch that spanned the passage from the nave to the tower. Another arch, decorated in the same way, separated the tower's interior from the choir. Carved beneath them were multiple bands in zigzag pattern. That, I knew, was characteristic of the Romanesque, but what about these burning beehives? Perhaps he had a point? Seen in a certain light, they did look like flowers.

Suddenly the afternoon sun shifted. Now seen in stronger light and close up, the beehives had to be flowers. In the centre of each was a semicircular disc covered in papillae. Arising from it like a halo of flames was a series of beautifully sculpted petals. The other carvings of vegetation in St Mary's were fanciful but not imaginary. They all had identifiable living sources. Having excluded the possibility of a sunflower, I was left with no other obvious identification but this – I was staring at a Romanesque lotus rainbow, and not notional lotuses but rather accurate depictions of the flower of *Nelumbo nucifera*, receptacle and all, cut across its middle. So much for my respite from the sacred flower – not even the Church could offer me sanctuary.

Nevertheless, I remained sceptical. Why would a Norman church have put a pagan exotic centre stage, made it the gateway to the godhead? How did the mason come by his source? Oaks and ivy I could understand, hops and grape vines too, but not a lotus. Most of the guides I consulted agreed that the motifs on the tower arches represented some unusual and possibly imaginary plant; one went so far as to say they were unique. Some pointed out that in the Middle Ages these stone blooms would have been painted, presenting a spectacle even more brilliant than John Piper's twentieth-century window. None of them ventured a guess at *Nelumbo* except Sir Nikolaus Pevsner and Jennifer Sherwood who, in their architectural companion to Oxfordshire, describe 'a wide outer order with a large stylised flower motif, probably a lotus'.

Some weeks later, the lotus-loving Alexander II, King of Epirus, put me out of my misery. I had read that he was one of the Hellenistic rulers to whom the Indian Emperor Ashoka sent Buddhist missionaries in the third century BC. Naturally, I wondered what became of those missionaries. What befell them in the West is not known, but their return to India is documented. So too is their eventual resting place, Sanchi, about 50 kilometres north-east of Bhopal, in Madhya Pradesh. There Ashoka built a great temple complex to house relics of the Buddha as well as the remains of his own emissaries. At its heart is the Great Stupa, a vast brick hemisphere which, after the emperor's death in 232 BC, was variously destroyed and rebuilt by rulers non-Buddhist and Buddhist. Among the latter was the Satavahana Dynasty who raised Sanchi to its present glory around 70 BC.

Around the Great Stupa they built four stone toranas, symbolic gateways to a sacred enclosure. Each consisted of two pillars transected by three broad bands, architraves of sorts. These were lavishly carved with scenes from the life of the Buddha and his followers, sacred emblems, wildlife, and examples of the various peoples within and around the Indian Empire. Among these last are Greek figures who may represent the Hellenistic cities that Alexander the Great founded in the Punjab, or who may be from further afield and either travellers or persons met by Indians while travelling.

Of all these swarming details none is quite so profuse or ecstatic as the lotus. On the inner face of the north torana, the plant becomes the main theme as well as the leitmotif. On the columns, within two squares, each over a metre square, *Nelumbo nucifera* soars from the neck of an elaborate vase, seven and nine blooms on each panel respectively, each held on sinuous stems and illustrating a stage of the lotus life cycle. There are fully ripened fruiting receptacles, tightly closed buds and open flowers. Still more intriguing are the pollinated flowers that are pictured sideways-on, their fading petals reflexed, their developing receptacles held uppermost and pitted with nascent seeds.

This last motif, the broad upturned arc of fleshy pod with its fringe of fluttering petals, recurs all over the Sanchi gates. I thought its frequency had to explain the sense of déjà vu that I was beginning to experience – after all, I had been looking at a great many photographs of Sanchi in my pursuit of Ashoka's missionaries. It was not until I turned these images upside-down while photocopying them that the real explanation became apparent. These pollinated blooms were essentially identical to the putative lotuses of St Mary's Iffley, with allowance made for the fact that the Oxford mason had inverted his flowers so that their petals pointed heavenwards and their seeds looked down on the aisle. My uncertainty about their identity had been caused by seeing them in this topsy-turvy state, and by misreading their original inspiration, which was not a transected flower seen in plan, but a bloom in side elevation. Pevsner and Sherwood could swap 'probably' for 'definitely' and take a bow.

I have discovered no other carvings quite like these sideways lotuses at Sanchi and Iffley. Their absence from churches is only to be expected; their rarity in Buddhist architecture is more of a surprise. Only when I returned to St Mary's for another look did I take the obvious step of scouring the church's exterior. The south door, I discovered, was where Iffley's anonymous genius really let rip. Far smaller than the tower's rainbow lotuses but rendered in greater detail, a mass of motifs surrounded the door, perfectly performed cameos from Nature and myth, past and present. Here were centaur and sphinx, Green Man and merman, St George and Norman knights, King Solomon and the reigning monarch and sometime Oxford resident, Henry II. The flora included English native trees, Continental roses, and yet another *Nelumbo*.

I found myself wondering what the Saxon congregation and Norman patrons of St Mary's would have felt about worshipping in a building full of Buddhist icons. Even if, as seems likely, they were unaware of the fact, they must have thought their strange stone blooms signified something. Would the Iffley flock have identified their floral arches with the Hebrew *Tse'el*, the lotus that shelters Behemoth, the primeval swamp monster, among the reeds in chapter 40 of the Book of Job? Precious few other lotuses are named in the Bible. Would St Mary's lotuses have struck a chord with members of the St Remy family who built the church and some of whom travelled east as crusaders?

'Masons,' said a friend on whom I disburdened myself over a drink.

I told him I was perfectly well aware that stonemasons were at the root of the puzzle.

'No,' he replied, '*Freemasons*. Say no more.'

I thought he was making a fanciful leap even if Freemasonry does claim roots in Middle Eastern antiquity and in the activities of mediaeval stone workers. Nonetheless, I pursued the matter as far as I could (not very far) and was surprised to find the cryptic craft has a curious affection for the lotus. The plant has an entry of its own and makes several other appearances in the standard encyclopedia on Freemasonry. With some justification, the same encyclopedia points out that many biblical 'lilies' may have been lotuses, among them the emblems that remain of paramount importance for Freemasons, the 'Lily Work' which adorned the pillars of the Temple of Solomon.

That still would not explain why the Iffley lotuses were identical to first-century-BC designs from a site in central India, the first great Buddhist temple. How did they end up in East Oxford in 1170? One hardly needs those fantasist's favourites, Templars and Freemasons, to see that these carvings present a mystery. Wandering home along the Isis, I reflected that Iffley completed the circle. Include the ritual uses to which Native Americans put their species, and *Nelumbo* becomes the only sacred plant to have circumnavigated the globe.

In a manner typical of the strange serendipity of my quest, Christianity had opened a door on Buddhism. I was beginning to realise that every detail of *Nelumbo nucifera* had been seized upon somewhere between Afghanistan and Japan, between the fourth century BC and the present, and imbued with mystical significance. An entire creed had been dictated by the plant's life cycle; a world view had been formed by the inspection of its anatomical features. Obviously, the seeds embodied reincarnation, and the foliage and flowers the transcendence of a muddy and polluting world by the virtuous or enlightened. But *Nelumbo* had permeated Buddhism more comprehensively. The flower was the Buddha's seat and halo, likewise those of his secondary and semi-divine incarnations, the angelic ministering Bodhisattvas. The lotus flower or leaf was the probable inspiration for Dharmachakra, the eight-spoked Wheel of the Law, which symbolises the Buddha's teachings. The circularity of these plant parts and the lotus life cycle as a whole also imbued Samsara, the wheel of being and becoming, a doctrine of transmigration which, as I had seen, would have rung bells for Pythagoras and Plato.

The lotus 'tree' of life that I encountered in the ancient cultures of Mesopotamia and the Indus Valley was reinvented as one of the most important Buddhist structures. Although it may appear to be nothing more than a tiered arrangement of discs, in origin the stupa is abstracted from the lotus plant, its leaves representing circles of being and stages of enlightenment, its flower buds the ultimate perfection of the Buddha's teachings. In Britain I found this connection between plant and pagoda credulity-stretching. Within a few weeks, however, Buddhist priests would confirm it. They would show me radically simplified towers which the uninitiated would not have associated with *Nelumbo* for a moment were it not for the lotus bud that crowned their summits. They would also show me altar decorations, either live flower and leaf arrangements or lifelike multi-stemmed lotus sculptures. These, they said, were stupas in their natural state.

To Dharmachakra, Samsara and stupas, we can also add mantras. The one mantra everyone knows is *Om mani padme hum*, six syllables of Sanskrit that possess a multiplicity of resonances which for many Buddhists are beyond the scope of the longest and deepest works of scripture. As with most mantras, its mystical potency resides not just in its meaning, or meanings, but also in its sound: recitation is all. There is, however, a literal, if reductive, translation: 'Hail the jewel in the lotus.' Since the fourteenth Dalai Lama is the reincarnation of the Bodhisattva with whom the mantra is associated, we can safely look to His Holiness for guidance on what this lotus means:

> The two syllables, padme, meaning lotus, symbolise wisdom. Just as a lotus grows forth from mud but is not sullied by the faults of mud, so wisdom is capable of putting you in a situation of non-contradiction whereas there would be contradiction if you did not have wisdom. There is wisdom realising impermanence, wisdom realising that persons are empty, of being self-sufficient or substantially existent, wisdom that realises the emptiness of duality – that is to say, of difference of entity between subject and object – and wisdom that realises the emptiness of inherent existence. Though there are many different types of wisdom, the main of all these is the wisdom realising emptiness.

Few Buddhist lotuses are so cryptic and compressed. I was beginning to discover that *Nelumbo* had inspired some of the most glorious religious artworks ever created. There were the Mogao Caves near Dunhuang, the Western Chinese gateway to the Silk Road, where 750 vaults were hewn from the Gobi sandstone over a period of 1,000 years beginning in 336 AD. Many are decorated with murals that depict ecstatic figures in watery states of flux and reincarnation. Lotuses are everywhere, painted in lapis blue and verdigris, and not just the flowers but also a myriad seeds shown at the point of germination. There was the *Lotus Sutra* itself, which also began to take its present translated form in western China a half-century after the Mogao Caves were begun. Was there ever a text so mind-bendingly surreal in its sense of space, time and number, so disinhibited in its opulence? There were the mandalas still created by Tibetan monks on temple floors, exquisite flowers a metre across, and teeming with divine figures and episodes. Made of rainbow-coloured sands painstakingly blown and brushed into place, these images were allowed to last no longer than a live lotus flower, and were then peremptorily swept away.

'How would you define a mandala?' I asked Yoko, my in-house Buddhist.

'A mandala is what I suppose you're making of all these bits and pieces you're collecting. I can only speak from experience, not expertise, but it's a picture or text full of fragments and people and stories from the scriptures; or perhaps showing a hierarchy of enlightened beings; or maybe heaven and earth, or the Buddhist paradise of the Pure Land. It's all sorts of things, but it often takes the form of a lotus, with a progression from the outer to the inner petals. Contemplating it is meant to lead to the discovery of some truth. It's a sort of stationary quest, if that makes any sense.'

She made perfect sense. But, lacking her talent for sitting still, I was beginning to feel the stationary aspect of my quest was leading nowhere. While these museums and libraries were all very well, it was time to visit a living lotus culture. But which? I wanted wild lotuses, lotus culture ancient and modern, and lotus horticulture, all ideally having developed in the same place without interruption. What about Japan, I wondered, where my three seeds had come from in the first place? Although I shared my life with a Japanese woman, had a garden full of Japanese plants, and had longed to go there since boyhood, I had never been to Japan. The lotus seemed a better excuse than any. I stepped outside to cast an anxious eye over my three tubs, now just beginning to sprout. Would they miss me for a month or two? Hardly, after three thousand years of waiting.

Returning indoors, I found Yoko online and staring at a press photograph of *Nelumbo nucifera*. It was a spectacularly large and luminous bloom that seemed, improbably, to be standing in an alpine meadow. Around it was an audience of admirers, the sort of crowd that would not have been out of place at a film premiere. As she translated the article that accompanied the picture, I became more convinced than ever that Japan was the place.

'Take a look at this. It's a newspaper report about a lotus that flowered last summer at a temple called Chūson-ji, in the far north of my country. It germinated from seeds that had been buried for 800 years. They found them during restoration work.'

'Look, I know I've got a bee in my bonnet, but I think it's really time we saw some lotuses in the field.'

'I'm ahead of you. I was just about to book the tickets when I saw this thing at Chūson-ji. Taeko-san is planning our itinerary. You have a fortnight to put your affairs in order.'

Naturally, I squandered it. While Yoko and Taeko-san finalised details and made preparations for our departure, I disappeared to the library again to see what other Westerners had made of the Lotus-Land I was at last about to visit.

9

Lotus-Land

On 29 May 1911 Captain Robert Falcon Scott attended a lecture. It was one of a series of evening talks with which he and his colleagues in the second British Antarctic Expedition regaled one another in their winter quarters at Cape Evans. Following other lectures on such subjects as parasitology, Mendelism and sledging diets, this occasion struck the party as an unusually frivolous and incongruous delight. Outside their benighted shed the temperature was minus 25 degrees Fahrenheit and falling, and the terrain one of towering ice cliffs beside fast-freezing sea. Inside, the magic lantern show transported them to another landscape entirely. As Scott recorded in his journal:

> To-night Ponting gave us a charming lecture on Japan with wonderful illustrations of his own. He is happiest in his descriptions of the artistic side of the people, with which he is in fullest sympathy. So he took us to see the flower pageants. The joyful festivals of the cherry blossom, the wistaria, the iris and chrysanthemum, the sombre colours of the beech blossom and the paths about the lotus gardens, where mankind meditated in solemn mood.

Ponting was Herbert Ponting (1870–1935), official photographer to the ill-fated second expedition. Following Scott's death, just eight months after this virtual stroll in the gardens of Japan, Ponting's images of the *Terra Nova* and its party, ponies and dogs amid ice packs, grottos and bergs became a haunting visual counterpart to the Captain's journals. Despite the fame it

78

brought him, the ice cap was not Ponting's natural artistic habitat. In his early twenties, he had forsaken England and a threatened career in banking for California and the life of a fruit farmer. When his ranch failed, he took to photography and travel, becoming, in his own words, 'a nomad who has worshipped at the shrine of Nature and Art in many lands'. Ponting spent three years in Japan, growing more devoted to the country than to any other of his many distant destinations – until, that is, he read Scott's *The Voyage of the 'Discovery'* while travelling on the Trans-Siberian Railway in January 1907. After that, the photographer only had eyes for Antarctica and the Captain. On 15 June 1910, Ponting's Far Eastern sojourn bore fruit when Macmillan published his first major book, *In Lotus-Land Japan*. The author was not present to enjoy the acclaim it received. That day the *Terra Nova* set sail from Cardiff Bay.

In Lotus-Land Japan makes explicit and implicit reference to Alfred Tennyson's *The Lotos-Eaters* of 1832 (and numerous subsequent revisions). Ponting was not alone in regarding this poem as authorisation for his Japanese reflections, despite its having been inspired by a contemporary European landscape and a Classical text. When he arrives in his narrative at the lotus itself, he includes a photograph of a kind which, before my own odyssey, I might have dismissed as posed to the point of fakery. It shows a pond filled with a massive double-flowered *Nelumbo* cultivar. On the bank are three women in traditional dress. At their feet stand two snowy egrets and a grey heron in a condition so far from flight that one begins to suspect a taxidermist's handiwork. I now know that scenes like this one are perfectly possible, right down to the becalmed waders. The lovely blooms of the lotus, says Ponting:

> *are the token for all that is best in man and woman; for, because the plant thrives best when growing in the foulest mud, and raises its great pink blossoms high above the poisonous slime below to open petals of surpassing loveliness to the morning sun, they typify a chaste and noble heart – unstained, unsullied, and untouched by the insidious breath of evil with which life is permeated – opening to the light of truth and knowledge.*

While Ponting sailed for Antarctic waters, *In Lotus-Land Japan* was accorded a warm reception. Amid all the plaudits, however, came one dissenting voice. In September 1910, an unsigned notice appeared in the *Geographical Journal*, organ of the Royal Geographical Society. Although the review was basically positive, its author picked a fight over the phrase 'Lotus-Land': 'The disadvantage of a fanciful title like this is that it so often connotes a valueless type of book, whereas Mr Ponting's is the opposite.' Strictly speaking, the reviewer was right to scruple. Not only was the title fanciful, it was also inaccurate. Homer's and Tennyson's lotos is not *Nelumbo* and their Lotos-Land is not Japan. But it is the very fancifulness of the phrase 'Lotus-Land' that is so telling.

Although largely accurate, the earliest Western descriptions of Japan and her flora, such as Engelbert Kaempfer's *Amoenitatum Exoticarum* ('Exotic Delights') of 1712, had presented a land that seemed to owe more to fantasy than fact. Between the 1630s and the start of the Meiji Period in 1868, this image became intensified in the Western consciousness as a result of Japan's deepening seclusion. Here was a different type of lotus-land, one whose denizens might not be prone to narcotic amnesia themselves but whose rulers wished to be forgotten. Time had certainly forgotten the country by the beginning of the Meiji Period when Japan opened herself to *gaijin*, foreigners, once more. Kaempfer's adventurer-successors discovered a nation that had achieved a high degree of civilisation without intervention or assistance from the West, and then had called a halt to progress, standing still somewhere in the early seventeenth century. The more romantic and less rapacious gaijin rejoiced to find an isolated idyll frozen in time. Many such nineteenth-century travellers had an education in the Classics and some knowledge of more recent poetry. Whether they took their cue from Homer's poem or Tennyson's, they were struck by a resemblance between Japan and the bliss-fully heedless land of the Lotophagoi. Revealed after centuries of secrecy was a captivating archipelago that had made captives of its natives and visitors and embraced a form of oblivion.

One plant, ubiquitous in life, stone, bronze, wood and paint, confirmed the connection for these foreigners and seemed to make a fact of the fancy: Japan was a place where, in Tennyson's lines, 'The Lotos blooms below the barren peak/The Lotos blows by every winding creek.' That it was not Homer's lotos – a gaunt tree that could hardly be said to 'bloom' or 'blow' and which is alien to watery places – did not matter in the slightest. The wanderers had encountered something altogether better, an enchanting flower, long known as 'lotus' in the West, that seemed worthy of Tennyson's muse and which was revered, grown, *eaten* at every turn. In *Nelumbo* Classicism met Orientalism and produced a syncretistic sensation. Of course Japan was

Lotus-Land. As if to put the matter beyond doubt, Herbert Ponting forged a further and still more striking identification. The first edition of *In Lotus-Land Japan* is prefaced by a quotation, purportedly from Tennyson:

> They saw the gleaming river seaward flow
> From the inner land; far off, a mountain-top,
> A silent pinnacle of aged snow,
> Stood sunset-flushed; and, dew'd with showery drops,
> Up-clomb the shadowy pines above the woven copse.

In fact, the poet wrote 'three mountain-tops/Three silent pinnacles of aged snow', a vista inspired by his wanderings in 1830 in the Pyrenees with his friend Arthur Hallam. This was of no use to Ponting, hence his down-scaling from three peaks to one. A country of mountains, his new-found real-life Lotus-Land boasted one pinnacle in particular, the soaring snow-covered summit of Mount Fuji. Perhaps he simply and felicitously misremembered the poet? But perhaps he knew exactly what he was doing when he narrowed Tennyson's focus from three European peaks to Japan's most singular sacred mountain.

In 1910 Herbert Ponting's book was merely the latest in a caravan of travelogues that referred to the living myth of the lotus. By now Japan was busily modernising and trading freely with the West; but her most popular export by far was her own image, her own romance, and *Nelumbo* was central to it. One of its most successful peddlers was the French author and naval officer Pierre Loti (1850–1923), a nom de plume that may well have been inspired by the lotus. His artistic connection with the flower began before he even reached Japan when his first successful novel, *Rarahu ou Le Mariage de Loti* (1880), provided inspiration for Léo Delibes's opera *Lakmé*. Written by Philippe Gille and Edmond Gondinet, the libretto is filled with the perfumed flora of faraway lands. Loti's signature species appears in the prelude to the Act One barcarolle that was a hit in 1883 when *Lakmé* opened and has remained so ever since, the famous Flower Duet:

Lakmé et Mallika: *Allons cueillir les lotus bleus. Oui, près des cygnes aux ailes de neige. Allons cueillir les lotus bleus.*

Sous le dôme épais, où le blanc jasmin . . .

Japan suited Loti's peculiar blend of exoticism and eroticism. Indirectly, his experiences there gave the world one of its most indelibly libellous images of the country – long-suffering and submissive womanhood in the form of

Madama Butterfly. The opera is based in part on *Madame Chrysanthème*, Loti's account of life and love in Meiji Period Japan which is altogether more plausible than Cio-Cio-san's warbling travails. As one might expect, chrysanthemums do appear in this 1887 novel; but it is the lotus that materialises at critical moments, as when Loti bids adieu to Japan and love in chapter 55, 'A Shattered Lotus Flower':

> *One night, in my cabin amid the Yellow Sea, my eyes settle on the lotus-flowers brought from Diou-djen-dji. They had survived for several days, but now they are shattered, and my carpet pathetically strewn with their pale rose petals. I who have lovingly kept so many faded flowers, fallen – alas! – into dust, snatched here and there, at moments of leave-taking in different countries; I who have kept so many of these love tokens that my collection of dried blooms is now an absurdly muddled herbarium. I try hard, but without success, to arouse some feeling for these lotuses, for they are the last living souvenirs of my summer at Nagasaki. Not without a measure of care, I gather them up and I open my porthole.*
>
> *From the misty grey sky an odd glow spreads upon the waters; a dim and gloomy dusk descends, yellowish upon this Yellow Sea. We sense that we are moving northwards, and that autumn is approaching. I cast the poor lotuses upon the boundless waste of waters, excusing myself as best I can for committing these natives of Japan to a grave that is so solemn and so vast.*

Madame Chrysanthème was a resounding popular success, which Pierre Loti tried to repeat in 1905 with another novel of Japan, *La Troisième Jeunesse de Mme Prune*. But his 1889 collection of non-fiction études, *Japoneries d'Automne*, had even greater impact. With essays that describe visits to see the innermost treasures of remote temples, an encounter with an Imperial princess, sacred mountains and fallen samurai, it seized the polite imagination. As with *Madame Chrysanthème*, the lotus makes an appearance wherever Loti is on the verge of prose poetry – notably in his melancholy description of the great shrine at Kamakura, spiritual citadel of Japan's mediaeval warrior capital, which he finds deserted, reclaimed by forest, and surrounded by lakes thick with lotus leaves yellowing with autumn's onset.

As a manifestation of Japonisme – the Western curiosity about and taste for things Japanese which burgeoned in the second half of the nineteenth century – the lotus had made appearances in France a decade before Loti set sail.

The Hamburg-born and French-naturalised merchant Siegfried Bing (1838–1905) began importing objets d'art from Japan in the 1870s, stimulating a Parisian appetite for both the imports themselves and the Western-made crafts they soon inspired. To sell goods of the second kind, in 1895 Bing opened La Maison de l'Art Nouveau, the shop whose name came to embody the movement that grew out of Japonisme. It was a movement, or perhaps more a confluence of styles and attitudes, which would develop simultane- ously elsewhere in Europe and North America – Liberty in London, Tiffany in New York. In each place and in every type of craftwork, the lotus motif linked the new art to its old and distant roots.

While Bing was busying himself with import–export, the artist Felix Henri Bracquemond (1833–1914) had already become a devotee of Japanese prints. In 1866, he joined forces with the ceramics dealer Eugène Rousseau (1827–90) to produce a range of hand-painted tableware that copied the natural history subjects favoured by Japanese printmakers. Launched at L'Exposition Universelle in 1867, Service Rousseau remained in production in France into the 1930s. One item became enduringly popular: adapted from a print made by Kyōsai Kawanabe in 1881, it was a plate that showed a turtle balancing on a lotus leaf. Bobbing on the water beside the leaf, however, is a yellow flower that does not belong to the lotus and which is not in Kawanabe's original image. This is *kō-hone* (*Nuphar japonica*), an aquatic plant closely related to the European spatterdock. The flower came to feature here via a strangely circuitous route. This same kō-hone was illustrated by Katsushika Hokusai in 1812, along with other plants and animals in one of his mass-produced collections of simple sketches or cartoons which, in the days long before the word became used for sophisticated comic books, were termed *manga*. Hokusai's manga were plundered by the makers of Service Rousseau for additional details and grace notes – a dandelion here, a dragonfly there. The designers assumed, through a misidentification or mistranslation, that his *Nuphar* was one and the same as *Nelumbo* and so added its flower to Kawanabe's lotus leaf.

Which would be of minimal interest had another artist not made a similar error. Édouard Manet was equally steeped in Japanese prints – partly through the collection of his friend and tutor in printing techniques Bracquemond, the artistic force behind Service Rousseau, but chiefly through the mass of material which another friend, his future biographer Théodore Duret, brought back from Japan in 1872. In 1876 Manet produced a series of illustrations for a limited edition of Stéphane Mallarmé's poem *L'Après-midi d'un faune*. At the front of the volume, above the legend 'Ex Libris' and the edition number, is a vignette of an aquatic plant that is freely copied from Hokusai's manga kō-hone, the yellow-flowered *Nuphar japonica*. The feeling at the time was that this image had to be a lotus. That was certainly what the painter and the poet desired and so Manet's solitary flower was coloured pink instead of yellow. It may have been a simple mistake – anyone but a Japanese native or a botanist could be forgiven for thinking Hokusai's sketch was a lotus. It may have been that the manga Manet was using had itself been wrongly coloured – they were produced in monochrome and often tinted afterwards. It may have been legerdemain, poetic licence of the kind that Ponting deployed with Tennyson's mountains. Whichever it was, Manet's and Mallarmé's plant needed to be something special, something suffused with the spirits of both Classical antiquity and the Orient – in other words, a lotus.

Around the time that Mallarmé was conjuring his vision of the faun roused and aroused in his nymph-populated paradise, others in France were arriving at the same *beau idéal* by different routes. A lawyer by training but with botany in his blood, Joseph Bory Latour-Marliac (1830–1911) established a nursery in 1875 on his family estates near the Gascon village of Le Temple-sur-Lot. In his twenties he had been bewitched by exotic waterlilies and lotuses in the Jardin des Plantes in Paris. Blooming in what was once the Sun King's physic garden, these Left Bank naiads were descended from the very lotuses that inspired the botanist Michel Adanson to coin the genus *Nelumbo* when he worked there a century before. By the late 1880s, Latour-Marliac's 4-hectare nursery was producing around 300,000 plants each year from 920 ponds. Most were *Nymphaea* hybrids, and they generated a craze whose enduring cultural impact is best exemplified by the garden and paintings made at Giverny by one of his favourite clients, Claude Monet. But a significant proportion of the nursery's production was lotuses, sourced from Japan, bred and selected in France and sold not just to conservatory owners in Paris and garden-makers in the Midi, but all over the world. The Latour-Marliac nursery still offers a range of *Nelumbo* varieties, among them a ruby-flowered cultivar that the firm introduced circa 1900 and which enjoyed a brief vogue in British conservatories. Although its bloodstock was Far Eastern, the name Joseph gave to this beautiful souvenir of fin-de-siècle lotus love was, and remains, 'Osiris' – the Nile dream as irresistible as ever.

These live specimens, together with a plethora of imported Japanese lotus artefacts, provided inspiration for the designers of Art Nouveau. Amid the frenzy of seemingly imaginary vegetation, flower buds, leaves and vaulting spans of veins can be found which are all identifiably *Nelumbo*-derived. The sacred flower of Japan was becoming *déraciné* or, rather, joining a new culture. The stained-glass bud lamp on its bronze leaf pedestal was now European and modern. Meanwhile, Parisians who wanted to see the real thing could always go to the Jardin des Plantes.

One frequent visitor was the painter Henri 'Le Douanier' Rousseau for whom the luxuriant contents of the botanic garden's glasshouses became a major source of inspiration. He was a homebody by nature, and all those rainforest fantasias were home-grown in origin: 'When I enter the hothouses and see the strange plants from exotic lands, I feel as if I were entering a dream.' In 1910, the year of his death, Rousseau gave the world his last dream, his extraordinary painting *Le Rêve*. In a moonlit jungle clearing, a naked woman lies on a brown velvet-covered couch. In attendance are she-lions, birds of paradise, an elephant, a worm-pink serpent and a dark-skinned snake charmer. Surrounding the odalisque's sofa are the leaves and lilac-mauve blooms of *Nelumbo nucifera*. Although Rousseau's 'Dream' is impossible to divine, it might be seen as the final and most florid flowering of the fantasy of nymph plus *Nymphaea* (or *Nelumbo*), the erotic watery dreamland that Mallarmé and Manet first pictured decades before. As if to confirm the connection, Rousseau's nude is an obvious homage to Manet's 1863 painting *Olympia*. In 1891 Rousseau had produced a portrait of Pierre Loti, fag in hand, fez on head and tabby cat at his elbow. The author was a friend and a source of inspiration for the studio-bound globetrotter. The Paris botanic garden showed Rousseau what lotuses looked like, but Loti told him what they were and meant.

Pierre Loti's *Japoneries d'Automne* was just the ticket for the drawing rooms full of aesthetes and chaise-longue exoticists who had been bitten by the bug of Japonisme. *Harper's Magazine* began seeking an English-language equivalent, starting a lotus-rush all of its own. The most famous of the magazine's Far Eastern agents was an American-Irish journalist born in Greece of Irish-Greek parentage who eventually took Japanese citizenship – Lafcadio Hearn who became Koizumi Yakumo. Hearn arrived in Japan in 1890, aged forty and with the *Harper's* commission in his pocket. He never left. By the time he died fourteen years later, he had married a samurai's daughter, fathered a family, and forged a career as a school teacher and university professor. A more thoroughgoing going-native it would be hard to imagine; but then, as Hearn said, as soon as he landed in Japan he sensed that he had simply been born and raised in the wrong countries. In his heart he had been Japanese all along. For many years his writings were the West's first point of literary contact with his adopted country. Here he describes his own pond in his essay 'In a Japanese Garden', published in *Glimpses of Unfamiliar Japan* in 1894.

> *There are iris plants growing along the bank, whose blossoms are prismatic violet, and there are various ornamental grasses and ferns and mosses. But the pond is essentially a lotus pond; the lotus plants make its greatest charm. It is a delight to watch every phase of their marvellous growth, from the first unrolling of the leaf to the fall of the last flower. On rainy days, especially, the lotus plants are worth observing. Their great cup-shaped leaves, swaying high above the pond, catch the rain and hold it a while; but always after the water in the leaf reaches a certain level the stem bends, and empties the leaf with a loud plash, and then straightens again. Rainwater upon a lotus-leaf is a favourite subject with Japanese metal-workers, and metal work can only reproduce the effect, for the motion and colour of water moving upon the green oleaginous surface are exactly those of quicksilver.*

But not even Lafcadio Hearn could satisfy the ravening appetite for dispatches from Lotus-Land. His articles merely served to stimulate a curiosity which, while expressed in the politest of terms, was of a pitch that one could imagine stimulated by the discovery of life on another planet. Japan was not just on the other side of the world; it seemed to exist in a parallel universe. More investigators were needed to furnish the stories behind the cargoes of silks and lacquerware, parasols and porcelain, netsuke and fans, folding screens and stone lanterns, bonsai and bronze cranes that were landing daily on Western docks.

None of these imports had so visible an impact as Japan's flora, a treasure house of horticultural novelties which, within a few decades, transformed the parks and gardens of Europe and North America. At first these were brought home by Western travellers. Before long, however, the Japanese would take a slice of what, after all, was their action. In 1907 the Yokohama Nursery opened a London office in Kingsway. Their stocklists from the pre-war period show that the company kept between 50 and 100 plants of *Nelumbo nucifera* on standby for dispatch to British gardens at any one time – a lot of lotuses. Never missing a trick, *Harper's Magazine* employed a new recruit to travel east and report on Lotus-Land's plants and landscapes. This was Alfred Parsons (1847–1920), an artist of distinction and creator of gardens which anticipated better-known Arts and Crafts designers like Gertrude Jekyll – painterly, romantic and profuse or, as his friend and client Henry James described them, 'nooky'.

Illustrated with his own watercolours, Parsons's articles on his Japanese sojourn appeared in *Harper's Magazine* between 1894 and 1895. They were then published in book form in 1896 as *Notes in Japan*. Although he defers at times to Pierre Loti, *cher maître*, there was really no need. Parsons observes with a closeness – a painter's eye – that was beyond Loti. Admittedly, he does not understand Shinto, 'the state religion' as he calls it, which he seems to envisage as some sabre-toothed equivalent of the C of E; or that its relationship with Buddhism could be anything but antagonistic. That apart, he is sympathetic towards his subjects in a sunny, very easy English way. He seems to have been a hit in Japan, taken into the confidence of his hosts, and to places where tourists were seldom encouraged. There is a natural fellowship among plant-lovers (if not always among gardeners), and especially in a nation that is not only dense with horticultural aficionados but where plants are so closely interwoven with the wider culture. Parsons's plantsmanship was the best possible passport.

In the third article in his series, or chapter three of *Notes in Japan*, Parsons deals with high summer, one of a sequence of Japanese mini-seasons that are defined by the blooming of a keynote plant and by characteristic weather. In this case the climate is one of tumultuous temperatures and humidity, brilliant sunshine and short-lived storms; the keynote plant is *Nelumbo*. This, as Parsons calls it, is 'The Time of the Lotus'. Following in Loti's footsteps, he visited the shrine at Kamakura. The lotuses were still there in their thousands and in full flower rather than autumnal dishevelment; but he found the sacred citadel very far from the scene of overgrown dereliction that Loti depicted. The place was thriving and full of bustle, so much so that the artist had to cordon himself off from the curious crowds with a length of string in order to paint Benzaiten's island shrine, seemingly afloat amid the flowers and spinning-plate foliage of *Nelumbo*. This watercolour was one of five that accompanied his article. Some feature lotuses in Kamakura where they thrive to this day; others show plants beside paddyfields long since absorbed by the outskirts of Tokyo. Here is Alfred Parsons in 'The Time of the Lotus':

> On the journey to Tokyo I saw my first lotus flowers in a lake near the railway, and I hurried off at once to the pond which surrounds the little temple of Benten at Shiba, where I found them in full glory.
>
> The lotus is one of the most difficult plants which it has ever been my lot to try and paint; the flowers are at their best only in the early morning, and each blossom after it has opened closes again before noon the first day, and on the second day its petals drop. The leaves are so large and so full of modelling that it is impossible to generalise them as a mass; each one has to be carefully studied, and every breath of wind disturbs their delicate balance, and completely alters their forms. Besides this, their glaucous surface, like that of a cabbage leaf, reflects every passing phase of the sky, and is constantly changing in colour as clouds pass over . . .

Contemporary with Parsons and over the next two decades, numerous Westerners would travel to Japan and join in the lotus quest. Those who recorded their observations in print and paint form a cast of characters so colourfully eclectic that they would have the makings of a passable murder mystery were we able to bring them together – perhaps in that home from home, Yokohama's Grand Hotel, where tinned meat from Crosse and Blackwell and Dundee marmalade could be reliably procured. They include the two indomitable daughters of a colonial governor, a fledgling barrister who would fly high before crashing, a dashing young architect, a brilliant American academic with a taste for antiquities, mysticism and beautiful women, various painters with their habitual troubles, the owner of a new and ambitious West End shop in search of goods to sell, a world-famous novelist, Britain's most successful arbiter of fashion, and, of course, the roving photographer who would shortly strike out for Antarctica. For some of these characters the Classical myth of Lotus-Land came true: having arrived in Japan, they either never left or soon returned and stayed for ever.

10

Honourable Foreigners

Gaijin literally means 'outside person' – harmless-sounding enough, although the insult implied in the mere fact of not being Japanese is evidently thought to be a grave one. It is not done to call foreigners *gaijin* any more, not to their faces anyway. The polite alternative is *gaikokujin*, 'foreign-countries people'. The term is old as examples of political correctness go, dating certainly from the second half of the nineteenth century and perhaps even further back than that. Having viewed foreigners with curiosity followed by suspicion and then contempt, Japan finally decided not only to admit them freely but to use them to beat the outside world at its own game. This change of view came, alongside so many other changes, after 1868 and the relatively bloodless revolution that was the Meiji Restoration. A new class of alien was actively recruited – promising persons of proven but as yet unpeaked skill and expertise who would help to modernise the nation. These were the *O-yatoi gaikokujin*, 'honourable hired foreign-countries people'. Several of them were distinguished participants in the nineteenth-century lotus quest.

In 1876 when he was just twenty-four years old, the British architect Josiah Conder was snapped up by the Meiji Government. Appointed professor of architecture at the newly founded Imperial College of Engineering in Tokyo, Conder was charged with a transformation that would have daunted the Emperor Augustus – of turning Japan's capital not from brick to marble but from paper, wood and stone to steel, glass, brick *and* marble. He and his students achieved this in grand style and at astonishing speed. Within two decades Tokyo was the architectural equal of many Western capitals. But Conder meanwhile had been ravished by Japan's unspoilt face, the face he had been employed to transform. Although surprisingly peaceful, the Meiji Revolution might have been cataclysmic. Japan's culture and identity might have been sacrificed in the headlong rush for Western modernity. They were, however, preserved – partly because of men like Conder who were bewitched by the very thing they were paid to exorcise.

As was often the case with O-yatoi gaikokujin, it was through Conder's foreign eyes that many Japanese learnt to recognise their native glory. For the young British architect this went beyond buildings. He became a disciple and then a close friend of the fiercely traditional painter Kyōsai Kawanabe (1831–89). He was with him when Kawanabe drew the image of lotus and turtle that would be used by the makers of Service Rousseau. How many gigots were served in France on that very plate by people who could have no clue of the circumstances behind its conception? Conder also became a devotee and student of Japanese gardens and flower arranging, and his writings on them were the first point of contact with these arts for many in the West. Published in 1891, *The Flowers of Japan and the Art of Floral Arrangement* contains a long account of the lotus. When it comes to flower arranging, says Conder, *Nelumbo* is not to be taken lightly, 'being suggestive of a spiritual life' and 'a suitable theme for religious contemplation'. The example he illustrates is very far from the artfully casual naturalism of most ikebana. Ascending from a vase, it is a multi-tiered tower of buds, flowers and leaves, a living stupa. Often made not with live plants but in bronze-gilt, similar compositions can still be found as altar pieces before sacred images in every temple and most homes in Japan. The foliage, says Conder, needs special attention:

> The Lotus leaves should be selected to express the idea of the three Buddhist divisions of time – Present, Past and Future. Past time is represented by a partly decayed or worm-eaten leaf. Present time by a handsome open leaf – often called the Mirror Leaf, on account of its resemblance in shape to that of a Japanese mirror; and Future time by a curled leaf, not fully open.

Strangely reminiscent of *Burnt Norton*, the greatest twentieth-century poem to contain a lotus, all this talk of time illustrates the seriousness with which Conder took his Buddhist studies. If 'conversion' is not too drastic, too sectarian a term for either Buddhism or Japanese religion in general, his studies eventually resulted in conversion. When he and his wife Kume died within a fortnight of each other in June 1920, they were interred together at Tokyo's Gokoku Temple. As I would learn soon after arriving in Tokyo, another, still deeper spiritual connection is hinted at in Conder's account. This is the comparison he draws between the lotus and the mirror, an ancient emblem which symbolises something far older than Japanese Buddhism – *Yamato*, the nation itself.

FILTH – failed in London try Hong Kong – is an acronym supposed to have been invented for lawyers who, unable to cut a dash at home, made careers at the Hong Kong Bar. What would be the equivalent for barristers who made such a hash of their careers in the former British territory that they were not just sent back to Blighty but doomed thereafter to impoverished ignominy? FECULENCE, perhaps – Far East cock-up London employment no chance ever. Sir Francis Taylor Piggott (1852–1925) was just such a character. His retirement ought to have come late and garlanded with plaudits. It came as soon as could possibly be contrived, accelerated by a Governor who found Piggott's bluntness and free thinking intolerable. It was a shock for Sir Francis. As Chief Justice of Hong Kong, he thought he was top dog and secure in his kennel. He had spent much and saved nothing. His passage home in 1914 had to be paid out of the poor relief fund. Three years before his death he was declared bankrupt.

In 1887, long before he started making things too hot for himself in Hong Kong, Piggott received a posting to Tokyo. The Meiji Period was now two decades old and its modernisation programme was well under way. The Japanese government appointed the thirty-five-year-old barrister legal advisor to Hirobumi Itō, who had become the country's first prime minister in 1885. Itō was working on a new constitution and it was here that Piggott proved his worth. Two years after his arrival, the Meiji Constitution was promulgated. The warmth of their relationship was reflected in the naming of the barrister's son, Julian Ito Piggott. Warmer still were his feelings about Japan's culture. He studied her music, graphic arts and gardens and continued to write about them even during his painful retirement.

His time in Japan coincided with the arrival there in March 1889 of four travelling companions. Charles Holme began trading British goods for Asian craftwork in the 1870s. He and his business partner, the designer Christopher Dresser, became pioneers of Japanese style and objects in Britain. In 1893,

Holme would provide these imports, along with home-grown avant-garde arts and artists such as Aubrey Beardsley, with a showcase in the form of *The Studio*, the magazine he founded and edited. The shop front meanwhile was provided by Arthur Lasenby Liberty whose store opened its doors in Regent Street in 1875. So far, Holme and Liberty, the twin generators of British Japonisme, had operated from a distance. In the spring of 1889, they journeyed to the source. It was an expedition that would result in a design revolution, and speed the lotus into British drawing rooms. Travelling with them were Liberty's wife Emma, a talented photographer, and a forty-five-year-old artist who, by the time of his death in 1913, would become Sir Alfred East RA, one of England's most highly regarded landscape painters.

Alfred East soon left his companions to embark on six months of wanderings commissioned by another promoter of Japonisme, the Fine Art Society. That summer, raging toothache forced him to Tokyo in search of a dentist. There he ran across Francis Piggott, the Japanese government's imported constitutional lawyer. East's time in the capital gave him an opportunity to visit Kamakura, which he described as 'this sunny lotus bit of landscape'. He also memorialised its lotuses in paint. Showing a sail-filled bay and a bloom-filled pool, one of these images is among four paintings of horticultural scenes by East that illustrate Francis Piggott's 1892 publication *The Garden of Japan: a year's diary of its flowers*. The book's monochrome figures are by Piggott himself and based on manga-type plant drawings of the kind Manet found so useful two decades earlier. They serve as a touching reminder that the lawyer was a sensitive soul capable of painstaking delicacy. But the strongest evidence that Piggott CJ was not such a beast is his account of seeing lotuses in 1890, shortly before leaving a country where he would have been wiser to remain:

> *August 20th. The lilies are nearly over, and Nature seems to rest until the Amaryllids are ready. The gap is filled with the scent of the Lotus, the wonderful sacred flower, which comes from afar across the heated plains . . .*
>
> *August 23rd. Belated at Shirakawa, and wandering through the country in the fierce heat of the midday sun, I stumble unexpectedly on a bed of Lotus, and I gaze for the first time on the lovely flowers, which, growing in the black mud, are to the Japanese the symbols of purity – 'A pure and beautiful woman in a haunt of vice'; 'A man of stainless honour in a wicked world'. Such exquisite tender colours, such perfection of form, such stately*

grace of growth – set round with mighty and shapely leaves with their under-colouring of pale blue, which seems in the sunlight to reflect the heavens – has the Lotus, that it is no wonder religion has set it on the highest pinnacle of its symbolism. The beautiful pencilling of the veins on the petals seems to have been the fount of inspiration for the old Buddhist artists, whose work was never perfect until the gold lines on the flower they loved to paint vied with Nature in her accuracy.

In the early morning the rising sun receives a royal salute of welcome from a hundred and one opening buds.

*

Unlike the hapless Hong Kong judge, Florence and Ella Du Cane knew just how to twist a colonial administrator round their little fingers. They were born in 1869 and 1874 respectively to Sir Charles Du Cane, then Governor of Tasmania. The sisters were a wild and gifted pair. Soon after their father's death in 1889 they began hatching travel plans. Records of these adventures would be kept – Florence doing the writing, Ella painting scenic watercolours. There would be no chaperone. Madeira, the Canaries, Egypt, China and Japan were all targeted and all, in time, yielded finely written and illustrated accounts as well as plants and design ideas for the gardens of the family's English estate, Mountains near Maldon in Essex.

Published in 1908, their *Flowers and Gardens of Japan* became an instant best-seller. In a chapter devoted to *Nelumbo*, Ella included three paintings of different lotus ponds and Florence referred admiringly to Alfred Parsons, beginning with his words 'the time of the lotus', a phrase which, since its appearance in the mid-1890s, had acquired talismanic status. In Japan, she says:

The 'time of the lotus' is suggestive of the damp hot August days when from earliest dawn the cicadas will be singing, if their discordant noise can be described as song, and the croaking of the frogs day and night, makes one wonder at last whether frogs never grow hoarse, or cicadas never tire of singing.

To Florence's eyes there was 'no more beautiful sight than a lotus bed at the dawn of a hot August day. Stately and yet tender is the beauty of the lotus blossom, and the great buds opening with a noise which is indescribable to one who has not heard it; and how quickly the delicate pink or white petals unfurl, as though hastening to make the most of their short life.'

But, warned Miss Du Cane, this beautiful sight and its strange attendant sound came at a price: 'For the true lover of the lotus there can be scarcely any night, for soon after midnight he must rise and start for the lotus pond to see their real beauty and hear the opening of the buds with the sudden touch of dawn.'

Like many others who made the lotus quest around the turn of the century, Florence Du Cane was captivated by the ethnology and theology that surrounded the flower. Of all the plants to be encountered overseas, only the lotus offered this holiday romance, this short break from Christian teaching and bourgeois proprieties. Its history, she says, 'is a very old one, for their beauty is sung in the old Buddhist sutra, and one passage describing the golden glory of Paradise tells of a pond where the lotus flowers large as a carriage-wheel grow'. This wheel imagery intrigued her and led her to the work of Sir Monier Monier-Williams (1819–99). She quotes the Oxford Sanskrit scholar and India specialist: 'its constant use as an emblem seems to result from the wheel-like form of the flower – the petals taking the place of spokes, and thus typifying the doctrine of perpetual cycles of existence.'

'No honour seems too great for this flower of Buddha,' is Miss Du Cane's conclusion. As confirmation of which, she refers to the fact that 'the Japanese dedicate their wonderful and awe-inspiring mountain Fuji-san to it, and call it Fugo Ho, meaning Lotus Peak.' She explains this honour by citing a description of the silent pinnacle of aged snow in the dawn. It comes from the writings of Mary McNeil Fenollosa, of whom more later:

Now far beyond the greyness, to the west, the cone of Fuji flashes into splendour. It, too, is pink; its shape is the shape of a lotus bud, and the long fissures that plough the mountain-side are now but the delicate gold veining of a petal. Slowly it seems to open. It is the chalice of a new day, and the pledge of consecration.

After that, Florence's observations on the role *Nelumbo* plays in the Japanese diet are, by her own admission, bathetic. Such culinary matters struck her as 'too unromantic to be associated with the lotus'. Much more to her liking was 'the Japanese phrase *ben po*, meaning lotus step, which they associate with the light step of a beautiful woman'.

As Liberty and Company approached the end of its first decade of trading, a new generation of artist-craftsmen emerged to turn the store from a bazaar filled with Oriental exotica into a pioneer of English Art Nouveau, or Liberty Style as it soon became known. Foremost among them was the designer Arthur Silver (1853–96) who was responsible in 1887 for the peacock print that remains the company's signature motif and best-selling fabric. Founded in 1880, the Silver Studio grew swiftly, becoming Britain's largest producer of designs for fabrics, wallpapers, carpets and metalwork and supplying numerous manufacturers and outlets in addition to Liberty. The firm's patterns are generally described as Art Nouveau, although they are often far from the worlds of the sinuous Hector Guimard or the Spartan Charles Rennie Mackintosh. Styles redolent of the European Middle Ages and Baroque as well as the Middle and Far East can be discerned in them, as can the more proximate influence of William Morris. Like Liberty, his most famous client, Arthur Silver looked to one source of inspiration above all others. His house was decorated with Japanese artefacts; he was quick to join the Japan Society when those erstwhile travelling companions Holme, East and Liberty founded it in 1891; he supported the magazine *Artistic Japan*; he even employed live Japanese artists.

One of these, a mysterious character by the name of Yamakawa Rinpo, produced several designs for Silver, the strangest of which has to be his personalised Christmas card for 1890. Within a border of holly and mistletoe-sprigged bamboo, it shows an immense lotus leaf floating on a sea of lotus flowers. A ring of bullfrogs sits around the leaf. They are in the midst of a riotous feast, some playing traditional Japanese instruments, others eating, all evidently in a state more often attributed to newts than frogs. At the centre is another leaf, forming a table on which is laid a banquet of the kind associated with Buddhist or Shinto fete days. With an especially bloated belly and bonhomous look, one frog is clearly meant to resemble Hotei, one of the Seven Gods of Good Fortune. The artist does manage, however, to remember that he is celebrating a Christian festival – just about. At the top of the leaf, dressed in a wardrobe of *Nelumbo* parts, the nursing Madonna appears. She too is depicted as a bullfrog, only slightly less grotesque than her companions. This unintended blasphemy recalls a Japanese Christmas tree decoration which, until recently, was made and sold in innocent confusion – Santa Claus on a crucifix.

In 1894, the Silver Studio produced a new best-seller. A fabric pattern manufactured by Warner and Ramm, it was a frieze of *Nelumbo* blooms, buds and leaves drawn in Japanese style. 'Waterlilies', as it was erroneously known, became Warner's most popular print of the nineties. Knowing a good thing when it saw one, the Silver Studio produced further lotus designs, for textiles, business cards and letter paper, culminating in 1900, a few years after Arthur Silver's death, in 'Evening Landscape with Mount Fuji'. Attributed to the designer John Illingworth Kay and printed on velveteen, this fabric pattern is Japonisme run riot. Fuji-san appears in silhouette against a starry moonlit sky. All around are the black clouds of pine boughs. Breasting the lower slopes of the mountain itself are giant lotus blooms. Seen in a small sample, it is a beautiful design. Endlessly repeated, it must have been hell to live with.

Much the same process was at work among arts and crafts on the other side of the Atlantic. American collectors had more spending power, and they also had a climate where, even as far north as New York, live lotuses would thrive outdoors. The sacred flower became an elite but familiar sight in museums, galleries, public gardens and the ponds of the rich. In 1891, William Goodyear, first curator of New York's Metropolitan Museum of Art and son of the inventor of vulcanised rubber, published *The Grammar of the Lotus*. Lavishly detailed, this 'new history of classic ornament as a development of sun worship' helped to lodge the sacred flower in the American consciousness. Although Goodyear focused chiefly on the iconography of the ancient Middle East and Classical world, his work fuelled the appetite for lotuses from Japan.

Before long, American designers were creating objects and patterns based on both imported artefacts and actual plants. Louis Comfort Tiffany adopted and adapted the metalwork lotus leaves that so impressed Lafcadio Hearn, turning them into lamp bases. The lampshades themselves were constructed of the coloured glass for which Tiffany was justly celebrated, and might either take the form of a single multi-petalled lotus flower or be composed of bouquets of them. Sometimes, he switched from free-standing lamps to hanging lanterns and from flowers to the outlines, subtle modelling and venation of the lotus leaf, producing objects that resembled hovering Chinese hats done in reticulated emerald. The earliest of these lamps date from around 1893, and they went into commercial production in 1895, produced by a staff of some 300 craftsmen. They were soon imitated by lesser artists, as they are to this day. The lotus lamp became as American as apple pie. Nonetheless, Tiffany's own creations retained their cachet and their cash value. A top-of-the-range lotus lamp produced by Tiffany Studios in 1906 sold for $750 when new. In 1997, the same model fetched $2,807,500 at Christie's New York.

In America the lotus also appeared in the fine as well as the decorative arts – although in Tiffany's case it seems absurd to distinguish between the two. Encouraged by that arch-Japoniste James Abbott McNeill Whistler, the young painter Theodore Wores (1859–1939) began to look east. At first he could afford to exercise his new-found Orientalism only by painting scenes of Chinatown in his native San Francisco. Then, in 1885, having secured a little success at home, Wores made the first of two visits to Japan. He returned with a cargo of canvases which were shown to great acclaim in New York and London. Among them was an oil painting from 1886 of the lotus pond at Shiba in Tokyo. It shows the lake, brimming with leaves, picked out with pink flowers, and surveyed from a wooden bridge by kimono-clad women and children. Although this is the most realistic of many lotus ponds captured by Western artists in this period, one critic remained unconvinced. Exhibited at the Dowdeswell Gallery in New Bond Street in 1888, the Shiba lotus pond and its companion scenes moved Oscar Wilde to proclaim in *The Decay of Lying*:

> *In fact, the whole of Japan is a pure invention. There is no such country. There are no such people. One of our most charming painters went recently to the Land of the Chrysanthemum in the foolish hope of seeing the Japanese. All he saw, all he had the chance of painting, were a few lanterns and some fans. He was quite unable to discover the inhabitants, as his delightful exhibition at Messrs Dowdeswell's Gallery showed only too well. He did not know that the Japanese people are, as I have said, simply a mode of style, an exquisite fancy of art.*

With allowance made for a few modifications to dress, the scene that Wores depicted can still be encountered across Japan. Rudyard Kipling, who read Wilde's comments shortly before arriving in the 'Land of the Chrysanthemum', declared him a 'long-toothed liar' and went on to demonstrate just how wrong he was in a series of published letters from Japan. 'Long-toothed liar' may be a little strong, but I cannot help wishing that Wilde had had an opportunity to travel further east than Ravenna – 'Ay! amid lotus-meadows dost thou stand' indeed.

The thrust of Wilde's argument was that rather than travel to the country itself, one would be better off staying at home and steeping one's self in its art. So steeped, one was just as likely to experience 'an absolutely Japanese effect' in a London park or strolling down Piccadilly. A painter who seems to illustrate this staying-put approach is the Pennsylvania-born Martin Johnson Heade (1819–1904). He did travel – to Europe in his youth to study, and later in Central and South America. But his most famous studies of exotica were produced in the comfort of his studio after he moved to St Augustine, Florida in 1883. Mysterious jungle scenes filled with moss-draped boughs, flamboyant orchids and darting hummingbirds, they were far indeed from the lambent landscapes, the New England salt marshes and seashores, with which Heade began his career. This Equatorial romance was informed partly by his early experience of South America, but chiefly by the horticultural feats that were possible in the Florida climate. Most of the orchids and bromeliads that Heade painted were being grown in gardens thereabouts. So too were the less uncommon flowers which he turned into divas, the popular solo artistes that provided him with a series of spectacular still lifes.

In this last group of paintings, from between 1885 and 1895, were *Magnolia grandiflora*, roses various, and the lotus, a subject to which he often returned. Usually portrayed with its flowers lying flat, singly or in a bunch and on a drapery of lotus leaf, Heade's favourite *Nelumbo* was a large pale rose cultivar whose petals are trimmed with carmine. It is an example of what we would call a picotee, or *kuchibeni*, as it has been known in Japan for about 400 years – 'crimson mouth', meaning lipstick. He chose the variety well. It is the closest a plant study can come to saying 'nude', closer even than his other fleshy favourite, the orchid *Cattleya labiata*. We do not know how this Japanese naiad came to be growing in Florida in the 1880s. It might have been shipped from Latour-Marliac in France; it might have arrived by another route. Whatever its source, Heade's lotus illustrates the fact that *Nelumbo nucifera* was established in US cultivation by the end of the nineteenth century. It was there that the sacred flower found its most comfortable niche outside the East and it was in Florida that *Nelumbo* 'Mrs Perry D. Slocum', the first hybrid between the Asian lotus and its American cousin, would flower in 1964.

In Europe lotomania came to an end with the First World War. Japonisme was suddenly trivial and old hat; its props were in any case largely unavailable, likewise the means of travelling to their source. Its Art Nouveau spin-offs now seemed cluttered, choking and unjustifiably extravagant. Something cleaner, sharper and sparser was in order. Horticulture was hit as garden staff and glasshouse fuel were directed to the Front. *Nelumbo nucifera* was one of countless exotic plants that all but disappeared from European cultivation. Herbert Ponting's career move from the bowers of Japan to the desolation of the Antarctic might almost be seen as a metaphor for the end of the Lotus-Land dream.

In the United States the phenomenon fared better, survived longer. The Asian lotus soon became a garden fixture, liking the Continental climate with its dependably long and hot summers even in northern States. Further south, it sometimes flourished on a scale seen nowhere else outside its native lands. It materialised en masse in the lake in Echo Park in downtown Los Angeles, where it remains to this day and has been the subject of an annual festival for some decades. Quite how it arrived there is a mystery. Records dating from the late 1880s (the eve of the park's birth) indicate a would-be lotus donor, and the colony was certainly thriving by the 1920s when the park became the pre-Hollywood locus of the film industry. One local theory, fondly cherished but probably fantastic, is that the seeds were brought from China by the evangelist Aimee Semple McPherson whose 5,000-seater Church of the Foursquare Gospel sprang up beside Echo Park in 1923. In the summer of 1910, however, when Sister Aimee was meant to be spreading the good word among the Chinese, she lost her first husband to dysentery, succumbed to the same disease, and then gave birth to a daughter – hardly lotus-gathering weather. Anyway, what would she have wanted with such an unashamedly heathen plant?

11

The Buddha among the Brahmins

It was on the East Coast while Echo Park was barely a whisper that the most surprising legacy of Lotus-Land began to take shape, precisely because the sacred flower was pagan. Born in Massachusetts in 1853, Ernest Fenollosa was one of the greatest O-yatoi gaikokujin. He went in search of Japanese culture, seeking out manuscripts, paintings and artefacts in shuttered temples and shrines, attending and recording performances of Noh, Kabuki, and traditional music, saving the artists and performers beloved of the *ancien régime* from the oblivion threatened by the new, progressive and Westward-looking order. In short, he told the Japanese that it was all right to be themselves – better than that, it was a winning formula in the eyes of the outside world. Why discard their greatest asset?

A Harvard-educated philosopher, Fenollosa was recruited to the cause by Edward Sylvester Morse, himself an honourable hired foreigner who had started work in Japan in 1877. Morse must be left in dots and dashes for the moment – it was his excavations that would lead me to the heart of the lotus mystery. We will return to him later. Arriving in Japan in 1878, Fenollosa began teaching politics, economy and philosophy at Tokyo's Imperial University. He acquitted himself well, rearing a brood of future luminaries whose rise through the ranks of the new order was so swift that Fenollosa became known as *Daijin Sensei*, 'The Teacher of Great Men'. Outside the lecture theatre, he immersed himself in Japanese culture, snapping up antiquities and more recent artworks.

Then, in 1881, the poacher began to turn first into the gamekeeper and finally into the steward of the entire estate. Fenollosa became a curious thing – a missionary who jettisoned his home-grown gospel and instead preached to his flock on their native ways. The following year he issued a manifesto. It took the form of a public lecture that was widely reproduced and debated. The burden of his message was that Japan's cultural heritage was uniquely great, but in immediate danger of being either erased or sold to foreigners. This heritage's proper place was at home, although the West undoubtedly needed to be told about it. As he wrote to his sponsor Edward Morse:

I expect the time will come when it will be considered necessary for a liberally educated man to know about the names and deeds of man's great benefactors in the East, and the steps in advance of their culture, as it is now to know Greek and Latin dates and the flavour of their production.

Three decades later, much the same point would be made by Fenollosa's literary executor, the poet Ezra Pound. Improbable though it seemed in the 1880s, Far Eastern culture would stand to Western Modernism as Classical Antiquity had stood to the European Renaissance.

In 1884, buoyed by the support his views received, Fenollosa founded Kangwakai. This Japanese art society had two main functions. It appraised and authenticated works from the distant past. It promoted the work of artists who were living or recently dead. It was Kangwakai, for example, that conferred new dignity and permanence on popular genres such as the prints of Ukiyo-e, the ephemeral effusions of 'the Floating World' – genres which many among Japan's elite had previously thought beneath consideration. In Tokyo Fenollosa had already organised and funded the first formal exhibition of these and more traditional Japanese art forms. Now this show became a regular fixture and spawned numerous events in imitation. Other art societies soon began to appear, many of them with Fenollosa's support and some of them welcoming gaijin as well as Japanese artists – Josiah Conder, Alfred East and Francis Piggott would all become active members.

At first Fenollosa's masters in the Meiji Government were taken aback – this was not quite what they had in mind when they hired him. But with his help a law was soon drafted requiring the registration and preservation of precious artefacts. Appointed Imperial Commissioner of Fine Arts, Fenollosa was charged with assembling a crew of connoisseurs and conservationists. In 1884, he and his treasure team inspected sacred sites in the ancient capital of Nara. When he asked to see the legendary glory of Yumedono, the Hōryū Temple's octagonal 'Hall of Dreams', he was shown a cupboard which contained what appeared to be a mummy. This was it, he was told, and nobody was allowed to see what lay beneath the wrappings. The last time anyone had attempted to look, there was a clap of thunder followed by an earthquake. Armed with his Imperial mandate, Fenollosa demanded that the mysterious figure be revealed.

'I shall never forget,' he recorded, 'our feelings as the long-disused key rattled in the rusty lock. Within the shrine appeared a tall mass closely wrapped about in swathing bands of cotton cloth upon which the dust of ages had gathered.' Fearfully, it was divested of its swaddling in the mote-speckled sun shafts of the octagonal hall: 'our eyes and nostrils were in danger of being choked with the pungent dust. But at last the final folds of the covering fell away, and this marvellous statue, unique in the world, came forth into human sight for the first time in centuries.' As the bandages – 500 metres of them – came off, the Commissioner was bathed in golden light.

This secret treasure was a 1.8-metre-tall statue of the Bodhisattva known as Kuze Kannon. Carved in camphor wood and thickly gilded sometime in the early eighth century, it had been displayed for around 500 years and then consigned to its cupboard ever since – not out of negligence but out of overly precious respect. As he gazed on its face, Fenollosa likened the Kannon's smile to the Mona Lisa's. Revealing more knowledge of the West than anyone could have suspected, the chief monk replied, 'No, no – I have seen the Mona Lisa's smile. It is shaded with troubles that are all too human.' For Fenollosa the statue's disrobing was an epiphany or, as a Japanese Buddhist would term it, *satori*, a moment of enlightenment. He implored the temple attendants to leave the Bodhisattva undressed and they agreed. Ecstatic, he pressed on with his nationwide progress in search of similar unseen master-pieces. His intention was not to transport them to Tokyo, let alone overseas. He simply wanted them to be left in situ, properly conserved and directly experienced.

Like most Buddhist statues, Kuze Kannon stands on a lotus-blossom pedestal. Behind the figure's head is a gilt-bronze halo shaped like a massive lotus petal. At its centre is a stylised circular representation of the lotus ringed with seeds and arabesques formed of typically Oriental dragons and unexpectedly Hellenistic palm leaves. From this inner wheel there rises a fringe of celestial fire. As he examined these motifs, Fenollosa found himself drawn into a mystery that he felt compelled to explore, if never to solve. In September 1885, the first phase of this exploration led to his being confirmed as a practising Buddhist. He was received into the Tendai Sect, the school whose cardinal text is the *Lotus Sutra*. The sacred flower would loom large in Fenollosa's consciousness for his remaining twenty-three years.

In the capital meanwhile, his powers as the Meiji Government's cultural overlord grew ever greater. He began formulating plans for the creation of the Tokyo Fine Arts School and the Imperial Museum of which he became director in 1888. He also began travelling to Europe and the United States to find new conservation and curatorial techniques and to bang the drum for Japanese culture. In 1886, on the eve of one of these trips, he was summoned to the Imperial Palace. After decorating Fenollosa with one of Japan's highest honours, the Emperor told him, 'You have taught my people to know their own art; in going back to your great country, I charge you, teach them also.' The professor obeyed the command perhaps a little too literally for his own good. Like Francis Piggott, he would have been wiser to stay in Lotus-Land; but he was not to know that at the time, and his belly, although sleek and black-waistcoated, was filled with evangelising fire. In 1886, he began laying his homeward path by selling his own treasure house of Japanese art to an American private collector on condition that it be permanently displayed in the Boston Museum of Fine Arts. Four years later he returned to Boston to become curator of the museum's Oriental department.

Tall, dark and bearded, Fenollosa cut a dash in the city that had given him his education. Born in Salem to a Spanish musician father, the professor now became a leading figure in Boston's intellectual aristocracy. While idiosyncratic and innovative, this class tended to run on hereditary and plutocratic principles uncommon among intelligentsias. Nevertheless the Brahmins of Beacon Hill suspended all scruples about background in Fenollosa's case. They loved their new-found Orientalist with his cargo of exotic objects and thinking, and he appears to have loved them back. For a caste largely descended from stout-hearted and no-nonsense Protestant stock, the New England Brahmins showed a surprising affinity for mysticism and foreign faiths. Theirs, after all, was the culture that had warmed not long before to the Transcendentalism of Emerson and Thoreau, both men whose insistence on the metaphysical unity of man and Nature can sound strangely like Shinto at times. For these grandees, one of Fenollosa's chief attractions was the fact that he could turn the old joke of their being Brahmin – in the sense of top class – into something more spiritual and worthy. He did this by introducing them to an unfamiliar cosmology, a world view that was partly spiritual, partly philosophical, but wholly centred on the flower that was sacred to real Brahmins as well as to Buddhists.

As Fenollosa lectured on the facts of Japanese art and Buddhism, he began to drift into a theoretical realm of his own inventing. He started by addressing what was generally understood about the Tendai Sect, its central text and its key icon, the lotus. This was magnetic stuff: the *Lotus Sutra* with its fantastically ornamented landscapes and language, its sensuality and suspension of moral condemnation, its sheer imaginative opulence, carried the audience to a faraway world of unparalleled colour and perfume, riches and liberty. Having transported the Boston Brahmins, Fenollosa proceeded to elaborate a vision of his own, a sort of Westernised Tendai for the Modern American. Central to this vision was the lotus, the emblem not just of his cosmology as a whole but of the individual within it. First, however, he dealt with the inclusiveness and the proven adaptability of the Tendai doctrine itself. Buddhism was not a religion in the Judaeo-Christian sense; it required no fundamental belief and no rejection of other faiths. It had no gods as such, let alone a single and jealous God. In short, Ladies and Gentlemen, it could harmonise with your existing mental furniture with minimal disruption. Moreover, the liberation from having to believe absolutely in supernatural or divine phenomena, taken with the sect's great ideas of flux and metamorphosis, meant that Tendai Buddhism sat comfortably with the new scientific thinking. It was the ideal spirituality for people who had decided God did not exist.

Even for those who wanted no truck with Buddhism, there was still something vital to be gained from its iconography and teaching. This, he explained, was the lotus. It had long been seen as a metaphor of the model human, learned, noble, unstained by worldly pollution. Now we had to modify that metaphor. Modern Americans still needed all the above lotus attributes, likewise the flower's time-honoured example as a lure towards perfecting of the spirit and eventual enlightenment. But they also needed to consider the lotus more closely. The Modern American, said Fenollosa, was a complex organism, as multi-layered as the lotus blossom itself. Nor should all these layers be identifiably American. Benign influences and components of character had to be sought and accepted from other cultures, and especially from the East. At a moment of critical uncertainty for the American identity, those cultures would provide just what was missing. Visualised in terms of objects, America with its material solidity, its rationality and unifying strength might be seen as an arch, whereas the Far East might be seen as the lotus itself. If they were to continue to evolve and to forge a new culture, Americans needed to combine the two. But, Fenollosa insisted, there was nothing collective about his symbolism of the lotus, nothing of the cult, despite his rallying and zealous tone. His lotus was a symbol of the individual and of each individual's quest to make the countless petal-like elements of personal identity cohere. In this, his vision recalled Emerson's description of his own lifelong preoccupation – 'the infinitude of the private man'.

Buddhism had been in the New England air for some time. Lilian Whiting, Boston correspondent of the *New Orleans Times-Democrat*, attended some of Fenollosa's lectures in the winter of 1894 and reported 'a power, a fervor, a splendor of spirited truth seldom equaled'. Slightly more wryly perhaps, she also observed that 'nothing so enchants Boston as mysticism' and that 'the term "American Buddhist" is not an uncommon one at date'. Not uncommon, maybe, but still elite. The scions of princely houses, young men with names like Adams, Bigelow, Cabot Lodge, Holmes and Lowell, were steeping themselves in Oriental art and mysticism, and in some cases packing their trunks and striking out for Lotus-Land. At Harvard, the response to all this lotus-gazing was decisive and far-sighted: Buddhism now became a serious subject of study. It was there, a decade later, that T. S. Eliot, a Brahmin once removed, would immerse himself in Eastern religion, so inheriting one part of Fenollosa's extraordinary bequest to modern English poetry.

William James (1842–1910), Harvard professor of psychology and philosophy and brother of Alfred Parsons's friend Henry, examined Buddhism in terms of its impact on the highly educated Western converts around him. At the time, he was amassing material for his 1902 magnum opus, *The Varieties of Religious Experience: A Study in Human Nature*. He and Fenollosa met and listened to each other lecture. The latter stressed that his vision of the lotus was pragmatic, anti-mystical, of this world, and far from the fashion for spiritualism, psychical experiments and Theosophy that was then taking Boston by storm. To his own astonishment and for all his scientific scepticism, James seems to have come away from these encounters with something like the very opposite of this earth-bound view. It might even be probable, he later observed, that 'there is a continuum of cosmic consciousness, against which our individuality builds but accidental fences, and into which our several minds plunge as into a mother sea or reservoir'. This sounds strangely close to one of the oldest ideas in Japanese Buddhism, the great common and infinite consciousness that takes the form of a lake in which individual identity germinates like lotus seeds.

In autumn 1894, the seed of Fenollosa's downfall was sprouting. At the Boston Museum of Fine Arts, the Curator of the Oriental Department had just taken on a new assistant. This was Mary McNeil Scott, a twenty-nine-year-old poet from Alabama. Her photographs show her to be a beauty by the standards of her day, a Gibson Girl with a soul. Fenollosa certainly thought so, but his new helpmate had another qualification that fascinated him. Her second husband (pneumonia claimed the first) had been US Consul in Kobe. She had lived with him in Japan before returning to America, whereupon she divorced him on grounds of domestic violence. The curator and his glamorous new assistant soon found they shared more than a passion for Japan. In October 1895, he divorced his wife of seventeen years. The Brahmins of Beacon Hill searched their consciences and discovered they were not that enlightened after all. They were scandalised. Fenollosa the philanderer was ostracised and his employment at the museum brought to an end.

Two months after the divorce, the outcast couple married in New York and stayed there, scratching a living from writing and lecturing. It was now that the oddest manifestation of Fenollosa's lotus obsession occurred. Earlier that year, he had started writing improving articles on art for the *New Cycle*, journal of the nationwide and 65,000-strong General Federation of Women's Clubs. As 1896 began, the Fenollosas were allowed to take control of the magazine. It was relaunched under a new title and packed, for the brief span of its five issues, with Mary's poetry and Ernest's editorialising on art and beauty, and on Japanese art and beauty especially. Now called *The Lotos* (and not to be confused with the distinguished New York literary club of that name established in 1870), the journal proclaimed its resurrection in February 1896 with a piece by Fenollosa titled, predictably enough, *The Symbolism of the Lotos*. The article covered ground that would have been familiar to any of his former Boston constituency, not that they would have dreamed of reading it.

In 1897, having tired of trying to transplant the lotus, the Fenollosas returned to its native land. The Meiji Government's one-time cultural commissar was appointed professor of English Literature at the Tokyo Normal Higher School. He had to take this comparatively lowly job for the simple reason that nothing more exalted was available. Thanks to him, there were now *Japanese* experts qualified to safeguard the nation's heritage. For a while he settled for the quiet life, pursuing old friendships and pastimes and delighting in new companions such as his fellow teacher and lotus-seeker, Lafcadio Hearn. Then he began shuttling between what Hearn described as 'the cloistered loveliness of old Japan', and the exhausting capitals of Europe and the United States, lecturing on Oriental art and philosophy. He never lost faith in the lotus. Even when not wishing to mention the flower by name, he found it impossible to banish its ghostly metaphorical presence. 'Thinking is *thinging*,' he wrote in a 1906 meditation on logic, 'to follow the buds of fact as they open, and see thought folded away within thought like so many petals.'

In London when he died in September 1908, Fenollosa was forced to endure temporary posthumous lodgings in Highgate Cemetery. Ezra Pound's remark that 'the Japanese Government sent a warship for his body' seems not to have been true. His ashes were, however, carried to Japan and interred at the place where he had studied to become a Buddhist two decades earlier, the Miidera Temple within sight of Lake Biwa. Other sacred buildings staged exhibitions of Japanese prints and paintings in his honour. At the Tokyo Fine Arts School, a monolith was erected in his memory. Carved by a friend and poet, its inscription described Fenollosa as 'the true discoverer of Japanese art for Japan'. The Emperor himself had said as much.

In 1899, Mary McNeil Fenollosa proclaimed her own love of things Japanese with a volume of verse, *Out of the Nest*. Learned, well-crafted, and patently sincere, it nonetheless crumbles to a sickly-scented dust in today's light. Here is a typical sample from one of her many poems evoking the flower her husband held so dear:

> For years, long years ago, on lake and river
> The Lotos bloomed, with petals curl on curl
> Close folded; and to full perfection never
> Had opened wide those lattices of pearl.

(Legend of the Lotos)

This offering was for a brief while *the* English lotus poem, widely cited, declaimed and anthologised. In her 1908 discussion of *Nelumbo* in *The Flowers and Gardens of Japan*, Florence Du Cane reproduces it in full. And yet the person who gave the world these antique japanned belles lettres was also, astonishingly, the midwife of modern English poetry. Within a few years of Ernest Fenollosa's death, his widow began casting around for a bright young literary talent to whom she could entrust his papers and unfinished projects. In 1912, she settled on Ezra Pound, then in his mid-twenties, with an unformed poetic voice, based in London and shortly to become the somewhat spiky amanuensis of William Butler Yeats.

Between 1913 and 1916, Pound and Yeats went to ground in a Sussex cottage. There, poring over the late professor's papers and notebooks, they found the answer to the questions that had been haunting them both. These might be crudely summarised as 'How, with all our gifts, do we avoid writing verse like *Mrs* Fenollosa's?' and 'Where do we take poetry next?' From the professor's studies of Noh, Yeats began to formulate a new type of verse drama. Still more revolutionary and with more lasting impact, however, was what Pound took from Fenollosa's fragmentary translations of long-dead Chinese and Japanese poets and his notes on *kanji*, the ideograms they used. This Oriental reading matter did for Pound what tribal African masks had done for Picasso a few years before. He described Fenollosa's notebooks as 'a ball of light'. Something old and alien had 'broken the mould' and 'made it new'.

Pound's later verse is about as new, or broken, as any poetry could be without descending into utter darkness. It includes not only a liberal scattering of real kanji but also clusters of apparently unconnected words which are meant to convey a single more complex or abstract concept when read together. This latter trick Pound styled the Ideogrammic Method. He derived it from Fenollosa's explanation of the way in which many kanji are formed – as assemblages of pictograms for other objects or phenomena. In Chinese and Japanese, for example, the characters for boat plus water plus knife plus man combine to give the kanji for a lake of the kind where lotuses grow.

As early as 1913, however, this same feature of kanji set Pound thinking about the resonances and relationships of words used sparingly, in lots of space and without fuss. In London meanwhile, the Imagists, a small group of poets, had already started producing haiku-like verses inspired by translations of Japanese masters. But they had yet to find their own idiom, and were still too Japonesque. Nor was it at all clear how a miniaturist's approach like theirs would handle a large subject. Upon them Pound descended, armed with the lessons he had learnt from the Boston lotus-seeker. He not only revolutionised the Imagist poem, he also showed how it might become the method of a more ambitious work. In 1915, he published *Cathay*, a collection based on Fenollosa's renderings into broken English of Tang Dynasty verses which had themselves been filtered through generations of Japanese scholars. The product of these Chinese whispers was a poetry that was new and Pound's own.

It had fallen to a thirty-year-old from Idaho who had never been further than Venice to realise the professor's dream and unite the arch with the lotus, fusing East with West. Whether or not it was quite what Fenollosa would have wanted, the result was a poetry that showed rather than told, a thing of suggestive juxtapositions and resonant phrases, of dislocations and silences, of conventions broken and reinvented, and far from Tennyson's great story-telling in verse.

Before long Pound applied the same method to an altogether larger project, *The Cantos*, which occupied him up until his death in 1972. Although the later phases of this often indecipherable odyssey are peppered with Chinese ideograms, Fenollosa's ghost is most evident in the early *Cantos* written between 1915 and 1924, when Pound was still making sense. *Canto* IV, for example, is dense with allusions to Homer's Ulysses and Lotus-Eaters, to Ovid's *Metamorphoses*, and to Japanese mythology. Its style likewise alternates between Classical epic and Oriental models:

> *Ply over ply, thin glitter of water;*
> *Brook film bearing white petals.*
> *The pine at Takasago*
> > *grows with the pine of Isé!*
> *The water whirls up the bright pale sand in the spring's mouth*
> *'Behold the Tree of the Visages!'*
> *Forked branch-tips, flaming as if with lotus.*
> > *Ply over ply*
> *The shallow eddying fluid,*
> > *beneath the knees of the gods.*

Pound believed this cultural hybridisation would produce something modern and vigorous. Fenollosa had thought the same twenty years earlier.

Both would be proved right – most resoundingly by T. S. Eliot who deferred to Pound as the better craftsman and adopted his patchwork approach. Had Fenollosa's widow not entrusted his papers to Pound, English verse in the twentieth century would have been entirely different. In evolutionary terms, the Brahmin bloom of the 1890s is ancestral to Eliot's lotos of 1935, the flower that materialises in the dry pond at an extraordinary moment in *Burnt Norton*:

> And the pool was filled with water out of sunlight,
> And the lotos rose, quietly, quietly,
> The surface glittered out of heart of light

III

Seeds of Eternity

12

Doctor Lotus

I had imagined that my own first visit to Lotus-Land would provide a conventional sort of case study – *Nelumbo* in Nature, garden and shrine furnishing tidy real-life illustrations of themes I had been pursuing in libraries and museums. What befell me in Japan was nothing like so systematic or segregated. Soon after landing at Narita Airport, I found myself immersed in a twelve-thousand-year epic populated with as many princes and poets as plant people, set in restaurants and DIY superstores as well as temples and wetlands, switching between scenes of sublime serenity and of tragic violence that even Kurosawa might have baulked at filming. Nor did this drama unfold in anything like a chronological sequence. Japan reveals herself in her own time and her own way – straighten things out or hurry them, and the picture becomes false.

It all began with what looked like a guaranteed disappointment – a visit to a sports ground that might have been anywhere in the world but which happened to be in Kemigawa, a town not far from Tokyo. This was not what I had wanted or expected. Nor did I understand why Taeko-san and Yoko were searching the turf in front of me as if for a lost contact lens. Then a cry went up: 'It's here. Quickly, Mark-san. We've found it!'

It was a small granite slab set in the middle of a large low-lying field that was desolate save for a cherry tree. On the slab were carved an arrow indicating due north and two lines of Japanese characters. These translated as 'Ōga's lotus digging place. Certified by the Geographical Society of Japan.'

Everything began to come into focus. So this was where it had all happened, this very spot. There was not much more to be done after gazing and reflecting. A flower laid on the stone might have been appropriate, but there was none to hand. In silence we wandered on, following the direction of the arrow and within five minutes found more than the makings of a wreath. It was a pond, tucked into the corner of the stadium. On its bank a notice-board explained all in Japanese. My companions began to translate, but there was really no need. I could see what was special about this pond: it was filled with heavenly pink lotuses, the same lotus I had nurtured at home, the very lotus Dr Ōga had discovered deep beneath the site of that granite slab fifty-six years earlier.

Burning one's boats has never been a particularly Japanese way of doing business, and few Japanese businesses have illustrated that quite so literally as Tōnen, the Tokyo Metropolitan Fuel and Forestry Industrial Association. Conventional fuels were in desperately short supply in the aftermath of World War II, so Tōnen began exploring for substitutes. Among these was a form of semi-carbonised peat, the remnant of erstwhile marshland and reed bed, which lay in compacted strata several metres down. One promising source of this black gold was an area of former wetland in the lower reaches of the Hanami River, a little to the south-east of the capital, in Chiba Prefecture. The land fell within the boundaries of the town of Kemigawa and formed part of what was then Tokyo University's Experimental Agricultural Station and Public Welfare Farm. Peat extraction began there in the spring of 1947.

It soon stopped, however, on 28 July of that year with the discovery of three large dugout canoes, two of them whole, the other in fragments, and six oars. All were found buried 5 metres deep. Fuel crisis notwithstanding, Tōnen realised that it had hit upon a major find: these boats were not for burning. Although the resources of the Japan Archaeological Institute and two of the capital's leading universities, Tōyō and Keiō, were swiftly dedicated to a formal excavation, nothing further of interest came to light – or so it was thought. The finds were removed to museums where it was determined that the boats were constructed from the timber of the Japanese nutmeg yew, *Torreya nucifera*. Other questions such as their age and method of manufacture proved less easy to determine. Some specialists believed the canoes had been made using iron tools, which would have placed them in the Yayoi Period of Japanese history, between around 400 BC and 250 AD. Others maintained that they were made with stone implements and were

114

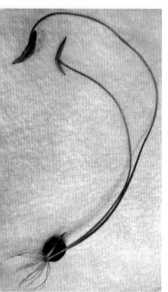

(*Top*) Dr Ōga's three thousand-year-old lotus - Nelumbo nucifera 'Ōga'.
(*Above left*) Seedling. (*Above right*) Fruiting receptacle holding beans.

Revellers on the Nile, a detail of the Praeneste Mosaic (Roman, c. 80 BC).

Mosaic detail from the House of the Faun, Pompeii (Roman, 2nd – 1st centuries BC).

(*Top*) Gold crown from Nimrud, near Mosul in Northern Iraq (Assyrian, 9th – 8th centuries BC). (*Above*) Gold ear-ring inlaid with lapis, turquoise and carnelian, lotus-shaped and bearing multiple lotus motifs (Achaemenid Persian, 558 – 330 BC). (*Left*) Silk tapestry created for the Ardabil Shrine in Northwest Iran (Persian, early 17th century AD).

(*Above*) Lakshmi attends
Vishnu at the birth of Brahma
(Indian, 18th century).
(*Right*) Krishna watches
cowgirls in their lotus bath
(Indian, early 19th century).

(*Top*) Shinobazu-no-ike, Edo's great lotus lake, now in downtown Tokyo.
(*Above*) The same scene depicted by Andō Hiroshige in the mid-1850s.

Classic Japanese Nelumbo cultivars, clockwise from top left –
Tenkyō; Zuikō; Myō-ren; Kōdai-ren; Makoto-basu; Taisaikin.

(*Top*) The Great Drum Bridge spanning Masako's lotus ponds at the entrance to
Tsurugaoka Hachiman-gū in Kamakura.
(*Above*) Lady Masako's white Genji lotus, planted in the early 1180s.

(*Above*) The altar of Konjiki-dō,
the Golden Hall at Chūson-ji
(early 12th century).
(*Right*) Chūson-ji-hasu, which
germinated in 1993 from seeds
buried with Yasuhira's head in 1189.

much earlier in origin, dating from the Jōmon Period, between around 14000 and 400 BC. As these arguments continued, peat extraction was resumed at Kemigawa.

That might have been the end of the tale of the Kemigawa site had one of the boats not been put on display at the Musashino Museum on the outskirts of Tokyo. There it fell under the gaze of a visitor, a frail-seeming, somewhat otherworldly sixty-five-year-old. This was Dr Ichirō Ōga, affectionately known as *Hasu Hakase*, 'Dr Lotus', around his home in the Tokyo satellite of Fuchū City and at Kantō Gakuin University where he was botany professor. It was a sobriquet that he had earned long before 1948. During Japan's occupation of Manchuria, Ōga had been government botanist to the Kwang-Tung Leased Territory and professor of botany at the Education Institute of the South Manchuria Railway Company. Soon after 1917, he began hearing reports of ancient lotus seeds unearthed by farming and peat cutting in an area to the north of his base in the city of Dalian. Intrigued by the extravagant ages and magical properties ascribed to these seeds, he decided to investigate. His quest took him into the Pulantien region of Liaoning Province in North-east China and to the Paozhi Basin in the Liaotung Peninsula. A dry terrain of peat beds, it was once the site of a vast lotus lake which had long since been drained by the action of an earthquake.

Ōga was blessed in his choice of guide, a local farmer, Liu Guai, who led him to sites where seeds had been discovered and helped him to dig for more. Within a few years and through Liu's efforts, Ōga's cache amounted to some 7,000 specimens, among them lotus seeds that had lain buried for centuries. By combining oral history with his own astute observations of local topography, Liu even presented the botanist with an estimate of the timing of the great quake that had caused the Paozhi Lake to drain away. This cataclysm which left Manchuria's Lotus-Land high and dry happened about 400 years ago, or so the farmer surmised in 1920. We now know that an event measuring 6.75 on the Richter Scale befell the region in early 1484. If we assume that the disappearance of the water and ensuing collapse of the lotus ecosystem would have taken a few decades, Liu's estimate was spot-on. As Ōga was the first to admit, the farmer was a man to treasure. Liu's fellow countrymen did not agree, however. He later paid the ultimate price for his work with Dr Lotus, executed as a collaborator at the end of the Japanese occupation.

Ichirō Ōga had found his *raison d'être*: he would be a palaeobotanist, a specialist in ancient plant remains. But rather than take the more trodden path of looking at fossils of plants that were long extinct, he would concentrate on the later relics of a species which, while ancient in origin, was still extant. Capable of lying preserved while all around them decayed, denatured or disappeared, lotus seeds struck Ōga as ideal markers of relatively recent geological upheavals. By narrowing the focus of his study to a single species, he hoped to enter a field of inquiry that would prove immense in its breadth and offer connections to a host of other disciplines.

Around the end of the First World War, Ōga asked himself two obvious questions: Why were these ancient seeds so well-preserved? Could they still be viable? Although lotus seeds had a reputation for great longevity, he thought it unlikely that his Manchurian finds still contained the stuff of life. Nonetheless, he decided to try nicking their hard shells and floating them in lukewarm water after the fashion of generations of Japanese and Chinese lotus growers before him. In the autumn of 1923, he succeeded in germinating some of the Pulantien seeds in the plant physiology laboratory of Johns Hopkins University where he was by then a graduate student. The *Baltimore Sun* reported that they 'had been found under layers of peat, some of them 15 feet deep, in the bottom of what was once a pond on the edge of the Gobi Desert'. The article ventured that the seeds might be as much as 500 years old – a conservative estimate as it would turn out, but still sensational so far as the newspaper was concerned. It was the first of many appearances that this shy and unassuming academic would make in the world's media.

In 1927, Ōga, now back in Japan and aged forty-four, obtained a doctorate from Tokyo University with a thesis titled *A Study of Ancient Lotus Seeds in Pulandian, South Manchuria*. In it he detailed his attempts to collect lotus seeds, to age them, to use them as indicators of change in climate, vegetation and terrain, and, above all, his attempts to germinate them despite their great age. In this last objective his success tended to be short-lived: he was a first-class sprouter but a poor cultivator thereafter. Not so his companions and colleagues. A small circle of antique lotus-lovers developed around the doctor and he was happy to entrust his treasures to them. Two of these characters would play important parts in the tale of Ōga's greatest discovery. One was his friend Shigeru Ihara, a soy sauce brewer by trade and a lotus grower by nature. The other was Dr Ralph W. Chaney, a palaeobotanist at the

University of California, Berkeley. Having received a batch of Ōga's Manchurian seeds in the late 1940s, Chaney passed some of them to Dr George W. Harding of the National Capital Parks in Washington DC and the remainder to the father of radiocarbon dating, Dr Willard F. Libby at the University of Chicago. In 1951, all came home to roost. The Washington donation germinated to huge acclaim at the Kenilworth Aquatic Garden. In Chicago meanwhile, Libby completed his tests and published the results: the seeds were about 1,040 years old, allowing for a century or two either way.

On Monday 1 October 1951, Ōga made his second appearance in the US prints. *Time* ran a feature titled 'Long-Lived Lotus' heralding the exciting new arrivals in Washington DC. The magazine reported that at first it was believed the seeds might be as much as 50,000 years old. This extreme age had been suggested by Chaney; Ōga himself favoured a mere 500 years. Oddly, both scientists seem to have based their estimates on similar evidence adduced from geological strata. According to *Time*, either age would have been deemed over the top before the radiocarbon revolution:

> *Most botanists were skeptical. The lotus seeds keep their viability for a long time, they said, but 150 or 200 years is about the limit. While the infant lotuses flourished in their Washington greenhouse, another batch of the seeds was sent to Dr Willard F. Libby of the University of Chicago. Libby decided to check their age by measuring their content of radioactive carbon 14. In the current issue of* Science *Dr Libby reported his findings: his tests on 19 of the lotus seeds had proved that they are 1,000 years old, give or take a couple of centuries. This is nothing like 50,000 years, but it makes the seeds the oldest of any species that have yet been known to sprout after such a long sleep.*

Ōga was said to have been unmoved by his sudden fame. Some of that can be put down to his self-deprecating character, but a more likely explanation was that he had moved on. By the autumn of 1951 his focus had shifted from Chinese to Japanese lotuses.

By the early 1950s Ichirō Ōga was the world's first and foremost authority on a plant the whole world thought it knew. Botany was still AD, ante-DNA, so far as taxonomy was concerned, and scanning electron microscopes and gas chromatography-mass spectrometry, both indispensable lotus illuminators, were but a dream. Nonetheless, he investigated every aspect of *Nelumbo* that was accessible to the techniques at his disposal, producing a cascade of learned papers. Some of these are as astonishing in their simplicity as they are in their results. For example, the entire rhizome system of a mature living lotus was exhumed intact and washed down. In its rigidly regular herringbone ramification this beached specimen resembled a child's drawing of a fir tree vastly magnified and sculpted in ivory. Observing that the rhizome's branching pattern was more redolent of a long-lived woody plant than a herbaceous perennial, Ōga began to question the lotus's long-assumed affinity with waterlilies. Systematic botany has since proved him right on both counts: the closest living relations of *Nelumbo* are plane trees and proteas, not *Nymphaea*. Other papers detailed his experiments in germination, his attempts to unlock the secret of the seed's longevity, his observation of the lotus's unique leaf insertions and growth axis, his taking a flower's temperature, minute by minute, as it opens and closes, is pollinated and fades. Rarely can any biologist have subjected a single species to such sustained scrutiny. Meanwhile his friends kept him supplied with healthy candidates and his assistants battled to maintain order in his collection of seeds, dried and pickled specimens. These filled a small private museum-cum-laboratory which had come to resemble the workshop of a peculiarly hectic and monomaniacal apothecary.

In choosing this of all subjects, *Hasu Hakase*, 'Dr Lotus', had let himself in for more than clinical anatomising. The seed of something larger than pure botany had been sown during his colonial sojourn in Manchuria. Ōga's fascination with the lotus was fast becoming as anthropological as it was botanical. He developed a desire to explain how in this one plant natural history had engaged so profoundly with human history. This parallel interest in the numinous and the natural, the palaeontological and the archaeological, in the human realm and the plant kingdom, in faith and fact, came to characterise his later work. A properly sceptical scientist to the last, he never muddled the one type of inquiry with the other; but he was convinced that both sides – the lotus as organism and artefact, species and symbol – were essential to a full understanding of the plant. Beyond the life story of the lotus was the part it played in our own story, what it revealed about us. At certain points the two stories converged, as in man's role in expanding the lotus's distribution or his gravitating to places where lotuses abounded. *Nelumbo* had been so intimately connected with us for so long that any botanical portrait would be incomplete without some consideration of the human factor. In this imaginative latitude, this non-partisan preparedness to switch between science and the humanities, the certainties of biology and the mysteries of belief, he bore comparison with the great French entomologist Jean-Henri Fabre who felt that the ancient mythology surrounding the sacred beetle was as important an aspect of his investigations as his minute observations of live scarabs. Ōga's approach might also be seen as anticipating the flowering, a little later, of ethnobotany, the study of humankind's relationship with plants.

On the eve of his Washington triumph, the doctor was stooped over an exhibit of the Kemigawa boat discovery in the Musashino Museum on the outskirts of Tokyo. He had gone along out of curiosity: the boats had been hailed as an important find, made barely an hour from his doorstep. Displayed alongside the canoes was a sample of the substrate on which they had rested for so long, a fragment of their bituminous berth. Black, treacly and squashed beyond recognition, it resembled a block of badly preserved figs or tamarind. Then the doctor looked more closely and began to discern the patterning of plant tissues. There were honeycomb-like apertures and parasol-like spokes, outlines of compressed organs that would have been top-shaped before they were ironed flat by centuries of sediment and humus. There could be no doubt: these were the receptacles of the lotus.

In 1932, Ōga recalled, he was given a single lotus seed that was discovered inside a Stone Age pot at Namekawa, not far from the site of the boat excavation. The seed had germinated and lived for a while, until one of his more zealous assistants overfed it. But he assumed this find was a freak or perhaps even a fraud. Botanists, himself included, believed that the lotus had been introduced to Japan from the Asian mainland towards the beginning of the first millennium AD and then again in waves with the arrival and spread of Buddhism. This was why he had always concentrated on China. But the Kemigawa boats were far older than the events which formed the standard account of the lotus's introduction from abroad. Could one of Japan's greatest signature plants actually have been native? What if, below its topsoil, this area of Chiba concealed the remains of a vanished lotus habitat and of human ancestors who once lived on and among the immortal flower? Had the answers to the questions that drove his career been buried beneath his home turf all along?

The doctor raced from the museum and set about making inquiries. With delight he learnt that a mass of plant debris had been discovered under the boats and that an entire bucketful of lotus seeds had been sifted from it and taken to Tōyō University. With despair he heard that the university care-taker had seen fit to empty and clean said bucket, discarding the contents. This was, after all, just a few years after the war and folk had more drastic priorities than hanging on to what looked like a stew of rotten acorns. Ōga's next thought was for the site itself. Obviously, there was only one thing to do – reopen the excavation. Here he ran into a fresh obstacle. The peat-mining company had finished with the Kemigawa Public Welfare Farm and now its owner, Tokyo University, had earmarked the site for a sports complex. Work would begin any day. It would involve draining, churning up and level-ling the land; there would be new topsoil, hard surfaces and buildings. The first thing to go would be the earthworks left by the fuel company – it was useless as a swimming pool and no athlete needed a pit that deep.

After a flurry of negotiations, the doctor obtained a stay of execution for the site. He was told he had one month before the builders moved in. It was now late February 1951. One of the happiest aspects of the tale of Ōga's lotus is the team that converged in a matter of days on the peaty precipices of the Kemigawa dig. Word had shot round the universities and outlying communities of the capital and the fragile sixty-five-year-old suddenly found himself in charge of a legion of volunteers and donors. In addition to Ōga's usual circle of lotus-loving disciples, there were officials from Chiba Prefecture (the site's local authority), senior academics and undergraduates from Tokyo University, farmers willing to lend a hand, neighbouring house-wives and, when work permitted, their husbands too, and pupils from nearby junior high schools who, unusually for Japan's rigorous education system, had been granted exeats to join in the dig. The would-be builders of the sports complex also pitched in, and perhaps to greatest effect: the Hozumi Construction Group would do all the heavy work, leaving others to scruti-nise and sieve whatever was unearthed. Shigeru Ihara, the soy sauce maker, saw to it that food and drink were carried to the pit each day and provided accommodation for the workers (Ōga among them) as time ran out and the pace of the dig accelerated.

Most professional archaeologists would consider this scenario a nightmare – an army of amateurs trampling over a site and against the clock. Ōga con-sidered himself blessed. The corporate, come-one-come-all nature of the new excavation remained for him the most felicitous feature of the Kemigawa adventure, an affirmation that the lotus did indeed belong to the Japanese people and that everybody had an interest in seeing its ancestors returned to the light.

Before long, everybody was feeling decidedly dispirited. The new excavation had begun on 3 March. The great hole had been widened and deepened, scoured and sifted by Ōga's army of prospectors. A month had passed – the only month they had – and not a thing had been found. The team redoubled its effort, in inverse proportion to its morale. The doctor, by now insomniac, off his food, and a real worry to his friend Ihara, prepared to throw in the trowel. In a final bid to find something, the excavators returned to the original position of the boats themselves and dug deeper. They were now 6 metres below the surface, about a metre deeper than the canoes had been. This, it seemed to Ōga, was a measure as pointless as it was desperate. Scores of prehistoric lotus seeds had already been found in that exact location, and thrown away by an overly fastidious caretaker. Surely that spot had been mined to death and could hold no new discoveries? Then, on the evening of 30 March, one day before the excavation was due to end, the doctor received some startling news. A girl from Hanazono Junior High School, Nishino by name, had returned to the pit with her friends for one final go. Between 6 and 7 metres down she had found a seed of some kind. Ōga rushed to the site. Miss Nishino was right – it was a seed, a lotus seed.

Heartened by the girl's discovery, the authorities extended the term of the dig. On 6 April, two further lotus seeds were found at the same level together with fragments of an oar. The shovelling and screening might have continued, but if the team's goodwill was boundless, their time was not. People had jobs to do and educations to complete. Tokyo University and the Hozumi Construction Group wanted to press on with the sports project. Most pressing of all, the site's past as prehistoric wetland was beginning to reassert itself. The pits were flooding and their walls becoming unstable; some had already collapsed, narrowly missing the schoolchildren whose zeal had brought the venture to fruition. Enough was enough.

Dr Ōga had testimony that large quantities of lotus seeds had been found under the canoes at a depth of between 5 and 6 metres. There were the semi-fossilised fruiting receptacles that had formed the bed on which the boats were found. Now, a little deeper and in the same spot, three more seeds had been discovered along with further remains of human activity. All in all, it was quite enough to demonstrate the hypothesis the doctor longed to prove: Japan's relationship with this plant was old. It reached beyond the earliest recorded incursions from the Asian mainland, and far beyond the arrival of Buddhism, the faith that made the lotus its own. From there he might even be able to go further, to suggest that the lotus was an aboriginal native of Japan or, if an import, an introduction that dated from the earliest waves of human settlement.

Japan's special relationship with plants, and with the lotus in particular, now presented Ōga and his colleagues with a dilemma. The proper thing to do with a plant was to cherish it or, if just a seed, to coax it into life. This was especially true of the seed of a species which both Buddhism and Shinto revered as a symbol of resurrection, and above all when that seed appeared to be as old as Japanese civilisation itself. Spirituality, love and plain curiosity apart, there were also good scientific reasons for wanting to see whether the three Kemigawa lotus seeds were viable and, if so, what type of lotus they would produce. The motivation for attempting to germinate the seeds could not have been stronger. Against it had to be set the possibility of dating them.

As the Kemigawa excavation was taking place, Willard F. Libby was publishing the astonishing results of his radiocarbon dating of Ōga's Manchurian seeds. The obvious course was to send the new Japanese finds to him for analysis. His technique at that time, however, required the destruction of the seeds themselves – to age them accurately was to lose them for ever. Dr Ōga and his colleagues could not bring themselves to dispatch these Japanese Ur-lotuses to Chicago. What they ought to have done is sacrifice one of the seeds, or take samples from their shells prior to germination. But everyone around them, beginning with their regiment of helpers and sponsors and now, thanks to the media, extending to the entire nation, wanted all three lotuses to be given the strongest possibility of living. Few Japanese would ever regret Ōga's decision not to send the seeds away to certain death and certification. But it would leave the finds vulnerable to doubters and challengers all over the rest of the world. To this day the science surrounding this most sacred of plants requires something of a leap of faith.

By the beginning of May two of the Kemigawa seeds were rousing themselves as if an age-long coma had been an afternoon nap. Then, just as suddenly, their unfurling first leaves grew crooked and spotted, slowed to a halt and began to deliquesce. Within a few days, both revenants were nothing more than a putrid mess. Just one seed now remained. Not wishing to bear responsibility for all three, Ōga had given it to Tokyo University's Experimental Agricultural Station where it had sat and sulked, by common assent a dud. Having been exposed and soaked, this last seed was no longer even of use to Dr Libby as test material. It seemed the great Kemigawa lotus quest had ended in failure.

13

Ōga-hasu

All good gardeners know that the best way to make a recalcitrant plant perform is to threaten it. In early June, just as the lifeless-seeming third and final seed was destined for the bin, it sprouted. That summer it grew apace, more vigorous than anyone could have anticipated of an embryo that had been entombed for so long. Come autumn it shed its leaves, as is the custom of *Nelumbo*. While its guardians fretted that its resting rootstock might be rotting, the new plant passed a peaceful winter. The following April, the rhizome was lifted from its muddy cradle, cleaned off and divided into three parts. Two were kept by the agricultural station and the third and largest was given to Shigeru Ihara, who had victualled the dig. Ihara's favoured lotus containers were the large iron cauldrons in which his family had once brewed the soy sauce that was still making their fortune. Planted in one of these, his portion of the surviving treasure produced a healthy crop of bloomy sea-green leaves. By early July the first flower buds were appearing. As their spearheads slowly became tipped with pale and glaucous rose, Dr Ōga began a daily commute of 25 miles from his Tokyo home to Ihara's yard in Kemigawa. After a while, he took up temporary residence with his old friend.

The two men began a vigil; the sauce could look after itself. They sat in the yard beside the cauldron and watched. Lovingly proffered and despairingly retrieved, a succession of rice bowls, tea pots and sake flasks grew cold beside them. At dawn on 19 July 1952, the first flower opened. It was pearly carmine turning to pale magenta-pink with age, highly fragrant and with a boss of golden stamens. In shape and colour, it reminded Ōga of the ancient lotuses he had discovered in Manchuria; it was also similar to some natur-alised or – as he had begun to think of them – native populations of *Nelumbo nucifera* that he had encountered in more remote regions of Japan. This was no disappointment: he understood the pace of plant evolution and knew to expect nothing astonishingly different from this prehistoric seed, nothing dramatically primitive. If anything, the Kemigawa lotus's similarity to others on mainland Asia and in Northern Japan was an illumination. Of course they were all alike – this was the North-east Asian lotus in its aboriginal state.

The lotus was, however, sufficiently distinctive to merit a name of its own. The doctor wondered if Chiba Prefecture, or the town of Kemigawa, or Shigeru Ihara might deserve the honour. But the nation had already made up its mind. This ancient novelty was becoming known everywhere as *Ōga-hasu*, 'Ōga's lotus', or, to give it its formal cultivar name, *Nelumbo nucifera* 'Ōga'. It has remained so ever since, despite the efforts of one or two mischief-makers to suggest that it is identical to a Chinese cultivar. It is nothing of the kind: the world's best-known *Nelumbo* variety, and for a while the world's most famous plant, is uniquely Ōga's lotus.

That first flower in the July dawn was swiftly followed by dozens of others chez Ihara and Tokyo University's Experimental Agricultural Station, and then hundreds more as the original plant was divided and the seeds it soon produced were shared. Today, Ōga's lotus blooms by the thousand, having been distributed all over Japan and the rest of the world. These plants are directly and exclusively descended from that one seed found in the Kemigawa excavation of 1951, and often by as little as a single generation. Some may even be clones produced by division of the original plant and as such can be said to have germinated from that solitary surviving seed. The immediate and international demand that Ōga-hasu stimulated is easy to understand. As I had discovered, to grow it is like possessing a hybrid between a time machine and the Alfred Jewel. It is a thing of astonishing and emblematic beauty which serves as an epitome of an entire culture and connects the present with the distant past by having lived in both.

As he did his best to live down his success, Ichirō Ōga began pondering *the* question: how distant was that past? Dr Libby had radiocarbon dated his Pulantien lotuses to around a thousand years old. The Kemigawa lotuses had been found with artefacts which indicated a far greater age – at least 2,000

years old if the canoes belonged to the Yayoi Period, possibly older if they
were made in the Jōmon Period which preceded it. At the time, however,
archaeologists seemed unable to agree on the period to which the boats
belonged. Ōga himself favoured a technique for estimating the age of strata
based on the relationship between alterations in protein and soil temperature. Deploying this formula, he placed the seeds and the boats at around
2,000 years old – Yayoi Period, in other words. But then the same method
had led him to believe the Pulantien lotuses were only half the age that
Libby's radiocarbon dating later indicated. Ōga's technique was clearly a blunt
instrument. Nevertheless, his tentative opinion became rumour, and rumour,
as it will, became reported fact. *Time*, which covered the Washington germination of the Manchurian lotuses and their dating by Libby in October 1951,
now turned again to Ōga's exploits. On 11 August 1952, the magazine ran
a piece under the headline 'In Silent Beauty', in which it described the
doctor's vigil 'as anxious as an expectant father' and the opening of the first
flower of the Kemigawa lotus. The plant, *Time* asserted no fewer than three
times in 500 words, was 2,000 years old, an estimate arrived at by Dr Lotus
himself.

For a while, that seemed quite old enough – the oldest-known seed to have
proved viable. Then all changed on Ōga's receipt of a letter from his distant
but admiring colleague, Ralph W. Chaney. He had met the California-based
palaeobotanist in Tokyo in the winter of 1951 and given him a parting gift
of wood samples from Kemigawa boats. On 20 May 1953, a year and a half
after that encounter, Chaney wrote to Ōga explaining what had become of
those fragments and what he thought it meant for the seeds they had covered:

> I have just received the following letter from Dr W. F. Libby from the Institute
> of Nuclear Studies at the University of Chicago:

> 'As I mentioned last week in Washington, we have been measuring the two
> pieces of wood from the canoe found at Kenigawa [sic] in 1948. You wrote
> on January 30, 1952: "Dr Ohga is rather excited, and I share his interest,
> in the recent discovery of three viable lotus seeds associated with the remains
> of a wooden canoe 20 feet below the surface and not far from Tokyo. He
> gave me specimens of this canoe adequate for testing, and I shall send them
> to you if you care to make an analysis. The age of the canoe as determined
> by archaeologists is 2,000 years."

*'We measured pieces of wood from the canoe with the following descrip-
tion: "Two pieces of wood (Torreya nucifera) from a canoe found at Kenigawa
in 1948. This is 8 miles east of Tokyo. Many lotus receptacles and three
fruits were collected in April 1951 by Ichiro Ohga. Transmitted by R. W.
Chaney."*

*'Our results were 3,052 +/– 200 and 3,277 +/– 350, for an average of
3,075 +/– 180 years, on two successive measurements on your wooden
canoe sample.'*

*It is of great interest to know that your Japanese lotus fruits are approximately
3,000 years old . . .*

Willard Libby's publication of these results, in volume 119 of the journal
Science on 29 January 1954, took the form of the most laconic shorthand.
It was one dating among many others for all manner of remains that he was
analysing at the time. Nonetheless, it resounded throughout the botanical
world. There had already been eighteen months of brouhaha surrounding
the discovery and flowering of Ōga's lotus. Now it turned out to be even
older than anyone had imagined and the man saying so was one of the
greatest scientists of the age, an unimpeachable expert who, six years later,
would be awarded the Nobel Prize for Chemistry. Of course, Libby was not
quite saying that. He had only tested the canoes and it was these that were
3,000 years old. The assumption, however, was that the seeds and receptacles had to be of similar age. It was an assumption that Libby and Chaney
shared, although many have sought to question it since. The seeds themselves were not tested and that is unfortunate only in so much as it means
we cannot be completely confident about their age. Their location, deep
beneath a large expanse of what had been undisturbed land for centuries
and under objects that are certifiably 3,000 years old, is persuasive. There is
nothing to suggest that subterranean upheavals, whether seismic or hydraulic,
had moved the boats out of the stratum in which they first came to rest, or
secreted younger remains – the lotus receptacles and seeds – beneath them.
But doubts have been expressed, giving rise to more damaging conclu-
sions – chiefly that the lotus, as per the old theory, was not a Japanese plant
at all but a more recent arrival there from China. This seemed to me the
question that was really worth settling once and for all, not the playground
stuff of 'my lotus is older than yours'. My own inclination as I walked the
site, examined the evidence, met people who knew and worked with Ōga,

and saw other examples of ancient, if not 3,000-year-old, lotuses was to believe in the antiquity of his find. What finally convinced me was my encounter, a day later, with the people who made the boats that had come to rest on Kemigawa's lotus bed. They, I would soon discover, had lived with, on and sometimes even for the lotus, and nobody doubted Willard Libby's dating of their handiwork.

Dr Ōga professed himself moved to tears by Ralph Chaney's communication and not quite able to accept the enormity of its implications for the lotus in Japan. Although he would live for another decade, he confessed to feeling exhausted by a long career in the field and the recent drama of the Kemigawa dig. He dearly wanted to fulfil Chaney's and Libby's requests that he conduct a new excavation, perhaps a series of them, and to supply bushels of Japanese lotus seeds for testing. He longed to put the matter beyond question. But his powers were ebbing. Those who cared for him felt the old man had achieved more than enough; that experts would argue as experts always will; and that the age of Ōga-hasu should become a matter of trust and belief. Their priority now was conserving Japan's best-loved botanist. He could have honours and acclaim; he could sit in the sun with Ihara-san and watch the soy sauce cauldrons brim with blooms; he could be helped to write up all those half-finished papers. But there would be no second dig. Nor has there been – partly because the Kemigawa sports ground is up and running but chiefly out of respect for Dr Lotus.

When it flowered in the summer of 1952, Ōga's lotus made headlines around the world. In the British Press, the reincarnated aquatic bubbled under the accession of Queen Elizabeth, opening reviews of *The Mousetrap* and the end of tea rationing. In the United States, *Time* paid homage in August. Not to be outdone, *Life* magazine devoted a special feature to it in the issue of 3 November 1952. Accompanied by a pink pin-up portrait of Ōga-hasu and a black-and-white, step-by-step guide to the resurrection, the article was headlined 'The Oldest Flower: buried 2,000 years, lotus seed finally gets chance to bloom':

> *Most lotus plants bloom every year, but the lotus above waited 2,000 years to produce its first blossom. Until a year and a half ago, its seed had lain in a Neolithic canoe which was buried beneath 18 feet of earth in a peat bog not far from Tokyo. While digging for the peat, some Japanese workmen*

discovered the canoe and turned it over to some archaeologists. The archaeologists in turn discovered the 2,000-year-old seed and turned it over to Japan's lotus expert, Dr Ichiro Ohga, who placed it in a tank of water to see if it would sprout. This summer, after a year of germination and growth, the seed developed into a beautiful pink flower. Although it is the oldest seed ever to blossom, it did not overwhelm Dr Ohga who has had similar success with 1,000-year-old seeds. 'It's quite a flower,' he said, 'but not different from lotuses today.'

The article's inaccuracies, such as understating the seed's age, were less important than the impression the plant created, or its propaganda value. One of America's best-known windows on the world was a showcase for a good news story from its former enemy and occupied territory and new ally. In the same issue, the magazine covered the unravelling of an older empire in the form of the Mau Mau rebellion, but *Life* was otherwise optimistic, indeed futuristic. Dr Ōga's lotus appeared among announcements of an ultrasonic carving machine and a monorail in Cologne, another post-war phoenix. There were glossy advertisements for deluxe Chryslers and Wrangler jeans, and heroic reports of the Maryland and Michigan State football teams. Above all, there was the issue's cover. A departure from the usual portrait photographs, it depicted the newly completed UN General Assembly Building. Although the UN's soaring monochrome spars could not have been further in visual terms from the refulgent pink of the lotus, both seemed to be conveying the same message. After years of conflict and deprivation, life held new promise, and *Life* was feeling decidedly upbeat.

Nobody heard that message more clearly than the Japanese themselves. Ōga's lotus flowered a few months after the end of nearly seven years of US occupation. Japan was coming to terms with governing herself again and facing a new and uncertain start. In this time of deep and mixed emotions, Ōga-hasu was embraced as an emblem not just of renewal but of reconciliation between past and present. Press, radio, cinema newsreels and a new thing called television all reported its flowering as an omen of national rebirth – a portent, moreover, that was a Japanese flower which always had symbolised peace and regeneration. Ōga, the doctor in attendance at the rebirth, became a national hero.

But its reception was not all bunting and *banzai!* Both Ōga-hasu and the media fanfare that heralded its flowering in the summer of 1952 provided material for more solemn reflections and enduring accounts. The greatest of these appears in Yasunari Kawabata's 1954 novel, *Yama no Oto* (*The Sound of the Mountain*). It is not the only plant to feature in Kawabata's novel, merely the most important and haunting of a cast of vegetable characters that includes ginkgo, cherries, maples and *Fatsia japonica* as well as less familiar species such as the black-flowered *Fritillaria camtschatcensis*. These plants mark the novel's seasons and moods, giving the narrative shape and the characters objects of psychological transference. They reflect or project the emotions of human protagonists in a way that is not so much uniquely Kawabata's as typically Japanese, the product of millennia of cohabiting with the green world, of using, contemplating and revering it. As I was to discover in the weeks to come, however, in a flora of around 7,000 native species of vascular plants 40 per cent of which are endemic and many of which have some connection with humankind, none has the power to elicit personal identification quite like *Nelumbo nucifera*. This certainly seems to have been Kawabata's view in *The Sound of the Mountain*.

The novel's main protagonist is Shingo Ogata, a Tokyo businessman who lives in Kamakura. He is in his sixties, aware that his powers are fading, and troubled by the fact that his grip on the recent past grows ever shakier while memories of long-lost love and opportunities present themselves with increasing vividness. He may simply be exhausted; he may be entering senile dementia. He becomes sensitive to portents, principally an eerie nocturnal rumbling that emanates from a mountain near his home and the flowering of Ōga's lotus. Ogata-san's household consists of a no-nonsense wife (the sister of the girl he wished he had married), a stroppy daughter who has left her feckless husband, and a dissolute son. Finally there is Kikuko, the son's long-suffering wife, beautiful and biddable to a fault. The ageing Shingo dotes on his daughter-in-law in a way that is partly fatherly and protective and partly to do with feelings of a kind he has not experienced since youth. Nonetheless he fails to protect her when she and his rakehell son conceive a child. Kikuko decides she cannot risk bringing a baby into such a marriage; she also fears that pregnancy might kill what remaining attraction she holds for her husband. The only answer is a short break from her wifely duties which camouflages an abortion.

So a sad tale, but a very ordinary one told with infinite delicacy. Life will go on in the Ogata household much as it always has done, even with death materialising in various forms. The plant imagery confirms this – there are changing seasons, climaxes and traumas, flowers opening and leaves falling, all bound in a relentless natural cycle. All except the booming mountain and the blooming lotus. These are preternatural events that present Shingo with fell realisations beyond the normal range of epiphanies. Kawabata wrote the novel as the lotus story was unfolding in Chiba and the USA. Although he usually refers to plants with haiku-like brevity, Ōga-hasu comes in for two extended treatments each running over several hundred words. Shingo reads of its flowering in a newspaper article headlined 'Lotus in Bloom, Two Thousand Years Old'. There follows an outline of the Kemigawa sensation in which much is made of Dr Ōga's excitement. It ends:

> *Below the article was a photograph of the bespectacled, seemingly grizzled doctor holding the stem of the opening lotus. Re-reading the article, he saw that the doctor was sixty-nine.*
>
> *After gazing at the photograph of the lotus for a while, Shingo took the paper into Kikuko's room . . . There seemed to be a scent of perfume. 'How are you? Don't you think it would be better if you didn't get up?' He sat down at her desk. Opening her eyes, she gazed at him. She seemed flustered that he had told her to stay in bed. Her cheeks were faintly flushed. Her forehead was pale and tense which made her eyebrows look beautiful.*
>
> *'Did you see in the paper that a two-thousand-year-old lotus has flowered?'*
>
> *'Yes, I did.'*
>
> *'You did,' Shingo muttered, and said, 'If only you'd confided in us, you wouldn't have had to overdo it. It can't have been good for your body, coming all the way back here on the same day.' Kikuko looked startled. 'It was last month, wasn't it, that we talked about your having a child? I suppose you already knew by then.'*
>
> *Kikuko shook her head and said, 'No – I didn't know. But if I'd known, I'd still have been too ashamed to talk about it.'*

It is a small episode of epic sadness. Here is Dr Ōga, an elderly gent like Shingo, who, unlike Shingo, seems to have power over life and to have taken boundless pleasure in watching a birth. The lovely Kikuko has lotus-like qualities herself, chiefly her ability to rise above the mess of her marriage. And yet she lacks the greatest lotus quality of all, the capacity for propagation in the face of appalling odds. Even the lotus itself cannot display this capacity unless somebody has first provided the right environment. Shingo Ogata feels he has failed in this duty of care and cultivation, whereas 'the lotus doctor', as he calls him, has triumphed. In the tight-lipped Ogata family, nothing has been said about Kikuko's pregnancy and abortion. But, as he reads the article, Shingo makes a heart-breaking connection between the recovered seed and the discarded foetus. He realises that he has been aware of his daughter-in-law's condition for some time, and, more recently, of the operation she felt compelled to suffer.

Time passes; people recover. Towards the end of the novel it is Kikuko's turn to offer her father-in-law a lotus. By now the story of Ōga's find has progressed and to it have been added various other accounts of ancient lotuses. All of these have been reported in the press and Kikuko keeps two of the articles to show to Shingo. As he reads them, he takes us through the different discoveries and the efforts to date the seeds; he scoffs at the disparity between two of the ages proposed for them (1,000 and 50,000 years); he notes that the articles had been filed by Washington correspondents – however traditional their family life may be in Kamakura, the post-war influence of America is never far away. Then he begins to reflect, not on Kikuko or her lost child but on his own condition:

> Shingo nodded. 'A thousand years or fifty thousand, the life of a lotus seed is very long, isn't it? Almost an eternity, compared with a human life.' And then he looked at Kikuko. 'It would be good if we could rest underground for a thousand or two thousand years without dying.'
>
> Kikuko spoke in a half-mutter: 'Rest underground!'
>
> 'Not in a grave. Not dying. Just resting. If only we could rest underground. We would wake up fifty thousand years later and find all our problems and society's problems resolved. The world would have become a paradise.'

The Sound of the Mountain won Yasunari Kawabata international recognition which culminated in 1968 in the Nobel Prize for Literature. Ōga's lotus is perhaps the only flower to have captivated the stern judges of the Swedish Academy. Kawabata immortalised the immortal flower, saved it from the piles of yellowing newsprint as Ōga had saved it from the strata of peat. But what appeared to be one man's literary invention, this longing for sleep and a better awakening, was in fact a long-established and widespread Japanese belief. I first read Shingo's yearning for lotus-style slumber in the plane to Tokyo. A month later, on a mountain far from the metropolis, I would see it put into practice, a lotus reborn in place of a human life that had been lost eight hundred years before.

14

Lotus-Eating

'*Kai-seki*,' said Yoko, shaking out her umbrella, 'literally it means "to hold a stone". I think the idea came originally from Zen. During long stints of meditation, monks sometimes kept a pebble tucked into the waistline of their robes. It would warm up with their body heat and act as a sort of false full stomach, a placebo for extreme ascetics.' We stepped into the restaurant from the neon-painted rain-washed street. Its cedarwood interior glowed amber in light diffused by the pearly paper of shōji screens.

'I think that's right,' added Taeko-san, returning the maître d's bow, her angle a friendly but commanding 45 degrees fewer than his. 'Then it was adapted by practitioners of the tea ceremony and perfected by the great master Sen no Rikyū in the sixteenth century. Of course, they used real food, not pebbles, and it was for looking at and eating, not hiding in clothes, but they wanted to make a connection with the contemplative spirit of Zen so they borrowed the phrase. Kai-seki became tea ceremony food. Like the flower arrangement that one would make for a tea house, it had to be perfectly chosen, prepared and served but at the same time seem spontaneous, and very very simple – perhaps just one superb example of something. I say "seem" simple because it was anything but that in reality. It took enormous skill and style to pull it off. Our modern chefs took it from there.'

We were in Taeko-san's home town of Ōmiya, not far from Tokyo, in Saitama Prefecture. So far I had proved a sadly maladapted specimen, able to sit cross-legged on the floor only for short spells of mounting anguish before rising oh so slowly to seek relief by hobbling around, much to my host's distress. As I entered the restaurant, I was struck by a rare and thrilling sight – tables and chairs and with legs measured in feet not inches. I did not know then that, outside cars, trains, libraries and cafés, the seat at which I now threw myself would be pretty much my last for a month and that my coccyx would have to learn to lump it.

Given what I had just heard, I imagined kai-seki would be the epitome of *wabi-sabi*, the aesthetic of rustic simplicity and time-worn elegance that is essential to the tea ceremony and some gardens, as it is to many other aspects of Japanese culture. I had been trying to picture the eating equivalent of – say – a solitary *Camellia sasanqua* flower arranged with a sad blade of autumnal grass in a rough-cut sleeve of tortoiseshell bamboo. When the food arrived, I discovered I could not have been more wrong. The minimalism was there, certainly, as was the painstaking choice and presentation of the ideal ingredient, the *objet juste*. Otherwise, what followed was a performance of virtuosic polish, a banquet lavish in every respect except the size of the offerings, for which fact I was grateful since it ran to twelve courses. Each involved materials that were either of great rarity and value and so prepared with as little fuss as possible, or more commonplace but transformed by dazzling culinary alchemy. Each arrived at its own ceremonial moment in a long sequence of calms and climaxes that resembled a ritual drama. They were borne to us by three girls in traditional dress who aspired to a delicate invisibility, an aim in which I found it impossible to help them. I was similarly ill-bred in respect of the tableware, a collection of lacquer and ceramics, differing from each other and yet harmonising with each dish, that seemed better than many I had seen in British museums. It filled me with covetous curiosity.

Two courses in particular attracted Taeko-san's attention. One was a fillet of Kobe beef as soft as mousse and the colour and shape of a perfectly cooked Chateaubriand, except that it was little larger than a matchbox. To its side, as greenery beside stone in a miniature garden, was a tuft of glossy pinnate leaves, *sanshō*, Japan's lip-tinglingly aromatic pepper equivalent, *Zanthoxylum piperitum*. The meat was not the excitement so much as the dish that accompanied it. A black lacquer bowl contained a heap of lotus rhizomes sliced into sections to show the pasta-maker perforations of their air vessels. They were mantled in a gleaming viscous reduction of beef broth, sake, honey and soy sauce, and sprigged with the pale mauve flower spikes of *shiso*, Japanese basil. These farthing-sized discs, Taeko-san told me, were not only the new season's lotus rhizomes, but the rhizomes of an especially small and tender cultivar. 'Not much flavour,' Alfred Parsons had remarked of his own lotus-eating, 'except that of the sugar with which they are boiled, but they are crisp in texture and pleasant to munch.' I wished the wandering artist could have joined us in our kai-seki. Pleasant – yes, intensely. Bland – no.

But even these wafers of rhizome were not as young and tender as another course that consisted of three black cubes seated on a juvenile lotus leaf within a raku bowl. The cubes were painstakingly papered with satiny seaweed, edges straight, corners perfectly tucked in, an accomplishment that made me reluctant to destroy them as they were barely bigger than poker dice. When I finally applied the chopsticks, I found each contained a nacreous gel of chilled fish stock with, at its centre, an emerald green comma. This was the embryo of a lotus excised whole, on the verge of germination and without a tear or bruise – an operation that must have required a combination of brute strength and microsurgical precision. These the chef implanted in the gel to make pseudo-seeds of the diminutive parcels. I had barely dispatched the first of them when Taeko-san began:

'I wanted to say something about that Greek material you sent. It fascinated me because of the similarities between the way they saw the lotus and the way we did. Herodotus said the pods were like a wasp's nest with their little holes and chambers, didn't he?'

'That's right,' I said, marvelling at her talent for sticking to the agenda. 'And then about a century later Theophrastus said the seed head was like a round wasp's nest and described the way the beans projected slightly from the cells in its upper surface. Great description, but what of it?'

'Well, we call the lotus *hasu* in Japanese as you know, and hasu is an interesting word because it's very old. It appears in the earliest Japanese writings, but it has to be older than they are. It may even go back, perhaps, to the beginning of our civilisation. Hasu is a corruption of *hachisu* which meant and still means "honeycomb". In seventh-century texts, you'll even find the two words used interchangeably where people mean lotus, especially in poetry. So the early Japanese were thinking along the same lines as the earliest Western botanists. They saw the lotus in the same way.'

'How early do you mean exactly?'

'No one can say, but if hasu or hachisu is what we call *Yamato kotoba*, an ancient and native Japanese word, which it seems to be, then we are certainly talking about our prehistory and perhaps even about the people whose old stomping ground we visited today. I thought you might enjoy the East/West coincidence.'

'I do. I do. I've a passion for rooting out these correspondences between folk botany and formal biology. I think it's wonderful that a hunter-gatherer and the Father of Botany looked at this plant, perhaps at around the same time, and noticed much the same thing. But what about your other word for lotus, *ren*, is it?'

Yoko joined the symposium:

'That came later, from the Chinese word for lotus, *lian*. You see, civilised though we were, we don't seem to have had a writing system of our own. That's why we can't date old words like hasu with more confidence. All we can say is that it does not seem to be related to words for lotus in the languages of the Asian mainland, so it is probably aboriginal. In 1113, the poet and calligrapher Minamoto no Toshiyori produced a manual of poetry in which he stated very clearly that hachisu and hasu were ancient words for lotus and that they were so called because of the way lotus seed heads resembled the nests of bees or *hachi*. I see no reason to doubt him. *Ren*, which you ask about, probably became established in our language sometime between the fourth and sixth centuries, as we adopted the Chinese method of writing, the ideographic characters we call *kanji*. With these characters came an influx of Chinese words and pronunciations. We had just the one written form, the one kanji, for lotus, but we had a choice: we could read this imported character either in our own original way, as "hasu", or as "ren", which is our way of pronouncing the Mandarin *lian*.'

'So is there any difference in meaning,' I asked her, 'between hasu and ren? Or are they just two ways of saying the same thing?'

At this point there was a whisper of silk and a screen of iris-patterned kimono sleeve interposed itself as a waitress placed a small urn of crackle-glazed celadon porcelain before me. She lifted the lid to release a vapour reminiscent of warm white truffle. It contained solid savoury custard with a trio of stewed ginkgo nuts embedded towards the base – more prehistoric seeds for our post-modern tea ceremony. The girl breathed an apology. I wanted to tell her not to worry, that things could not be better, but that was not the point. The graceful interruption and the soft sibilant 'Sumimasen' were part of the ritual. They served to concentrate the serenity of the proceedings as they unfolded in the sanctuary of a room that had become a drum for the summer storm. Now Taeko-san joined in the word games:

'No difference in meaning, but certainly a difference in tone. Ren is the form we tend to use in compound words, especially when they refer to something rather basic. *Renkon*, which you have just been eating, is "lotus root", or lotus *rhizome* as you would call it. Hasu is the pronunciation we use when talking about the lotus itself, particularly as something remarkable or beautiful. The plant Ōga-sensei discovered and which we saw today is Ōga-hasu. Sometimes the "h" hardens to a "b", *basu*, to make it easier to pronounce. So the lotus in Linnaeus's herbarium is, we think, a specimen of one of a group of dwarf cultivars known as Chawan-basu, "tea bowl lotuses". Those are two good horticultural examples of hasu; but, as I said, it's an old word which you will also find in poetry. Writing in kanji has an elegance and grandeur, but you could say we keep our original tongue, our native speech, for special occasions and for things close to the heart.'

I swallowed the last of my renkon and asked her for more instances of the lotus in Japanese compound words.

'There are lots,' said Taeko-san, 'but the most interesting are the vernacular names of plants that, botanically speaking, have nothing to do with *Nelumbo*. We call *Nymphaea*, the waterlily, *suiren*, "sleeping lotus", because its flowers open quite late in the day whereas those of the true lotus open at dawn. As this is not a proper lotus but an impostor, it is ren and not hasu, ren being the term, as I said before, that is preferred for lowly contexts. Now, the waterlily has a remarkable relation in Japan, a purple-flowered plant with enormous floating leaves that are covered in spines. You call this plant *Euryale ferox*. We call it *oni-hasu*, "the devil lotus".'

'Now why is that one hasu and not ren?' I asked.

'I imagine because it's a real giant which suddenly appears in swamps and then disappears almost as quickly. So it's rather marvellous to our eyes. Now we come onto dry land. Our large-flowered magnolias are known as *mokuren*, "woody lotuses", which I find easier to understand than their Chinese name *mulan*, which means "woody orchid" – after all, Chinese orchids have quite small flowers. Next we have *renge* which means "lotus flower". Renge is the term we Japanese use for a Chinese-style soup spoon, because its shape resembles a lotus petal. Renge or *renge-so*, "lotus-flower-herb", is also the name we give to a clover-like plant, *Astragalus sinicus*, with heads of pink flowers which look like tiny lotus blooms. On cliff faces and near the sea, you will find a strange succulent with cupped rosettes of petal-shaped leaves. We call this *iwa-renge*, "rock lotus flower". In fact, botanists took this old Japanese name as the basis of the succulent's scientific name: *Orostachys iwarenge*. *Kirengeshoma palmata*, a perennial I've seen in British gardens, takes its name from the Japanese ki-renge-shōma, which might be translated as "the yellow lotus-flowered woodland herb with compound serrate leaves".

'There are even more. You see where all these false lotuses get us? Other plants were measured by the genuine article and its name was often borrowed for completely different species. To me this suggests something very like your own observations on the lotus in the Western world. At a certain point our *Nelumbo* or hachisu or hasu, or ren – whatever you want to call it – stopped being a reality and became an ideal.'

The three girls were returning bearing trays. On them was an assortment of hasu dishes, no longer virtuoso kai seki but simpler fare, served in our honour as an extraordinarily thoughtful afterthought. There were small bowls of pearly rice porridge sown with shelled lotus seeds. Heaped on blue and white saucers were discs of rhizome from different *Nelumbo* cultivars. Each with properties as distinctive as apple or potato varieties, they had been prepared in different ways – fried as tempura, stewed in soy sauce and mirin, steeped cold and raw in vinegar. On a scarlet plate there was a reconstructed lotus flower: balls of rice boiled with lotus shoots were cradled in the concavities of eight real petals arranged in a wheel of pink around a bowl of peeled and simmered seeds. There were various sweetmeats made of candied seeds and powdered renkon. To accompany them was a single long-stalked lotus leaf and a flask of sake. Taeko-san explained that the idea was to perforate the navel-like midpoint to create a natural funnel. Sake was then poured onto the leaf and the end of the stalk placed in the mouth. Since the petiole was hollow, the wine percolated into the mouth, cooled and flavoured by its passage through the tube of living tissue. It was, she said, the customary way of making toasts and sharing libations at lotus festivals. You could always suck if the process was proving too slow.

'To lotus-eating. Kanpai!' I said, making a dribbling idiot of myself.

'Yes,' said Taeko-san, 'to lotus-eating – not that you must forget any of this. Now, if you've finished, we really must be getting back. We have an early start tomorrow.'

The rain had stopped and large bats wheeled before a milky moon. Everywhere exuded an odour of newly damped-down hothouse. We wandered home past numerous smallholdings in the interstices of shops and apartment blocks, survivors from Ōmiya's time as a famous centre for agriculture and horticulture. Their black and steaming earth contained a mixture of both types of growing. There were rows of *niwaki*, ornamental trees and shrubs planted long before as an investment, one day to be sold at a premium, having been pruned and trained by generations of horticultural sculptors. Their arabesque trunks and manicured foliage pads contrasted strangely with the massive arrow-shaped leaves of taro sprouting alongside. They did not strike me as nearly so strange, however, as the smallholdings that had fallen into disuse. Here jungle had taken possession in dense thickets of banana and bamboo, the barrel trunks and shuttlecock crowns of *Cycas revoluta*, the giant's handspans of *Tetrapanax*, *Fatsia* and windmill palms. This moonlit vegetation produced a complicated sense of simultaneous claustrophobia and elation. Call it horticulture shock.

'Where are we going tomorrow?' I asked Taeko-san.

'Even further back in time – there are some people you should meet.'

15

Refugium

The next day, at the Edo-Tokyo Open Air Architectural Museum in Fuchu City, they pushed the boat out for me. It was a dugout, midway between a family-sized canoe and a peculiarly cumbersome punt, 6.2 metres long, just under a metre across, and cut with stone blades from a single trunk of the yew-like conifer *Torreya nucifera*. Its sides were shallow and curved slightly inwards; at one end was a low and tapering prow, at the other a rough standing platform. The boat, I later learnt, was usually held in climate-controlled storage, but the curators had retrieved it just for me, an uncommon courtesy of a kind with which I would grow familiar in Japan. I knew at once that this was *the* boat, the best of the three that were found by accident in 1947 when Tōnen, the Tokyo Metropolitan Fuel and Forestry Industrial Association, dug down into the meadows of Kemigawa in search of semi-carbonised peat. This was the craft that launched Dr Ōga's journey. At around 3,000 years old, it was made during the Jōmon Period. Meaning 'cord-pattern' and describing one of the period's characteristic pottery motifs, the name *Jōmon* was coined by Edward Sylvester Morse, the American biologist, anti-quary and 'honourable hired foreigner' who first unearthed Japan's oldest culture in 1877.

On dry land, there is only so much one can do with a 6.2-metre canoe. Having paid my respects, I began looking at the artefacts in a series of glass cabinets nearby.

'What are these?' I asked one of the curators.

'The pierced objects are earrings, and the others are charms or amulets. They've been found in a number of excavations around here. Both types are motifs that were common among the people of the Kantō Plain in the Early to Middle Jōmon Sub-Periods. That's between 5000 and 1500 BC.'

They were discs crudely fashioned in earthenware and between 2.5 and 4 centimetres in diameter, like clay coins or petrified biscuits. They were of two kinds. In the first, the discs were solid and their upper surface pebbled with papillae, much worn but still prominent. In the second, the discs were pierced with a roughly radiating pattern of perforations. These holes were not round and arbitrary piercings, but artfully asymmetric vacuoles edged with minute engraved lines that suggested severed fibres. The discs with bumps on their upper surface looked exactly like the top of a lotus receptacle as the seeds reach ripeness. Whoever had fashioned them even went to the trouble of making some of the bumps larger and more protuberant than others. Meanwhile, the perforated pieces looked exactly like renkon, the sections of rhizome I had been eating only the previous night. If these were Nelumbo-inspired artefacts, they were as old as, or older than, any from Mesopotamia or the Indus Valley Civilisation. The Jōmon, prehistoric denizens of the hinterland of present-day Tokyo, were beginning to look like the world's oldest lotus culture. I said as much to the curator who calmly replied:

'Why not? Don't forget the boat and the stratum in which it was found. This whole region was once marshland, full of lotuses. The Jōmon are often called hunter-gatherers, but for much of their time they were quite settled people. They lived where food supplies were richest, plant foodstuffs especially, which is why they have also been called "affluent foragers", a phrase that paints a more accurate portrait. Imagine them here on the Kantō Plain surrounded by all these lotuses, a huge and unending food supply. They would have paddled among them in a boat like that one, spearing fish and harvesting rhizomes to supply themselves with something not that unlike our diet today. It's not at all surprising that they made images of one of their most important staples. But tell me, what do you make of this?'

'This' was one of the most enchanting objects I have ever seen. It was a clay sculpture of a circular flower, 10 centimetres in diameter and 6 centimetres deep. At first sight, it recalled a densely double rose. Wafer-thin volutes spiralled within an outer bowl. Each in turn formed swirls and scrolls, petals that coalesced around five inner buds. Around these were empty spaces, openings that accentuated the object's three-dimensionality and imparted a suspended fragility to its intricate modelling. Enfolded at its heart and projecting slightly from the innermost bud was a small diamond-shaped device, the eye of this petaloid vortex. There was something very familiar about this supremely esoteric and exotic talisman. It struck me as looking neither prehistoric nor Oriental. In its brooch-like circularity and the rapturous complexity of its convolutions, it appeared Celtic or Saxon. Even on its own ground, the bloom seemed to present a problem of time. Not only was it far finer than its companions, the earthenware discs of lotus rhizome and receptacle, but so too was the clay from which it was fashioned. The petals had a delicacy that one would have thought possible only in porcelain. Still more sophisticated and seemingly anachronistic was the fact that they were coated in what appeared to be lacquer, still cinnabar red after all this time.

'It seems such a polished production,' I remarked to my guide. 'I don't see how it relates to the other exhibits. It looks like another time and culture entirely.'

'It relates all right,' she replied. 'The Jōmon were here for a very long time. We now think the Jōmon Period lasted from around 14000 to 400 or 300 BC, depending on where you are excavating in the Japanese archipelago. This piece dates from the Late to Final Jōmon, 1500 to 300 BC, the same sub-periods as the boat. It is exceptionally beautiful and well-preserved, but it's not that unusual in terms of technique.'

'But what about the quality of the pottery, and the lacquer, if that's what it is?'

'They were a precocious people, the Jōmon. Of course, by the time this artefact was made, pottery this fine could be found elsewhere in Asia, likewise lacquer. But you could say the Jōmon had a head-start. The archaeological evidence points to theirs being the oldest-known pots in the world, and the earliest use of lacquer. A hunter-gatherer, or an affluent forager, is not necessarily an uncultured savage. Go back long before the Jōmon and the Paleolithic Japanese were making ground and polished stone tools perhaps as early as 30000 BC. The rest of the world seems to have waited another 20,000 years before catching up. Technology, you see. We have a bit of a thing about it. But what do you make of this object? Is it a flower, a lotus flower even?'

'I don't know,' I said. 'It's so marvellous, it could just be a fantasy flower or an abstract design. On the other hand, you have all these earlier lotus artefacts from the same place and culture so why shouldn't the tradition culminate in this? If the Kantō Jōmon had a flair for accurate depiction of natural phenomena, then you have to ask yourself what other real flower like this they'd have known to sculpt. You can rule out double roses. They might, at a pinch, have seen camellias with multiple petals. But the simplest construction to put on this piece, made and lost as it was here in the marshlands, is that it is a final flowering of the iconography we see in those earlier and simpler artefacts. In other words, it's a lotus.'

The Jōmon story begins in the Last Glacial Maximum, around 20,000 years ago. Over its geological history the landmass that produced present-day Japan has shifted greatly in shape. What began as a large Asiatic peninsula metamorphosed into an archipelago due to rising oceans and tectonic activity. Then, between 150,000 and 20,000 years ago, as sea levels dropped again during the last Ice Age, many of its islands became joined to each other and to the continent by land bridges. So linked, they formed what was effectively an arc or loop of land projecting from the Asian continent into the Pacific and making an inland sea of what is now the Sea of Japan. Due to their latitude and the warming influence of the ocean, the lowermost three quarters of this loop – later to be inundated, divided and stranded as the islands of Honshu, Shikoku and Kyushu – were not so gravely affected by the final Ice Age as their neighbouring areas in what today is the Asian mainland. They remained green and relatively equable while much of the adjacent land mass was drastically changed by drought and cold.

North-east China became a patchwork of tundra and alpine desert. Central China and Korea became dry steppe. The future Japan, however, survived as a mixture of open woodland, typically boreal in the north and on high ground, more luxuriant in the south and at lower altitudes. In ecological terms it was a vast refugium, a safe house for species that would otherwise have succumbed to climatic change. This explains the remarkable diversity of Japan's flora today. It also accounts for the preponderance of broad-leaved evergreens, the beautifully named luciphyllous – 'shining-leaved' – forest characteristic of the southern half of Japan but rare elsewhere in the Northern Hemisphere, and for the survival of living fossils such as the umbrella pine *Sciadopitys verticillata* and the cycad *Cycas revoluta*.

Lotus fossils dating from the Late Cretaceous to the start of the Cenozoic (99 to 23 million years ago) have been found at several sites, north and south included, in what today is the Japanese archipelago. The exact relationship of these palaeo-lotuses to *Nelumbo nucifera* has yet to be determined – they may be ancestral, if not identical, to the species we know today. Less ambiguous are the quantities of more recent fossil remains of lotus leaves, fruiting receptacles and rhizomes discovered at a range of sites which includes the cities of Yokohama and Kyoto, and Shimane and Fukushima Prefectures. These are identifiably *Nelumbo nucifera* and they date from the Pleistocene Epoch, the period between 1.8 million and 10,000 years ago which ended with the beginning of the Jōmon ascent. In other words, *Nelumbo nucifera* was among the beneficiaries of Japan's Ice Age sanctuary and was growing there when the Jōmon arrived.

Physically, the Jōmon seem to have had more in common with some relict indigenous peoples of South-east Asia and with Australian aboriginals than with most modern Asians – hairier and with a rugged facial topography more suggestive of Caucasoid and Australoid than Mongoloid. Who they were and where they came from are still disputed. The safest generalisation is that they were survivors of an archaic Asian population, probably southern in origin, who were thriving in what became Japan at least as long ago as the end of the Ice Age. It was then, around 18,000 years ago, that their environment began to improve still further. This gave rise to an interval of high temperatures and rainfall, which corresponded with the marked population expansion and cultural flowering of the Early to Middle Jōmon (5000–1500 BC). Tender elements of Japan's flora that had retreated south during the Ice Age now began to regain their northern territory, providing the gatherer rather than the hunter side of Jōmon subsistence with an unprecedented array of plant resources.

Sea levels rose at the same time as temperatures, peaking between 6,500 and 5,000 years ago in a process known as the Jōmon Transgression. As a result, the scimitar of land that the earliest settlers had penetrated became a necklace of islands once more. This brought access to a wealth of marine and brackish fauna which became their principal protein source. But the flood also served to isolate the Jōmon and the plants and animals that became their co-castaways. In ecological terms, islands are often Prospero's: magic happens within their seclusion. The Jōmon Transgression might be seen as the catalyst in the formation of Japanese identity, geographical, biological and cultural.

A vast number of plants supported them as foodstuffs, the raw materials of buildings, boats, basketry, tools, fabrics and lacquer, and in medicine and magic. Many of these were only available at certain times and places, like-wise the animals on which the Jōmon preyed. As a result, theirs were initially mobile populations, travelling to wherever their needs could best be served according to season. This pattern of life changed when they began to make clay containers. At around 16,500 years old, the earliest of these are the oldest-known pots in the world. Food storage and preparation now became more sophisticated. Next they began to secure and to systematise the wealth of the wilderness by associating themselves with natural repositories of useful plants and husbanding them to some extent – a swamp full of edible lotuses would be an obvious choice. Then they took the step of cultivating certain staple crops. This was yet another development that seems remarkably precocious, especially given their isolation.

Throughout much of their territory, the Jōmon diet consisted chiefly of fish, shellfish and vegetables. It would have been recognisable, if not neces-sarily palatable, to Japanese today. Even rice, whose introduction is usually credited to their successors, the Yayoi people, makes an occasional appear-ance from the Middle Jōmon Period onwards, alongside other cereals such as millet. While such grains would have been wild-collected at first, a form of primitive cultivation eventually emerged. Other Jōmon plant resources were more certainly cultigens and under production as early as 4000 BC, among them bottle gourds (Lagenaria), buckwheat (Fagopyrum esculentum), hemp (Cannabis sativa), and the ancestors of modern azuki (Azukia angularis) and soya beans (Glycine max). Sufficiently well-known, the pulses can speak for themselves. Hemp, used for rope and cloth, became and remains a signa-ture plant of Shinto. The cannabis leaf may signify narcotic rebelliousness in the West, but in Japan it is a traditional token of good fortune approved by the religious Establishment. The gourds too are still of cultural import-ance, but nowhere near so important as buckwheat, the raw material of soba noodles. Equally significant is the early cultivation of shiso, Perilla frutescens var. japonica. Without the aromatic, antiseptic and preservative properties of shiso, modern Japanese cuisine would come to a standstill. To judge by the seeds and stalks they left behind, the Jōmon held this basil-like annual in similarly high regard.

Nelumbo nucifera is one of the best examples of the Jōmon practice of proto-cultivation, a process of living in close association with useful plants, selecting the best among them and protecting them from their predators and competitors. From this practice emerged actual cultivation and the principles of plant propagation, domestication and transportation. So the Jōmon lotus may have been a quasi-cultigen, a native plant resource highly valued and to some extent marshalled through human intervention. Others included the giant nettle-like herb *Boehmeria* which was the main source of twines and textile fibres before the spread of hemp, and the chestnut *Castanea crenata*. In the latter case, wood remains have been discovered which indicate the mass planting of genetically uniform trees some 5,000 years ago – prehistoric forestry, in other words, involving a single proto-cultivar.

Growing nuts is one thing, but what I found credulity-stretching as I looked more closely at Jōmon artefacts is that a Stone Age people could have noticed another tree, not just inedible but highly toxic and liable to cause dermatitis at the most glancing contact, and somehow made the leap to lacquer. But leap they did and, it seems, without any help from elsewhere. At least as early as 5000 BC, the Jōmon were using the refined sap of *urushi* (*Rhus verniciflua*) to make lacquerware and colouring it with iron oxide, cinnabar and soot. The technology has been with the Japanese ever since, as have its signature colours, scarlet and black.

Among their favoured climbers were wild grapes and *Actinidia polygama*, Japan's Chinese gooseberry counterpart, for their fruit, and yams and *kuzu* (*Pueraria lobata*) for their starchy tuberous roots. Many of these wild plants continued, continue, to be of economic importance long after the Jōmon, as did many of the herbaceous perennials that they culled either for culinary or medicinal reasons. The most spectacular of these is probably the lotus, but we also know, for example, that *warabi* – bracken – was valued for its new shoots, as was *gobo* (burdock) for its roots, and various lilies for their bulbs.

All of this goes to show the extraordinary intimacy of the Jōmon with the green world around them, perhaps the most important of numerous characteristics that have never gone away. All of these plants are still eaten or used in some way. Even in modern industrialised Japan, there is a sense of jubilant urgency in spring and early summer as people take to the wilds to look for 'mountain vegetables'. It is a drive, amounting these days to a spiritual impulse, that they have been experiencing for over 10,000 years.

Jōmon beliefs were animistic and shamanistic, based on maintaining an entente with a living world inhabited by sacred spirits, the supernatural mediated by the natural. In this they might be thought to prefigure key aspects of Shinto, Japan's endemic religion. Clay masks, stone swords or sceptres, shell-bracelets, stone phalluses, and comma-shaped gemstone 'jewels' are among many ritual objects found in excavations. Most revealing of all, however, are the countless *dogū*, 'clay idols'. These clay figurines evolved over 10,000 years from barely recognisable anthropoid blobs through a phase of endearingly squat and owlish crudeness reminiscent of the terracotta multitudes of Antony Gormley's 1991 sculpture *Field*. Their development climaxed in Northern Japan in the Final Jōmon Sub-Period (1000–300 BC) in statuettes with elaborately decorated bodies, ornate topknots and ellipsoidal slitted eyes that are often likened to goggles but which, if we must be anachronistic, look more like coffee beans. What most dogū have in common is breasts. That feature, coupled with the evidence of burials of heavily adorned elite women, suggests a strongly female flavour to Jōmon spirituality – a mother or fertility goddess cult possibly served by priestesses.

In all likelihood it was Jōmon women who gathered and grew useful plants and processed their products. The knowledge and skills possessed by women alone gave Jōmon society its structural permanence, stood between it and the old terrors of wandering and hunting, scavenging and starving. In addition to being priestesses and plantswomen, it also seems that they were responsible for the greatest Jōmon achievement of all – making the pots.

They were not only the first pots ever made, they were also among the most richly complex, the most enigmatically symbolic, and the most beautiful pots ever made. They have earned their makers the alternative name *Doki Shakai*, 'The Pottery Society'. It began with primitive vessels which, like all Jōmon pots, were shaped by hand and without a wheel. These were simply decorated, either by scratching the surface with a stick or by marking it with objects such as shells and seeds or the end section of a split bamboo cane. The patterns were abstract, geometric lines or serial impressions.

Next, as they mastered plant fibres, the containers were decorated with impressions made by twine, rope and fabric. The designs became more lavish and the pots often assumed a deep vase-like shape. By the Early to Middle Jōmon (5000–1500 BC) there was an imaginative unleashing, an explosion of invention and iconography. The pots now incorporated all the earlier techniques, but to these was added a new and highly expressive design vocabulary. There were serrations and crenulations, spirals and swirls, writhing waves and labyrinthine ribs, petaloid starbursts and networks that resembled anastomosing leaf veins. Many of these were sculpted in appliqué clay on a basic pot body that had become funnelform and with a broadly expanded bowl-like aperture, like the corolla of some unfeasibly exotic flower. The rim itself might be crowned with tooth-like projections and surrounded by handles which were sculptures in their own right, three-dimensional arabesques that would have struck even the most florid practitioner of Art Nouveau as a trifle de trop.

'Fire-flame' is the term archaeologists often use for this dynamic style. While it is safe to assume that fire played a ceremonial part in Jōmon life, as it continues to do in Shinto, I rarely found myself able to see flames. The decoration of the most decorated Jōmon pots suggests vegetation. Sometimes it verges on realistic representation – the parasol-like leaf ribs of *Nelumbo*, or some edible tubers, an unfolding fern crozier, or the needles of a conifer such as *Torreya nucifera*. At other times it is semi-abstract, generalised – a mesh of venation, the sinuous stem of a vine, the rhythmic regularity of bamboo canes, or the promise of some plump bud. Either way, these pots seem indivisible from the green world; they are ceramic odes to growth, fruition, regeneration. But then, as a botanist, I would say that.

For Yoko this vegetation was the best proof that the potters were women and that Jōmon society was, if not matriarchal, then certainly one where women carried the greater cultural and technological burden:

'Surely you'd need to be very familiar with plants to make these designs? That's woman's work. And it wasn't only plants that they modelled. There are plenty of snakes, for example. For us they're creatures of good omen which have always been associated with female deities and powerful women. By the time we go home, I'll have introduced you to one of the strongest women in the history of any nation. You can't approach her shrine – a shrine she built to a goddess, by the way – without confronting snakes, not just pottery snakes but real ones. I think this identification of women with mystical powers and serpents may have started as long ago as the Jōmon Period. And what about *Shussan-doki?*'

Shussan-doki, 'birth pottery', is one of the rare instances of human images appearing on Jōmon vessels. In the best examples, a vagina is modelled slightly below the pot's bulging midline. From it the baby's head emerges, a ball perhaps 3 centimetres in diameter, its mouth a startled-looking 'O', its narrow eyes uptilted at 45 degrees in an expression that seems happy, vital. A clay shamaness might project from the rim, overseeing the birth. There was no need, said Yoko, to depict the mother's face because the pot was the mother, 'the vessel itself is the female body or the womb. That, I think, is the essential symbolism of all Jōmon pots, even where there are no images of people.'

Earth mother to earthenware matriarch was an easy enough connection to make. It was confirmed by what I learned next. Jōmon adults were usually buried in graves, uncoffined but entombed in shallow chambers. Dead children, however, were ritually returned to the womb by being buried in pots with uterine bodies and, aptly enough, cervical necks. These funerary urns were not Shussan-doki, the elaborate birth pots that heralded sublunary life, but simpler creations often bearing plant motifs and with their bottoms ceremonially broken. At the Fuchu City Museum, I saw several such vessels with broad, fabric-patterned bodies and necks lovingly modelled in the likeness of an open *Nelumbo* flower. In the course of my quest I would encounter many emblems of rebirth, but none was as moving as this childbed for the afterlife which was also a lotus.

16

Through Looking Glass and Keyhole

The 13,000-year Jōmon hegemony came to an end with the arrival of incomers from the continent. These were the Yayoi, members of a racial group akin to the great majority of present-day North-east Asian people, who began their migration to Japan from the territories that are now Korea and China around 500 BC. With intensive rice-growing and metal-working, the Yayoi were capable of rapid and sustained population growth. Their culture soon overtook the Jōmon and furnished Japan with the ruling house and national identity that she maintains to this day. The Yamato ascendancy, the triumph of the Yayoi-derived *Wa-jin*, or the true Japanese as they saw themselves, was described in *Nihon Shoki*, a compilation of myth, oral tradition and historical records produced in 720 AD. These chronicles make very clear the Yamato attitude to the native, non-Yayoi population: they were *tsuchigumo*, 'mud spiders', to be exterminated or subjugated.

In the Dark and Middle Ages, descendants of these aboriginal arachnids who had managed to survive in the north were known as *Emishi*, barbarians who were geographically and politically beyond Imperial rule and so 'foreign'. It was these people that the court had in its sights in the eighth century when it fashioned the role and title *Sei-i-tai-shōgun*, 'Great General who beats barbarians'. As I was to discover, their eventual conquest contained the greatest lotus tale of all. Before Morse's excavations in the late 1870s, the Japanese took the view that the pre-Yayoi legacy had been either annihilated or marginalised. In any event, it was 'nothing to do with us'.

Opinion soon began to change, however, as more Jōmon sites came to light. Although science was not yet in a position to prove a direct link between the modern Japanese and this prehistoric people, excavators noticed uncanny presentiments of later and even present-day Japanese civilisation. Perhaps the Yayoi had not so much routed the Jōmon as assimilated them? Perhaps they adopted their cults, customs and crafts and their knowledge of flora and fauna? After all, this new-found archipelago had vastly greater biodiversity than the shores they had left behind. How else could one explain the many examples of Jōmon beliefs, arts, motifs and foodstuffs that survived into modern times, let alone the strange singularity of the Japanese language?

Since then the intriguing suggestiveness of memes has been borne out by the hard evidence of genes. Between 10 and 20 per cent of the genetic stock of the modern Japanese is identifiably Jōmon, the proportion increasing as one travels north and east – that is, further away from the original entry point and radiation of the Yayoi and into regions where the Jōmon lasted longest without change. Anthropological and archaeological data paint the same picture, not of sudden subjugation or extinction but of gradual integration and hybridisation. The answer to the question 'What became of the Jōmon?' is all around you in Japan: they never went away.

I now wanted to know what became of the lotus between the end of the Jōmon Period and the arrival of Buddhism in Japan a thousand years later. The Jōmon were the oldest lotus culture I had seen, but had any part of it continued to the present day? The answers, I was told, could be supplied in a few hours spent in Tokyo's museums. There would be no kai-seki tonight: I should brace myself for an early commute on the morrow.

According to *Nihon Shoki*, Japan's Three Imperial Regalia, the mirror, the sword, and the jewel, were given to Ninigi no Mikoto by his grandmother the Sun Goddess Amaterasu. She wished him to descend from the heavens to impose peace on a troubled land and to introduce rice cultivation. Sanshu no Jingi, 'The Three Sacred Treasures' would help him to achieve these goals and act as symbols of his divine authority. Of the three, the mirror was especially dear to the Sun Goddess. It was with this object that she had been lured from the cave to which she retreated after being offended by her brother – a spectacularly umbrageous umbrage-taking which plunged the world into darkness. Without this mirror, Amaterasu would never have emerged again and all life would have expired.

Equipped with his three treasures, Ninigi descended and set about his mission somewhere, it is believed, in Kyushu, the southernmost of Japan's main islands. Later, his great-grandson Jimmu extended divine rule further north. Crossing to Honshu, Jimmu progressed along the Inland Sea, overcoming local tribes. Eventually he arrived in the region known today as the Kinki which extends due south of Lake Biwa and includes Kyoto. He settled on the Yamato Plain where, in 660 BC, he is said to have founded a confederation of Uji, tribal clans. This was known as Yamato, a name which the Japanese still use to convey the essence of their national identity. Jimmu was its first emperor. All 124 emperors since have claimed direct descent from him and all have looked to the Sun Goddess's gifts of the mirror, the sword and the jewel as the emblems of their authority.

These myths reflect historical events. The founding and expansion of a new state in the middle of the first millennium BC fits the archaeological picture of the subjugation of the Jōmon by newly arrived migrants from the Asian mainland. The Sun Goddess's emphasis on the role of rice cultivation in taming the barbarous nation is mirrored by the main Yayoi innovation after metal-working.

The three treasures might be seen as a heaven-sent post hoc justification for conquest and colonisation, but they also hint at a gentler and more reciprocal process. Sacred swords, mirrors and jewels were by no means the prerogative of the imperial line. They were common in the ceremonial life of other tribes. Nor did these emblems necessarily arrive from the Asian mainland. Metal-working was introduced by the Yayoi, and the sacred swords were made of iron and the mirrors of bronze. But the Jōmon had used stone swords in their rituals, and comma- or cashew-nut-shaped gemstones. These Jōmon gems are similar to those held sacred by the Yamato ascendancy. Quite possibly, they are much the same as *the* jewel of the present-day and impenetrably guarded Three Imperial Regalia – although proving as much would require an appalling breach of 2,500 years of protocol. Furthermore, the clan leaders who became subject to Yamato rule included regional queens whose chief function appears to have been spiritual, recalling the sacerdotal matriarchy of the Jōmon. By the third century AD, the role of the monarch-priestess seems to have extended to members of the ruling house. Pre-eminent among them, and possibly an empress in her own right, is one of the most enigmatic figures in Japanese history, Himiko, the third-century-AD sorceress queen of Yamatai.

The location and extent of Himiko's kingdom are hotly debated. Yamatai may have been in northern Kyushu, or it may have been in central Japan in the Nara Basin – in other words, the accepted site of Yamato. Early Japanese sources are strangely silent about her, but Chinese chronicles dating from a few decades after Himiko's supposed death in 248 detail her enthronement by a people tired of inter-clan strife, her empire of thirty dominions, her necromancy, her seclusion within a stockaded palace, her thousand maidservants and solitary male attendant, her difficulties in subjugating part of neighbouring Korea, and her burial in a vast tumulus.

This last detail is the first mention of the keyhole-shaped mound tombs that were created for Japan's rulers from the early third century onwards. Known as Kofun, these tumuli gave their name to the era that immediately followed the Yayoi Period and which lasted from 250 until 538. Unique to Japan, Kofun might be seen as a magnificent elaboration of the Jōmon cult of the womb-tomb, the grave as the childbed of the afterlife. The body was laid with goods in a slender passage, a birth or rebirth canal, deep within a mound that was broad and circular at its head and then narrowed to a stem-like neck. In dealing with Himiko, the Chinese chroniclers also describe exchanges of ambassadors and gifts between the Emperor of Wei (then one of China's Three Kingdoms) and the Queen of Wa (then China's name for Japan). Among the gifts sent to her by the Wei Emperor Cao Rui in 239 were 100 bronze mirrors. These were the perfect tribute to the female leader of a nation where mirrors were identified with the Sun Goddess herself.

Around 500 *Shinjūkyō* – bronze ceremonial 'deity and beast mirrors' – have been discovered in Kofun tombs across Japan, usually placed beside the head of the deceased and close to swords and gems. Some closely resemble Han Dynasty mirrors and were almost certainly manufactured in China. Many more, however, have design features that only faintly echo Continental models. These are likely to have been made either in Japan or in what were then her closest trading partners and colonial possessions in present-day Korea. This perplexes archaeologists and historians in their continuing search for Himiko's identity and the location of Yamatai. Find a sizeable cache of Chinese third-century mirrors, they reason, and you pinpoint the Emperor of Wei's gift and thus the queen's elusive kingdom. Where my own quest was concerned, however, the existence of home-made rather than imported mirrors proved illuminating. They are the strongest evidence of what became of the lotus between its celebration by the prehistoric Jōmon and its consecration by Japanese Buddhists a thousand years later.

In 1997, archaeologists excavated the Kurotsuka Kofun in Nara Prefecture. Dating from the middle of the third century, this tumulus contained no fewer than 33 bronze mirrors, the largest single Shinjūkyō find to date. In the geographical centre of historical Yamato, a royal tomb contemporary with Himiko had yielded treasures that suggested a portion – a third, no less – of the Chinese Emperor's famous gift to the Queen of Wa. The discovery was greeted with wild excitement and rejoicing except in Kyushu which had long been a contender for the honour of having been Himiko's seat. Then the mirrors were more closely examined, by Chinese as well as Japanese antiquaries, and pronounced unlikely to have originated from the court of the Wei Emperor. Once more the mists enveloped the sorceress queen.

What is 'wrong' with the mirrors found in the Kurotsuka Kofun, as with so many others found in Japan, is that their decoration is too uniformly distinctive to be Chinese, too stylised and floral.

Their perimeters are patterned with one or more concentric rings of trian-gular teeth. This same pattern can be found in numerous Jōmon pots, a few Chinese artefacts, and in abundance in Indian art. In the Indian tradition, it is lotus-inspired – the flower seen in plan and composed of whorls of acute-tipped petals. The same zigzag motif travelled west as well as east. At many removes, it accounts for the chevron arches of that least likely of lotus temples, the Romanesque church of St Mary the Virgin in Iffley.

The 33 mirrors are bronze dishes each some 20 centimetres across and edged in rings of petal-derived triangles. At the centre is a boss, far more prominent than those found in Chinese examples. Surrounding it is a circular zone, usually decorated with gods, mythical beasts, swirling waters and ideograms. Here we are closer to Chinese models – here is reason for faint hope that we may be looking at Himiko's mirrors. But in this same middle zone we also encounter a fatal problem. China's Han Dynasty and Three Kingdoms Period mirrors often have four accessory knobs arranged around the central boss and signifying geomantic compass points, the elements, or some zodiacal pattern. In the Japanese examples, these lesser protuberances are more numerous and randomly dispersed. The inner field is sometimes peppered with them. Often, moreover, some effort has been made to suggest that these lumps are discrete objects. They are ellipsoidal and slightly pointed; their bases are submerged, it seems, in sockets. They almost appear to have been inserted into the surface. They look like beans, and that is what they are – lotus seeds protruding from the central receptacle of a brazen bloom.

My first encounter with Shinjūkyō was in a gallery where they had been placed between Jōmon ornaments that imitated the receptacle of *Nelumbo* and items such as roof tiles and priests' breastplates from early Buddhist Japan which depicted the same subject. The sense of continuity, of transmission, was staggering. The bronze mirrors may not tell us who Himiko the enchantress was or where she ruled, but they do reveal something just as important. Japan's original lotus cult no more expired than the Jōmon did. Rather it underwent a metamorphosis from clay to metal, from pot to tomb culture.

Not all Kofun Period rulers are as elusive as Himiko. Yūryaku (418–479) is acknowledged as the 21st Emperor of Japan. Swords excavated from tumuli bear inscriptions that record his titles such as King of Yamato. Japan's earliest histories detail his life and loves, as do her oldest anthologies, for he was a prolific poet. Compiled around the end of the seventh century, the annals known as *Kojiki* contain an episode concerning Yūryaku which shows that the lotus in this era was not all sacral smoke and mirrors and that Japanese as well as Chinese emperors made gifts to lonely women:

> As a youth the emperor was playing beside the River Miwa one day when he spotted a beautiful girl who was washing her clothes. He asked her name and she replied, 'Hikitabe no Akaiko, Your Majesty.' Enchanted, the emperor told her, 'Wait until I summon you, and don't get married in the meantime.' Then he returned to the palace. The girl did as she was told and waited.
>
> Eighty years passed and she thought to herself, 'I'm so shrunken and wizened that there's no chance now of ever receiving the royal summons. But I would just like to tell him that I did as I was told and waited.' So she made her way to the palace, dressed in her scarlet girlhood finery and loaded down with small tokens of appreciation for His Majesty.
>
> The emperor, who had quite forgotten his youthful encounter, said, 'Who the hell are you, old woman?' She replied that she had been waiting for eighty years just as he had ordered and now, although she knew she had no chance

of winning his favour any more, she just wanted to let him know that she had been loyal to his command.

The emperor felt wretched at having made her waste her life in this way. For a while, he even considered keeping her in the palace. Then he thought better of it – she was so very old. Instead he decided to send her home laden with gifts and two poems which he composed specially for her. When she heard them, she was so moved that tear drops fell on her scarlet sleeves. She composed two poems in reply and here is one of them:

> *How I now envy that young and healthy girl who bloomed like a lotus at Kusakae-no-irie on the banks of the River Yamano.*

The 21st emperor's own verse appears in the great anthology called *Man'yōshū*, 'The Album of Ten Thousand Leaves', the oldest-surviving collection of Japanese poems. The earliest of its 4,500 entries date from the middle of the fourth century AD, while the majority of the verses were written between 600 and 759. The authors range from emperors like Yūryaku to high-ranking courtiers, merchants, artisans and border guards. There is also a high proportion of women poets. The Album of Ten Thousand Leaves presents an astonishing cross-section of Japanese life over a period when the nation underwent immense changes, indeed could be said to have taken recognisable shape.

There is no greater token of this evolutionary dynamism than the way the poems are written. Although their language and literature were ancient, the only method the Japanese had of recording them was kanji, the ideograms that had been imported from China early in the first millennium. They had no home-grown alphabet or syllabary. The Chinese system posed grave problems. It was pictographic rather than phonetic; it was not even a system, more a mass of complex icons whose individual meanings had to be memorised and whose sounds were far more alien to the Japanese than most European languages would be to the English. Sometime in the fourth century, poets began selecting ideograms that approximated to Japanese sounds and using them merely as phonetic building blocks. It no longer mattered what the characters ha, chi and su meant in Chinese. What mattered was that, spoken together, they formed the Japanese word 'hachisu' – lotus. This method is especially well-developed in *Man'yōshū* and so it became known as *Man'yōgana*, 'Ten Thousand Leaves Writing

System'. The great anthology reveals not just Japan's poetic worldview between the fourth and eighth centuries, but also a nation struggling to find its own voice.

The bouquet of antique lotuses contained in The Album of Ten Thousand Leaves gives glimpses of changing attitudes over the four centuries. Some of these hachisu poems are earthy. Here a poet beholds the beauty of his friend's wife and thinks less than graciously of his own:

Now this is what a lotus leaf should really look like. Compared with yours, mine is more like taro.

Naganoimiki Okimaro, Volume 16, number 3826

Taro is a root vegetable whose large leaves might be considered a coarse and common version of lotus foliage. The blokes have no monopoly of jokes, however. Some women in ancient Japan were evidently of a mind with Rudyard Kipling's heroines – except that for them kissing a man without a moustache was less like eating a boiled egg without salt than visiting a lake destitute of hachisu:

Yes, I know Katsumata Pond and there aren't any lotuses in it – in the same way that you don't have a moustache.

Anon. Volume 16, number 3835

We can assume that nothing came of the proposed assignation, and that the would-be seducer went home with head hung low to work on his handlebar. Not every gallant in Man'yōshū faces such frustration. Sometimes the geta is on the other foot:

Although my mother warned me not to sleep with you, I followed my heart, unsure where it would lead me. I ran out of control like a drop of water on a lotus leaf in Tsurugi Pond. Now my heart is as settled as the bottom of Kiyosumi Pond: I will not be able to stop thinking about you until I sleep with you again.

Anon. Volume 13, number 3289

I would discover that it is almost always wrong to imagine that the Japanese enforce a distinction, Christian-style, between sacred and profane. But as Yoko led me through this 1,500-year-old anthology on the purse-sized

Sony Vaio which – she insisted – was her true travelling companion and the apogee of Japanese civilisation, I could detect a change in attitude, a shift in the treatment of the lotus from sexed-up to ethereal. The poems became simpler, softer, and more contemplative:

I am waiting for rain, as I love to watch the downpour turn to beads on a lotus leaf.

Anon. Volume 16, number 3837

When I asked Yoko if and why she thought that was the case, she replied that it was because the greatest revolution in Japanese history had occurred halfway through the time span of the poems included in The Album of Ten Thousand Leaves. 'Not a bloody revolution,' she added, 'I mean the arrival of Buddhism.'

17

A Thousand Petals, a Million Prayers

In 406 a Chinese translation of the *Lotus Sutra* was produced for Yao Xing, Emperor of the Late Qin state. Its author was Kumarajiva, a Buddhist scholar-monk born in the Silk Road oasis kingdom of Kucha. He was trained in Kashmir before being spirited away by a China that was then as curious about the 'new' religion as Japan would be 200 years later. Kashmir is also where the sutra itself seems to have been set down, in the first century AD by proponents of the movement which would come to dominate East Asian Buddhism. Offering universal compassion, the intercession and aid of deity-like incarnations of the Buddha known as Bodhisattva or Kannon, and the possibility of rebirth and redemption through Samsara, the great transmigratory cycle of being and becoming, this new movement presented an achievable and optimistic everyman's alternative to the self-reliant strictness of monastic practice. It became known as Mahayana, 'The Great Vehicle', a term that first appears in the *Lotus Sutra*. Although the lotus was already well-established as one of Buddhism's principal icons, it is difficult to avoid the notion that this new scripture, in which the flower looms larger than ever, was influenced by its birthplace. Both its earliest compilers and Kumarajiva, its greatest translator, worked close to the *Nelumbo*-filled waters of Lake Dal.

As Kumarajiva was working on his translation, Buddhism was beginning to gain purchase in Japan. Immigrants from Korea and China were allowed to practise the faith. There is even a record of a mission to Fusang, 'the Country of the Furthest East', undertaken in 467 by five monks from the

Indian kingdom of Gandhara. They were said to have had a benign effect on their flock: worldly goods were renounced and enlightenment sought. According to *Nihon Shoki*, the new faith arrived in Nara in the autumn of 552 in the form of a gilt statue of the Buddha and a collection of sutras sent to Kinmei, Japan's 29th emperor, by the king of the Korean state of Baekje. The first two decades of its life in the imperial capital were beset by factional squabbles and fears that the *kami*, the gods and sacred spirits of Shinto, would be affronted or even ousted. Before long a typically Japanese accommodation emerged, a syncretism in which the Buddha and his attendant deities lived alongside the native gods and became kami of sorts, not beating but joining.

The Empress Suiko put this relationship on a formal footing in 594. Soon after she ascended the throne and shortly before becoming a Buddhist nun, she announced that the new religion would enjoy the protection of the state. The implementation of this decree fell to Suiko's nephew, the twenty-year-old Prince Shōtoku who ruled as regent from the moment of the empress's retreat. By the time of his death in 621, there were 46 Buddhist temples, 816 monks and 569 nuns in Japan. Among the temples were some of the nation's greatest religious complexes, including Hōryū-ji in Nara, dedicated by Shōtoku and his aunt in 607. It was in Yumedono, Hōryū-ji's octagonal 'Hall of Dreams', that Ernest Fenollosa unwrapped the golden Kannon 1,277 years later and so experienced his own moment of enlightenment.

Prince Shōtoku investigated and propagated Buddhism partly for the good of the state and partly as a field in which his own intellect could roam, or soar. As his writings demonstrate, it was an exciting field, a new system filled with esoteric learning, foreign texts and exotic iconography. To advance his project, he recruited sages and craftsmen from Continental Asia. He also strengthened relations with China – it was in his regency and in diplomatic correspondence that Wa, the 'lowly' or 'subordinate nation' in China's eyes, became Nihon, 'the Land of the Rising Sun'. In the course of importing all this learning, Shōtoku added a further ingredient to the syncretistic Japanese mix, Confucianism. This he regarded in the spirit for which the *Analects* were intended, as a guide for the principled conduct of men of rank. When it came to forming a vision for his entire nation, however, he looked to Buddhist scripture and to one text especially, the *Lotus Sutra* in Kumarajiva's translation.

From it Shōtoku took his two big ideas. The path to enlightenment was not a prerogative of the priesthood. Enlightenment was a thing of this life, a process of engagement with the world through compassionate deeds and attitudes rather than a mystical goal attained by withdrawing from life. As a result, the entire laity was set on the Buddha's way and enjoined to travel it by means of forbearance and mercy. These qualities were to be shown not just to one's fellow humans but to all living beings. This empathy with the natural world struck a chord with Japan's existing beliefs. So too did the central image of the lotus itself. While the *Lotus Sutra* is a text of dazzling opulence and dizzying dimensions, its main metaphor, the flower that embodies the law itself and blooms endlessly throughout its verses, was an easy thing to grasp: it was already everywhere in Japan and already sacred. The ease with which such pre-Buddhist icons were shared with the new faith was itself seen as a manifestation of the *Lotus Sutra*. Universal tolerance is its main message, and that goes for beliefs as well as living creatures. It was only proper that in Shōtoku's Japan the lotuses of the Jōmon, Yayoi and Kofun should have cross-pollinated the lotus of the Buddha and produced a hybrid bigger and more beautiful than any of them.

That meant the beginning of an extraordinary proliferation in which the leaves, flowers and fruit of the lotus began to appear everywhere in paint, wood, metal and stone in both temples and secular buildings. During Shōtoku's regency the practice, still widespread in Japanese architecture, of ending house gables with roof tiles fashioned as *Nelumbo* flowers and receptacles became common. Under those lotus-ornamented roofs, *O-Butsudan* began to appear, the 'Buddha altars' commonly called family shrines in the West but which, strictly speaking, are small domestic temples. Each had its complement of lotuses, sculpted or real, standing in vases or providing the Buddha's seat and halo. They still do, and in quantities that could only be calculated by the mathematical wizardry of the *Lotus Sutra* itself.

In 606, the retired Empress Suiko gave her wealthier and better-educated subjects an annual rite that focused on these household altars – Obon, now Japan's most important holiday after the New Year. This great high-summer festival of the returning dead cannot be celebrated without lotuses in some form and in Suiko's day that meant live lotuses. Seventh-century records show poor rustics finding sudden wealth. The swamp full of *Nelumbo* adjoining the paddy-field was now a source not of rude carbohydrates but of sacred props. Carried to the capital at the right time of year, a small load of lotus leaves, flower buds and rhizomes was worth any amount of rice. Some farmers began to pay their taxes in lotuses alone, leaving their cereal income intact. It is hardly surprising that the lotus poems of Man'yōshū became less raunchy and more respectful around the time of Shōtoku's regency. In 636, some years after his death, the official records gave the flowering of a double-headed lotus in the Tsurugi Lake equal billing with news of a comet.

Buddhism elevated the people as well as its signature plant. Temples sponsored by the prince and his aunt performed a wide range of social as well as sacral functions. They were universities for the newly imported learning, centres for the arts, dispensaries and infirmaries, and charitable operations for the poor, lame and orphaned. In the next century, Shōmu, the 45th Emperor of Japan, extended this principle across his domain and made it the core of his political as well as spiritual philosophy. In 741, he ordered the construction of a nationwide network of temples organised in a hierarchy that culminated in great religious complexes under his patronage in Nara, the capital. Some regard this venture as the first and most thoroughgoing attempt to convert the whole of Japan to Buddhism. It was less an assault on Shinto, however, than an attempt to control Buddhism, and the nation through it. For a model of governance, Shōmu thought in terms of that most Buddhist of schemes, the mandala, the visual and usually hierarchical representation of the heavens and earth in microcosm. Many mandalas are lotus-inspired and so was Shōmu's; but his was verbal rather than visual. It came from a passage in the text (again translated by Kumarajiva) known as Bonmōkyō in Japanese, or the *Brahmajala Sutra*.

Here Vairocana, the ultimate embodiment of all Buddhas and Bodhisattvas, the personification of the infinite and universal, sits at the centre of a thousand-petalled lotus flower. On every petal there sits a further great Buddha who is also a personification of Vairocana, enthroned in the midst of a discrete world. Every one of these thousand worlds contains 10,000 million worlds each with its own lotus-seated Buddha presiding. In some readings, these 10 trillion worlds encompass their own worlds in turn, the implication being that the pattern is repeated again and again, progressing from trillions to infinity with each petal sporting its own lotus rosette and a new world on every petal. For some monarchs the hive was a popular way of visualising the social organisation of a state, for others the human body or the garden. For Shōmu it was this flower, whose petals divided an innumerable citizenry into communities centred on temples, those communities into provinces with their own principal religious houses, and those provinces into whorls

163

of ever-increasing importance around the emperor and his arch prelates. As he saw it, the entire nation was a lotus.

In 752, Emperor Shōmu presided over the dedicatory eye-opening ceremony of a statue of Vairocana watched by 10,000 guests at Tōdai-ji, his 'Great Eastern Temple' in Nara. It was, and remains, the largest bronze sculpture of the Buddha in Japan, and the hall that houses it is the largest wooden building in the world. The figure itself is 15 metres tall. At 10 metres wide and 3 metres deep, his seat is the largest lotus sculpture. Its petals depart from convention in being upturned and cupped rather than outspread. Each of them is engraved with myriad subsidiary Buddhas and lotuses as per Shōmu's favourite text, *Bonmōkyō*. In case anyone misses the point, before the sculpture are two bronze images of lotuses arranged in vases. Measured from the top of the vases, their stalks stand 5 metres tall and the individual flowers are as much as 1.5 metres across.

When the emperor commissioned this Colossus, his realm was not as orderly as his political vision might suggest. There had been earthquakes, outbreaks of smallpox, several rebellions, famine, and the death of his son by a consort chosen from the Fujiwara family – the first of many such unions between the imperial line and this aristocratic house. With so much to pray for, it is little wonder Shōmu made his icon a large one. A decade in the making, it nearly beggared the nation. By the time Shōmu saw the great Buddha's eyes opened in 752, these troubles were no longer officially his. He had abdicated three years earlier, becoming the first of many emperors to seek the seclusion of the Buddhist cloister.

Like the Empress Suiko, Shōmu's daughter occupied the Chrysanthemum Throne in her own right and not as an imperial consort. She did so twice. Between Shōmu's retirement in 749 and 758, she reigned as the Empress Kōken. She then abdicated in favour of her cousin, only to change her mind and dethrone him, ruling again from 764 until her death when she was granted the posthumous name of Empress Shōtoku, so linking her in memory to the princely pioneer of Japanese Buddhism. In the six-year interval between her reigns, the empress had become a nun, and so she remained on returning to power. Unsurprisingly, her second reign saw a deepening of Japan's commitment to Buddhism and a growth in the might of temples and monasteries.

In 764, a new smallpox epidemic threatened her nation. Salvation, it seemed to the empress, lay in *dharani*, the mantra-like incantations with which her favourite monk Dōkyō had cured her of the same disease. If only her subjects were able to receive this balm, they might be not only spared the plague but also convinced of her authority as a Buddhist ruler. She consulted one of her courtiers, a scholar called Kibi no Makibi who had travelled in China and returned with examples of printing. These printed images and texts, she understood, were rarities, produced with difficulty and at great cost; but would it not be possible to improve the technology, to streamline production and to print a prayer for every one of her subjects? Unsure how many exactly that meant, she seized on a good roundish figure. Say a million, she told her astonished courtier; and of course these paper prayers would need protection – what if every one of them were housed in its own miniature pagoda?

Kibi no Makibi assembled a team of 157 craftsmen – wood turners, paper makers and printers. The small scrolls that would bear the prayers were cut from sheets of paper made from laid hemp (*Cannabis sativa*), produced in quantities and to a uniform standard never seen before. Probably cast from clay stereotypes, the metal stamps with which the text was printed had a durability that likewise broke the mould. Kibi no Makibi also simplified and systematised the technique of using parts of Chinese characters for their sounds alone. He had little choice. Dharani are esoteric texts, composed in Sanskrit. Even if it was unintelligible to most Japanese, each syllable was held to contain the properties of a magic charm and had to be read out loud. Not pictographic but phonetic, Kibi no Makibi's solution to this problem was another step towards the evolution of Japan's own writing system a half-century later.

Over a period of five years and eight months, his team printed 1 million mantras and made 1 million lotus-capped canisters for them, finishing the project in 770, the year of the empress's death. The pagodas became known as *Hyakumantō Darani*, 'The Million Dharani Towers', after the texts they contained. Prayers for freedom from disease, war, and physical and mental torment, four different dharani were printed, each housed in its miniature wooden pagoda with four of these toy-sized towers making up one set. Encased in a vastly larger tower, 25,000 of these sets were then sent to each of Japan's ten principal temples. Once they had received their complement of 100,000 towers apiece, the temples could either store them as a great generator of prayer power, or disseminate them among the congregation.

'Pagoda' conjures soaring splendour, storey upon storey of upturned gilded roofs. Nothing could be further from the smooth simplicity of these pint-sized artefacts. Just 21 centimetres tall and 10 centimetres wide at the bottom, they are constructed from two pieces of wood turned on a lathe: the conical body of Hinoki cypress (*Chamaecyparis obtusa*), and the slender spire of Katsura (*Cercidiphyllum japonicum*). The result is an object so minimalist, so essential and unadorned as to appear Modernist. Ascending from a broad circular base, their tiers are of two kinds – widely spaced and discus-like below, coin-sized and closer together above. At the apex is a stalked ellipsoidal knob a little under a centimetre across. Looking at one of these towers, I was reminded of porcelain bushings, those concertina-shaped ceramic insulators used on overhead cables. The similarity is apt: channelling energy was its intended purpose.

I was told that the pagoda, or stupa to give it its rightful name, was an object of meditation, a sermon in sculpture. Its various tiers progressed through precepts such as generosity and moral restraint, culminating in the Buddha's compassion at the top. Their circularity was also intended to represent cycles of being arranged in a hierarchy that journeyed through the stages of enlightenment, growing ever narrower, ever more focused and refined towards the summit. As the mandala took its physical inspiration from the lotus flower, so these circles were suggested by the same plant's foliage. In effect, the stupa was a radically simplified and semi-abstract representation of the lotus. Conversely, the bronze, wood or living lotus flower and leaf arrangements that can be seen in every Japanese temple and almost every home are stupas in their pre-abstracted state. As if to confirm this identification, I was told that the knob that crowned the miniature pagoda was meant to be a lotus bud. The ultimate emblem of Buddha's infinite mercy, its infolded petals contained all the teeming ranks of life symbolised by the circles beneath it.

The priest who explained this also told me that the different widths of tiers fell into distinct zones. These, moving from the base up, represented *Roku-Dai*, 'the Six Great Elements' – earth, water, fire, wind, space and consciousness. When I pointed out that I could only see five such zones, I was told that the sixth element, consciousness, hovered over the stupa and animated the other five, physically embodied zones in a metaphysical percolation. And still there was more to come from this 21-centimetre spindle. When meditating on the stupa, people should replicate its form and mirror these bands of elements – legs/earth, chest/fire, head/space. In other words, they should assume the lotus position.

I would have been happy to leave it at that. Of all the artistic representations of *Nelumbo* I had encountered, none could equal this tiny tower in
distilled potency. But then my guide pointed out an astonishing fact. Any
one of the empress's surviving dharani might plausibly be described as the
world's oldest printed book. That accolade is usually granted to a version of
the *Diamond Sutra* discovered in the Mogao Caves in North-western China
and now owned by the British Library. Its primacy rests on the fact that its
date – May 868 AD – is made explicit in the text itself. Unlike the *Diamond
Sutra*, none of the Empress Shōtoku's scrolls was dated, but their containers
were. The one I was looking at was dated 23 April 768. At a little over
50 centimetres long, the dharani are far smaller and simpler than the 5-
metre-long Mogao treasure, but they are still entire and lengthy texts. The
Chinese sutra was a one-off, a unique and uniquely beautiful artwork. A
century before it was printed, the empress's million scrolls were already a
feat of mass production that would be judged phenomenal even by today's
standards.

Nara Period Japan was a place of real-life lotus miracles. In addition to
the giant bronze bloom that cushions the Tōdai Temple's 15-metre Vairocana,
there were prodigies of manufacturing such as the Taima Mandala, a glori-
ously coloured and detailed wall hanging of the Pure Land of the Amida
Buddha which dates from 763. Not only is it filled with depictions of the
lotus, but it was originally made from *Nelumbo*. One hundred horse-loads of
lotus stalks provided the fibre from which the first version of this mandala
was woven. It does not matter whether, as legend has it, the process really
only took three days and the labour of three nuns (two of whom were believed
to be the Buddha and Kannon in disguise). What matters is that the ideal
medium for creating this two-dimensional lotus-land was judged to be the
lotus itself. This image, so full of figures in the process of being born or
reborn from lotus flowers, could only be born of the sacred flower. At the
temple of Taima-dera in Nara, the mandala became and remains an object
of pilgrimage. Within a few years of its making, copies of it could be found
throughout Japan. It was *the* map of the Buddha's paradise. But to my eyes,
neither Vairocana's gargantuan seat nor the Taima Mandala was a match for
the 1 million towers of the Empress Shōtoku. Around 50,000 survive today.
Some still contain the scrolls that resulted from the world's first instance of
mass-produced printing. All of them remain the most intriguing and revolutionary of lotus artefacts.

18

Sacred and *Profane*

In Empress Shōtoku's day, Japanese Buddhism was dominated by six great sects based in Nara. All of them resorted to lotus iconography and scripture to some degree. The Hossō Sect, which established itself in the capital in 660, was greatly exercised by the nature of consciousness and thus of coming into being, awaking, germinating. Like the Harvard psychologist-philosopher William James 1,200 years later, Hossō adherents explored the idea of a primordial seam of common and latent consciousness. It was visualised as a lake bed, or perhaps a peat stratum like the one at Kemigawa, that contained dormant seeds from which natural phenomena and aspects of human identity developed.

The philosopher-monk Kūkai (774–835) was fascinated by language. After long immersion in Sanskrit and related scripts, he finally devised kana, the phonetic writing system that freed the Japanese language from Chinese ideograms. His linguistic interests are reflected in the name he gave his sect – Shingon, 'True Word', from the term for esoteric texts like the Empress Shōtoku's dharani, texts of the kind that had led him to his greatest invention. For Kūkai the lotus seed with its impenetrability, capacity for prolonged dormancy, and talent for phenomenal germination and proliferation served as a metaphor for the cryptic complexity and spiritual potential of language: in the beginning was the word, and the word was lotus seed. The task of the True Word scholar was to make that seed germinate.

Other sects took a less intellectual approach. Another great scholar-monk,

Saichō (767–822), travelled to China with Kūkai in 804 and returned with new learning and a new perspective. As the Emperor Kanmu became persuaded of the merits of his teachings, Saichō's hermit hovel on Mount Hiei near Kyoto received state recognition and soon grew to become Enryaku-ji, one of the nation's greatest temples and its spiritual beacon. Its growth was assisted by the fact that in 794, the emperor had moved his palace. This move marked the beginning of a decline in the power of the six great Nara sects and ushered in the historical period that would bear the name of the new imperial capital – Heian, or Kyoto as it later became. Saichō's school was a hybrid. To Chinese T'ien-t'ai Sect teachings he added Zen, the precepts enshrined in the *Bonmōkyō*, and aspects of Shingon mysticism. Vitalising these elements like the invisible but transforming consciousness that hovers over the empress's wooden stupas was the *Lotus Sutra*.

Saichō called his new sect Tendai-Hokke, a combination of the Japanese names for T'ien-t'ai and the *Lotus Sutra*. It was a winner. It resolved or swept away the jarring diversity of the other sects that had proliferated: all were welcome, all reconciled. It did the same to the priesthood and the laity: this was everyone's religion. All were able to seek salvation in a flawed and declining world. All were engaged in Samsara, the great cycle of metempsychosis. Karma, the law of cause and effect, remained important: what came around still went around, people got their just deserts in the next life or lives if not in this one. But this was presented less as a process of judgement (bad man becomes worm) and more as an evolutionary dynamic (bad man needs to become worm to become good man). Through this engagement, the world's and our own rebirth in some happier form would become more likely as, ultimately, would the prospect of Nirvana, enlightenment. While there were rites, scriptures and dogma that remained the province of priestly experts, the day-to-day pursuit of this goal was a relatively simple matter of good deeds performed in public and good thoughts harboured in private.

The manual for priest and lay person alike was the *Lotus Sutra* where tolerance and compassion, the primary values of the Tendai Sect, are endlessly articulated. In the thirteenth century, the sutra's formal invocation, *Namu-Myōhō-Renge-Kyō*, became the main precept of a new school of Buddhism which developed from the Tendai Sect. For its followers, simply stating the *Lotus Sutra*'s title was the *summum bonum* – just chant or write the magic words; all life, all ceremony and all teaching are encompassed by them. The name taken by this new sect's founder, and given to the sect itself, was

Nichiren, 'Sun Lotus'. The 'Sun' in question was Japan herself. Once more, the nation was a lotus.

There was a hitch, however, and a large one. As the Tendai Sect took root, so the belief became common that the world was entering its final phase, a 10,000-year period of decline in which Buddhist practice would decay and it would become ever more difficult to attain enlightenment. The Buddha himself had predicted this end time, the world's autumn. Already a powerful concept, evanescence now threatened to oppress the Heian Period sensibility. Rather than live with the prospect of slow disintegration and extinction, the Japanese added a further ingredient to the mix. In the tenth and eleventh centuries, the Amida Buddha began to take centre stage. The reason for his promotion was simple: this Indian incarnation of the Buddha presided over the Pure Land or Jōdo, a paradise situated in the imaginary far west. Anybody, no matter how corrupt or base, was eligible for rebirth in this ultimate lotus-land provided that before death he or she accepted the Amida Buddha and invoked him with the chant *Namu Amida Butsu*. As a result, pure faith became a basis of Japanese Buddhism, complementing or sometimes replacing the duties of virtuous deeds, learning and ritual practice. This world might decline, but otherworldly redemption was promised at its end.

The Amida Buddha was often given central prominence in Tendai temples, and especially in those sponsored by the Fujiwara, the clan which came to dominate court and culture in the Heian Period. So far as the lotus was concerned, the mix was potent fertiliser. Its blooms loomed large in both the *Lotus Sutra* of Tendai Sect and the Pure Land of Amidism. Both doctrines offered paradisiacal visions of a landscape not only replete with *Nelumbo* but where the flower was also a vehicle of redemption: the reborn were visualised either as emerging from its buds or as being synonymous with them. The plant and its heavenly habitat became much more than the stuff of scripture. For the Heian emperors and aristocracy they were blueprints for living and spending. They began to appear everywhere in the arts, often in media whose opulence strove to emulate the teeming, 24-carat terrain of the *Lotus Sutra*. For the rich and powerful, these arts became a proper focus for extravagance, an investment in immortality. The gardens they made, the temples they built, the poems they wrote, and the gold-illuminated, flower-flocked libraries they commissioned all imitated the lotus-filled landscapes of scripture. Although I did not realise as much so soon after my arrival in

Japan, it was the Fujiwara clan's attempts to realise the visionary world of the sutra and the Pure Land paradise that would provide the main plot and denouement of my lotus quest.

One member of this clan left the most vivid picture of the impact of the *Lotus Sutra* on Heian life. In doing so, she proved a pioneer to equal the Jōmon potters and the empress-publisher. As I arrived in Japan, the country was preparing to celebrate the thousandth birthday of *Tale of Genji*, the world's oldest novel and still, by any measure, one of the best.

Its author Murasaki Shikibu (c. 973–1014) is often linked with Sei Shōnagon (c. 966–1017), whose *Pillow Book*, a collection of journal jottings, vignettes and lists, was composed in the same period. These two courtly Heian ladies are popularly imagined as bitter rivals, two exquisite pedigree cats in a silk brocade sack. Certainly Murasaki seems to have had little time for Sei Shōnagon, or just time enough to note in her own journal that she was smug, presumptuous, a shoddy literary craftsman, overly demonstrative, obsessed with novelties, and frivolous. *The Pillow Book* gives us the lighter side of the lotus cult. Sei Shōnagon loves the contrast between crimson lotus blooms and the blue of a lake. Short of paper but wishing to send a note to a friend at court, she writes a poem on the underside of a lotus petal. The coin-sized leaves of a fledgling lotus are among the lists of favourite things whose praises she sings like some sexy, sophisticated Sister Maria. Other items in the adorable category are wild pinks, duck eggs and a child eating strawberries. The cool compress of a lotus leaf on her cheek in summer sends her into raptures. The lotus should count itself blessed – Sei Shōnagon is even more passionate about things that do not meet her approval. What makes her irresistible is also why Murasaki found her so objectionable. The author of *Tale of Genji* thought more gravitas was in order when writing about the sacred flower.

Plants abound in Lady Murasaki's epic of the life, loves and posterity of her hero Hikaru Genji. Many of its fifty-four chapters are named after them; the seasons and hours are told by them; moods and events are epitomised by them. The species involved are real, diverse and often endemic to Japan. Murasaki weaves them into the fabric of life and text in ways that are, likewise, uniquely Japanese. Compared to her use of plants, the Victorian Language of Flowers is monosyllabic, verging on mute. In *Tale of Genji*, they not only set the scene and provide a focus for the action, they are characters themselves.

After this profusion of plants and the astonishing fact that something written circa 1008 has every appearance of a modern novel, the third most striking feature of *Tale of Genji* is the role played by acceptance and transience. The hero, Hikaru Genji, is the illegitimate son of an emperor and yet he is accepted and loved. Hikaru means 'shining'; he is literally a shining example of aristocratic Japanese manhood, but no cardboard gallant – he is also a shocking *coureur de dames*. His large appetites, however, are usually accepted as the downside of his manifest virtues. You cannot have the one without the other. When his father effectively severs him from the imperial line by granting him the surname Genji or Minamoto, he accepts his new rank with good grace. When later this playboy paragon discovers that his own heir is another man's son, he accepts that too. After all, he has visited the same wrong on plenty of other husbands, including his father the emperor; it is only Karma. Death is accepted, indeed assiduously prepared for, except in the case of his favourite lover whom Hikaru cannot bear to lose. Genji's own departure occurs three quarters of the way through the book, baldly announced in a brilliant stylistic coup, and yet we must accept it and read on.

Even in spring, with the characters fresh from their love-making, surrounded by blossom and feasting on newly harvested wild vegetables (these are very affluent foragers), there is an atmosphere of ephemeral fragility. This sense of passing, of disintegration and decline, deepens after Genji's death and is embodied by his legal heir, an anti-hero who is not only not of Hikaru's blood but also a poor imitation of him. Only in non-Japanese eyes is this a sad conclusion, or indeed any kind of conclusion. In the same way that the story continues once the protagonist has left the stage, Murasaki Shikibu herself seems to have felt that the novel never ended. There was no last page. Even within the existing pages, relationships and plot lines echo each other in a way that suggests life is a series of transfigured repetitions, endless variations on a theme.

With plants put on an equal footing with humans, the acceptance or interchangeability of differing views, ranks, roles, and fates, a sense of impermanence, and a strong intimation that all of the above will continue or be repeated, sometimes declining, at other times shining, as if in a great natural cycle, *Tale of Genji* is the novel as mandala.

In addition to numerous mentions of the *Lotus Sutra*, the plant itself makes eleven major appearances. Unable to live together in this life, star-crossed lovers pray that they will be reborn sharing the same lotus in the next. Water droplets on lotus leaves sometimes evoke human transcendence, a fugacious thing to be striven for by renouncing the world, chased like quicksilver over and beyond the mundane orbit of the leaf. At other times these droplets represent the impossibility of earthly devotion matching the purity of the sutra: 'However piously she might behave, how could this flawed and fickle woman turn the dew on a lotus leaf into the shining jewel of Buddha's law?' There are elaborate descriptions of rites involving decorations and sacred offerings of food made from lotuses. There are also growing lotuses, as, for example, when Genji visits his favourite lover and unofficial wife, Murasaki, who has been battling a grave illness. She is installed in a somewhat ramshackle mansion (beautiful decrepitude again), and Genji has had its overgrown garden put in order to cheer her up. Now he joins her to admire the results:

> The pond looked very cool, filled as it was with blooming lotuses whose fresh green leaves glittered with gem-like dewdrops.
>
> 'Just look at that,' said Genji, 'when I see water droplets like that, I feel as if only lotuses really understood what coolness meant.' Murasaki propped herself up and gazed at the pond. He continued, 'Being here, looking at this garden with you is like a dream. Sometimes, you know, I feel the sadness of it all is going to kill me.' There were tears in his eyes – a very rare occurrence. Murasaki felt sad too, and sad for him. 'Life,' she said, 'is often compared to droplets on a lotus leaf, but now I'm beginning to wonder if mine will last as long as the dew.'
>
> 'Let me make this promise to you,' said Genji, 'we will always be as close to one another as dewdrops on a lotus leaf – in this world and the next.'

This scene takes place in chapter 35. By chapter 41 Murasaki has died and the grief-stricken Genji is in steep but stately decline. On a broiling summer day, he returns to her mansion and sits beside the lotus pond which is now in full flower. As he looks at the leaves, the first thought that comes into his mind is, 'How can there be so many tears?' True to his promise, he is dead by the following chapter.

19

Secret Lake

The flyovers leapt and looped over a flashing black circuitry of rivers and channels, reminders that Tokyo was once a floating city canalised on a Venetian scale. It was not yet dawn when we made our descent, dropping below the water level before emerging from a tunnel in the heart of the capital to skirt the leafy bulwarks of the Imperial Palace. 'Tell me,' I asked, 'what does Shinobazu mean?' I was told it was an old name, probably even older than the palace, and that people argued about its meaning. The consensus favoured the idea that it was derived from *Shinobugaoka*, meaning 'Hill of Secrets'. When it was nothing more than a forested mound amid marshland this place was a favourite venue for clandestine meetings. It retained something of that reputation even after it was turned into a park. So it was a belt of wilderness which, if I understood correctly, became a park where people met in secret. Familiar-sounding ground – but were these skulking couplings in the style of Hampstead Heath or the covert, carnation-and-*Times*-toting rendezvous of St James's Park? They were both, I was told, less than helpfully. I fell to pondering what kind of encounter awaited us.

Ten minutes' drive north of the palace, we arrived at Ueno Park, the latter-day site of the Hill of Secrets. Walking among cherry trees and maples, we were soon accompanied not by a park's usual early-morning population of joggers, dog-walkers and derelicts, but by a dressy and festive cast of characters who were labouring under nothing worse than a sunhat, a camera or a small hamper. They were moving in the same direction as we were, clearly magnetised by something out of the ordinary. I had suspected a surprise was in the offing as soon as I was booted from my futon, but I had been kept in ignorance of our and, now it seemed, everyone else's purpose. It was not until we were deeper into the park and the sun rose that all became clear.

An ocean of lotuses extended before me. Their leaves were so dense that the waters of the lake could only be heard, not seen. Save for a glinting shrine at its centre, my eyes roved across this vast and perfumed plain of sea green, rose and ivory without interruption until they met the Tokyo skyscrapers. Mistily pink, these loomed from the distant shore as if they too were rooted among the hasu. Our fellow strollers had joined us on the bank. We stood in silence, waiting for what the novelist Yasunari Kawabata describes as 'the beguiling dawn explosion of lotus buds at Shinobazu-no-ike'. We waited as had others on summer mornings for centuries before. As the sun filled the park, we were rewarded with the sight of a myriad flowers opening, and their sound like a frenzy of furtive kisses.

In the Jōmon Period the area now occupied by Ueno Park lay deep under Tokyo Bay. By the end of their hegemony, sea levels had fallen, exposing an immense tract of marsh. Aptly enough, it was a fragment of this lotus-land that would become Shinobazu-no-ike, Japan's most famous lotus lake. As the Edo Period dawned in the first half of the seventeenth century, what remained of this landscape – the wetlands and the bosky Hill of Secrets – was suddenly of interest to the government for the simple reason that it lay just two miles to the north of Edo Castle. This was the recently acquired headquarters of the Tokugawa Shogun, Japan's executive ruler as opposed to the emperor who was based in Kyoto and was by now a monarch in little more than title. Around that time, the shogun ordered the creation of an island shrine in Shinobazu's great and largely untamed pool. It was dedicated to Benzaiten, the goddess of love, language and all that flows, who is often associated with lotuses and aquatic sites. The shrine was reached by causeways. Soon afterwards other low and narrow land bridges were made that divided Shinobazu-no-ike into three, allowing visitors to walk, as if on water, among the head-high hasu and reeds. Other sacred buildings began to appear on the lake shores, among them temples and a further Tokugawa shrine. As the eighteenth century dawned, this ancient lotus swamp in the centre of the nation's new capital became a focus of horticultural attention.

Daimyō – feudal lords – sponsored the development of Shinobazu-no-ike and its surrounds. The marshy causeways were raised and embanked and their margins lined with willows, maples and flowering cherries. Tree peonies were planted in the temple precincts. Most of these plantings, or their later replacements, grow there still, ensuring that even when the lotus is out of flower there is always something to see, some special plant event to mark the season. Around the shrines and temples, for example, are varieties of Kan-botan ('winter tree peonies') which flower months earlier than most Paeonia suffruticosa cultivars. In Ueno they bloom just when we in Britain would expect to see (at best) winter-flowering pansies in our parks. These precocious peonies are housed in small thatch wigwams. No matter how deep the snow, their side-flaps are opened each morning to reveal the massive, silken scarlet and coral flowers that glow within. Like the plants they protect, these straw teepees have not changed in 300 years, and every February they still attract swarms of visitors eager to view their chilly peep show.

The shady Hill of Secrets evolved into the urban Eden of Ueno Park. No plant played a greater role in this transformation than the lotus. Already a stronghold of Wa-basu, wild Japanese lotuses, the lake began to teem with Nelumbo cultivars donated by feudal lords from their domains all over the country. As they spent more and more time pacing its shores and planting its shallows, these magnificoes developed a shortened form for Shinobazu-no-ike. They called it Shinobu-ike, 'The Secret Lake'. A wonderfully enigmatic name for such a public attraction, it implied that the lake's patrons alone were aware of the true value of the living treasures they consigned to its bottom. The same species that had inhabited the region since soon after it surfaced from the Pacific now became the park's raison d'être. By the mid-eighteenth century, Shinobazu-no-ike was hailed as one of the most glorious sights of the Japanese summer. So it would remain. Published in 1834, Edo Meisho Zue ('A Guide to Famous Places in Edo') illustrates two samurai and their consorts upon a covered deck which projects over the bloom-filled waters. The guidebook says that they are engaged in Shinobazu-no-ike Hasumi, 'Shinobazu Lake lotus-gazing', and that the iki thing – the superior, suavely, secretively smart thing – to do is to get there before dawn, sit in a tea house, watch the flowers open, eat rice simmered with lotus seeds off lotus leaf plates, and then retire. Little about the ritual of hasumi, lotus-gazing, has altered since 1834, not even the breakfast fare.

The lake itself, however, has changed in shape and size. Following the fall of the shogunate in 1868, the hinterland of Shinobazu-no-ike became

176

an advertisement for Japan's newly modern and outward-looking credentials. Tokyo University sprang up nearby. Within the perimeter of Ueno Park, the nation's great museums arose. To accommodate these, the lake had to shrink and to be sealed and sanitised to some extent – although to no extent great enough to leave me anything other than overwhelmed. Of its three divisions, today the western part is a boating pond and the northern part is called *U-no-ike* after the cormorants that fish there. To the south, partitioned from this bird sanctuary by Benzaiten's Island, is the largest of the three divisions, often called the lotus pond, although 'pond' hardly seems the word for an area some 55,000 metres square. This was the site of our hasumi that morning.

High summer is *the* time for lotus-gazing at Shinobazu-no-ike, but not the only time. Between late autumn and the turn of the year, the decline and collapse of *Nelumbo* leaves and seed heads are judged almost as moving an attraction as the flowers. To the Japanese their stranded parchment-like skeletons speak strongly of *mono-no-aware*, the pathos of passing things.

At Shinobazu-no-ike this melancholy spectacle is the setting for the crucial episode in Ōgai Mori's great novel of 1911 to 1913, *Gan*, usually translated as 'Wild Geese'. Although it occurs almost at the end of the book, the incident provides the work's central metaphor, a single image that could betoken either soaring escape for its hopeful young hero or inescapable entrapment for its compromised heroine. Since Japanese makes no distinction between singular and plural nouns, the *Gan* of the title might stand for one or the other or both of these characters. It is a deliberate ambiguity – Wild Goose and Wild Geese – that succeeds in capturing two astonishingly contradictory states, killing two birds with one stone. The novel is set in 1880 and, like its author, the character Okada is a gifted medical student during the revolution in learning that occurred with the wholesale introduction of Western science and technology in the Meiji Period. Here he is with two fellow students, the nameless narrator and the impish Ishihara, at Shinobazu-no-ike, walking the watery groves of the new Japan's Lyceum.

'What are you watching there?' I asked.

Ishihara pointed silently at the lake. Okada and I followed the line of his finger through the grey and sordid evening light. There were reeds growing everywhere from Komizo to the waterside where we were standing. Towards the centre of the lake, the dead leaves were becoming sparse, rag-like leaves of lotuses and their sponge-like receptacles. They were scattered across the lake, their leaf stems and flower stalks bent at various heights, towering acutely and adding a bleak effect to the scene. Among the bitumen-coloured stems, about ten wild geese were drifting over the blackened water, casting obscure reflections. Some of them stopped and remained stock still.

'Could a stone reach that far?' asked Ishihara, watching Okada's face.

'Yes, it'll reach,' he replied, 'but I'm not sure it'll hit any birds.'

'Why don't you give it a go?' asked Ishihara.

But Okada said, 'Look, they'll be asleep soon, and it's a pity to go throwing stones at them.'

Laughing, Ishihara replied, 'You're much too sensitive to mono-no-aware. If you won't throw stones at them, I will.'

Reluctantly Okada picked up a few pebbles and said, 'In that case I will throw them – but only so the birds take flight.'

The stones flew with a faint howling sound. As I followed their trajectory, I saw that the neck of one of the wild geese, held high before, now suddenly drooped. As this happened two or three of its companions scattered, skating across the water crying and flapping. But they did not take off. Meanwhile the stricken goose had not moved. It simply floated there.

In the complex plant iconography that most Japanese hold in common almost as a matter of second nature, those 'rag-like leaves', 'sponge-like receptacles' and 'bitumen-coloured stems' bespeak mono-no-aware more than any other species except, perhaps, for the wind-blasted autumnal flower plumes of susuki, *Miscanthus sinensis*. It may seem a strangely morbid honour to award to a plant which, for much of the time, is identified with purity, reincarnation and immortality. For the Japanese, however, the two sides of the story, summer and winter, are inseparable. The bud-burst at dawn and the withered leaf at dusk may say different things but they speak with the same voice.

And yet the more I learnt about Shinobazu-no-ike, the more I was struck by the very opposite of transience. Despite being little more than a metre deep for much of its enormous breadth, this lake has survived everything – millennia of climatic and geological change, the rise of Edo as the shogun's seat and its transformation into Tokyo, the emperor's and the nation's modern capital, the encroachment of a railway station, a racecourse and a zoo, wartime service as a paddy-field, firebombing, post-war attempts to make a baseball stadium of it, earthquakes, and even being punctured by the burrowing of the subway system. It has existed almost as long as the Japanese themselves, playing host to *Nelumbo* for much of that time and throughout all these upheavals.

Despite which the Secret Lake's elevation in the seventeenth century as the centre of the lotus cult was sudden and spectacular. As we breakfasted among the hasu, I asked Taeko-san and Yoko what had caused it. They told me that the phenomenon was the product of much deeper and stronger forces than horticultural fashion. To understand it properly was to see to the very heart of samurai and shogun. It was a striking instance of garden history being synonymous with social and political history.

In the second half of the sixteenth century, Japan's inter-clan feuding metastasised into a civil war in which warlords competed for the office of shogun. *Sei-i-tai-shōgun*, 'barbarian-crushing generalissimo', was a title originally conferred by the emperor in the early Heian Period (794–1185) on military leaders who distinguished themselves by subduing the Emishi, the relict Jōmon-descended population of Japan's north-east. Over time its shortened form, *Shōgun*, came to refer to the nation's executive ruler or, as he is sometimes and somewhat reductively described, military dictator. Although the office was granted by the imperial court and depended on it for spiritual authority and rubber-stamping, the shogun's rule was absolute in practice. Yoko described his relationship with the emperor as resembling that between a European monarch and the Pope in the fifteenth and sixteenth centuries. The shogun's administration was called the *Bakufu*, 'tent government', a reference to its battlefield origins.

The last bout of inter-clan competition for this post culminated in 1600 in the Battle of Sekigahara and victory for Ieyasu Tokugawa (1543–1616) who was appointed shogun in 1603. The historical span of his shogunate and those of his heirs and successors is known as the Edo Period after the city that Ieyasu made his seat of government. In 1868 the fifteenth and final Tokugawa shogun fell from power and his capital was renamed Tokyo by the Emperor Meiji. For *Nihon no dento engei*, 'Traditional Japanese Horticulture', as for so many other arts, the intervening 265-year period was a golden one.

Horticulture had long been considered a suitable activity for men of power, learning and influence. Ieyasu himself was described as 'a lover of flowers'. Of his son, the second Tokugawa shogun, one chronicler noted, 'Hidetada has a plant habit.' He collected plants from all over Japan for his gardens and was especially devoted to *Primula sieboldii* and camellias. Hidetada's son and successor Iemitsu was so obsessed with bonsai that one of his senior advisors had to throw a favourite tree on the ground and smash its pot to force him to concentrate on affairs of state. Most Tokugawa shoguns shared this passion for plants. The eleventh, Ienari (1773–1841) thought of little else. Like his forefathers, he was what the Japanese call an *otaku*, a fanatical fancier or compulsive connoisseur. Since his authority was absolute and his reign was unusually long at fifty years, it is hardly surprising that the late Edo Period saw the most dramatic expansion of ornamental horticulture in garden history, a phase during which plants could be said not only to have dominated the nation's arts but also to have driven science, politics and the economy.

Among the ruling orders, many who were not already followers of Nihon no dento engei decided to follow the shogun's example, becoming patrons of plantsmanship if not plantsmen themselves. At the topmost level, they divided into *daimyō*, the feudal lords of *han* (quasi-autonomous provincial domains), and *hatamoto*, 'banner-holders', liegemen appointed by the shogun and usually in his service. One of the ways in which the Bakufu maintained control over these feudal lords was *Sankin Kōtai*, the rule of 'alternate attendance', which required daimyō to spend every other year residing in Edo waiting on the shogun's pleasure.

This practice had a profound impact on horticulture. Aristocratic townhouses began to spring up around Edo and gardens with them. The daimyō needed something to occupy them during their metropolitan captivity – what better than plant fancying, a pastime enjoyed by the shogun himself? A disconnected archipelago of highly diverse and regionalised flora and gardening customs suddenly had a centre in which its various botanical and horticultural resources were not just able but compelled to converge. New plants, and new ways with plants, flooded into the capital. Once there, they were exhibited and discussed, sold or exchanged. In Edo's new princely compounds, men who just a generation or two before might have met on the battlefield now met to argue about each other's favourite flowers. Horticulture was war continued by other means. When the time came for the daimyō to return to their home domains, unfamiliar plants and horticultural practices would travel with them, revolutionising the nation's gardens.

If an ideology could be said to have underpinned life before 1603 at the regional level, it was bushidō, the warrior code, with its emphasis on bonds of personal and clan rather than national loyalty. At the state level it was a reactive realpolitik that lurched from crisis to crisis under the cover of an imperial, and thus divine, mandate. Ieyasu Tokugawa dealt with both ways of thinking fairly directly – with the first, by making it clear through sheer might that every daimyō was now his vassal; with the second, by establishing the Bakufu, his administrative and military capital, in Edo and far from Kyoto. So distanced, the imperial court started shrinking to a constitutional monarchy. But Ieyasu also wanted the Tokugawa shogunate to last and so he needed a new ideology, a system of governance that would help him to build a stable state.

Neo-Confucian thought, and especially the work of the twelfth-century philosopher Zhu Xi (Chu Hsi), had entered Japan long before with Zen monks who visited China. It did not flourish, however, until the scholar Razan Hayashi (1583–1657) became one of the new shogun's most trusted advisors. As his thinker-in-chief, Hayashi presented Ieyasu with a tantalising model. It was a pyramidal hierarchy in which, beyond the immediate bonds of family, all duty was owed to the rank above and, ultimately, to its pinnacle, the shogun. Its basis was civil rather than military, secular rather than theocratic. Although compartmentalised, it was completely centralised – all roads and all taxes led to Edo and no province was truly autonomous. It was administered by cohorts of highly educated and culturally accomplished men who could attain their positions through ability as well as heredity.

Tokugawa Neo-Confucianism dovetailed neatly with the beliefs of Shinto and with pre-existing hierarchical values. It also fostered a new spirit of rational inquiry which amounted to a scientific revolution not dissimilar in spirit to the European Enlightenment. The Chinese philosopher Zhu Xi had been an indefatigable explainer of natural phenomena who elevated pure investigation and played down the role – if any – of the divine. Since the Japanese are nothing if not attuned to Nature, this analytical aspect of the sage's work found as much favour in Edo as his ethical and political discourses. In the shogunate's new colleges and away from temples, scholarship was diverted from the study of Buddhist scripture. Nature took precedence over Supernature. A generation of natural historians and encyclopedists emerged who were encouraged to describe, name and classify organisms objectively and for learning's sake.

One of the most famous of these new scientists was Ekiken Kaibara

(1630–1714), a scholar, translator and author of the first Japanese flora. This work, alongside his numerous other systematic treatises, led to his being hailed as 'Japan's Aristotle' by the botanist Philipp Franz Von Siebold. Encyclopedic and taxonomic, the new approach had an impact on horticulture as well as botany in the Edo Period. The Bakufu commissioned plant-collectors to scour Japan for new species which might be of scientific interest, economic use or ornamental value. Formerly the prerogative of physicians, the task of describing and illustrating these discoveries now fell not only to high-ranking samurai and natural philosophers, but also to any other of the callings and classes that made up the ranks of otaku, the fanatical plant connoisseurs.

Discriminating between different species and then between variations of the same species was a vital aspect of the new intellectual project. People set out to calibrate the diversity they found in their gardens as well as in the wild. As early as the mid-seventeenth century, we find categories such as *engei-hinshu* (garden variety or cultivar) and *gei*. Literally meaning 'performance' (a geisha, for example, is a 'performance person'), in the horticultural sense gei indicates a group of related cultivars with similar attributes – plants which 'perform' in the same way. Modern taxonomy would not formalise the scientific equivalents of these concepts – cultivar and group – until after 1953 and the appearance of the first *International Code of Nomenclature for Cultivated Plants*. Japanese plant hybridisation and selection were similarly precocious in the Edo Period. Countless new crosses were made, many of them remarkable in their ambition and ingenuity. Variability, selfing, clones, back-crossing, line-breeding, seed races, filial generations, compatibility and sterility are plant breeding concepts that we associate with the post-Mendelian world. All were known to plant otaku as empirically observed and manipulable phenomena if not yet as elements of anything understood as genetics. Within the natural limits they were mapping and probing, anything seemed possible to Edo horticulturists.

Theirs was an art as well as a science. The living artworks they created formed symbiotic relationships with other fields and genres. Poets were employed to coin cultivar names that were exquisite miniature lyrics. Potters created containers that included some of the finest ceramics of all time. Goldsmiths produced gilded cages to protect prize plants that were either being exhibited or accompanying daimyō in their palanquins between Edo and home. Painters were commissioned to produce portraits of favourite plants too fragile to commute. The martial arts were also evoked. Before admiring some horticultural masterpiece, samurai would wash, change into fresh clothes, and cover their mouths with a slip of rice paper to mask their – as they saw it – polluting breath. For centuries this same ritual had attended the handling of a new sword. The posters that reported and ranked the cultivars in each otaku genus were modelled on Sumo wrestling league tables. In design, the exhibitions at which those cultivars appeared owed much to classical drama, and, like the stage, they became mass attractions. Under Tokugawa patronage, Nihon no dento engei, Traditional Japanese Horticulture, became the highest expression of culture.

Although the new Edo spirit was essentially secular, the ancient spiritual and mythic resonances of Japan's flora were not lost. The sacred trees of Shinto remained sacred; in temples, the lotus still belonged to Buddha; the various other species associated with rituals, festivals and special seasons maintained their mystique. To extirpate these plants and the ideas they represented would have been to attack one of the deepest-rooted strands of Japanese identity. The Bakufu was not about to attempt that. Some plants, however, were promoted as emblems not of spirituality but of spirit, as virtuous tropes within the Neo-Confucian scheme. Omoto, the strappy-leaved lily relation *Rohdea japonica*, came to represent fortitude and endurance. Fūkiran, the small, white-flowered orchid *Neofinetia falcata*, betokened the understated nobility of the ideal samurai. Many other plants beloved of Nihon no dento engei became emblematic, were held to say something to and about their fanciers. And one above all was singled out by the Edo government as a living object lesson. No other plant taught integrity or advertised its owner's integrity quite like the lotus.

20

Lotus Love

During the civil wars that preceded the Edo Period it was commonplace for the aristocracy to grow *Nelumbo* in *hasu-ike*, 'lotus lakes' that were also castle moats. The plant's role in these defensive pools was only partly ornamental or spiritual. It was also there to provide food in times of siege. Brave retainers would swarm down the ramparts under cover of darkness and then, if lucky, clamber back with a rucksack full of rhizomes to the relief of their starving clansmen within. Ieyasu, the first Tokugawa shogun, had good reason to know their strategic value. More than once during his struggle for power these emergency-ration lotuses had caused him to linger longer than he would have wished outside an enemy's walls. They had been introduced to the moats of Edo Castle, built in 1457 during particularly turbulent times. They were flowering there still in the late summer of 1590 when, after a series of prolonged sieges, it fell and became Ieyasu's new headquarters. The same lotuses thrive there to this day. Backed by vast stone walls, their gulleys of swaying rose blooms are a haunting sight in downtown Tokyo, in the castle's latest incarnation as the Imperial Palace.

Once Ieyasu had prevailed and set about restructuring society in the early seventeenth century, lotus cultivation no longer needed to be so brutally utilitarian. The ruling classes were now in a position to make gardens again and the lotus was invited through the castle gates or, more likely, into the precincts of *buke-yashiki*, compound-like samurai mansions. There the sacred flower could enjoy pride of place, a thing of wonderment rather than desperation. Its renewed value as an ornamental was soon magnified and given an ideological underpinning as the subject of the shogun's favourite Neo-Confucian parable, a lesson propagated by the new schools and taken to heart by anybody hoping to be somebody. Now it was not only a pleasure to grow lotuses, and a living domestic reminder of Buddhist teachings, it was also the politically correct thing to do. This flower above all others epitomised the *kunshi*, the model man in the eyes of the new regime.

The authorisation for this pre-eminence was a short prose meditation which remains one of the most famous Neo-Confucian texts, familiar to millions in the Far East where it is still learnt by heart in childhood. It was written in Song Dynasty China by the Master of Lianxi, Zhou Dunyi (1017–73), a scholar-sage who, as a result of his revival of Confucian teachings and his rational reworking of mystical Taoist cosmology, came to be revered as the forefather of the new philosophical school. It is called, simply enough, *Ai Lian Shuo*, which literally translates as 'Lotus Love Thoughts':

> *While adorable flowers can be found among many herbs and trees of land and water, in the Jin Dynasty, Tao Yuan-ming only had eyes for chrysanthemums. On the other hand, more worldly people have adored the peony ever since the Tang Dynasty. But my special love is for the lotus which grows out of the mud but remains unsoiled, is cleansed by pure rippling water and which, for all its beauty, remains free from seductive guile. With neither branch nor tendril, its stalks run hollow but straight to the heart of its leaves. With a floral fragrance that is subtler at a distance and borne aloft on slim clean stems, it is best appreciated from afar and not treated with too much familiarity. I maintain that the chrysanthemum is like a scholarly recluse and the peony like a person of high rank and wealth, whereas the lotus is like a gentleman. Sadly, one rarely hears of people loving chrysanthemums except in the case of Tao Yuan-ming. And where are the people who love the lotus as I do? As for peony-lovers, well they, of course, are everywhere.*

Tao Yuan-ming or Tao Qian (365–427) was China's first great nature poet, a man who threw over his career as a public administrator for a life of impoverished rural seclusion. He found solace in the landscapes around his country retreat, and especially in the chrysanthemums that grew in his garden and which, like an autumn sunset or the wine of which he was so fond, were an affirmation that the simple life was best. By contrast, the tree peony became the object of a cult from the Tang Dynasty (618–907) onwards, as new varieties of ever more lavish colouring, shape and size were bred. These were usually displayed in containers in city homes as signals of wealth and sophistication. By the time Zhou Dunyi wrote his reflections on the lotus, tree peony cultivars were associated with persons of power and rank, chief among them China's emperors. It was a plant not of contemplation but of worldly ambition. So the Master of Lianxi is presenting a moral taxonomy or a floral morality in which a plant is identified with a type. His own type is the *junzi*, the ideal Confucian gentleman, perfectly illustrated by the lotus. If only there were more of us, the Master laments.

The rulers of Edo Period Japan, for whom *Ai Lian Shuo* was a cardinal text, took the sage at his word and decided to recast the samurai in this gentlemanly image. In most cases little was needed in the way of recasting. Theirs was already a highly educated and cultured class whose accomplishments were more than a match for any Chinese models. But Zhou Dunyi's favourite flower was the perfect propaganda tool, battening as it did on centuries of Japanese tradition in which the lotus had been exalted as incorruptibly virtuous. All the shogunate's academics had to do was deftly divest the flower of its sacral robes and relaunch it as a secular symbol. The teachings of a highly respected Chinese master were a ready-made pretext for doing so. But this symbol was to be more than a paper flower, it was to have a life beyond the page and mind. In his short study *The Sinologue*, W. Somerset Maugham describes a scholar so steeped in the writings of the Tang Dynasty that text overcomes reality: 'The tragic splendour of the lotus moves him only when its loveliness is enshrined in the verse of Li Po and the laughter of demure Chinese girls stirs his blood but in the perfection of an exquisitely chiselled quatrain.' Ever practical, the shogun and his retainers would suffer no such detachment. Their lotuses would not only be real, they would grow them themselves.

But what was so desirable about being a *junzi*? I was told that the equivalent Japanese concept, *kunshi*, is noble in the sense of innate and/or cultivated nobility rather than blue blood, a person of dignity, probity and sound judgement, wise without being calculating, managerial without being Machiavellian, and often humane, especially by the harsh standards of Edo times. Although kunshi occupy a high position in society, they are unimpressed by material wealth and by power for power's sake. They lead by example and their dominion is purely ethical. For the Tokugawa regime, the beauty of this ideal – already long-established by the time Zhou Dunyi's lotus became its poster plant – was that it set a limit on worldly ambition but removed all limits from personal development. In a strictly hierarchical and compartmentalised society, it still provided scope for aspiration and leadership. Every town, village and family needed its kunshi, and the shogunate needed them too. As with the learned legions of the Chinese bureaucracy, lotus men rather than rusticating chrysanthemum or grasping peony men were required to fill the countless offices within Japan's new hierarchy of government.

The philosophical basis for that ideal was Chinese, and so, before long, were many of the lotuses themselves. In the early Edo Period most *Nelumbo* grown by samurai would have been Wa-basu, Japanese in origin. By the 1680s they had begun sourcing cultivars from China where – *pace* Zhou Dunyi – lotus breeding had become every bit as frantic and flashy as the materialistic cult of the tree peony that the Master of Lianxi lamented. The arrival of these unfamiliar varieties is itself an indication of the Bakufu's lotus love. The flow of imports started and continued throughout periods when the Japanese government imposed a comprehensive ban on foreign trade and looked upon China with especially suspicious eyes. A Chinese lotus, however, was different. It carried with it the one message from the mainland that the shogunate wished to hear. So it remained permissible, no, de rigueur to import ornamental lotus rhizomes at a time when smuggling more basic Chinese goods could result in crucifixion or decapitation.

By the end of the seventeenth century this influx of new plants had seized the fancy of that emerging Edo Period profession, the horticultural encyclopedists. They recorded much the same observations – native Japanese lotuses (Wa-basu) were large plants, usually with rather open and bowl-like single-petalled flowers in white, pink or carmine. Chinese lotus cultivars (*Kara-basu*) could be large, medium-sized or small enough to grow in a pot. Their flowers were often more pointed in outline (we might say 'tulip-shaped'), commonly double-petalled and sometimes very densely so, giving them a ruffled, antique rose appearance. They encompassed a wide range of colours – greens, whites, creams, pinks, reds and rosy mauves – and more than one hue might be present in the same flower: a white picotee edged in puce, for example.

Lotuses grow fast and flower within a year or two of germination. In no time at all the Japanese were hybridising these Chinese plants with each other and with their own Wa-basu. A new range of cultivars began to emerge, identifiably Japanese but drawing on Chinese bloodstock or models in its early days. As with the other specialities of Nihon no dento engei – Traditional Japanese Horticulture – such as maples and orchids, the introduction of these new lotuses was usually a matter of percolation from aristocratic amateur or professional nurseryman to an illustrious client (the shogun, perhaps) or to a society of otaku and thence, at long-awaited last, to the wider public. The process was regional with certain clans or domains making lotuses their forte. Appropriately enough for a cadet branch of the imperial family, the Takatsukasa bred cultivars whose names were literary allusions to life in the courtly heyday of the Heian Period. Higo, a domain in Kyushu's present-day Kumamoto Prefecture, decided to deploy the same legendary breeding skills on lotuses as it had already on irises and camellias to such astonishing effect. True to form, the region produced some of the most unfeasibly flamboyant varieties, among them 'Higo-shibori' ('Higo Batik'), a white flower whose petals were tipped with scarlet and emblazoned with jade.

As had happened long before with tree peonies imported from China in the Heian Period, these new lotuses underwent a curious Yamato transformation in the hands of otaku. They were stronger, more elegant and more upstanding than their Chinese counterparts and with clearer colours – characteristics that can be variously attributed to Wa-basu genes and the experimental gifts and good taste of the breeders. Some forms were so small that they could be grown in a tea or rice bowl – hence their collective name Chawan-basu. It was a pressed specimen of one of these dwarves that we had encountered in Piccadilly in the Linnaean Herbarium and which had sown the seeds of my lotus quest. Others were vegetable leviathans, suited only to hasu-ike on the estates of the grandest grandees. Their flowers could be single, semi-double or extra-double, slender and starry or as densely layered as a crepe rosette. They ranged in colour from deepest carmine to palest apple blossom, from cool limes and lilacs to hot magentas and scarlets, from sparkling whites and golds to sombre burgundies and blood reds, and every permutation thereof. Often their ground colour was complemented with stainings and stripings, blushes and brushmarks of second or third tones.

As if that were not variety enough, there were further criteria for discrimination and appreciation. Some were obvious, such as fragrance, how long a flower lasted, and whether its colour changed over time. Others were more arcane or monstrous – an inner ring of petaloid stamens that gave a flower an anemone-like centre; the freakish development on a single floral receptacle of several smaller flowerheads wrapped within an outer whorl of guard petals; 'Buddha's toes', a clutch of malformed ovules protruding from the receptacle like a miniature hand of bananas. All these mutations were deemed horticultural coups and reasons to celebrate. By the mid-eighteenth century at least 50 new lotus cultivars of Japanese making were in general cultivation. To that total can be added the untouched Chinese imports and a handful of Japanese proto- or archaeo-cultivars – morphologically distinctive Wa-basu associated with localities such as moats and temples and introduced there as ornamentals centuries before.

It was one thing to do what the Japanese had been doing since before the nation's foundation – scatter seeds over a lake shore or stick a rhizome in a pond bed and await the results. It was another thing entirely to marshal and husband all these new varieties, and especially those that were amenable to cultivation in tubs. Wild or semi-tamed for millennia, *Nelumbo* had suddenly metamorphosed into a horticultural entity, *hana-basu*, 'flower [meaning *ornamental*] lotus'. It was a plant that could be collected and selectively bred, transported into the home and from town to town. Despite Zhou Dunyi's advice about keeping one's distance, it could now be admired at close range: lotus-loving had become an intimate affair. Not only had hana-basu joined the ranks of Nihon no dento engei, with all the shogunate's Neo-Confucian propagandising it had gone straight to the head of them. Advice was needed on how best to accord these plants due honours and so Edo horticulturists began to set down the curious rites of lotus germination and cultivation. Over 200 major works and innumerable pamphlets on garden plants were published in the Edo Period, many of them making reference to *Nelumbo*. An early example of these guidelines for happier hana-basu comes from *Ka-Fu*, the three-volume 'Flower Book' published in 1694 by Ekiken Kaibara. He is writing early on in the Japanese craze when Chinese cultivars were still a novelty.

In recent years many Chinese lotuses have been appearing around the place. Some claim they are better plants than Japanese lotuses. Certainly, if you plant and feed them well, they will flower very quickly – usually within a year from seed. They are easily grown in bowls, and will flower freely even in quite small bowls, although the smaller the container the smaller the leaves. As with Japanese lotuses, the flowers of these Chinese plants fade and wither after three days.

Here is how to grow these Chinese varieties –

In early March, grind both ends of the seed and shave away the hard outer coat using a small knife. Take care not to cut too deeply and hurt the flesh within. Leave the seed to soak in a small vessel of water. It will soon produce its first three leaves – even so, do not be tempted to plant it in mud yet. It will rot if you plant it before it has produced its first white root. When this has happened and you are ready to plant, allocate one seedling to a pot or bowl no matter what the size of the container. Even in a large tub, two seedlings planted together will not flourish. The container should be half full of mud, half full of fresh water. Even in a large expanse of mud – a pond, for example – a Chinese lotus will die out if it has to compete with a Japanese lotus.

If growing Chinese lotuses from rhizomes rather than seeds, just plant a single length of two nodal sections per pot. In this way the plant should flower in the same year. If you plant longer rhizomes or more rhizomes per pot than that, the plant will not thrive. Deep pots tend to encourage long leaf- and flower-stalks; shallow pots shorter stalks. In the end, a large pond is probably best as it will allow the lotus to spread rapidly – but be careful not to mix varieties. Chinese lotuses come in many colours. There are whites and crimsons. Some are brushed with different shades or edged with red like lipstick. Others have the tawny tones of persimmon. In my book, the white and lipstick varieties are elegant; the brushed and crimson types are tasteless and vulgar.

Within a century of Kaibara's 'Flower Book' appearing, the lotus craze had spread from Japan's ruling classes to most of society, and especially urban society. While grandees continued to amass, breed and describe cultivars (for example, the daimyō of Fukuoka, Saisei Kuroda, catalogued his own collection in a glorious *Ren-pu*, 'Lotus Book'), lotuses came within everyone's reach. Thanks to the discovery that these bulky and rampant plants could be confined to containers, even those who had no gardens could join in the cult. Easier to obtain and faster to perform than most other plants of Nihon no dento engei, lotuses began to appear among the pot plants that decorated many Edo shop fronts. The most modest homes made room for them on their *engawa*, their wooden verandahs, and in their *tokonoma*, their interior display alcoves.

At first these containerised lotuses were offered makeshift accommodation. Wooden barrels were filched from bath houses, sake sellers and coffin-makers.

The kitchen and table were raided for ceramics. Charcoal-burners were extinguished. Goldfish were evicted from their bowls and ginger jars emptied with heart-burning rapacity. Although many poorer lotus-lovers continued to improvise in this way, potters soon began to manufacture special lotus containers. As with pots created for other hallowed plants, these vessels came in different styles and offered lotus-growers a choice in what they said about themselves. One could be wabi-sabi, artfully rustic and samurai-austere with a broad bowl that was raw or simply glazed in earthy tones; or one could plump for the hasu equivalent of the parvenu gin palace – a curvaceous body, wavy rim and ornate but outsize feet, all pimped with a spree of impasto gilt and lurid appliqué. Most seem to have steered the middle course – porcelain bowls, glazed and tall-sided, that stood on modest feet and were patterned with blue and white motifs. This model became the standard pot for displaying lotuses within the home and at exhibitions. Even so, the subject of the blue and white pattern still offered scope for making a statement. There were scenes from the Chinese classics, Persian-influenced arabesques, beloved sights and creatures of Japan (Mount Fuji, for example, or a flight of cranes), family crests, and bold geometric abstracts that seem eerily to anticipate Modernism. Sometimes the hasu pot was ribbed and sculpted in imitation of a lotus leaf. Although Edo craftsmen could hardly have known it, this same *Nelumbo* vein motif was favoured by Jōmon potters thousands of years before them.

Not that one needed to grow hasu to enjoy them. As the craze blossomed, ancient lotus lakes were revived in the grounds of temples and shrines and new ones were developed in public parks. Among the latter, Shinobazu-no-ike swiftly became paramount. Seasonality had a great deal to do with the affection in which this and other lotus lakes were held. The Japanese are intensely aware of the seasons and especially as marked by different plants. A token of this is the fact that the various species which form the canon of Nihon no dento engei, Traditional Japanese Horticulture, are often seen as a living calendar that starts at the New Year with fukujuso (*Adonis amurensis* or *A. multiflora*), and ume (*Prunus mume*), runs, most famously, through cherries in spring and maples in autumn, and ends with pines and red-berried evergreens like *Ardisia*. The lotus filled an awkward gap in this calendar, flowering as it does in the sultry days between the end of wisteria and irises and the beginning of maples and chrysanthemums. Not only did it fill the gap, it did so with extraordinary flair: this was a performance plant. Phenomenally fast to develop, flower and fade, more sensuous and overwhelmingly physical than any other perennial in the repertoire, the lotus was an event.

And it spawned events. From the end of the eighteenth century onwards, public festivals were held to celebrate its flowering. In July 1792, for example, the Neo-Confucian scholar and *homme sérieux* Yamamoto Hokusan inaugurated *Kanren-setsu* 'lotus-viewing time' at Shinobazu-no-ike. Although this spectacle seems at first to have been attended by intellectuals, it and similar events soon became the pretext for Homeric lotus-eating. The literati and the iki enjoyed the exclusivity of the dawn, were evidently still doing so in 1834, and might even claim to do so in the 2000s. But once the sun was overhead, the lotuses were fully open and the elite had departed, visitors of all kinds would arrive in their tens of thousands. *Chaya*, 'tea shops' that were more like French cafés, sprang up on the lakeshores, most of them with balconies that turned horticultural appreciation into a mass spectator sport. Reminiscent of the bulging bark that bears the carousing Seven Gods of Fortune, boats laboured under cargoes of flower-gazers, some drunk on sake, all intoxicated by the perfume of the lotus. Elsewhere, shielded from view by parasol leaves, were moored punts, pale hands trailing in water, low laughter and loosened kimonos. This one aquatic plant and the celebrations associated with it came to epitomise *Ukiyo*, the hedonistic 'floating world' of the mid- to late Edo Period. Ukiyo-e artists made prints of lotuses in close-up, lotuses in pots, lotuses in lakes and that most popular and apt Edo pairing of all, lotuses beheld by beautiful women. Sensational but short-lived, what better flower for a floating world?

21

The Mansion of a Thousand Autumns

In Lotus-Land, to wander is to embark upon an endless flow of transmigrations: megalopolis in the morning, wilderness in the afternoon; breakfast with urban professionals, lunch with peasants whose families have been working the same land since the days of the shogun; check out of an air-conditioned hotel in a subtropical city, check in to an alpine inn where the drinking water is freshly melted snow.

The reason for these time-warps and contrasts is also, for a naturalist, the single most important fact about Japan: three quarters of its landmass is immune to development and so not only unspoilt but sometimes virgin to an extent difficult to believe of an ultra-modern industrialised country. This immunity is conferred by topography. To journey just a little way into the interior is to enter a vast longitudinal tract of mountain and forest, the one so contoured and the other so dense that even small-scale agriculture can be hard to practise and the construction of a minor road can be a feat of Brunel-confounding complexity. It is a terrain of daunting natural constraints which have combined with the innate conservatism of the Japanese character to produce a way of life that, give or take the benefits of technology, has scarcely changed in centuries.

This struck me first on the Tōhoku Expressway, the great road north that follows the eastern flank of Honshu's central mountain ranges. Their peaks started to materialise as vaporous oyster-coloured outlines even before we had disentangled ourselves from the floodlit flatlands of twenty-four-hour golf driving ranges and love hotels that form Tokyo's outer suburbs. As we drove on, they grew nearer to the road, becoming less of a mirage by the mile. Soon new ranges appeared behind them, layer upon layer of summit and slope that produced a hypnotic sense of infinite reduplication and regression. Two hours from the capital, we were in a world I had assumed was done to death decades ago if, indeed, it ever existed – not the floating world of Edo, but the watercolour world of the poet-painter.

The peaks themselves were a patchwork of coniferous forest and mixed woodland still brilliant with the bloom of the new season. Now and again, at home yet incongruous beside the boreal-looking firs, a great sweep of golden bamboo was let into this fabric. As the eye followed the descent of the mountains it seized upon the most striking feature of their vegetation, its rhythmic verticality: the trunks of sugi (*Cryptomeria japonica*) and the canes of bamboo appeared to march down to the valley floors in a wilderness of columns, the one kind stout and sombre, the other slim and shining. They came to a halt a little above the precious, cultivable low-lying land which, being flooded, had the appearance of a serpentine shore with numberless creeks and coves. Here were networks of paddy-fields, just planted with sprigs of rice and flush with water from snow-melt cataracts. Their divisions had the haphazard order of some natural phenomenon. Sometimes rectilinear, sometimes curving and looping, and progressing from major segment to minor cell, they resembled the veins of a leaf or, in their shimmering reflectivity, the wing of a damsel fly. Within each inland cove an island floated among the paddy-fields like a giant breaching turtle. Approached via a wildflower-spangled causeway and a Torii gate, it bore a dense grove of sugi with a Shinto shrine at its centre. Some of these shrines were so old and plain that they scarcely aspired beyond the status of a shack. Others were ornately carved, gilded and lacquered, a visual ambush of splendour amid the rusticity. All were newly dressed with white banners, fluttering petitions to the gods for a successful harvest.

A little above the rice-growing level, tucked into the sinus of two slopes, would be the hamlet itself. Rarely more than ten households, these settlements looked at a distance like some precious enamel jettisoned among the greenery. Their jostling roofs shone in shades of turquoise, oxblood and bronze. The houses stuck rigidly to traditional lines despite having been rebuilt down the years in the wake of upheavals, both social and seismic, that seemed unimaginable in this idyll. No design detail conveyed a stronger sense of this continuity than the ceramic circular lotus motifs that provided the final flourish for their dazzling sweeps of tiles.

Athwart all the natural profusion, these farmsteads boasted rigorously controlled gardens complete with cloud-pruned trees and rows of treasured pot plants along their paths and verandahs. Occasionally a huddle of homes would come into view that had survived earthquakes and other disasters and which were exactly as they would have appeared to Hiroshige when he was illustrating scenes of country life. These were timber and rammed-earth long-houses with high-pitched and low-slung roofs covered in shaggy thatch. Often the thatch was colonised by *Iris japonica* whose fans of evergreen leaves fell forward and overlapped one another, forming natural tiles. These hermitages always seemed to be secreted in woodland niches. All in mottled browns save for their iris waterproofing, they brought to mind a covey of partridge sheltering in a covert. No matter what the age of the house, from almost every roof there rose a slender strand: wood smoke is the signature scent of rural Japan, even in summer.

'This place is paradise,' I said. 'Where are we?'

'Just entering Fukushima Prefecture,' Yoko replied. 'It's the beginning of what we used to call *Oku*, the Deep North, or what today is called the Tōhoku Region. I'm glad you like it – my family used to be landowners here.'

'What possessed them to give it up?'

'They didn't have much choice. Like a lot of samurai loyal to the shogun, we lost some of our estates after the Meiji Restoration in 1868. We lost the rest, I think, during the land reforms after the Second World War. But we weren't the only landlords in these parts.'

We had suddenly been engulfed by a blizzard: a series of peaks breasted the road, their slopes covered in orchards of cherries, apples and peaches all in full blossom. Fukushima, I learnt, was famous for its fruit. Grown in terraces that were covered by bamboo laths as protection against late frosts, the trees were pruned to a tabletop flatness. Now wild plants appeared, glimpsed in flashes beyond and between the orchards: a stand of pines draped in wisteria; a sunny bank of *Miscanthus* mingled with the silken shoots of crimson bush clover; a rocky bluff encrusted with scarlet azaleas; a spontaneous shrubbery of *Kerria*, *Forsythia* and *Deutzia*; bamboos embowered with the great white briar *Rosa multiflora*; a spinney blushing and bridal with Japanese maples and *Magnolia kobus*. Of course, these were not all in flower as we drove past; but they were all there and thriving in concert, the natural models and materials for gardens the world over. Sometimes the peaks parted to reveal swampy strips that bordered the mirror mosaic of paddy-fields below. Rising from these sumps, clearly discernible against the turbid water, were the sea-green scrolls, still tightly rolled, of the lotus.

'In the eighteenth century,' Yoko continued, 'this was the domain of a great lord called Sadanobu Matsudaira. It's where his career officially began and he often returned when he wasn't needed in the capital. His agricultural reforms saved the region from collapse. But crops weren't the only plants that interested him, and that's why we're here. A little clue – you remember you told me about a British barrister whose career went smash in Hong Kong?'

'Sir Francis Piggott, yes. Poor chap.'

'This is where he said he saw his first lotuses – Shirakawa.'

The Tōhoku Expressway roughly follows the first leg of the most famous Japanese journey – that embarked upon by the poet Matsuo Bashō in the spring of 1689. It resulted in Japan's most famous literary work, Bashō's travelogue in prose and verse, *Oku no Hosomichi*, 'The Narrow Road to the Deep North'. What I had not yet realised as we entered Fukushima was that my journey would follow his, and that the poet would continue to materialise at intervals like a ghostly guide ultimately leading me to the lotus of lotuses. Bashō arrived in Shirakawa in late May of 1689, just under a century before Sadanobu Matsudaira took charge of the faltering domain. He noted that, both physically and psychologically, the place marked an important border between the familiar South and the unknown North. To cross this point, to make a gateway of a barrier, would be a transformation in itself. Others had crossed it before him and written poems filled with fiery leaves and chill winds. These now swarmed into Bashō's mind, causing him momentarily to see the region not in summer verdure but in its autumn colours.

No sooner had the poet recovered from this literary delusion than a botanical one presented itself. All around him were the white blooms of *unohana* (*Deutzia crenata*) and *no-ibara* (*Rosa multiflora*) in such profusion 'that I felt as if I were trudging across the border through snowfall'. A subtle death-in-life irony underlies this plain-seeming observation: unohana is celebrated in Japan as a herald of summer, a vibrant beginning, not a frozen end. Bashō was unsure which outcome awaited him on the journey ahead. These plants also confirm the idea that to walk through the gateway at Shirakawa amounted to a spiritual ceremony. *Shide*, the hanging tapers that mark a holy space in

Shinto, are white, so too are the rose and the deutzia. Their garlands signified a natural sacred boundary. All of which, the poet records, left him feeling too filled with sensation to write verse, a temporary blockage with which anyone who has seen this landscape can only sympathise. Finally, having crossed the barrier, he managed to produce a haiku:

Fūryū no hajime ya Oku no taue uta
The starting point of poetry, these songs of rice planters in the North

Fūryū is a densely packed idea which means something like 'showing a discerning relish for life as a whole by appreciating art'. In its original sense, the inspiration and possibly the medium for the art were derived from Nature. This is often still the case, hence the high esteem in which gardening is held in Japan. Other arts that evince *Fūryū* include flower and landscape painting, the tea ceremony and calligraphy. In Bashō's case it was *Fūryū inji*, 'the elegant, Nature-loving, life-embracing culture of words', or poetry for short. Although it is a process of refinement, *Fūryū* should remain rooted in Nature. In horticulture the connection is obvious, as it is in the tea ceremony with its artful rusticity, earthy ceramics and seasonal flower arrangements. Even a Japanese calligrapher will view the characters he draws as dynamic or organic entities, their overall composition in terms of landscape, and his materials as precious gifts from the living world. 'Nature,' as Emerson said, 'is loved by what is best in us.' Given this need for rootedness, there is a special poignancy about the fact that it was rice-planting songs, primitive ancestors of Japanese poetry, which inspired Bashō's polished haiku after his short spell of writer's block. The poem and its occasion are about beginnings: the origins of poetry ancient and modern, the planting of a new season's crop at the start of summer, the gateway to the North and to the year, the departure point of a journey into terra incognita. It is Bashō at his most concentrated, a beautiful illustration of the way in which he could make something very small assume multiple layers and sweeping proportions.

In Shirakawa the deutzia and the rose were still making May-tide avalanches of the roadside banks. But I had arrived a little too late in the year for the rice-planting songs. It was not until near the end of my own journey, deep in the north, that I would hear the tunes that Bashō thought were poetry's beginning.

*   *   *

197

Sadanobu Matsudaira, one-time lord of this beautiful domain, was born in 1759 in Edo Castle, the grandson of Yoshimune, the eighth Tokugawa shogun. Although his own father had been passed over for the shogunate, hopes persisted that the young Sadanobu would succeed one day to the post of Japan's executive ruler. This was a likely prospect since the office did not have to fall to the next in line and it was not unknown for a shogun to die young or to retire early. As a result, Sadanobu was prepared for power from an early age. For some years it appeared that these preparations were not in vain: not only was Sadanobu a brilliant scholar and a courtly young warrior, but several members of the Tokugawa family touted as likely successors to the shogunate either died or proved themselves unsuitable. He was moving up the line with *Kind Hearts and Coronets* rapidity but, surprisingly, with none of the bloodshed. All that was needed was his official adoption as the shogun's heir.

It was never to happen. Despite his obvious eligibility, Sadanobu and his sponsors found themselves repeatedly blocked by a faction within the government led by the shogun's chancellor, Okitsugu Tanuma. Behind problems of protocol and precedence was the chancellor's horror of a very new broom from a side of the clan whose political philosophy was the opposite of his own. Tanuma was a promoter of manufacturing, trade and overseas contact. He was also no stranger to corruption. Sadanobu, like his father and grandfather, held business in aristocratic contempt, was suspicious of foreigners, and inclined to the view that the price of a backhander was beheading. Between his late teens and early twenties, it became clear that Sadanobu would never be shogun.

Something had to be done with this unwanted flower of the Tokugawa clan – ideally something that would keep him busy to breaking point and far from the capital. It was arranged that he would be officially adopted as heir not by the shogun but by one of his kinsmen, Sadakuni Matsudaira, daimyō of Shirakawa. A large but impoverished and troubled domain in what today is Southern Fukushima Prefecture, Shirakawa was the gateway to *Oku*, the Deep North. Although close enough in modern eyes to the capital and by no means the frozen wasteland that it sounds, the Deep North was a region wreathed in ideas of remoteness, hardship and exile. Okitsugu Tanuma wished all three on the young pretender, Sadanobu Matsudaira, as he became on his adoption.

Succeeding his adoptive father as daimyō of Shirakawa in 1783, Matsudaira set about restoring the domain's fortunes. He removed corrupt officials, cut wages and imposed price restraints on merchants. He expanded education, promoting Neo-Confucian texts. He exhorted agriculture and horticulture as the route to financial and social recovery. Within four years, Shirakawa was verging on prosperous: peasants' rice bowls were full again; merchants had learnt to grasp a little less; official pockets were no longer being lined but they were being worn with samurai dignity.

In 1787 Sadanobu Matsudaira helped his friend Ienari to become the eleventh Tokugawa shogun. Ienari was the otaku shogun, famed for his profligacy and love of plants. He was not always a byword for extravagance, however. Beset by inflation, shortages and mercantile venality, the nation he inherited was like a macrocosm of Matsudaira's formerly ailing domain. Now, with his friend's help, Ienari set out to restore its health and fortunes. First to go was the disgraced Tanuma. The twenty-eight-year-old Matsudaira succeeded him as chancellor, introducing the economic measures known as the Kansei Reforms. The Neo-Confucian thinking on which the Tokugawa Bakufu had been founded was reaffirmed as the state orthodoxy. Trade, especially foreign trade, was dramatically reduced. Agriculture was promoted as the greatest common good and agricultural workers were banned from migrating to cities. Merchants were required to write off debts owed to them by the shogunate and daimyō. From Edo Castle to the remotest fief, spending at all levels of government was curtailed except where education, defence and agriculture were concerned.

And horticulture. It was Matsudaira's greatest love, and one he shared with the shogun Ienari. But there was more than self-interest to this exemption from penny-pinching. In the new chancellor's view, horticulture was a properly Japanese art associated with the imperial court and the Bakufu since the earliest times. The love of plants also sat comfortably with his Neo-Confucian principles, and the love of the lotus especially.

Reared to aspire to the ideal of the kunshi, the scholar-gentleman of unimpeachable integrity, Sadanobu Matsudaira had been fed a diet of Chinese classics since early childhood. Of these his best-loved was Zhou Dunyi's 'Lotus Love Thoughts'. While he grew to manhood, his favourite extended metaphor was busily becoming a nationwide reality. Close to his home in Edo Castle, the Secret Lake was developing into a centre for lotus-growing and -gazing. Before long the labyrinthine lanes he would have negotiated to visit Shinobazu-no-ike also had their share of hasu, grown in bowls and barrels in porches and along shop fronts. When he moved to Shirakawa, a domain whose wild flora and horticultural prowess were the antithesis of its economic troubles, he began to grow different varieties of *Nelumbo*. Some of these were already named and known to the Edo beau monde. Others were new to the official ranks of cultivation, having either been bred by Matsudaira himself or collected by him in the course of his travels among wilderness, farmland and temples.

In naming his new introductions, Matsudaira combined the concentrated, *mot juste*-seeking spirit of the haiku writer with the loving scrutiny of the plant otaku. Some of the epithets he coined were allusions to literature, history and myth; others were place names; others again were purely descriptive – a few choice adjectives, a reference to a time of day or season, a comparison with a flower such as the peony or with a creature, perhaps legendary like the phoenix or as real as a crab. As I had discovered, lotus love was no more solemn than any other Japanese passion, grave and rule-ridden though these arts sometimes seem to outsiders. Matsudaira permitted himself a joke or two. Aware that he was already known as a princely proponent of Neo-Confucian values, he named one of his Shirakawa cultivars 'Kunshi'. Was it tall and pure, the unblemished embodiment of the virtues he strove to attain? No – it was small, looked like a blighted rosebud and had the colouring of a choleric colonel. In his portraits Matsudaira appears pale, lean and elegant. Nonetheless, he used this cultivar to lampoon his own pretentiousness: 'The lotus is the kunshi's plant and I may be *the* kunshi, but a kunshi is not always as lofty as he would like and neither is his lotus.'

In the Tokyo National Museum are two volumes, roughly Folio in size and each comprising 52 pages. The first is titled *Ken* ('Heaven'), and the second *Kon* ('Earth'). Together they form the work known as *Seikō-gafu*. I was told that its name meant 'Fresh Fragrance Picture Book', and that in this context *seikō* – fresh fragrance – was a poetical synonym for lotus.

In total the flowers of 52 named and 6 unidentified *Nelumbo* cultivars appear painted by hand on spreads of nacreous paper. Beside each flower, the cultivar's name, its synonyms, and a word or two about its origins are inscribed in cinereous ink. At the back of the second volume are studies of the lotus's anatomy and life cycle. A little further on and in the same elegantly cascading hand as the captions is an anthology of hasu texts both Chinese and Japanese. Chief among them are Zhou Dunyi's 'Lotus Love

Thoughts' and Ekiken Kaibara's 1694 prescription for successful *Nelumbo* cultivation, apparently still considered current many years after it was first published.

Yoko began translating the captions for me. In 'Earth' (volume two), we found a single flower – pale rose combed with alizarin crimson and labelled 'Fujitsubo-ren'. 'This new variety,' said the legend, 'was bred by the Takatsukasa, a cadet branch of the Imperial Family.' Fujitsubo was the step-mother and lover of Hikaru Genji, hero of Murasaki Shikibu's *Tale of Genji*. It was not the only literary lotus. In 'Heaven' (volume one) we found a golden-eyed double white with an inner ruff of lacy petaloids that gave it the appearance of some glorious albino peony. Its name was 'Man'yo-ren', a reference to Man'yōshū, Japan's oldest collection of poems, which includes early mentions of hasu. Next a pair of densely double-flowered lotuses appeared. Pale salmon, tipped with deep blush, they were labelled 'Gyokushū-ren also known as Hokke-ren', *gyokushū* meaning 'precious embroidery', and *Hokke*, its synonym, being the Japanese name of the *Lotus Sutra*.

As we progressed, I found cultivars whose plumage had evidently taxed even this skilful painter. 'Zuiko-ren', 'the first light lotus', was one such defiant beauty. A deep bowl of white flushed with gold at the base and kissed with cochineal at the rim – a dawn flower that sang its own aubade. The cultivar I liked best and which best seemed to suit the pearl and pastel refine-ment of *Seikō-gafu* was filed under 'Heaven'. Named 'Shinobu-ike byakuren' ('the white lotus of the Secret Lake'), its petals were large and snowy except for their tips which were brushed with the elusive lavender that is the legendary lotus blue. As its name suggests, this variety was a speciality of Shinobazu-no-ike. It is believed to have come to grief during World War II when the lake was commandeered for rice production. Despite its talent for immortality, it seemed the lotus was a wild goose of a plant, not always able to escape circumstance no matter how beautiful.

Sadanobu Matsudaira created *Seikō-gafu* in 1822, working either alone or in collaboration with one or more of his in-house artists. I was told the text was in his lordship's hand, and that there was good reason to suppose a high proportion of the painting was as well. Accurate and accomplished though they were, the pictures had a naivety and unevenness which suggested an inspired amateur rather than a day-in-day-out professional; a man who was moved to paint by love of his subject alone. The personal record of what was once the world's largest lotus collection, *Seikō-gafu* is the most important illustrated work on *Nelumbo* ever produced and the progenitor of almost all that have followed.

There are two scrolls in the National Diet Library in Tokyo. The first consists of nine panels and is 40 centimetres by 748 centimetres; the second consists of ten and is longer at 861 centimetres. They are the work of Bunryō Hoshino (1797–1846), one of a small stable of artists employed more or less full-time by Sadanobu Matsudaira. Painted in 1822, the same year as *Seikō-gafu*, they present an astonishing record in plant portraits and panoramas of the haven he created for his lotus collection. The scrolls are called *Yokuon Shinkei* ('True Scenes of Yokuon'). An allusion, perhaps, to the great oceans of beneficence described in the *Lotus Sutra*, Yokuon means an in-flowing of blessings or glory. It was the name Matsudaira gave to his estate on Reigan-jima, an artificial island in the mouth of the Sumida River that lay just two miles east of his offices in Edo Castle but whose view of Tokyo Bay ran clear to the Pacific Ocean. He named the compound that he built there Senshu Kan, 'The Mansion of a Thousand Autumns'. Around it, between the early 1790s and 1829, he developed the collage of open landscapes and passages of intensive cultivation known as Yokuon-en, 'The In-flowing Blessings Garden', which many regard as the climax of Edo horticulture.

The Mansion of a Thousand Autumns is shown as a glorified buke-yashiki, or samurai compound, that resembles a small village in its sprawl of teal-tiled rooftops. In a gravelled yard just outside its stockaded rear entrance is the *maetei* or front garden, a place for intensive cultivation – pot plants, miniature landscapes and small, perfectly judged assemblages of shrubs and perennials – that takes its origins in *senzai*, the close-to-home areas of aristocratic gardens in the Heian Period. Here stand a small thatched shelter for orchids and other delicacies and open benches for bonsai and *yose-ue*, containerised plantings of seasonal perennials. Before these is a series of bays surrounded by low bamboo fencing. Within them are *hasu-game*, dozens of bowls containing different lotus cultivars, their flowers ranging in colour from ivory to blood red. Nearby is a small pavilion with a projecting verandah or engawa, a space, the legend informs us, designated for lotus appreciation, study and painting.

Although fewer cultivars appear in the lake – mainly sturdy whites and shades of pink – they fill its amoeba-like outlines, colonising creeks and marching under a rainbow bridge before finally congregating in a great pool around an island that is home to a majestic maple draped in wisteria.

Conventionally enough, this pool is described as a hasu-ike, 'a lotus lake'; but its wider setting, a basin formed by man-made mountains and filled with ornamental trees and shrubs, is named Tamomono-ike, 'the lake of precious gems'. In other words, in designing his garden Matsudaira extended the concept of the lake full of treasures – the secret lake – to the whole landscape, wet and dry.

An ideal is at work in this samurai equivalent of the Elysian Fields – of cultivation held in balance with Nature. Around the Mansion of a Thousand Autumns are carefully pruned pine trees, passages of cleverly coordinated shrubbery, and Matsudaira's gallery of lotus tubs. As one moves away from the house, so the garden becomes more rustic. Orchards and thatched pavilions appear and lakeside irises are planted in ranks to suggest paddy-fields. Beyond and forming an arena for all this husbandry is an artificial mountain range, a Shangri-la of peaks and gulleys capped with pine trees and clothed in wild shrubs and herbs. All three aspects – groomed and contained civilisation, the managed fecundity of farmland, and the lyrical wilderness – cohere in Bunryō's composition as they did in the garden itself; they are elements of a continuum. Within a short distance of the shogun's capital, Matsudaira constructed his own world, Japan in microcosm. This was his ideal, a nation harmonised by cultivation. It was an ideal whose inspiration was the sublime landscape of Shirakawa, Matsudaira's rural domain. The flora that grew on these man-made peaks, the folds, crossings and openings of their slopes, their ever-mistier diminution to the vanishing point were all unmistakable: they were copies of the mountains that had lined our route north that day in Fukushima.

Convinced he had done his best and that the best thing a politician could do was to know when to quit, Matsudaira resigned as chancellor in 1793. At thirty-five, he was young for the role of elder statesman, but he played it with relish. He devoted himself to writing, painting, gardening, and to the hasu collection which had made Edo the lotus capital of the world. This, he was more than happy to accept, was his greatest achievement. He was happier still to share this hobby that was also an object lesson in ethics. His garden at Yokuon-en was no Selfish Giant's orchard. This upholder of a rigidly stratified society welcomed visitors regardless of their rank. Any surplus plants soon found homes elsewhere. His writings and paintings told their recipients what they were and what to do with them. Those without access to Matsudaira's *Seikō-gafu* or to the expanded versions of it his artists produced such as *Yokuon-en-renpu* ('The Lotus Book of Yokuon Garden', 1822–28) were still able to consult him indirectly – he encouraged other authors to reproduce his images and text in a crop of publications devoted to lotuses and in horticultural encyclopedias like Kan'en Iwasaki's 96-volume *Honzō Zufu* ('Illustrated Herbal'). It was fortunate that Matsudaira was such a passionate sharer, so absolute a believer in the gardener's maxim that the best way to keep a plant is to give it away. In early 1829 a fire that began in Edo's Kanda District destroyed his house and garden. He died in the summer of that same year, aged seventy. The Mansion of a Thousand Autumns had barely lasted forty.

Pondering Bunryō's paintings of Yokuon-en, I found it hard to believe that anything so beautiful and substantial could have gone up in smoke. The mansion maybe, but what of the hills and lakes that Matsudaira sculpted? Had the one been used to fill the other? Was nothing left? I was told that the artificial island had changed shape as Tokyo expanded and had been joined by others spilling from the river mouth into the bay; that a naval academy had occupied the site and then a fish market. I was warned not to look and so, naturally, I did. I went to the area now called Kayabachō and found a grid of tower blocks and canals, as if Wall Street had been superimposed on Venice. As a landscape it was not Yokuon-en, but it was beautiful in its own way, and exciting. And of course there were plants, as always and wherever the Japanese live or work – potted, petted and in some cases perching perilously close to the water. In the doorway of a noodle shop a lotus grew in a dragon-painted ginger jar. Its flowers were deep carmine and rather small. I cannot be sure and its owner neither knew nor cared, but it looked like 'Kunshi'.

22

Hasu-gari

Level land suitable for development is in short supply in Japan. It is also where lotuses are most likely to have grown. As a result, ancient seeds sometimes turn up when treasures, human or natural, are the last thing on anyone's mind. In 1951 Ōga-hasu came to light in a peat cutting that was destined to become a sports complex. Twenty years later, in Gyōda City in Saitama Prefecture, a plot was earmarked for a rubbish incinerating facility. As it was cleared, the rains began. When work resumed, a wealth of Jōmon pottery was discovered, revealed by the action of bulldozer and downpour. Soon afterwards, as the summer heat arrived, the building site began to sprout. By 1973, no fewer than 52 flowering-sized lotus plants had been salvaged from seeds which, unlike Ōga-hasu, had needed no assistance in germinating other than their rude exposure. All alike but subtly different from other Wa-basu, they were named Gyōda-hasu, or *Nelumbo nucifera* 'Gyōda'.

Based on the Jōmon pots with which, and in which, they were found, the age of these seeds was estimated at between 2,500 and 3,000 years. Much of the site was now irreparably disturbed and the deepest and oldest strata had been churned to the surface, yielding their treasures. Nonetheless, in 1974, the lotus specialist Dr Kiyonobu Toyoda and his students undertook two digs in the upper layers of what little remained untouched. Both excavations produced seeds which, when germinated, proved identical to Gyōda-hasu. In other words, the site was a colony consisting of a single and distinctive lotus variety which had thrived there for millennia. In 1975 the Japan Radioisotope

Association radiocarbon dated a sample of the seeds Toyoda had found in the upper and more recent strata. These relative Johnnies-come-lately were 1,400 years old, give or take a century.

While there is an understandable reluctance in Japan to do anything to detract from the unique value of Dr Ōga's lotus, the likely reality is that it represents one of thousands of colonies of ancient lotuses that lie buried beneath cities and agricultural land. Heaven forfend that the nation's littoral plains be stripped of civilisation and rotavated by some giant hand. If they were, however, fields of hasu would spring up after centuries of slumber to take the place of humankind.

Yōzō In'nami told me he thought such action unnecessarily drastic, and I agreed with him. But he also maintained that not all of Japan's sleeping lotuses should be left to chance and the bulldozer's deftness of touch. By profession, he is a distinguished park director in Utsunomiya, the city 100 kilometres north of Tokyo that is the capital of Tochigi Prefecture. In this civic role, and in his gentleman-scholar appearance, he has more than a little of the kunshi about him. By passion, he is not only a lotus-lover but also a prospector for ancient buried *Nelumbo*. Soon after Taeko-san introduced us, I found myself asked – for the second time since my arrival in Japan – to pay close attention to something I would normally ignore. This time, it was not a sports stadium but the surface of an inner-city car park. 'I know they're down there,' said In'nami-san, pointing at a patch of oil-stained asphalt. 'We dug just over there last year and came up with nothing, but I'm convinced they must be here.'

In May 1868 Utsunomiya Castle was the scene of a decisive battle in the Meiji Restoration, the toppling of the shogunate and the return of the emperor to direct rule. It took place over four days and resulted in defeat for the shogun's forces. Since the castle had become a stronghold of troops loyal to the Tokugawa Bakufu, what survived the battle was razed by the new Meiji Government as an example to others. Today only grass-covered bulwarks, a wall and two restored gate towers remain of what was once one of the greatest defensive buildings in Japan. In its heyday the castle had a particularly elaborate system of moats, four major circuits of water and numerous lesser tracts. On old maps, they define the stepped battlements like blue contour lines, growing smaller and tighter towards the citadel. As was common with castle moats, these were naturalised with lotuses to provide decoration and spiritual elevation in times of peace, and famine food in times of siege.

Utsunomiya's martial lotuses had disappeared with the castle. The ramparts had been levelled and built upon to form the new city centre. The car park we were scrutinising lay over what was once the widest moat and most prolific lotus site – or so In'nami-san had concluded after poring over maps and records, pacing out the land, persuading technicians to take sonar measurements and receiving reports of buried lotus pollen from soil analysts. Although the first dig had produced nothing, there would be others, and in this very spot. Here in the car park was where the castle lotus would see light again. He was not alone in this belief. Taeko-san was convinced, and In'nami-san had a growing band of supporters in the city itself. Tired of peering under Hondas, we went to meet the most vocal among them, Nobuo Itō, the Gyōza King.

I had always known them before as Chinese dumplings. Why so, I cannot imagine. Dumplings by rights should be fatty and farinaceous, suety fibroids bobbing in a mess of pottage. In Britain Chinese dumplings tend to look more like the newly farrowed litter of a peculiarly anaemic pasty. But in Utsunomiya they are delicious and not called dumplings but *gyōza*. The city has numerous claims to distinction. Turbulent military history notwithstanding, it was a favourite stopover for pilgrims and gaijin tourists en route to the great Tokugawa shrine at nearby Nikkō. Today it is crammed with jazz dives and cocktail bars, the improbable descendants of the watering holes those travellers frequented. It is also filled with practitioners of bronze-work, lacquer and wood-carving, and is the hub of one of the nation's busiest horticultural regions. But the boast that Utsunomiya makes most proudly of itself is that it is the gyōza capital of Japan.

In a city with a population of half a million, there are over 200 restaurants which serve dumplings and nothing else. To be Gyōza King in such a place is to be emperor and shogun rolled into one. And yet Nobuo Itō wore his crown lightly. It was a chef's hat of slightly naval appearance. He had the look and carriage of the boss of some great conglomerate and many around him behaved as if he were; but the charm and care he showed his clients suggested no such rank. In'nami-san was one of his most honoured customers. The Gyōza King had high hopes of him. He said as much as we took our seats in Min Min, the restaurant that is his court: 'How are our lotuses doing? Have you found any yet? No? Don't give up hope, my friend – we'll dig up the whole damned town if we have to.' They made an unlikely pair, the shining-faced chef in brilliant whites, and the reserved gentleman-scholar, *soigné* but ascetic in navy mohair suit and knitted silk tie; but they were clearly comrades in arms.

'You see this man?' the Gyōza King proclaimed. 'He is leading us on a great *Hasu-gari*.'

'Hasu-gari?' I asked Yoko *sotto voce*.

'Lotus Quest.'

The perfect gyōza arrived, served to general astonishment by the monarch himself. For a while Min Min, small, noisy, heaving, seemed to turn into a *salon privé* where only lotus business could be discussed. Concern was expressed that In'nami-san should eat heartily. He needed to keep his strength up. The entire Gyōza Kingdom was depending on him. I began to realise that there was enormous popular support for his subterranean investigations. Nobuo Itō and a handful of other local worthies were supporting the excavation practically with food, finance, labour and whatever pressure they could bring to bear on intransigent property owners; but there was a great deal of cheering going on from the sidelines too. Utsunomiya's university and schools were watching keenly and waiting to pitch in. The sense of collective anticipation and collaboration between all generations and walks of life reminded me of the tales I had heard of the discovery of Ōga-hasu. The city wanted its lotus, or, rather, wanted its lotuses back. The Utsunomiya Lotus Pond Revival Committee had been formed; there was even talk that one day the castle moat itself might be restored, and filled again with the very lotuses that grew there in the days of the shogun.

'You know,' I said to Nobuo Itō, 'the chances are that if In'nami-san does find hasu buried beneath the city, they may not be that old. They'll probably date from the Tokugawa Shogunate when the castle was last thriving. I think you'll be talking centuries rather than millennia.'

'But isn't that old enough?' he replied. 'Isn't that the whole point? We're interested in history not pre-history. Lots of people make a fuss of thousand-year-old lotuses. What we want to see is something that reminds us of the city's glory in the Edo Period. Ours are samurai lotuses, not Jōmon lotuses, and we're going to see them again soon – aren't we, In'nami-san?'

I hoped so, for everyone's sake. A little way outside Utsunomiya lay Mizuho no Mori, a public area of nature reserve and landscaped gardens of great beauty, administered by Yōzō In'nami. There he showed me a new lake, an arc as slender and brilliant as a new moon. It was negotiated by a bridge that was almost at water level and consisted of a series of platforms. These squares of decking were linked at haphazard angles, like scattered playing cards. 'It's a traditional Japanese bridge design,' In'nami-san explained. 'The idea is that your progress should be disrupted, that you should be momentarily disoriented and forced to pause, taking in a different view from each platform. Later, I'll show you my lotuses at home. Some of those may end up in this lake. But, of course, what we really hope is that we'll have Utsunomiya's own antique lotuses to plant here one day.' Standing on the bridge amid the irises and air-kissing carp, I longed for him to succeed. Ravishing as it was, the lake had the look of a frame without a painting.

Afterwards we went to Yōzō In'nami's home, a villa of traditional design set high on a bluff. As dusk descended, we sat listening to the plunging and singing of frogs. They evidently believed themselves the rightful occupants of the glazed bowls which lined the driveway and precincts of the house. In fact, the bowls belonged to lotuses. Comprising 70 cultivars in all and hundreds of individual specimens, that evening In'nami-san's collection was still missing the one plant that would complete the set. Not that I felt its absence. We were surrounded by hasu. In the twilight, their massed buds appeared to float and glow, an avenue of lanterns.

'So you're saying goodbye to Taeko-san for the time being,' said In'nami-san. 'Where will your travels take you next?'

'I don't think we know where immediately,' said Yoko, 'but in the end we're heading north, for Chūson-ji; although I'm not sure who to contact there. It's rather daunting.'

'I have an idea,' he offered. 'Let me see what I can do.'

There was a certain amount of talk about Kyoto, but Yoko would have none of it. Time was limited, she said, and Kyoto was sufficiently well-known. It could wait for another day. We should go no further south of Tokyo than Kamakura.

'Ah,' said In'nami-san, 'in Kamakura you'll find a very old lotus moat still full of the original plants.'

'Yes,' she said, 'and a proper lotus story, at least as far as I'm concerned.'

All I knew about Kamakura was what everybody knows – that it is home to an enormous seated statue of the Buddha.

In Ōmiya the next morning we said goodbye to Taeko-san. As we were loading the car she asked if we would mind making room for a parting gift. It was a box containing the sprouting rhizomes of ten *Nelumbo* cultivars – the pick of her collection, swaddled in damp tissue paper. She secured it on the back seat with all the care of someone handling a newborn baby. I risked a valedictory kiss, clearly still a shocking gesture in Japan even for the widely travelled. Then I compensated for my gaffe with a low bow and 'Sayōnara'. She seemed completely delighted: 'Perfect! You've managed it at last.' Ever since my arrival, sayōnara was a word she had been at pains to have me get right. It was, she said, a shibboleth, something the whole world thought it knew but which hardly any gaijin could pronounce. The first syllable should sound like 'sigh' and be uttered like a sigh. The 'yō' needed to be played down. There had to be a sudden syncopation of the 'nara', with the 'r' done slightly à l'Écosse. Despite this final flourish, the objective was a wistful, rather quiet evenness of tone. After many a leave-taking lesson on the thresholds of restaurants, gardens and museums, I had finally pulled it off. But not to my satisfaction. To my mind there was no proper way to bid farewell to so much kindness.

More than a year has passed since my meeting with Yōzō In'nami. Although we corresponded for some months, I did not want to press him on whether he had made any progress in his hasu-gari. This spring the bulletins from Utsunomiya stopped, and I began to worry that this most thoughtful and dedicated of lotus-hunters had abandoned his quest. I imagined the Gyōza King urging him not to give up hope, offering a dish of consolatory dumplings, threatening to buy and dynamite the car park. I need not have worried – In'nami-san was simply busy. Today he sent me an email:

> This spring we returned to the car park we visited last summer. By now our lotus restoration committee had grown from 9 to about 100 members. We were also fortunate in being joined in our efforts by students from Utsunomiya University and pupils from local schools, some of whom were very young but marvellously enthusiastic and hard-working. So the project came to feel as if it belonged to everyone – which, of course, it does.
>
> Just one metre below the surface of the car park, we began to find the mud of the castle moat and remains of lotus stalks, receptacles and rhizomes which had been preserved in it. On 5 April we encountered the first lotus seeds. These were buried at depths of between 2.7 and 1.9 metres below the surface and in exactly the same place I showed you last year.
>
> We found 16 seeds in all. Some have been sent for radiocarbon dating and we await the results. Five were kept for germination. Two of these have

Above left) Terracotta fertility
goddess from Pakistan (Indus Valley
Civilisation, 2,000 – 1,500 BC).
Above right) Clay plaque of Astarte
from Beth Shemesh near Jerusalem
(Phoenician, 1,500 – 1,200 BC).
Right) Puabi's gold head-dress,
crowned with the eight-pointed lotuses
of Inanna, from Ur in Southern Iraq
(Sumerian, 2,550 – 2,400 BC).

(*Top*) Coin from Croton, Southern Italy, minted around the end of Pythagoras's lifetime (circa 480 BC).
(*Above*) Relief from the Apadana Palace, Persepolis, showing the Persian half-lotus motifs that inspired the Greek lotus palmette (Achaemenid, late 6th to early 5th centuries BC).
(*Right*) Red figure ware drinking vessel with lotus palmette motif (Greek, 400 – 300 BC).

(*Top left*) Stone relief of a winged genie tending
a ceremonial lotus 'tree', from Nimrud,
Northern Iraq (Assyrian, 9th century BC).
(*Top right*) Fragment of a fretwork ivory lotus 'tree'
from Nimrud (Assyrian, 8th century BC).
(*Above*) 9th century AD stucco relief from Samarra, Iraq.
(*Left*) Relief of Sargon II from Dur-Sharrukin,
Northern Iraq (Assyrian, early 8th century BC).

(*Above left*) Darius the Great holding the lotus of kingship, from Persepolis (Achaemenid Persian, circa 515 BC).
(*Left*) Column base at the site of ancient Lidoma, near Persepolis, Iran (Achaemenid Persian, 5th century BC).
(*Above*) Silver lotus leaf phiale or libation bowl (Achaemenid Persian, 6 - 4th centuries BC).

(*Top left*) Relief on a stone gate at the Great Stupa, Sanchi (Indian, circa 70 BC).
(*Top right*) Detail from one of the lotus arches at St Mary's, Iffley (Norman, 1170).
(*Above*) Nelum Pokuna, a 12th century granite lotus bath in tiers of eight petals
at Polonnaruwa, Sri Lanka.

Clay artifacts from the Early to Middle Jōmon Period (Japan, 5,000 – 1,500 BC):

Lotus-lipped urn.

Model of a receptacle with seeds.

Ear-ring fragment depicting
a slice of rhizome.

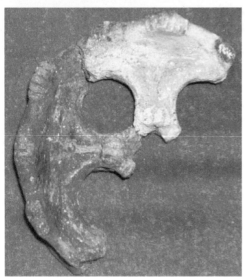

Lotus receptacle toggle.

Early Kofun Period
ceremonial bronze mirror
(Japan, circa 250 AD).

Earthenware lotus bloom roof tile
(Japan, 7th century AD).

Semi-abstract lotus tiles installed in 1609 at
Zuigan-ji, a Zen temple in Matsushima.

Jūichimen Kannon, the eleven-faced and lotus-armed bodhisattva, a famous but seldom-glimpsed Ninth Century wooden statue in Hokke-ji, Nara's 'Temple of the Lotus Sutra'.

sprouted and grown rapidly. They are now producing standing leaves rather than floating juvenile leaves, and I believe they have a good chance of flowering next summer. Until then we can only wait and guess what colour their flowers might be. I shall tell you when we know, likewise the age of these seeds once we learn it.

Utsunomiya, 21 September 2008

IV

Tales of Genji

23

The Hall of the Lotus King

In the end Yoko relented. I was allowed a flying visit to Kyoto before doubling back and heading north via Kamakura. Lotuses abound in the old imperial capital – painted and sculpted in the fabric and adornments of every temple, alive in many of their precincts, some of them unchanged in over a thousand years. Growing in willow-banked ponds, a few specimens greeted me as I entered the compound of the sacred building that I came to see as seminal to Japan's most dramatic lotus story. Their flowers echoed the dusty rose colonnades that marched in either direction from the temple's gatehouses. It was an appropriate greeting: the name of this place was Rengeō-in, 'The Hall of the Lotus King'.

Erected in 1164 and still the longest wooden building in Japan, the hall is a single gallery 120 metres long, 22 metres wide and 16 metres high. It is composed of 33 sections of walling, painted white and divided by beams of hinoki cypress (*Chamaecyparis obtusa*), a warmly aromatic timber that was uncommon and precious even in the twelfth century. The number of sections is significant. In the *Lotus Sutra* and related texts Kannon, the 'Thousand-Armed' Bodhisattva of mercy to whom this Tendai Sect temple is dedicated, can adopt any of a multitude of guises and skills to come to the aid of those in need. For this reason, the deity is usually depicted with multiple hands, each holding a different useful or holy item. Thirty-three is the magic number often mentioned in connection with these quick-change acts of clemency and assistance, although their upper limit, says the Sutra, exceeds infinity.

This sacred numerology explains the unofficial name by which Rengeō-in is better known – Sanjūsangen-dō, 'The Thirty-three Sections Hall'. What makes the building such an artistic tour de force, however, is the statuary that lines the back wall of the gallery and projects outward on a series of stepped shelves that form a stage filling two thirds of the floor space. Sculpted in cypress wood and heavily gilded, at the centre is a single statue of Kannon seated on an immense open lotus flower. This figure has forty-two arms, one main face and ten others, the total of countenances giving a third of thirty-three. It stands 11 *shaku* tall, again a third of thirty-three. Yoko explained that a shaku was an old unit of measurement equivalent – I learnt with a distinct frisson – to 30.3030 centimetres recurring. In other words, the statue is 3.3 metres tall, not that its maker could have known that. Could he? Above its various heads another lotus hovers, a celestial lamp fringed with dishevelled chains of gold which resemble Spanish moss subjected to a peculiarly expensive form of electro-plating. Charms hang from these glittering filaments, among them ormolu models of lotus seeds.

That, you might think, would be quite enough to establish this place as the Hall of the Lotus King. It is barely the beginning. To either side of this central figure is a forest of standing statues of the same deity, again in gilded wood. Each has a sunburst behind its head and 40 hands, two of which are joined in prayer or greeting with the remainder proffered around and behind in a corona of arms. Although these writhing limbs and the spokes of the sunbursts do not touch, they do seem to connect, giving the ensemble an overpowering sense of homogeneity and complexity. These figures are all 1.65 metres tall and they appear identical until one notices variations in their expressions and in the objects they hold in their haloes of hands. As with most representations of Kannon, however, one thing that many of them hold in common is some part of the lotus – rhizome, leaf, bud, bloom, or seed head – and all stand on pedestals styled as open lotus flowers. In ten tiered ranks, 500 of these statues extend in either direction from the midpoint of the Hall of the Lotus King, bringing the total number of Kannon, the principal image included, to 1,001.

It all seems of such a glorious piece, so wonderfully calculated – all except the number of limbs, which surely is out of order with the numerology. This too has an explanation. Altogether there are 40,042 Bodhisattva arms in the building. Subtract from that sum the hands that are empty or holding duplicate objects and one is left with 33,033 different items, each fitted to a specific need or function, 33,033 possible metamorphoses that the Kannon can assume to help us. Or so it is said. I did not count them, but any number in that region would be in keeping with the arithmetical magniloquence of the *Lotus Sutra*.

Following their ranks across and up and down, the eye is first confused then overwhelmed. These statues ought to look like the matriculation photograph of some angelic host; but they have been arranged in slightly diagonal files so that they perform a perspectival trick. Appearing to grow ever more numerous as they recede, they dispel the notion that there might be anything so mundane and limiting as a back wall. Before this bank of gleaming idols stand 30 further figures. These are the gods of wind and thunder and 28 guardian deities, each portrayed in the midst of some avenging act. They perch not on lotuses but on riven boulders that have been sculpted with astonishing verisimilitude as have the demon warriors themselves. Allowing for the fact that some have flames for hair and boar's tusks for teeth, these figures are more lifelike, more anatomically astute than anything created in Europe between the fall of Rome and the Renaissance. Modelled in ungilded and ferrous-looking wood, their infernal grimaces and gristly musculature are decidedly earthbound, or suggestive of some darker place beneath it. They are there to protect the Kannon and to remind us of the brutality of life led without their succour and example. They succeed in both: since they stand in the corridor rather than on the staging, one has to look them straight in the eye (sometimes glass and horribly staring) before daring to gaze beyond to the golden army of heavenly helpers.

'What genius was responsible for this?' I asked Yoko.

'His name was Tankei,' she said. 'He was a great sculptor of the Kamakura Period. He and his students finished the most magnificent figures here just two years before his death in 1256. He would have been about eighty-two years old at the time.'

This troubled me. On entering the Hall of the Lotus King, I had been told it was finished in 1164, some twenty-eight years before the beginning of the Kamakura Period and in the violent twilight of the Heian Period. Yoko confirmed that was true but said the temple had been largely destroyed by fire in 1249. A little over 10 per cent of the original statues survived the blaze and the rest had been newly created by Tankei and his disciples over a span of sixteen years. The restoration was a pet project of the Kamakura shogunate and was judged a considerable improvement on the original – so

217

much so that some of the artists took the unusual step of signing their various Kannon.

'All the same,' I said, 'much of the credit for the vision must go to the men who first commissioned the Hall of the Lotus King. Who were they?'

'An emperor called Go-Shirakawa and a clan chief called Taira no Kiyomori. Credit them if you must, but I think they were two of the biggest shits of all time.'

Heian Period emperors were a philoprogenitive lot. They fathered children by any one of a number of official consorts and innumerable concubines. They also had a habit of abdicating and becoming *Daijō Hōō*, 'cloistered emperors'. For some that meant a genuine retreat from government and the world, perhaps to a life of scholarship, poetry or spiritual contemplation. For others it was a form of retirement in which the erstwhile monarch could pontificate and puppeteer without any of the burdens of office. This practice meant that at any time there might be one occupant of the Chrysanthemum Throne and one or more former occupants all alive and well in Kyoto and each with numerous offspring and a large household. By the ninth century, the capital was awash with superfluous sons, most of whom viewed each other with competitive unease, and all of whom required to be kept in the style the gods had ordained for them.

The time had come to prune the family tree. Emperors granted new surnames to sons and grandsons who were not directly in line to inherit the throne, in the hope that they would found aristocratic dynasties of their own, be satisfied with their new rank, and grow distant from the imperial purse. In some cases these noble houses were given an even stronger inducement to establish their independence, by being dispatched to the provinces as regional rulers. Confusingly, the same surname was sometimes given by different emperors to different offspring. The Emperor Saga (786–842) called his seventh son Minamoto. In 916, the same name was granted to Tsunemoto, the grandson of Seiwa (850–880), the 56th emperor. Already a proven fighter and provincial governor, this second imperial prince was finally given his own show to run and his own route to immortality. He now became *Minamoto no Tsunemoto*, 'Tsunemoto of the Minamoto', the style appropriate to a clan chief. His newly created noble house was known as the Seiwa Genji from the name of the emperor who was its grandsire, and Genji, an alternative way of reading the characters for Minamoto. In terms of historical importance, the Seiwa came to eclipse the Saga and other Minamoto lines. As a result its members were often referred to simply as *The* Genji, while the form 'Minamoto' was restricted to the chief and his immediate family.

These real persons should not be confused with the fictional Hikaru Genji, hero of *Tale of Genji*. In calling her princely character Minamoto/Genji, Lady Murasaki was simply using a surname that emperors had bestowed on much-loved but second-ranking sons. In reality, by the time she was writing her novel, the Seiwa Genji clan was already a byword for a gravitas that was the antithesis of Hikaru's dazzling but dilettante charm.

Such nomenclatural niceties can be tiring even for taxonomists; but before reaching the main tale of sex, violence and lotuses, it is important to consider another of these lopped-off branches of the imperial tree. Around 825, a grandson of Kammu, Japan's 50th emperor, was granted the surname Taira and encouraged to found his own aristocratic house. His clan prospered and became known as the Heike, an alternative reading of this prince's new family name which stands to Taira as Genji stands to Minamoto. In time, the Genji and Heike clans became bitter rivals and ultimately fought each other for control of the nation. The tale of their massively extended family dispute is taught as if it were Japan's equivalent of the Wars of the Roses. As I was to discover, the Genji's greatest champion would have considered the comparison apt, although she would have quibbled over the choice of flower.

By the 1150s, the Seiwa Genji had established themselves as aristocratic rulers throughout the Kantō Region, the 'East' of the country as seen from the then capital Kyoto, hence the title of the clan's great chronicle, *Azuma Kagami*, 'The Mirror of the East'. Among their number were distinguished poets and thinkers and several generals who were employed by emperors to impose order on remote regions. In this they showed a combination of fair play and ferocity that became a famous Minamoto, or Genji, characteristic. Remoteness and disinterest were also hallmarks of Genji conduct at court. Bracing austerity, loyal service and an independent spirit were the clan's watchwords. They harboured no obvious ambition to control the throne.

None of which could really be said of the Heike clan. They established their power base in the western provinces. They remained close to the court in Kyoto where they lived in extravagant style. They sought repeatedly to influence the policies and choice of emperors, backing retirees over their reigning sons and vice versa according to whichever candidate would gain them greater advantage. Their ruses ranged from marrying into the imperial line to seeking, or seizing, high office and, ultimately, to running a kind of protection racket in which their forces infested the capital on the pretext of policing it. Inevitably, Genji loyalty collided with Heike self-interest. The two sides had clashed before, but only ever in the provinces. In July 1156 they confronted each other in Kyoto. At the end of this conflict, known as the Hōgen Rebellion, the Genji chief Minamoto no Tameyoshi (b. 1096) lost his head, while his Heike counterpart Taira no Kiyomori (1118–81) won the capital.

The background to these hostilities was a power struggle between Sutoku, a cloistered or retired emperor, and his brother, the reigning Emperor Go-Shirakawa (1127–92). It presented Tameyoshi's son Yoshitomo (b. 1123) with a conflict of his own. The Genji leader aligned himself with Sutoku on the basis of merit: he may have been a cloistered emperor, but his integrity far outstripped his brother's. For his son Yoshitomo, however, duty to a reigning monarch took precedence over filial loyalty and better judgement. A victim of his own Genji code of honour, he was forced to oppose his father and to join cause with the Heike clan. They, meanwhile, were promoting Go-Shirakawa's interests not for reasons of courtly protocol but because the emperor was their creature, and a fairly repugnant one to boot.

At the end of the Hōgen Rebellion, the victorious Heike chief Taira no Kiyomori ordered Yoshitomo to decapitate his own father and, when he refused, gave the task to another Genji warrior. Kiyomori then took all the spoils and preferment that the grateful Emperor Go-Shirakawa could offer him. Meanwhile, the Seiwa Genji had gained nothing, having sacrificed their men, leader and honour. This breakdown of gratitude and reciprocity, I would discover, was the one thing most certain to attract Minamoto wrath. Yoshitomo, the new Genji chief, bided his time for three years, rallied his surviving troops and sought allies among the Fujiwara, the ancient courtly dynasty that had furnished him with a wife and which now, he thought, offered a solution to all this in-fighting between semi-imperial clans.

In the winter of 1159, Kiyomori, the Heike chief, was away from Kyoto. Yoshitomo seized the opportunity to invade the capital. His forces abducted Go-Shirakawa (by now cloistered but still young, vigorous and acting it), and his son, the sixteen-year-old Emperor Nijō. They replaced the Heike-friendly chancellor with the pro-Genji Fujiwara no Nobuyori. Then they occupied the palace. By January 1160, however, both imperial hostages had escaped and sought Kiyomori's protection. With unwonted unanimity the two emperors ordered the Heike chief to take back the palace and kill the traitors. He sent a raiding party through the main gates to tempt the Genji into giving chase, and then crushed them as they emerged. It was a rudimentary trick that could only have deceived soldiers enervated by becoming hostage-takers in a siege that was not just long but amounted to treason and sacrilege. But then some say the Heiji Rebellion, as these events became known, was one big trick from start to finish, that in leaving Kyoto and his two imperial protégés so vulnerable to attack, Taira no Kiyomori had set a trap for the Genji.

By the end of February 1160, the Genji leader Yoshitomo and his two oldest sons had been killed. His third and last legitimate heir was being prepared for execution when Kiyomori's stepmother intervened. The boy reminded her of her own favourite son who had died young. Would Kiyomori spare his life for her sake? He did, sending the thirteen-year-old into exile. His two half-brothers were also spared, dispatched to monasteries. Since only a son born to the Genji chief and his official consort could become leader of the clan, these two were no threat to the Heike. Having dealt with the head, Kiyomori addressed himself to the body, using an imperial mandate to strip the Seiwa Genji clan of their titles and lands. Only those who had sided with the Heike in the rebellions would retain their rank and property, and then only if they agreed to serve him as vassals.

Now the Heike leader dominated court and national life. He began in deceptively dignified style. Go-Shirakawa appeared to have thrown himself into scriptural study and was at last showing signs of becoming a truly cloistered emperor. Wishing to encourage his imperial ally's renunciation of worldly power, Kiyomori built a temple in the grounds of Hōjūji-Den, the Buddhist compound that Go-Shirakawa made his retirement base. This was Rengeō-in, the Hall of the Lotus King. Soon chafed by his gilded cloister, the retired emperor began seeking greater sway than he had ever held on the throne. The Heike chief responded by playing the conniving Go-Shirakawa off against the peevish Emperor Nijō, diverting tax revenues to his own coffers, and filling the offices of state and provincial governorships with his placemen. The greatest of these offices he reserved for himself: in 1167 Kiyomori became *Daijō Daijin*, chief minister and chancellor, a post that had been occupied in one form or another by members of the Fujiwara clan for over 400 years. So far as Kiyomori was concerned, however, those traditional bastions of the imperial court were history that was even more ancient than the Genji: 'If you are not Heike,' he was fond of saying, 'you are not human.'

Aged twenty-two, the Emperor Nijō fell ill, abdicated and died in the summer of 1165. He was succeeded by his son Rokujō who, being less than a year old, was in no position to defend himself against the machinations of the Heike chief and his grandfather Go-Shirakawa. Three years later the infant emperor was deposed in favour of Takakura, Go-Shirakawa's son by Kiyomori's sister-in-law and kinswoman. Next the chancellor engineered the marriage of his own daughter to the Emperor Takakura, a union that bore fruit in 1178 in Prince Tokihito. Anxious to ensure his grandson's succession, Kiyomori exiled his few remaining opponents, replacing them with friends and family. He also replaced Go-Shirakawa's cloister with incarceration. The retired emperor began to realise that he had backed a Machiavel even more manipulative than himself. Finally, in 1180 Kiyomori compelled Emperor Takakura to abdicate in favour of his son. Fifty per cent Heike and less than two years old, Prince Tokihito became Antoku, the 81st Emperor of Japan. Since the new emperor was but a babe-in-arms, his grandfather Kiyomori had no choice but to appoint himself regent.

These were the events and personalities that gave rise to that most exalted and exquisite of buildings, the Hall of the Lotus King. I was about to discover that they were also the seeds of the greatest of all the lotus stories I would hear in Japan. Its main protagonist overturns Western, Pierre Loti-style stereotypes of Japanese womanhood. In the same way that she seems astonishingly modern, so did the source where I first encountered her, although it was composed during her lifetime. As Yoko translated it for me, I found it hard to believe that anything so fresh and forceful could have been set down eight centuries ago:

'You look exhausted,' said Masako, 'what's the matter? Haven't you slept?'

'I've had that nightmare again,' her sister replied. 'This time it was worse than ever. Can you believe it? I actually ended up married to him.'

'Then I'll take it,' said Masako, remembering an old custom that had amused them in childhood; that a nightmare sold was a sweet dream bought. 'What would you like for it?'

Her sister bartered the nightmare for a kimono that she had been coveting. It was a beautiful thing and, as she took possession, she found herself *wondering at Masako's generosity and the speed with which she proposed the exchange. But then Masako always had been an odd girl who was not much given to dressing up and who clearly had no intention of marrying anybody, let alone the condemned man, that phantom who had visited her in her dreams last night.*

Masako's father was Tokimasa, chief of the Hōjō clan who controlled Izu. Until the second half of the twelfth century, this peninsula to the south of Mount Fuji was considered remote and backward, part of the wild east. Although he had Taira blood and was a Heike loyalist, Tokimasa preferred to keep himself and his men off the battlefield. Instead he led the life of the feudal lord in peacetime, practising swordsmanship and archery, riding, hunting and fishing. To general astonishment, he was accompanied and often bested in these pursuits by his favourite child, Masako, who was born in 1156. The girl had proved herself such a budding samurai that Tokimasa bought her the best possible tutors in the martial arts. He encouraged her to eat with his retainers rather than with the womenfolk; to join in their councils; and, most improbably of all, to use the syntactically distinct and bark-like locutions that were men's language. When challenged over the propriety of her upbringing, Tokimasa would ask what could possibly be the problem: the girl was beautiful; there was no mistaking her gender.

Then, much as he loved her, he began to suspect he had blundered. As she grew to womanhood, Masako gave short shrift to every would-be wooer her father could find for her, and they, horrified by this Amazon, were only too pleased to receive it. Tokimasa feared she was becoming not just immune to admirers but something of a loner. He had received reports that she rode off for hours by herself whenever business took him from his domain. She was such an adept at steeplechasing and guerilla tactics that even his best men had no chance of following her. He had no doubt Masako could look after herself, but was it seemly now she was twenty-three, old enough to be a wife and mother?

Tokimasa had two further problems which, for the moment, seemed unrelated to his warrior princess. In Kyoto his distant kinsman and liege lord Taira no Kiyomori had taken control of the court and was using his own grandson to seize the throne. He had deposed two emperors, imprisoned a third, and quite possibly killed a fourth. He was rumoured to have been embezzling for years, but now he had given himself a divine right to do it.

Not sure that he could stand to be related, however remotely, to this usurper, Tokimasa was finding it harder and harder to travel to the capital to make his obeisance.

But even at home, it was difficult to avoid Kiyomori's contamination. In 1160, at the end of the Heiji Rebellion, the Heike leader had given Tokimasa a difficult duty to perform and he was still performing it. A thirteen-year-old boy, the last legitimate heir of the last Seiwa Genji chief, had been sent into exile in Izu. He had arrived with his old nurse and two retainers. It was Tokimasa's job to keep this sad ménage under a loose guard in a sort of rural open prison, and to permit the last heir to live out his days in the frugal dignity for which, after all, the Seiwa Genji were famous. More importantly, he had to prevent his prisoner from communicating with anyone outside the domain and from producing any legitimate heirs of his own. Quite how well he succeeded in these aims, the Hōjō chief could not be sure. His charge always seemed suspiciously well-informed of events in the capital. The nurse had been allowed to receive messages from her family outside the domain and that was the most likely explanation. But, he comforted himself, what harm could an old woman do? She could hardly have had access to any intelligence of real value. Of one thing he was certain: nobody inside the Hōjō household had been leaking. Tokimasa was even more certain that he would succeed in the most vital aspect of his task. The prisoner could have as many mistresses as he liked, but he would never be allowed to take a wife. The main line of the Seiwa Genji would die with him.

That thirteen-year-old boy was now thirty-two, just a decade younger than Tokimasa himself, and he rather liked him. On the one hand he was reserved, with an ascetic elegance much emphasised by his pallor and habitual black dress. On the other hand, he was formidably tough, a general manqué. There was a lot of the court in bygone days about him: he had spent much of his childhood in Kyoto where his mother was a Fujiwara no less. But he also had the self-denying strictness that was characteristic of his forefathers. It was going to be odd to watch him grow old in his hermitage; but then he probably would not have to: at any moment Kiyomori would remember that the last Genji was alive and now an adult, and order Tokimasa to kill him.

It was Masako herself who solved all three problems, not at a stroke but by starting five years of continuous swordplay. In 1179 she told her father that she had been on intimate terms with his captive for some time and that she would consider marrying nobody but Minamoto no Yoritomo. The lonely horse-rides were suddenly less mysterious. Her sister shuddered again at the thought of the least eligible bachelor in Japan, stroked her new kimono, and knew for a fact that she had got the better part of the dream bargain.

Tokimasa knew that the marriage would incur Kiyomori's rage and might spell the end of them all. But he had no desire to lose Masako. He consented to the match after a pre-betrothal interview with Yoritomo that was more like a council of war. He would distance his clan from the Heike and back his would-be son-in-law in a Genji uprising if the opportunity arose. The couple married that same year, without impediment from Kyoto where Kiyomori was too busy contriving Emperor Antoku's accession and his own regency to keep an eye on the provinces. Tokimasa habituated himself to the idea that he and the Hōjō now owed fealty to the Seiwa Genji, a greater clan of imperial descent which had suddenly been revivified by his wayward daughter. He proposed setting up Lord Yoritomo and Lady Masako in a domain of their own. They chose Kamakura on the coast to the north of Izu. Typically, Yoritomo favoured the place because one of his greatest ancestors had built a shrine there in 1063, whereas Masako liked it because it was a natural fortress, an east-facing bay shielded to the rear by an arc of mountains. It was agreed that they would settle there the following autumn.

The winter passed with frightening tranquillity. Then, on 9 April 1180, a message arrived from the capital, delivered by Yoritomo's uncle Yuki'ie Minamoto. It described the travails of Yorimasa Minamoto, a warrior and poet of great distinction who belonged to the Settsu Genji, a clan that had continued to provide the court with faithful champions throughout all these reversals. Yorimasa had finally sickened of Kiyomori. Having served the emperor and the Heike clan as a general, he had retired into the contemplative life. There he had witnessed the destruction and pilfering of Kyoto's temples by the Heike clan and the murder of dissident monks. All of which had compelled him to take up arms again, this time against the government. Yorimasa was, however, a devout man who was loyal to the Chrysanthemum Throne and so he had needed an imperial mandate to rebel. Since, unlike the Seiwa Genji, he had been free to operate inside Kyoto, he had managed to secure one. It came from Prince Mochihito, the second son and rightful heir of Go-Shirakawa who was enraged at having been first imprisoned with his father and then passed over in favour of Taira no Kiyomori's eighteen-month-old grandson, Emperor Antoku.

With the message came a letter from the prince. Deciding that he should

now conduct himself with the decorum befitting the leader of the Seiwa
Genji, Yoritomo followed the proper etiquette for receiving such a letter. He
changed into the formal but radically simple black garb that would become
his trademark and prayed to Hachiman, the Shinto god of war and protector
of the Japanese people. Masako and Tokimasa waited anxiously during these
preparations. At last Yoritomo opened the imperial letter and began to read:

> I order the Genji clan to destroy Taira no Kiyomori and his followers as
> quickly as possible since they are now in open revolt.
>
>   Kiyomori and his second son used military force to seize the capital,
> claiming that they acted under imperial orders. As a result they have brought
> ruin upon the nation. Using whatever pretext they wished, they arrested the
> Emperor Go-Shirakawa, and killed, exiled or imprisoned those who stood in
> their way. They have plundered the exchequer and removed its officers,
> imposed impossible taxes, awarded sinecures to relations, falsely accused and
> punished all opponents. Scholars and monks who have spoken out against
> them have been jailed and the tithes of rice and silk due to the temples have
> been sent instead to Heike clan members and mercenaries. They are destroying
> the Imperial Family, beheading the Emperor's ministers and defiling Buddhism.
> They are traitors who flout our great tradition. The Imperial Family is
> unhappy and so are the people. Therefore I, the second son of Go-
> Shirakawa . . . will demonstrate my legitimate title to the throne by destroying
> those who have seized power . . . I order the noble clans of the Genji and
> Fujiwara to rise up together and avenge themselves on these usurpers. If you
> do not comply you will be exiled or beheaded in the same way that we will
> punish the Heike clan. If you succeed, once I ascend the throne you will be
> rewarded with the restoration of the honours and possessions that are right-
> fully yours and with more besides.

Yoritomo folded the letter, bowed to it and handed it back to his uncle:
'You know where all the others are. Take this to them. Let them read it.'
Masako looked at Tokimasa: 'Well, Father, I think that settles it. Don't you?'

24

The Wars of the Lotuses

Refraction made it difficult to judge, as did its wave-like motion, but the snake looked about 2 metres long and, at its well-fed median, as thick as my wrist. It swam towards me, head held above the water with mesmerising dignity, its body threading through the lotus stalks. Set in a mask of coppery green, its eyes were topaz. They made contact with my own and sustained it. The approach quickened and I formed the view that it might be the prelude to an attack. With a few obvious exceptions, I had always operated on the basis of the old saw that, no matter how frightening the creature, it was probably more frightened of me than I was of it; that, unprovoked, it would not put itself in conflict's way. Now this snake was subverting that wisdom as he glided relentlessly in my direction. He actually seemed to be taking me on. A voice behind me said, 'Don't be alarmed. He only wants you to feed him.' I made a rapid assessment of my companion's English. There was no doubt that this serpent wanted to be fed, and by me; but by what part of me and with my consent or not? Then it became clear: the snake was tame, or as near to tame as such a creature could ever be.

Someone should have warned me that Lady Masako has snakes like San Marco has pigeons. Or perhaps I was meant to work it out for myself. They are, after all, completely in character for her – beautiful, dignified, unstoppable, predatory. This public space was once Masako's private garden. The snakes and lotuses have been there since 1182. It was a remarkable garden, even after all that time, and it somehow remained defiantly and exclusively

Masako's no matter how many visitors filled it. This was where she plotted, prayed and sometimes danced for victory, and where her stratagems were physically mapped out in the form of plants. This was where lotuses, eternal emblems of peace and resurrection, became battalions in horticultural war games.

The priest who watched over the garden explained that this type of snake was known as *Aodaishō*, 'the Blue General', 'blue' describing its verdigris scales and 'general' being a suitable rank for a creature of such dangerous dignity, and especially one so closely associated with the First Shogun, general of generals. I had to agree with him. The name was certainly better than Japanese rat snake or *Elaphe climacophora*, as this reptile is known in the West. He also pointed out that the snake had only appeared to have an unflinching visual fix on me. In reality he hunted chiefly by smell, tasting the air with his flickering tongue. 'But don't worry,' the priest continued as if he had insulted me, 'the Blue General had definitely chosen you. You were his target. Er, how to put it? You must, if you will forgive me, be differently scented to the usual visitors to the ponds. He doesn't approach them unless he can smell that they have some food for him. Their persons do not interest him. Yours does. You are honoured.'

Voracious rather than venomous, this colubrid is a creature of good omen. Farmers love him for his ratting skills, as do the inhabitants of traditional homes. The under-floor space of a Japanese house can be rodent heaven until the Blue General takes command. In Lady Masako's garden, however, he holds a more elevated office. The snake is a sacred animal of Benzaiten or Benten who became one of the most important Shinto deities, having arrived in Japan from India and via incarnations in the Vedic and Buddhist traditions. The goddess of flowing things, among them water and dance, music and language, wisdom and love, Benzaiten has an indefinably wide dominion. In Shinto mythology, she emerged from the sea at Enoshima, an island not far from Kamakura. It was this that led the founder of the department store and promoter of Japonisme, Arthur Lasenby Liberty, to describe the goddess as 'the Japanese Venus' when he visited the ancient capital in 1889. As far as any description of her could go, it is difficult to beat Liberty's Classical analogy: the water-born Benzaiten is a deity of beautiful things who is physically beautiful herself, but not without grit and guile, and a shape-shifter.

I conceded defeat in my staring competition with the snake and wandered off through the gardens of which he was master. Quite how anything so beautiful and immaculate in its execution could have been accomplished at such a time was beyond me. The landscape that prefaces Kamakura's Tsurugaoka Hachiman Shrine was not only designed by Yoritomo and Masako during a civil war in which they were protagonists, but the couple also planted much of it themselves. I was unsure what their determination to create such a paradise amid so much strife and uncertainty meant. Was it a token of their confidence in their ultimate victory, a refuge from the daily demands of battle, or an elaborate exercise in seizing the day? Yoko and the priest conferred and declared that it had probably been all three; that, even when faced with defeat, a samurai achieves victory by making the present as close to perfect as possible and reconciling himself with its passing. There was also, said the priest, another motivation behind all this gardening, at least on Lady Masako's part, and we would come to that shortly.

The events that led to the garden's creation were hardly propitious. On Prince Mochihito's orders and supported by his father-in-law and his new bride Masako, Yoritomo mounted a Genji rebellion against the Heike clan in the spring of 1180. There followed nineteen major battles and hundreds of lesser skirmishes in a five-year conflict which became known as the Genpei War, after the first syllables of the names of the two principal clans involved. After the first of these battles, Kiyomori, the imperial regent and Heike chief, decreed that all Genji who had received Prince Mochihito's seditious letter should be killed and by anyone who was in a position to do so regardless of rank or judicial process. Yoritomo was no longer an exile on borrowed time but a wanted man.

While Masako was giving birth to their first child, her husband went on the run. It was not a passive flight, however. He followed a strategy of hide-and-seek guerilla tactics, using a small troop of crack samurai to destroy the bounty hunters who pursued him and to impose Genji control on the various mountain villages where he sought refuge. Emboldened, he returned to his father-in-law's domain in Izu in late summer 1180 to see his new daughter Ō-Hime and to prepare for his family's long-awaited move to Kamakura. In the capital, Kiyomori caught wind of their departure for the new Genji head-quarters and sent an army to intercept them. The two sides met at Ishibashiyama in the Hakone Pass near Mount Fuji. It was the first full-scale battle in which Yoritomo led the Seiwa Genji as their clan chief. He lost and Masako's elder brother was killed. Convinced that he had dealt the Genji and Hōjō clans a fatal blow, Kiyomori decided not to press home his advantage and hunt down Yoritomo and Tokimasa. It would prove to be a bad decision.

Having regrouped, Yoritomo, Masako, family and retainers finally moved to Kamakura in October 1180. Their first action on arriving was to find a new location for a shrine to Hachiman, the great Shinto war god, that Yoritomo's ancestor Yoriyoshi had originally built in 1063 and which had long since been lost to fire. They found a suitable site on a sea-facing slope called the Hill of Cranes and began building the shrine that would be known as Tsurugaoka Hachiman-gū. They made their own home on the plain at the base of the hill, within the precincts of the new sacred compound. Contemporary records show that gardens were a priority for them even within a few months of their arrival in Kamakura, despite all the chaos outside their gates.

So far as the imperial court was concerned, the Genji chief and his lady now lived the life of provincial aristocrats with limited means and very much on sufferance. In and around Kamakura itself, however, people spoke already of Yoritomo's *Bakufu*, his 'tent government', and the Genji and Hōjō clans continued to plot their rebellion. Within a few months, much of the east was tending towards the rebel cause and accepting Kamakura's rule. Then in 1181, Taira no Kiyomori, the old Heike leader and imperial regent, died of surprisingly natural causes, precipitating the next phase of the Genpei War. Kiyomori's son and successor Munemori decided to exterminate the Genji and, foolishly, to do so on their home ground. The plan was already poor, but what would make it a disaster for the ruling Heike clan was the emergence of Yoritomo's two half-brothers, Yoshitsune and Noriyori. In 1160, they had been dispatched as infants to monasteries while the thirteen-year-old Yoritomo had been banished to Izu. Now they reappeared, aged twenty-two and twenty-five respectively, ready to become the Genji chief's most brilliant commanders.

'Now you know all that,' said the priest, 'we can return to the gardens.'

In the spring of 1182, Yoritomo ordained that the marsh at the foot of Tsurugaoka Hachiman-gū should be turned into a moat where rice could be planted and fish released as an offering to the gods. But Masako had a different idea, and as usual prevailed. There would be water, but it would take the form of two roughly circular ponds lying east and west, one on either side of the main avenue. These would be connected by a slender canal in a configuration that looked like a dumbbell in plan. Announced by a Torii gate, a great rainbow bridge would span the canal with an arc of sealing-wax red, marking the beginning of the compound. In other words, having crossed water to approach the Genji shrine and citadel, one would immediately feel encompassed by water. Around the gateway and ponds, the couple planted junipers and willows, some of which not only survive but are in astonishingly youthful fettle, having been pruned and groomed down the centuries. Masako alone, however, took responsibility for the contents of the two ponds. They were her garden and she threw herself into their creation with a fervour out of all countenance with the turmoil that threatened her new home or the fact that she was heavily pregnant with Yoriie, their second child and first son.

She had small islands constructed in both of them, but only in the eastern pond did any of these islands have a purpose. On the largest she built a small shrine to Benzaiten, reached by a smaller version of the great red rainbow bridge. An exquisite cottage in cinnabar and gold, the goddess's new home mirrored the bridges in colour and construction. Before it Masako erected a pergola covered in wisteria (*fuji*), symbol of longevity and a nod to her husband's Fujiwara ('Wisteria Field') blood. All around the shrine she planted cherry trees. In their shade she set up dovecotes: when the cherries were out of flower the trees should still be dressed with pure white plumage. Like improbably large blossoms, doves fill their boughs to this day, rarely leaving the island. Not that these birds are purely decorative. Like the Blue Generals that bask on the pond's shores and wind their way through its waters, they are sacred animals – in their case not to Benzaiten but to Hachiman, the god of war. Serene though it seems, nothing could be further in spirit from Christ's injunction to be 'wise as serpents, and harmless as doves' than this moated aviary. Above all, the doves were – are – white, not just the colour of Shinto purity but of something far more important in Lady Masako's view.

All of this might have been expected, was no less than it ought to be, even if it was happening in peculiarly interesting times. Shrines dedicated to the Japanese Venus were often created in watery places and as substations of larger religious complexes. Inevitably some of these were pools and sometimes colonised by lotuses. It was a tradition that began before Yoritomo and Masako took possession of Kamakura and it would continue long after them, culminating in Benzaiten's Island, created by the Tokugawa Shogunate in Shinobazu-no-ike, Edo's lotus-filled Secret Lake. Where Masako's garden differed was in the contents of the ponds themselves. She chose to plant lotuses where there were none before, borrowing a Buddhist emblem for a Shinto scheme. Moreover, her lotuses were directed to a very specific and worldly purpose. In the eastern pond around the goddess's shrine she planted a white variety. In the western pond she planted crimson. White was the clan colour of the Seiwa Genji, her family by marriage and former overlords of eastern Japan. Red or crimson was the colour of the insignia and livery of their hated foes the Heike, the megalomaniacal masters of the west who had triumphed over the Genji on their way to seizing control of the nation. In Yoritomo's Bakufu, the white lotus came to signify the home team while the pink stood for their adversaries. It was an identification that would endure for centuries afterwards.

Unable to ride into battle herself, Masako had decided to create a massive living diorama of the conflict using lotuses instead of troops. But it was more than an al fresco war room model: the garden was a place of prayer, ritual and offerings. She saw it as a spiritual generator whose energy could be marshalled towards eventual Genji victory, and she spent almost as much time there in religious observance as she did in calculating military strategy. There was one other important feature of this landscape – the water itself. For a realist who was always on the qui vive, Masako set great store by dreams even by the heady oneirocritical standards of her day. Around the time that she conceived her garden, Masako dreamed that Genji victory over the Heike would be secured not on land but water. The Genpei Ponds, as they became known, were a physical enactment of this dream. Three years later her lotus prophecy came true.

In March 1184, Yoritomo's half-brothers, Yoshitsune and Noriyori, destroyed the remaining Heike garrison in the Battle of Ichi-no-Tani at Suma near present-day Kobe. A natural fortress even more impregnable than Kamakura, it was taken by dividing the Genji samurai into three. One regiment attacked in conventional fashion from the coast, drawing the brunt of the Heike strength. The other two approached from the rear, ninja-style through the thickly forested slopes. It was a battle that would confirm Yoshitsune's reputation for tactical brilliance. In Kamakura meanwhile, Yoritomo and Masako planned and plotted, he with ink and paper, she with water and lotuses. The whites were doing well against the reds, but there was a great deal of blood still to be shed.

Led by Yoshitsune, the Genji now spent a year harrying the rump of the Heike troops and chasing them west along the Inland Sea. On 24 March

1185, they were brought to bay on Honshu's southern tip at the naval battle of Dan-no-Ura in the Shimonoseki Strait. It was conducted on an immense scale with all the available forces of both sides, a clash between 1,300 ships, 800 of them Genji, 500 of them Heike. Before long the conflict had spread from the fleets to the shallows and shores of the strait itself. With each samurai wearing either the white banner of the Minamoto or the red banner of the Taira, their watery mêlée at last made Masako's lotus dream materialise. The core of the army of Japan's ruling clan was shot down by Genji archers or died in sword fights, all in the space of a morning. It was a rout that had been heralded by the arrival of two white doves which are said to have settled on the leading ship of the Minamoto fleet. Hachiman, the god of war, was smiling on Yoritomo.

His arch-opponent, the Heike chief and imperial regent Taira no Kiyomori, had died of illness four years previously. It was left to his widow Tokiko to provide the extraordinary coda to the fall of his house. She had fled the capital with the Heike troops, accompanied by the six-year-old Emperor Antoku and his mother, Kiyomori's daughter the Dowager Empress Tokuko. As the battle turned against them, all three jumped overboard along with most of their entourage. The Genji managed to save Tokuko, but her son the boy emperor was drowned, as was Tokiko. The widow of the once all-powerful Heike chief disappeared beneath the waves clutching Kusanagi, the ancient sword which, with the mirror and the jewel, is one of Japan's three sacred imperial regalia. Desperate to deny the Genji authority, the surviving Heike attempted to consign the remaining regalia to the deep before drowning themselves. The jewel and the mirror were saved. According to the Genji chronicles, however, the sword remained on the Shimonoseki sea bed along with the Heike dead. Many believe that Japan's Excalibur lies there still. Not that Yoritomo felt the need of this trio of emblems to assert his supremacy: after Dan-no-Ura, his rivals were finished and Japan was his. Meanwhile, Masako prayed at Benzaiten's shrine and saw with pleasure that her lotuses were making faster progress than usual that spring.

'All the same,' I said to the priest as he explained these events, 'she was taking a risk. White lotuses are generally reckoned to be weaker than the ordinary pink variety.'

'I know,' he replied, 'but she seems to have chosen her white Genji lotus very carefully. As you can see, it's enormously strong. It fills the eastern pond and it even spreads along the canal and under the bridge towards the western pond. If we didn't discipline it from time to time, the white east would eventually overrun the pink west – which, I suppose, is exactly what Lady Masako intended. There is no record of this white variety ever having been replaced. It is exactly the same plant that Lady Masako chose – what? – 826 years ago and it has been living here all this time. Meanwhile, the pink Heike lotuses in the western pond never seem to do as well and have had to be replaced or augmented down the centuries.'

There was something odd about the Genji lotus. Its leaves were brighter green than most I had seen, not bluish or glaucous but a grasshopper green and very large. The flowers were smaller than one would find in the general run of cultivars and single, but they were produced in great abundance, pure white and held clear of the foliage in what can only be described as a constellation. And the plant was clearly possessed of formidable vigour. *Nelumbo* shuns the shadows and yet Lady Masako's lotus was as happy under willow boughs as it was at the water's shining heart. Its steady infiltration of the dark canal that joined the eastern and western ponds, and its lurking guerilla-like beneath the rainbow bridge before charging into Heike territory were feats of shade tolerance that I had seen in no other lotus. By comparison, the pink hasu in the Heike pond were a sorry sight. They did not seem to stand a chance against these white-bannered Genji insurgents.

Allowing for the fact that they are smaller, the Genpei Ponds today are much as they would have been when Masako created them, and the eastern pond especially – the willow-fringed, snake-charmed bowl of virginal lotuses with Benzaiten's shrine, dove-haunted and scarlet-beamed, at its centre. There is, however, one important difference between the Genji pond now and in the Middle Ages. In creating her garden, Masako had invented an unbeatable victory machine, a schematised, colour-coded sacred landscape that acted as a focus for winning strategies. On her lotus-skirted island, Benzaiten, the irenic goddess of shifting things, underwent a metamorphosis herself. Associated with Masako and the Genji ascendancy, Venus became rather more like Nike or Victoria. Over time she acquired a prefix, Kijō-Benzaiten, 'Benzaiten of the battle banner'.

It is a name that is taken literally at the Genpei Ponds. Warriors wore their colours into battle in the form of a rectangular flag that was supported by a cane and attached to their backs with the short ends top and bottom, like an immensely long menu card. Around the shores of the Genji pond and on Benzaiten's island there are hundreds of such flags, their canes inserted in the ground in forests of fluttering fabric. They are all the same colour – Genji white, of course, the linen land-born equivalent of the lotuses they surround. But every flag bears a different legend dramatically inscribed in cataracts of black characters. These are prayers and petitions to the victory goddess which can be had in exchange for an offering to the shrine. Written at the centre of each is an invocation of the deity herself; all around it are details of the favours being asked of her, the names of the petitioners and the date of their supplication. Walking among these legions of pleas, I was astonished at their specificity: Company X prays for success in a forthcoming takeover bid; Mr Y faces a life-or-death operation; Miss Z is worried about her exams. They ranged from couples who were having difficulty producing children, to parents who devoutly wished their offspring would leave home. It was an army of human troubles seeking peace around a sea of lotuses. I asked one of the flag-planters, a large-browed man of academic bearing, if he set much store by this ritual: 'It's always worked for me in the past. I do it every time I start writing a new book.'

Writing the flags was the task of the Shinto priest who is the guardian of the Genpei Ponds, the man who led me through their history and mysteries with such smiling patience. In late middle age and wearing brilliant white robes, he sat for much of the time in a kiosk beside the bridge to Benzaiten's shrine, surrounded by photographs of lotuses and jars of seeds and seed heads. Before I dared to disturb him, I sat on the bank for a half-hour watching as he first listened to a young couple's whispered worries, then produced an inkstone and brush and finally painted their petition in beautifully sweeping characters down a length of fabric. He appeared, I thought, more like a therapist than a votary, subjecting the couple to a concerned but penetrating scrutiny accentuated by his evident intelligence and wire-framed spectacles. Sitting in lotus-land all day making dreams come true was serious work and, as I discovered, underpinned by an immense knowledge not just of ritual and doctrine but also of past events and present realities. When at last I approached the priest, I found he was prepared to give me everything he knew, from the dietary habits of the Blue General to the ins and outs of the Wars of the Lotuses – everything except his name. He was, he said, simply a servant of Lady Masako's shrine and as such he had no name.

25

The Hill of Cranes

Masako's was not the first lotus I saw in Kamakura. Early that same day we had barely arrived in the city when I encountered a worried-looking businessman at the taxi rank outside Ōfuna Station. Beside his briefcase was a plastic bag containing a young hasu, three leaves and a fat magenta flowerbud. When he spotted me admiring his plant, his frustrated haste and compressed anxiety thawed into the sort of expression one would hope to be able to muster for a long-lost friend. He said he had just come from an early-morning plant sale in Yokohama and was running late. He was sorry that he could not give me the lotus; he would have liked to, but it was a cultivar that he had been particularly eager to find. He hoped I would understand. Now he was concerned about how the plant would cope with eight air-conditioned hours in his office. He explained that he grew many other varieties and would gladly give me some if we cared to visit his garden after work. Destined for the North that night, I had to decline. Troubled, he insisted that I should try to find a lotus somewhere since it was 'a happy plant'. I promised him I would do my best; but at that moment nothing could have made me happier than this evidence that the Edo Period plant-lovers' sodality was still in the pink.

Breakfast happened in a *kissaten*, a coffee shop that is more café than caff. On the wall beside me, an art deco poster showed a Japanese flapper and her brilliantined beau whispering sweet nothings to each other over a plate of brown sludge. Slowly I deciphered the name of the product being advertised from the faded katakana characters:

'*Ro-ma-n'-chi-kku-ka-ré, romanchikku karé*, hang on a minute – *Romantic Curry?* Have I made a mistake?'

'No, no,' said Yoko, 'it's a well-known brand, still available, I think, after seventy years. Would you like some? Or toast perhaps?'

Toast, I had learnt, was another import that exerted a fascination over the Japanese which many in its homelands would find hard to share. Some days before, I had discovered a magazine devoted to it – top-shelf toast, that *otaku* thing again. I stuck with *ampan*, the brioche buns filled with sweet adzuki bean paste that had become my morning staple.

Alongside the poster for Romantic Curry were signed black-and-white photographs of movie stars. Many of Yasujirō Ozu's company were there, actors whom I could not name but who had become familiar to me in the course of watching the director's bittersweet studies of life in post-war Tokyo and Kyoto: the lean moustachioed gent who always plays the long-suffering father; the pert daughter who reconciles rebelliousness with duty; the wry executive who has done better than his high-school chums and therefore chairs their endless sake-soaked reunions. Not snarling but smiling, an unusu-ally at-home Toshirō Mifune seemed to have forsaken sword and topknot for sports car, pipe and Harris Tweed. Near him hung a portrait of Isuzu Yamada who played his terrifying spouse in Kurosawa's 1957 film *Kumonosu-jō* ('Cobweb Castle') – Lady Washizu, for many the best-yet Lady Macbeth. I had difficulty placing her at first. The Noh mask make-up had been wiped away to reveal a face that was almost motherly in its fresh and open charm. The court kimono, whose hissing trail along the corridors of the doomed castle announces her Nosferatu-like entrances, had turned into twinset and pearls. Scattered among these cinematic greats were the framed dust jackets and autographed title pages of novels and volumes of poetry, among them *Yama no Oto* ('The Sound of the Mountain') in which Yasunari Kawabata meditates on Ōga's lotus.

The café's faded movie stars and first editions revealed much that was the making, or remaking, of Kamakura in the twentieth and twenty-first centuries. Until recently, the city was a centre of the film industry and home to actors and directors. It was also, and remains, a colony for writers and intellectuals, an off-site, sunny Quartier Latin an hour or so from Tokyo. The presence of talent has shaped Kamakura in the modern period almost as much as the exercise of power did in the Middle Ages. The glamour of the one and the relics of the other make for a strangely chimerical city, as does its location, hidden in a horseshoe of dense mountain forest which embraces one of the country's most beautiful bays. Beyond, an apparition floats mid-sky like a vast white lotus bud – the distant summit of Mount Fuji, visible even from the beach and snow-capped even when it is too hot to sunbathe.

The city was not always so urbane. From the seventeenth century onwards, a surprising number of foreign visitors made the pilgrimage to see Kamakura's most famous sight, Daibutsu, the 13.5-metre-tall bronze image of the seated Amida Buddha which was erected in 1252. Allowing for the facts that a tsunami had washed away his protective hall in 1498, leaving his head bare to the elements, and that the earliest (English) tourists had carved their names on his hollow interior, they found the Buddha a vision of serene composure. They rarely reported the same of Kamakura itself. Access to the city involved negotiating one of seven passes – narrow gorges, steep-walled and thickly overgrown, through the mountains that surrounded the coastal settlement. When the sightseers emerged blinking on the other side, they found themselves confronted not by the great sweep of civilisation Kamakura's reputation had given them to expect, but by a natural amphitheatre that was even more densely wooded than the terrain they had just left.

Deep in the thickets, they spotted bamboo-punctured roofs and regiments of vine-strangled statues which hinted at fallen palaces. Once great avenues had diminished into forest tracks; shops and houses had dwindled to the condition of sparse country shacks. And yet here and there, soaring amid all the vegetation and dilapidation, was a temple or shrine. The tourists noted that apart from a few inn-keepers, the population consisted chiefly of priests, monks and nuns who lived among these buildings in an unchanged state as if they were an isolated tribe. By the second half of the nineteenth century Kamakura was that favourite thing of travellers – a lost city, guarded by a stockade of peaks and an army of trees, abandoned by all but a time-forgotten priestly caste, its glories largely ruined and returned to Nature. Its mysteries moved Kipling to poetry and furnished Pierre Loti with the elegiac centrepiece of his *Japoneries d'Automne*. Most of my Victorian lotus-seekers had savoured its jungly dereliction. Many remarked on the Genpei Ponds, although unaware of the woman who made them.

These past glories, but not the manner of their passing, were all to the credit of Masako and Yoritomo. Within a decade of settling in Kamakura, the couple had brought the entire country under their control and their home had become its administrative capital. By 1192, when the court finally granted Yoritomo the title of shogun, the nation had been his for some years. A half-century later, Kamakura was not only Japan's largest city but one of the largest in the world. Its might was secured as much by Masako as by the Genji chief himself. When Yoritomo, sick and exhausted, died in 1199, Masako took Buddhist vows and donned the robes of a religious recluse. In practice, however, she remained out of the cloister and in the shogunate's ministries, hatching strategy, chairing meetings, pooling intelligence and pronouncing judgement. In her early forties the warrior princess and shogun's widow was reborn as one of the most remarkable figures in Japanese history. Shaven-headed and prepared for a life of prayer and contemplation, Masako now wielded more temporal power than ever, and would do so right up until her death in 1225. She acquired the nom de guerre by which she has been known ever since, Ama Shōgun, 'The Nun Shogun'.

The fishing-village-turned-metropolis flourished until 1333 when the administration that the couple founded fell, bringing to an end the era known as the Kamakura Period. Then came the long years of decay and hypertrophy that culminated in the picturesque spectacle of Japan's forsaken capital. Despite this the triumph of Yoritomo and Masako was a revolution that transformed Japan and shaped the Japanese character. Its political innovations – chiefly the division of powers between the shogun as executive ruler and the emperor as constitutional monarch – lasted for over 600 years until the restoration of the Meiji Emperor to direct rule in 1868. Many would say its repercussions can still be felt. Its ethos and ethics are certainly flourishing.

Although he was not the first commander to be named Sei-i-tai-shōgun by a margin of about 400 years, Yoritomo was the first to use the honour – which originally referred only to subjugating the barbarous north – as a charter for ruling the whole of Japan. For this reason he is often described as the First Shogun. It was Yoritomo too who first elevated the idea of a battlefield command post to the status of a permanent regime with nationwide dominion that ran parallel to the Chrysanthemum Throne it ostensibly served. As he intended its name – Bakufu, 'tent government' – should suggest, this form of administration would never lose sight of its roots in warfare.

There was more to this continuous battle-readiness than actual strategic need or bloodlust. Yoritomo owed his ascendancy to a new class of retainer-cum-warrior, the *bushi* or, as they are more familiarly known, samurai. He counted himself one of them and he planned to control the nation by using them as the agents of his system of centralised feudalism. They would run Japan rather than the old aristocracy or the new class of sycophant-turned-protection-racketeer that had come to dominate the imperial government; and they would run it with the peacetime equivalent of *bushidō*, the chivalrous, honour-bound code that had served them so well in war. For a society that was so hierarchical and so conscious of lineage, theirs was a meritocratic elite. Commoners and even Emishi, the Jōmon-descended 'northern barbarians', were among Yoritomo's best-respected officers. A first-class nobody from the back of beyond was far more likely to gain favour than a third-class somebody from Kyoto. Excellence in their allotted roles, ability to act collectively, adherence to the warrior code and unswerving loyalty were what conferred their nobility, and confirmed their samurai status.

In theory, the role that Yoritomo negotiated for himself was one of limited powers. The emperor and his advisors would govern Japan from Kyoto. Based in Kamakura, at a self-imposed distance from the court, Yoritomo would enforce their mandate, using imperial authority and his own military might to defend the nation, to bring an end to territorial and clan disputes, and to secure tax revenues through a system of tight governance and surveillance. In practice, he was soon very much more than the emperor's strong man; in fact, he was never really the emperor's man in any sense. But he was no Cesare Borgia either. He seems to have had no interest in wealth or love of power for power's sake, and certainly no designs on the throne. His ambitions were for the nation itself, a vision of orderly rule and steadily improving conditions. These would be imposed by strata of society who until recently had been little more than mercenaries and servants: his samurai were still an elite, but they were a far more extensive and earthy elite than the functionaries of the imperial court. He also made a point of living beneath his means and station and of instilling his cult of simplicity in those who were close to him. Spartan rather than Philistine and purist rather than puritan, this cult was a long-established Genji attitude that had been sharpened during his years of exile and guerilla combat. If provincial rulers had reasons to resent paying taxes, the idea that Yoritomo was living like a king would not be one of them.

Compiled during his lifetime and with astonishing candour, the official Bakufu chronicle *Azuma Kagami* is full of instances of Yoritomo's love of life – his gardening, hunting and womanising. But it also details his passionate austerity. In one such episode a senior official is summoned to discuss a matter of great importance with the shogun. The vassal arrives for his audience wearing a kimono in multicoloured silk with sleeves that trail on the floor. Before the man has a chance to kneel, Yoritomo draws his sword and lops off these gaudy sleeves, leaving his retainer's hands and arms unscathed: 'That's all I wanted to say. You can go now.'

But by far the most important manifestation of this pared-down approach was the physical form his government took. Yoritomo separated rule from ritual, focusing on the former and leaving the latter to Kyoto. Gone was the Hydra-headed bureaucracy of the Heian court with its semi-imperial and self-interested ministers squabbling over matters of no practical importance and its effete cohorts of eunuch-like placemen. Gone too were engorged and grandiose henchmen like Kiyomori, the late Heike chief.

Instead the entire burden of government was placed on just three main bureaux – the Office of Retainers, the Administrative Office and the Office of Inquiry. These dealt with domain and military issues, finance and projects, and judicial matters respectively. None of them occupied anything larger than a single wooden building and each was staffed by a small personnel selected on the basis of ability. The method of these streamlined ministries was collective responsibility: a question had to be debated and a consensus reached before a recommendation was presented to the shogun, *primus inter pares*, for ratification. This method has remained Japan's favoured approach to decision-taking ever since, whether launching a new car or awarding a prize to a pot plant. There was only one higher counsel, one final court of appeal, the opinion of Lady Masako. Although she had no formal role within the administration, *Azuma Kagami* makes it clear that her instincts and judgement often either gave rise to policy or were sought to test it. Even the most powerful officials and battle-hardened warriors went in awe of her. The pillow talk of the shogun and his lady resulted in a nation's conception.

Yoritomo's ostentatious modesty only went so far. The man in black was still capable of magnificence and especially where the arts were concerned. But, as with his wife and her lotus ponds, he needed to find meaning in it, and a proper occasion for it. He found both in designing the beacon of his new capital, the complex of buildings and landscapes that form Tsurugaoka Hachiman-gū, 'The Crane Hill Shrine of Hachiman'. His new creation would honour his ancestor Yoriyoshi who first built a shrine to Hachiman, the eight-battle-bannered god of war 117 years earlier on the coast nearby, a shrine that had long since disappeared during the Genji nadir. It would

241

provide a spiritual hub from which administrative and military initiatives could radiate as if with kami-generated energy. It would give his fast-expanding city a focus of inescapable grandeur that would be not so much its heart – Kamakura's topography would not allow that – as its head held high.

He built the senior shrine on the sea-facing slope of the Hill of Cranes, the central and largest of the peaks that guarded his stronghold. Seated on an eminence skirted with massive cut boulders, it dominated the landscape with strategic command: this was a shrine to the god of war that was also an unassailable citadel. From the midpoint of its inner sanctum a line proceeded down the ramparts in the form of a vast stone stairway, extended through a lower courtyard which housed the junior shrine, and crossed the plain to form the main avenue of the complex before exiting between Masako's lotus ponds. This great axis then became a boulevard of Haussmann-like proportions which ran to the sea and the site of Yoriyoshi's original shrine. As the Bakufu prospered and Kamakura grew, this road was transected by others, all of them bevelled to avoid flooding and lined with ornamental cherry trees. Within a few decades, the grid formed by these highways would teem with more than a million souls. Meanwhile, inside the precincts of the sacred citadel, Yoritomo's and Masako's home and the offices of government barely transcended their original humility – wood and paper, lightly ornamented if at all, and sheltered by the mountain groves that the couple had first declared to their liking in 1179.

No such restraint was shown when it came to the shrine itself. The avenue that is the city's spine sweeps through the compound of Tsurugaoka Hachiman-gū before marching up the mountainside in the form of 61 giant steps. Looming from the luciphyllous forest at their summit is the senior shrine, a massive construction in scarlet-lacquered wood detailed with gilt and turquoise. Tiled in unglazed ash-grey ceramic, its swooping roofs catch the sunlight and shimmer like old silver. Each row of tiles ends in an embossed disc fashioned in the shape of a lotus seed receptacle, and the stone lanterns that surround the ramparts are likewise representations of the lotus.

Atop its stone staircase, I found this structure distinctly unnerving, almost Aztec in its power. The awe it produces is, I suspect, what Yoritomo and Masako intended. If so, we would have been in a minority of three that day. The hundreds of other visitors, pilgrims and petitioners, were sunny-faced without exception. Like many Shinto shrines, Tsurugaoka Hachiman-gū is a happy place, not only a venue for prayer and life's rites of passage, but also a forum for meeting, idling, doing the *passeggiata*. Seated on the tatami-covered floor of the senior shrine's reception hall were family parties of all generations. In their arms, dressed in pristine miniature kimonos and strangely quiet, were babies undergoing the ritual of *Omiyamaira*, the first shrine visit which is comparable to baptismal blessing. Within the junior shrine at the foot of the stone staircase, a wedding ceremony was taking place, a beauti-fully choreographed public rite accompanied by a small *Gagaku* orchestra, a classical court ensemble of the kind that has been playing there, instruments and sheet music unchanged, since Yoritomo's time. Their sound followed me wherever I went in Tsurugaoka Hachiman-gū, into the innermost chambers of the hilltop sanctum, all through the surrounding woodlands. Gagaku seemed to me to be a kind of unfolding landscape, a sequence of spaces and discoveries that was the shape in sound of Kamakura.

At the foot of the stairway on the left-hand side soars Dai Ginkyō, the Great Ginkgo, a living pagoda some 50 metres tall, its trunk girt with the hempen ropes and white paper *shide* that declare this tree is sacred. This specimen of *Ginkgo biloba* was already a giant, at least 200 years old, when Yoritomo built his shrine above and around it. Along with the terrain's strategic advantages and propitious geomancy, the mysterious presence of this sacred tree was a deciding factor as he looked for a site for his head-quarters. He was right to think it portentous, but not in the way that he would have wished.

On a snowy February night in 1219, Sanetomo, Yoritomo's second son and the third Kamakura Shogun, was cut down by an assassin who had been hiding behind the ginkgo. The killer was his own nephew, dispossessed and disenchanted. Rules of succession within the Seiwa Genji were peculiarly strict – only a legitimate son of the last chief could inherit his title and control of the family. The murder of the childless Sanetomo deprived the clan of any hope of a future head. Although Masako, the Nun Shogun, and her Hōjō kin would battle on, the main line of the Seiwa Genji expired in the snow at the foot of the Great Ginkgo. But while the clan was decapi-tated in 1219, I was about to discover that the Genji themselves were alive and well.

26

And the lotos rose, quietly, quietly

Late that night we arrived in Sendai. Spread on a plain between mountains and the Pacific, this settlement of around a million souls is the capital of Miyagi Prefecture and the largest city in Tōhoku, the northern region of Honshu. In Yoko's family home, I was led to a suite of rooms constructed in traditional style which would be our base for the next few days. Decanting my belongings into a cupboard, I disturbed what appeared to be bolts of cloth wrapped in paper. I lifted a corner and found layer upon layer of silks of different weights and colours. 'I see you've found my kimono collection,' said Yoko, whom I had never seen wearing Japanese dress in our entire time together. 'Have a look. This one might interest you botanically. It's for a wedding – not my wedding, you understand, but for me to wear at the marriage of a member of my family.'

She lifted out a fantasia in heavy peach crepe which shimmered in the low light of the lamps dotted around the floor. Its bottom half was decorated with a frieze of plants and creatures of good omen – cranes and turtles, bamboo and iris, chrysanthemum and wisteria – as if the kimono were the collapsible version of a painted screen. It was not the fauna and flora that held my attention, however, but a small emblem printed on the reverse of each sleeve and, again, between the shoulders. I knew enough to know it was a *mon*, a personal mark, or a *kamon*, a family crest.

These devices are far from the complex symbolism and quarterings of European coats-of-arms. They are simple motifs, often derived from Nature.

The kamon, for example, of the Fujiwara clan shows two tresses of stylised wisteria (fuji) blossom, a visual pun on their name. The personal, rather than clan mon of Minamoto no Yoritomo was the *sasarindō*, a design in which three flowers of rindō (the Japanese gentian, *Gentiana scabra* or G. *makinoi*) sit above three leaves of the shrubby bamboo *Sasa*. The gentian was characteristic of the damp grassland flora of Southern Japan, while the bamboo was a signature plant of the North. This elegant posy is iconographic code for the shogun: the North is subjugated by the South; the country united under his military authority. The Heike clan took the swallowtail butterfly as their badge, suitably flamboyant and fugacious for the high-rolling tribe routed by Yoritomo's Genji.

Studying Yoko's kimono, I felt I had seen the same insignia somewhere before and recently. It was circular and faintly reminiscent of the imperial chrysanthemum motif but with a prominent hub and thick radiating divisions. I looked again and began to form the notion that it might be based on the leaf veins or the transected rhizome of the lotus. She knew me well enough to know what this small seizure of interest meant.

'I hope you don't mind my asking, but what is that?'

'It's my family crest.'

'I know that, but what is it?'

'I can see where this is going. No, it's nothing to do with lotuses. You see them everywhere. Thank God you're not researching phallic emblems. It's a wheel. Can't you see the spokes? We call it the *Guruma*.'

'I see now. When were your family granted it?'

'You mean my ancestors. Rather a long time ago.'

'And what does it mean, this wheel?'

'I'm not entirely sure. It's called the Genji Guruma. Different families use different versions of it. That doesn't mean they're all Genji, but in my family's case, I'm afraid it does.'

'Why've you never mentioned this before? Why didn't you say so at the shrine?'

'It was all such a long time ago. Try not to think about it.'

Although there are excellent cultural reasons why an artist might wish to settle in Sendai, it was characteristic of Yoko's father, Hōyō Ōtsuki, that he should have owned to simpler motives. This man who, by the time of his death in 1993, was hailed as one of the greatest calligraphers in a nation where calligraphy is one of the greatest arts, found some first-class spots for fishing along Sendai's rivers and seashore. Since this pleasure was, he insisted, an essential adjunct to creativity, he decided to bait his hooks and put down roots. Unlike Tokyo, this northern city also granted Ōtsuki-sensei a *sine qua non* even more vital than angling, something that was not so much a respite from his art as an indispensable second outlet for it. In Sendai the master found space to make a garden.

In Japan the connection between word, image, music and garden is deep. They are all aspects of the same aesthetic, all awarded the same prestige. My first glimpse of the calligrapher's private paradise convinced me, however, that it was an important garden by any culture's standards. It was full of a strange magic that I could sense but could not dissect. As she led me around it, Yoko's mother Toyo Ōtsuki explained that the key to this mystery resided less in the garden's components than in the spaces between them, the *Ma*. This was the key to much more besides: 'Grasp it,' she said, 'and you will understand our calligraphy, music and gardens.' With that she fell silent, gazing at a swallowtail butterfly that had settled to sun itself in calm ecstasy on a rock beside us. A better example of *Ma* I could not imagine.

At a third of an acre, the garden was large by Japanese standards. Before its high walls stood ranks of conifers, a mixture of sugi (*Cryptomeria japonica*) in the densely ball-forming cultivar known as 'Birōdo' ('velvet') and hinoki (*Chamaecyparis obtusa*). Pruned into asymmetric shapes, these trees were sculptural experiments or essays in calligraphy. With pads and plumes of foliage on slender branches that snaked from ramrod trunks, each was a series of splashes of dark intensity thrown into space as if to be caught by the limbs of its neighbour. Graphic and idiosyncratic, they resembled a procession painted by Miró. At the feet of these trees ran evergreen hedging, pruned to achieve sinuous rather than straight lines, giving the appearance of movement, of being molten, in fact. It was made up of a wide variety of evergreens, from the broad glossy foliage of *Aucuba* to the small glittering leaves of azaleas. This, I discovered, had been the intention. Ōtsuki-sensei had been fascinated by the potential of monochrome and by textural variations: the hedge was all green, but its greens were all different. Here chlorophyll was calligrapher's ink.

From these walls, the garden sloped gently downwards to form an arena that faced the engawa, the low wooden verandah at the rear of the house. Here the master used to sit, drink tea and think or (far more important) *not* think. Nearby aged and leviathan koi once circled in a large pond, the garden's dominant feature, fed by a waterfall and a series of smaller pools, each traversed by stepping stones. Completely tame, the fish would gather and surface at the slightest sound emanating from the engawa, eager for food. Koi is a homophone for the Japanese word for affection. As old as or perhaps older than the calligrapher, these cupboard-loving carp died soon after him, mysteriously and certainly through no neglect. Since then the pond and its tributaries had been left empty. The only remaining water was a spout that fell from a standing stone into an overflowing *tsukubai*, a basin roughly hewn from granite and thick with moss. This slender cascade filled the garden with music.

Written in the eleventh century, the world's oldest surviving garden design manual, *Sakuteiki*, defines gardening as 'the art of setting stones'. Hōyō Ōtsuki had achieved a kind of lapidary calligraphy. Sometimes sombre and soaring, at other times supine and sun-soaked, stones were his ink as well as vegetation. He drew with them, defining spaces, dictating moods, punctuating passages of planting. Studying their arrangement, and the naturalism with which they had been graded from monolith to gravel, I realised the garden was an archipelago, a shoal of crags and shores each bearing its burden of greenery. The pleasure and fascination it exerted lay in the visual navigation of these islands glimpsed from the tatami-covered floor of the house and between half-open shōji screens. Although the largest rocks stood 6 feet tall, I was astonished to learn this was only half their actual size. Yoko's mother explained: 'We bury much of the rock. Earthquakes, you see. We have so many tremors. A house can fall and be rebuilt, but you make a garden for ever.' One evening when something sounding like a monstrous subway train passed under the house with a rattling of screens and a trembling of lamps, I noticed she did not even look up from her sewing.

'You make a garden for ever.' This seemed to be holding good in Ōtsuki-sensei's garden. The menhirs, marls, and miniature mountain ranges composed by this artist of the rooted world had merely weathered and grown more settled amid the cushions, colonies and corridors of foliage. Time and the slight dishabille that had overtaken the garden in the master's absence gave it the appearance of having long preceded him and Sendai city itself, a primeval permanence as of some dolmen or henge. And yet such was the discipline of the original design that cosmos had still not become chaos. Only the bone-dry pond betrayed his departure.

Along a sunny wall ran a series of low square bays. Brick-edged and filled with gritty sand, they looked like the remnants of cold frames in some long-abandoned English kitchen garden. These were the pond's filtration tanks. In happier times its waters were pumped through the sand, retrieved and recycled. 'I should really get rid of them,' said Ōtsuki-san. 'They seem point-less now the pond is empty. And they are not exactly beautiful. We used to stand pots of lotuses on the sand and their leaves would camouflage the edges. But that was then. I wouldn't know where to find lotuses now, and they're such big plants, such a lot of heavy lifting. It was my husband's thing, this garden, so you must excuse areas like this that haven't really survived him.'

I had begun to despair of the lotus rhizomes that Taeko-san gave me. They had been languishing unannounced in plastic bags and sodden lavatory paper in a corner of our suite. If the garden had been in full flight and the master still presiding, I doubt I would have dared to impose them on him. In his absence and with the garden frozen as a memorial to him in stone and tree, the notion seemed little short of sacrilege. But something had to be done with my charges, and so I took Ōtsuki-san's explanation of the filter bays as my cue, retreating indoors and returning with the lotuses in their two-ply stew. She recognised this offering at once, but did nothing to dispel my fear that I was the worst kind of house-guest, the man who arrives with a gift that demands attention and space, the well-meaning bearer of a Rottweiler pup. Without a word, Ōtsuki-san darted into the house, leaving me with the plants and a crushing sense that I had blundered. A few moments later, she reappeared, dressed, it seemed, for golf complete with eye-shade and footwear for tricky terrain. There was a fabulous smile, which put me back at ease, but then a very firm command:

'Quickly, Yoko-san – the car. I want to go to Daishin. Come on. There's no time to lose.'

I had expected another temple or shrine. I soon discovered that Daishin ('Big Push Forward') was a DIY superstore on the outskirts of Sendai. Here the gardener's customary weaponry – the spades and secateurs that are the same the world over – sat alongside endemic tools whose design and crafts-manship had not changed in centuries: lance-like saws for taming unruly trees, ampersand-shaped shears for performing keyhole surgery on bonsai, fiendishly clever hybrids of trowel and sickle for deep-rooted weeds. Their finely tempered, beech-handled blades looked antique, anomalous, like a samurai and ninja kit concession in the midst of an arms fair. My retail ethnology yielded some unwelcome surprises as well. All around me consumers were devouring English roses and hellebores – gaijin plants. Car boots were being loaded with bushels of half-hardy annuals, fodder for the non-Japanese Japanese gardener's latest obsession, the hanging basket, one horticultural confection for which hanging is surely too good.

These humdrum exotics should not really have surprised me. For much of the world, gardening is about borrowing other nations' plants and plans. Just a fortnight before, had I not noticed that my own local equivalent of Daishin was full of *Aspidistra* and *Cycas*, *Miscanthus* and *Hosta*, camellias and bamboos, all Japanese in origin? But that was no comfort. In the plants they house and the styles they espouse, British gardens have been omnivorous, international since Roman times. Their eclecticism is what characterises them. By contrast, the Japanese garden is largely home-grown apart from early Chinese influences, and to our eyes strikingly homogeneous. It is the product of a preoccupation with indigenous plants and native tradition, a flowering in seclusion. Why did it need Day-Glo petunias? For Japan's sake, I dreaded the possibility of these annuals becoming perennial favourites.

It took Ōtsuki-san to save me from vicarious chauvinism. She was waving at a row of ceramic bowls of various sizes, without drainage holes and, I could not help thinking, rather beautifully glazed for a DIY superstore.

'Here they are. Thank heavens – I thought we'd be too late. We'll need them all. Please hurry.' They were bowls for growing lotuses. We were indeed running late in the horticultural schedule and only ten of them were left.

'I'm sorry,' the shop assistant explained, 'we had dozens a few weeks ago, but we sell so many.'

'More than hanging baskets?' I asked.

'Yes,' the girl replied, 'many more than hanging baskets, in fact more and more as the years go by. That must seem strange to someone from abroad like you who must have seen how lovely hanging baskets can be. Perhaps that's why you're smiling?'

Having bagged the bowls for us, the shop assistant began loading me up with other lotus prerequisites – fishmeal (tuna, I suspect) with a bouquet so fine that it might have made a passable stock, and sacks of soil the colour and consistency of Christmas pudding but with a mass that put me more in mind of lead. While I staggered to the car, the girl danced alongside me explaining:

'I don't know how it's done elsewhere in Japan, but this is how we grow lotuses in Sendai. The black earth comes from a mountain not far from here. It's very special.'

It was not until some time later that I found myself agreeing with her, when I saw the source of this soil – Mount Zaō, a volcano whose slumbering crater stands some 1,800 metres above sea level. But even there in the car park, my multicultural misgivings were falling away. Never mind petunias, this was traditional Japanese horticulture.

Two hours later we were sipping tea on the engawa. Before us, basking in the lotus bays in the hottest part of the garden, were the ten bowls ranging in size from a tank to a tureen and in colour from ginger biscuit to forest green raku. In their bottoms we had spread a layer of half-rotten garden compost. Over it, to a depth of two thirds of each container, had gone the volcanic gold anointed with a dash of fish dust. Into this dark substrate, I had firmed the fragile rhizomes. Finally, Ōtsuki-san had filled the bowls with tap water, lotus poison in much of Great Britain, but perfect in a place where Mount Zaō and its kinsmen are just over the horizon. This had brought the first leaves bobbing to the brim. Now, with all completed, she turned to me and quietly said:

'I must apologise for having made you rush like that.'

'Apologise? Never. You were quite right to hurry. They needed to be planted. I should be apologising to you. After all, I've turned up here with these plants and imposed them on Ōtsuki-sensei's garden.'

'Ah – then you really haven't understood the need for all the urgency. If things go well, I will explain it to you later. As for my husband, he will love these lotuses. But let's wait and see.'

In late August, I received a letter that made it clear I had not misheard her:

Within a few weeks of your leaving Japan, the lotuses that Goto-san so kindly gave you had grown so much that it was no longer possible to see the bowls. I took great care of them. I attended to their water daily, even in the rainy season. You will think that odd or a trifle fussy, but the lotus for us is so wrapped up in ideas of purity, and our young plants needed to know that they were loved. By the beginning of this month, the leaves were as tall as my shoulders. Then, to my huge excitement and relief, I noticed the first flower buds. In this great heat we have had, the stalks developed at the rate *of a foot a day before stopping at about my height.*

It was now the beginning of the second week of August. As the flower buds swelled and began to show a little colour, I realised that I had a chance of achieving the goal I had in mind when I rushed you around the superstore in June. I promised then that I would tell you what the fuss was about. Now I can report success, here is my overdue explanation.

We have a ceremony in Japan, called Obon. It was first performed early in the seventh century by the female Emperor Suiko. I use that rather awkward phrase for her because she ruled in her own right and was not an empress in the sense of an imperial consort. She was also a pioneer of Buddhism in Japan, in which Obon came to play a major part.

For centuries afterwards, this ceremony was observed only by the members of the court, aristocrats, samurai and monks. This was for a very simple reason. Obon requires candles and was therefore very expensive. It was not until the Edo Period when candles became cheaper that it grew in popularity. By the nineteenth century this ceremony had grown into a national festival. Everybody celebrated Obon and that is still the case today – so much so that it is our main holiday after New Year and the nation becomes frantic as people return to their family homes to conduct the rites and prepare for the festivities. Obon falls over a period of five days and at one of two times: those who follow the old calendar mark it in July; the rest of us do so in mid-August. The latter is the more common time for the feast, but so popular is it that I sometimes think our country would seize up completely if we did not have the alternative dates. You will have noticed that it takes a lot to make us Japanese stop work. You can deduce the importance of Obon from that.

You must be wondering what it is that could do this to us. Obon is the time when the spirits of our dead ancestors and loved ones return to visit us. It is our duty, and our pleasure, to make their homecoming as easy as possible, to welcome and feed them, to pray for them, and then, after a few days spent in their company, to bid them farewell and speed them on their way back to the other world.

I will describe what all of this involves, but first let me explain my excitement and our panicky preparations in June. Candles and lanterns are integral to Obon, but so too is the lotus. We cannot celebrate this joyful reunion and sad departure without it. Every year many millions of cut lotus flowers and leaves are sold for the event throughout Japan. I usually buy

251

the flowers from florists; but, live as they are, these do not have the special potency of lotuses that one has actually planted and watched growing. You see, the longer and more painstaking the preparations, the happier the eventual homecoming. There is also the risk, the waiting and hoping for the flowers to open on time, and the feeling that their success, were they to hit the target, would be especially auspicious. After all, we couldn't be sure of succeeding with ten bowls of lotuses. August may be their flowering time, but the blooms last just for a day or two and the dates of Obon are fixed. Finally, I need not tell you, since it was why you came here, that the lotus is our symbol of rebirth. When I can watch the whole progress of the plant, see the leaves and buds develop, catch the flowers in the dawn at the moment of their opening, this becomes less like a symbol and more like a reality.

Obon begins for me in early August. This is when I start giving my late husband's grave – our family grave – and the area surrounding it a thorough clean. I do the same to the house and garden. On 12 August I close the doors of the family shrine. You must have noticed it, the cabinet standing here in the drawing room. Westerners tend to call it a 'shrine', I suppose, because it is small and private, devoted to family members only. In fact the daily rites we perform before it are Buddhist, so strictly speaking you might be safer calling it a temple. Whatever you wish to call it, I close its doors on the 12th. This is to stop the returning spirit of my late husband being received inside the shrine. 'Why?' you must wonder. Well, this is a great occasion and it is not done to welcome a loved one into the place where we pray every day: we want to keep him, just for a short while, outside the usual sacred enclosure so that we can be with him.

13 August, the day after this closing, is called Mukae bon, 'the welcoming of the spirit'. By now I have removed my husband's ihai, [his memorial tablet], and the altar fittings from inside the shrine. I place them on a specially constructed Bon shelf that stands like a table before the shrine. Traditionally this shelf is made from bamboo. In the past it would have been hung with red or white aubergines and herbs. In front of the ihai and altar fittings go two bowls known as Mizunoko and Akamizu. Both are lined with lotus leaves. In the Mizunoko bowl I must serve a mixture of diced aubergine, cucumber and washed rice grains. The Akamizu bowl is filled with pure water. Beside this water bowl, the ceremony dictates that I must place a bunch of misohagi [Lythrum anceps], a beautiful riverside herb with magenta flowers. This is used as a sort of whisk-cum-scoop. From now on, while

praying, I dip the misohagi in the Akamizu bowl and then use it to transfer the water, little by little, into the Mizunoko bowl. With this ritual we feed the returning spirit who is starving and thirsty after his journey from the other world.

But I am not yet done with the Bon shelf. On either side of it, I place vases filled with lotus flowers – this year, our lotus flowers. Elsewhere on the shelf I arrange offerings of incense and food, and especially things that my husband liked. This food is served on fresh lotus leaves – this year, our lotus leaves. To these I add two further vegetables, but not for eating. They are cucumber and aubergine, which are meant to be a horse and an ox respectively, both with wooden sticks pushed in for legs. The spirit is supposed to use the horse to come home swiftly and the ox to return to the other world slowly. Not every household is as happy as ours, however. Where the deceased are no more welcome than they were in life, the roles of these animals are reversed. These unfortunate spirits are invited to use the ox first and the horse second – arrive late, leave early. Or so, at least, I am told. You may believe it if you wish, or simply regard it as a Japanese joke.

Now the scene is set. On the afternoon of the 13th the family visits the graveyard. There we use a burning stick of incense to light a lantern. As darkness falls we carry it back to the house. The flame it contains is the returning spirit of the departed and with it we light another, special lantern on the Bon shelf. This personifies our loved one, home at last.

14 and 15 August are Bon chūnichi, 'mid Bon'. Over this period we offer our visitor the same food as the rest of the family, three times a day. We may ask a priest to visit the house in order to chant; we often invite family and friends to dine with us and the returned spirit. Above all, we are careful to keep the lantern burning.

The 16th is Okuri Bon, the day of leave-taking. Until dusk it proceeds much as the previous two days. After sunset, we light a farewell fire in front of the house and prepare ourselves for our visitor's departure. Remember he is the fire in the lantern, so with this same flame we light a candle. We put this candle within a cylinder or box made of translucent paper, together with a little of the offering food. Only now can the lantern on the Bon shelf be extinguished. To reach the other world, the spirits of the departed must cross water. So we place the candle in its paper house in a tiny craft – perhaps just a bamboo raft, although I have seen some rather showy model yachts in recent years. Then we carry our various boats en masse to the nearest *river and set them adrift. We call this farewell act Shōrō nagashi.*

It is a very moving sight, these little flotillas flickering and floating down-stream in the darkness. I am sorry you were not here to see it. I will confess, however, that I did not witness it myself this month. There is an alternative way of saying 'goodbye', a symbolic form of Shōrō nagashi for those unable to go to a river. This is the ritual I have just performed. Before extinguishing the lantern flame, I lit a stick of incense with it. While the incense burned down, I slowly filled a bowl with water – so slowly in fact that the bowl became full exactly as the incense expired. The water is the river, but some-thing must symbolise the loved one himself and his drifting away. The ritual demands that it must be lotus petals. These are placed in the bottom of the bowl and gradually rise and float as it fills. This year they were our lotus petals.

27

A Dream of Islands

'Take good care of yourselves,' said Ōtsuki-san with a knee-touching, broad-smiling bow that is Japan's equivalent of a farewell embrace. It was not yet four in the morning when we set out, bafflingly early even by local standards. The previous evening mother and daughter had held a council of war while I smoked in post-prandial peace beside our newly planted lotuses. Ōtsuki-san had learnt we were destined for Hiraizumi and its temple, Chūson-ji. This, she felt, was an excellent plan but one that could bear some improvement. If we wanted to see lotuses, we should head for a lake called Naganuma. But did I know that there was more to our route than lotuses? Was I aware that Sendai to Hiraizumi was the most critical leg of the most famous journey ever undertaken in Japan? Did Mark-san know Bashō?

He did. In fact, I had known Matsuo Bashō since boyhood. His haiku-illuminated, late-seventeenth-century travel narrative, *Oku no Hosomichi* ('The Narrow Road to the Deep North') was what first inspired my until now unconsummated longing for Japan. The problem with poetry loved in youth is that real life will intervene. Faced with the certainty of dis-appointment, we immunise ourselves. Part of me said that the places Bashō visited may never have been just as he described them. Part of me said that even if these places were once exactly so, they could scarcely have survived in any form that Bashō would recognise. So I had steeled myself to a kind of wilful forgetting. I had failed entirely to connect Hiraizumi with the wandering poet's destination and his Oku with the very region in whose capital I was now sitting. When Ōtsuki-san mentioned him, it was like being reminded of a dear but woefully neglected friend. 'You will not,' she promised, 'be disappointed if you follow in Bashō's footsteps. Let him lead you to the lotus.'

The roads became narrower and narrower. Before long their signs were in Japanese characters only. This, combined with night-time fog and my companion's refusal to answer questions, left me in the dark in every sense. After a half-hour drive north through wakeful fishing villages, the roads ran out. Yoko stashed the car on a woodland track and led me over a series of rooty, fern-covered slopes. Sliding silently downhill through the underwood seemed a peculiar way of going in search of a nation's greatest poet. Daylight was still a little way off as, grouchy and puzzled, I was ordered to dig in among pine trees on a cliff-top overlooking the Pacific. Only the occasional rhapsodising of some nightingale-like bird disturbed the stillness of the woods behind us. Below, barely discernible in the fog, there floated what appeared to be a large fleet, vast in fact, but unaccountably motionless and unlit. Then it began. A geophysicist or meteorologist would perhaps say it was no different there than anywhere else. A psychiatrist would probably put it down to suggestibility, inspired by the Japanese flag. I had never seen a sunrise like it. A scarlet disc levitated with disquieting speed in a sky that turned from petrol blue to milky white.

As the disc rose the fog dispersed and the identity of the phantom fleet was revealed – not ships but islands, scores of them extending as far as I could see. Some were large enough to sport the shining roofs of shrines and houses, a beach and perhaps even a bridge to an adjacent islet which trailed behind its larger neighbour like a dinghy. In others sea and wind had bitten into the pale rock, leaving the gargantuan likeness of an apple core, its vaulted sides unscalable, its plateau capped with an unvisited grove. Others again had been planed away to the slenderest of snags, white sails painted with the calligraphic flourish of a solitary tree. Whether single or in squadrons, the trees aboard every island in this petrified armada were *aka matsu*, *Pinus densiflora*, the red pine. Warm rust in the morning sunshine, their trunks and boughs were sinuous and gracefully inclined as if to greet the sea. Misty blue-green, their foliage was presented in tiered pads that looked as if they had been pruned by gardeners, not gales. I was studying a three-quarters-drowned mountain landscape which, in the scattering and sculpting of its stranded peaks and the disposition of its surviving vegetation, seemed to contain the inspirational germ of every man-made Japanese landscape. An entire archipelago seemed to have budded on the north-east coast of Honshu, as if the country had being trying to reproduce itself in miniature.

'I know this place.'

'We thought you might.'

'This is Matsushima.'

In 1643 Razan Hayashi, Neo-Confucian philosopher and scholar-in-chief to the Tokugawa shogunate, compiled a very short but very important catalogue, *Nihon Sankei*. In the closed world of the Edo Period, 'The Three Views of Japan' was the nation's equivalent of the Seven Wonders, three places of astonishing beauty that had to be seen before one died. They were the Itsukushima Shrine in Hiroshima Prefecture, whose scarlet torii gate appears to float upon the waters of the Inland Sea; Amanohashidate, 'Heaven's Bridge', a slender pine-covered sandbar some 3 kilometres long that connects the two shores of Miyazu Bay in Kyoto Prefecture; and, finally, Matsushima. Anywhere between 250 and 300 islands make up this miniature archipelago, depending on whether one counts the slighter skerries and splinters. Their characteristic vegetation is reflected in its name which means, quite simply, 'pine islands'.

The Three Views exert a psychological pressure which seems curious at first but becomes easy to understand the moment you encounter one of them. The Japanese feel a powerful need, amounting almost to an obligation, to see them at least once in a lifetime. In a culture much given to pilgrimage, Nihon Sankei are *the* three destinations. In the case of Matsushima, this pressure used to be intensified by inaccessibility. The north lay a long way from the main centres of population and the route was obscure and hazardous, sometimes fatally so. The suspicion arose that the least attainable of the Three Views had to be the most beautiful. This scattering of pine-clad islands gleaming amid the Pacific inspired yearning, and the fear that one might never make it. On their return, those who had made it did nothing to dispel the mystique. Matsushima, they said, was more beautiful than they could possibly have hoped.

So there arose this idea of Matsushima-lust. In the Japanese imagination, it became the elevated equivalent of Moscow for Chekhov's Three Sisters. It was the notion of a place one must visit but might not, of a life-transforming journey that seemed doomed to deferral, the endpoint of 'if only'. Yasunari Kawabata expressed this pine-island anxiety in his 1954 novel, *Yama no Oto*,

'The Sound of the Mountain'. Shingo Ogata, the novel's sympathetic hero, is much exercised by Ōga's lotus, whose flowering he follows in the press. But before that, in a chapter titled *Shima no Yume*, 'A Dream of Islands', he is haunted by a dream set in a place which he now realises he will never visit:

> *In the morning, he remembered only fragments of the dream; but the colour of the pine trees and the sea remained clear and fresh, and he was sure he had dreamt of Matsushima.*
>
> *Shingo was embracing a woman behind a pine tree on a grassy slope. They were hiding, frightened. They seemed to have left their companions. The woman was very young, a girl. He could not tell his own age, but he must have been young, judging by the way they ran among the pines. He did not sense any difference in their ages when he held her in his arms. He embraced her as a young man would. Yet he did not think of himself as rejuvenated, nor did it seem to be a dream of long ago. It was as if Shingo had remained in his twenties till the age of sixty-two. That was the mystery of his dream . . .*
>
> *After he woke, he did not know who she was. He had no memory of her face, figure or touch. Only the scenery remained vivid. But he did not know why it must have been Matsushima or why he should have dreamt of Matsushima. He had never been to Matsushima . . .*

Poor Ogata-san. He lives in Kamakura barely 320 miles from Matsushima, no great distance in 1954. 'What's stopping him?' one wonders. But that is not the point. If the pine islands were next door, they would still be remote. Stare them in the face, and they still seem like a dream.

In 1689 Matsushima was very remote indeed. To reach it from Edo (Tokyo) took weeks and very possibly one's life. In spring that year, Matsuo Bashō, middle-aged, unfit, unarmed, unhorsed, apparently penniless and accompanied only by a young disciple, set out from his hovel near the capital with the aim of realising his own dream of islands. 'I patched up my trousers and attached a new cord to my hat. I had moxa burned on my legs to make them stronger. But even as I made these preparations for my journey, I was already dreaming of the full moon over Matsushima.' His final act of preparation was to sell his cottage on the Sumida River: this was a journey from which he might not return.

On the doorpost of his cottage, Bashō pinned a verse for the new owners. It became the first poem in the *haibun*, the narrative in haiku and prose that is *Oku no Hosomichi* ('The Narrow Road to the Deep North'). It is worth pausing over these seventeen syllables of valediction and greeting. They tell us a great deal about the poet and his art in their maturity, and his state of mind as he set out on his pilgrimage. Transliterated into the Roman alphabet, the poem runs as follows:

> *Kusa no to mo*
> *sumikawaru yo zo*
> *hina no ie*

Here are two translations of it. The first was produced by Nobuyuki Yuasa in 1966:

> *Behind this door*
> *Now buried in deep grass,*
> *A different generation will celebrate*
> *The Festival of Dolls*

The second was made by Donald Keene in 1996:

> *Even a thatched hut*
> *May change with a new owner*
> *Into a doll's house*

What the poem literally says is, 'Even the door of plants to be changed in time a doll's house.' Which flurry of banal-seeming non-sequiturs entitles us to ask why this is a good, never mind a great, poem, and how Yuasa and Keene arrived at their versions. Consider first that 'door of plants' (*kusa no to*). Often translated as 'grasses', *kusa* means lowly herbaceous plants, wild-flowers, weeds. It was a key word for Bashō, occurring at critical stages throughout the narrative of his journey to the Deep North. It usually signifies Nature's reassertion of herself in humble but irrepressible form on a site formerly occupied and perhaps glorified by man – a ruined pavilion, for example, or a battlefield. Plants in this context are markers of time whose passage is the main theme of *Oku no Hosomichi*: 'Days and months are travellers of eternity,' the work begins, 'the passing years are likewise voyagers.' In the context of this parting poem, however, the 'door of plants' is saying something slightly different. *Kusa* here is a trope for the cottage and its owner. This one word compresses all we need to know about Bashō at this stage. He is solitary and not a little sad. He is increasingly ascetic, partly due to the hardships of life, partly due to his studies in Zen. He has come to renounce more and more, and now he plans to renounce his last non-portable possession, his home. This, he realises, is merely ephemeral in any case, a shack, a thing of weeds. At one level this 'door of plants' is the door of his hovel as he occupies it; but it also anticipates the overgrown state of his home after he has gone, and the places to which he will go: he is destined for the wilderness where the only walls are vegetation.

There we are – 250 words to explain one word of Bashō and to do it barely adequately. Much of him is like that. In Bashō's mature work, a vast amount is allusive and, if we are not careful, elusive. The plainest speech is multi-layered. How else could he express such complex ideas in seventeen syllables? Do not be fooled by English poets who throw down a handful of suitably plangent-sounding words and tell you that the art of haiku is simplicity. The real thing only seems simple.

What of the rest of this first and farewell poem? 'To be changed in time' is obvious. It looks forward to the new occupants and what they might do to the cottage. Less obvious is the 'house of dolls' into which the cottage will be transformed. This is a reference to *Hina matsuri*, the Festival of Dolls, a holiday that takes its origins in early Heian Period ritual, dedicated to the health and happiness of young female members of the family. It is also known as Girls' Day, and still celebrated by arranging ornate dolls of members of the Heian Period court from the emperor and empress down upon shelves covered in scarlet cloth. Into the bleak hermitage that he is leaving, Bashō projects an image of colour, youth, life and the future. The new owners may well have a family whereas he has none. There may be sophisticated dolls where before there was only the poet's one enduring possession, a simple statue of the Buddha.

Hina matsuri falls in spring and so its mention affords Bashō an ideal example of a quality he always sought in his haiku – *kigo*, the use of seasonal vocabulary. He liked to root his poems in time. Plant names are among his most frequent choices of kigo, but the Dolls' Festival was particularly apt. It coincided with his departure for the Deep North: out with the old, in with the new. This sense of a time-based contrast is the essence of Bashō's mature work. An existential sadness at the passing of things, it is the main theme of *The Narrow Road to the Deep North*. It is not necessarily a sad sadness; it may, as here, suggest renewal; sometimes it can be very funny. But it is always there, the melancholy-tinged message, the fragile human element. Bashō had several terms for this mysterious element according to the concentration in which it was used and the mood he wished to convey – *sabi* (loneliness), *shiori* (tenderness), *hosomi* (a thin or reduced quality, literally narrowness, as in *Oku no Hosomichi*). A quartet of haiku on the theme of the lotus goes some way towards illustrating what these different terms mean in practice.

The first poem was written in 1694, the year of Bashō's death at the age of fifty. Despite which, it illustrates some aspects of his earlier style, clever, teasing and enigmatic:

> Hasu no ka wo
> me ni kayowasu ya
> men no hana

(With that Noh mask in place your eyes can smell the perfume of lotuses)

The reason for the reversion to an earlier style is that this was an occasional poem, the occasion being dinner with a famous Noh actor. The two men were admiring a lotus pond. The poet could do this either with his eyes or with his nose, whereas the actor could see and smell the lotuses simultaneously with one and the same organ since the nostrils of a Noh mask are also its eyes. It is a synaesthetic conceit that was intended, and taken, as a compliment.

Written around 1688, the second poem illustrates the quality of hosomi, narrowness:

> Hasuike ya
> orade sonomama
> tama matsuri

(Uncut, a pond full of lotuses is offering enough for Obon)

This is a typical late Bashō sentiment – true spiritual feeling should be spontaneous, raw and inspired by living things rather than bound by ceremony, so let the lotus flowers and leaves alone and simply admire the pond instead. The poem is direct, simple and involves a shedding or narrowing both of literary complexity and the rituals of Obon. In this respect, the poem has a Zen atmosphere.

The third poem was written in the early 1680s on the death of a student's father. It exhibits the quality of shiori, tenderness:

Tamuke keri
imo wa hachisu ni
nitaru tote
(I offered root vegetables in your father's memory, not lotuses)

Bashō made an offering of sweet potato, kon'nyaku, taro and so on instead of the customary lotus (another rhizomatous crop) to the memorial tablet of his disciple's late father. This appears to be an insult – why not the sacred flower as custom demands? Is there something of the same Zen spirit of renunciation and questioning paradox about this gesture as surfaced in the last haiku? Far from it – there can be no question of the poet's wanting to offend the memory of the deceased or of his using death as the hook for a clever point. These coarse root vegetables are poor man's lotuses, given at greater cost to the hungry Bashō than the real thing. They are a pathetic offering intended to evoke pathos. What appears to be a perverse sentiment is in fact full of tenderness.

The last of this quartet was published in 1684:

Namu hotoke
kusa no utena mo
suzushi kere
(On a simple stand, Buddha's statue will feel cool in my weedy hut)

Here again is *kusa* – weeds, grasses, wildflowers – acting as a trope for Bashō's hovel. Ordinarily, a figure of the Buddha would be placed on a lotus-shaped pedestal. Bashō could not or would not run to that. Instead he scraped an alcove in the mud wall of the cottage and stood his treasured statue within it on a bed of gravel. The lotus is missing from the poem and the cottage, but it looms large in both by virtue of its absence. The real Buddha, Bashō implies, would have been more comfortable with these humble arrangements. After all, was he not a prince who renounced everything? That the Enlightened One will be at home even, or especially, without his customary plinth is only part of the point, however. Bashō is drawing a contrast between the dilapidation of the hut (and himself) and the sublime composure of the statue. This contrast is at the heart of sabi, loneliness. As Yoko's mother had promised, even where there seemed to be no lotuses, the poet would lead me to them.

Of these three terms, sabi was the quality that he regarded most highly.

Kyorai, one of Bashō's disciples, recorded his master's thoughts on the subject:

Sabi (loneliness) is a poem's colour. It does not have to refer to a lonely scene, person or event. For example, if an old man goes into battle wearing the armour of a youthful warrior or if he turns up at a party wearing bright clothes, there is something of sabi about him. Or perhaps I should say sabi is like that old man. It is an indefinable quality that exists in the poem whether it actually describes solitude or conviviality.

It is this 'colour', rather than extreme compression, ellipsis or allusion, that is ultimately lost in translation. It took Bashō himself many years to discover it, years of living the life of a young samurai, enjoying rakish literary *réclame* in the big city, experimenting with relationships, producing work that was ingenious, punning, conscious of its classical antecedents, and brilliant but contrived. Then as his forties approached so did sabi, which not only means loneliness but also maturity in the sense of weathered beauty and the patina of age, the quality Stéphane Mallarmé described as *la grâce des choses fanées*, 'the grace of faded things'. With it came a huge shrugging off which culminated in his pinning the poem to the door of his hut on that May morning in 1689. It was the end of a process of divesting himself not only of his possessions but also of the trappings of his earlier and gaudier literary manner. What remained was lonelier, more tender, more slender and radically simpler in style if not in substance. It was a form of fragmentary naturalism, a frozen moment, reality not in miniature but in microcosm.

A record exists of this gathering and shedding process in action. Appropriately enough, it involves the composition of Bashō's best-known poem. He was sitting with his disciples in the garden of his cottage on a mild March morning in 1686. Rain and cherry petals were falling and a pigeon was cooing, all of them softly. The only disruption was the occasional plunging of frogs in the margins of the river nearby. Bashō lifted his head and was delivered of the second half of a new poem. There was a strong collaborative, not to say competitive, aspect to these meetings of poets and so Bashō's disciple Kikaku leapt in with a proposed opening for the haiku, something self-consciously lovely along the lines of 'Among the golden rose flowers'. The master gave this some thought, politely rejected it and then produced his own opening. The poem was now complete:

Furuike ya
kawazu tobikomu
mizu no oto

Which translates literally as 'an ancient pond, a frog jumps, a sound of water'. Shikō, another disciple and the recorder of this event, says of it, 'The master's choice was more truthful because it was simpler. Only someone who has explored the mysteries of the universe could find a phrase like this.' But what interests me about this scene is the way Bashō chose to depart from truthfulness in order to achieve his new reality. The marshy river bank became an ancient pond. Although there were many frogs a-leaping that day, and Japanese makes no distinction between singular and plural, there is a strong sense of singularity, of just one jumping frog and the prolonged and isolated sound of its dive.

So happened the best-known splash in world culture before David Hockney. At my last count, there were over thirty published English translations of Bashō's seven words, starting with that indefatigable opener-up of things Japanese, Lafcadio Hearn (he pluralises the frog, unforgivably). The commentary on what this haiku may or may not mean amounts to a small industry. Everything, from the outbreak of civil unrest to the tolling of a temple bell, has been read into the animated amphibian. I incline to the view that it might just be a frog, unless it symbolises Bashō's words which are, after all, like depth charges.

He arrived in Matsushima in July 1689. A few days earlier, he had been in Sendai where he spent time with Kaemon, then the city's most noted calligrapher, painter and poet. Together they wandered the surrounding hills and plains, noticing pine woods, white rhododendrons and the newly emerging shoots of hagi, the bush clover *Lespedeza thunbergii* which is Miyagi Prefecture's signature plant and, to Bashō, a portent of autumn even in the salad days of summer. As they parted, Kaemon gave his guest two pairs of straw sandals whose laces were dyed with the dark blue of iris. The beauty of their colour struck Bashō as the strongest indication of the calligrapher's artistic nature; but the sandals were also a practical gift, much needed after a tramp of sixty days. So too were the paintings that Kaemon gave him. These were landscapes depicting the territory between Sendai and Matsushima. At a time when possession of a map could be a capital offence, it was only by comparing these paintings to the new terrain he was entering that Bashō was able to realise his dream of islands.

A Dream of Islands

We had ambushed Matsushima, approaching the great spectacle via one of the coastline's least-known bays and under cover of darkness. Bashō's approach was more stately. He took a boat from the fishing town of Shiogama and sailed among the islands for two miles or so before landing on the Ojima Peninsula. He was not disappointed:

Countless islands are scattered from one end of the bay to the other. The taller islands reach to the sky; the lower ones bow before the ocean swell. Sometimes islands are heaped upon islands in what appear to be groups. At other times, the islands seem linked one to another so that they resemble parents embracing their children or carrying them on their backs or walking with them hand in hand. The pine trees are of an astonishingly deep and verdant green and their branches curve in snaking lines, shaped by the wind that blows endlessly through them. The whole scene exerts the serene and enigmatic enchantment of the face of a beautiful woman. Matsushima, I could not help thinking, must have been made by the God of Mountains in the Time of the Gods. Who else could have created such beauty? And what poet or painter could capture such a masterpiece of divine artifice?

The answer to the last question is 'Not Bashō'. While he could address the view later in prose, no poem was forthcoming on the moment. That night, watching the islands by moonlight from the window of an inn, Bashō was so over-wrought that he could neither write nor sleep. He solaced himself by reading a collection of verses that his friends had given him on his departure from Edo – all of them, presciently, on the subject of Matsushima. He beat these poetic competitors by not even entering the lists and this admission of defeat is among the best things he ever did. It is a brilliant caesura within the narrative flow of *The Narrow Road to the Deep North*, a resounding silence amid the exquisite observations and poignant reflections accumulated over months of wandering. After the plunging frog, the one Bashō haiku that everybody quotes is meant to express the inexpressibility of the pine islands. It needs no translation:

Matsushima ya
ā Matsushima ya
Matsushima ya

In other words, he is lost for words. This poem does not appear, however, in *Oku no Hosomichi* and it always struck me as too obvious to be Bashō. In

Matsushima I was pleased to learn that it is now believed to be a fake. His silence is the genuine article.

Botanists are less easily hushed. Take our breath away and we can still describe the landscape, no matter how beautiful, in terms of what grows there. We lunched on tea-green noodles, stewed lotus rhizomes and flash-fried *haze* (a goby that is a Sendai delicacy) in a restaurant that was hidden like a hermit's retreat high in the woods and overlooking the bay. Leaving Yoko there, I plunged into the undergrowth.

Under the red pines, the slopes were clothed with Japanese maple, *Acer palmatum*, in larger and more elegantly tiered form than I had ever seen it take in Western gardens – immense trees with fan-like boughs which, in autumn, make a ritual fire dance of the shoreline. Beneath these grew mosses, ferns and sedges in a tapestry of intense greens. All around were the garnet-spattered leaves of *Tricyrtis*. The Japanese look at the foliage of these lily-like perennials and see the mottled breast plumage of a bird. They call it *hototogisu*, after their name for the lesser cuckoo, *Cuculus poliocephalus*. Our cuckoo tends to be most vocal soon after sun-up; hototogisu sings most loudly just before sunrise, as it had in the woods that morning. Liquid, sensual and nocturnal, its song has won the bird a prestige in Japanese literature comparable to the nightingale's in the West. Cuckoo 'hunts' – pre-dawn rambles undertaken in the hope of being serenaded by it – were a favourite early-summer pastime of Heian Period aristocrats. In her *Pillow Book*, Sei Shōnagon wrote of lying awake and listening out for it: 'I love anything that calls out in the night – well, anything except babies.'

The rocks were draped with the evergreen climber *Trachelospermum asiaticum*, in a smaller form than I had ever seen before. The colour of old lace, its sprigged flowers filled the air with an odour of gardenia which mingled with the scent of pine. Very occasionally a mass of dove-shaped flowers the colour of rose quartz and more sweetly scented than jasmine materialised above me like a bridal bouquet that had been tossed and caught amid the pine boughs. This was *Dendrobium moniliforme*, an epiphytic orchid that clings perilously to tree limbs without taking anything from them. Most remarkable of all were the ancient vines of *Wisteria floribunda* that snaked their way through the woodland and which were still in flower this far north. In places, I had to part veils of blooms to make any progress at all. Sometimes their stems spiralled around pines that extended over the sea, blue cascading to blue.

The tide was out, so I could see the cliff flora head on. I walked across the bay among clam-gatherers who wore the blue-and-white-patterned head-scarves and rough indigo linens that are de rigueur for manual labour in rural Japan. When not bent double, they skipped across the flats, sprightly as the sandpipers that accompanied them. They were, however, disconcerted by my presence – even more so than is usually occasioned by gaijin-shock. They watched my every movement. I clambered about the headland, gripping ledges that were filled with orchids and lilies and breathing in the fragrance of the vine as it trailed its racemes in rock pools. It was hard to believe this repository of rarities could have remained in such peace for so long. Perhaps the clam-gatherers were its guardians? Each time I looked around, their eyes were upon me and filled with concern. I had a strong sense of being an invader, or at least a suspect. Back at the restaurant and unable to keep the marvel of the maritime wisteria to myself, I pressed my fieldglasses on Yoko and urged her to take a look. 'Baka!' she said, a strong word that means something like, 'You idiot!' To which she added, 'Bakademic, in fact' – a hybrid term of her own devising inspired by Oxford life. I asked what I had done to deserve this scolding. She handed back the binoculars: 'Do you see that sign down there on the foreshore? It says, *Quicksand – extreme danger of death.*'

28

Lacustral

The Japanese language is careful with water. There are, for example, various onomatopoeic terms for different grades of rain. *Zāzā* is a dramatic downpour, drenching roofs, flooding streets, compelling a change of clothes and a patient retreat. *Shitoshito* (pronounced without the letter 'i') is finer than drizzle and heavier than Scotch mist, calm and constant, akin to the billowing atomised precipitation met along a seafront in spring or near the base of a waterfall. Shitoshito is good for the skin and for tree-dwelling orchids. Then there is *potsupotsu*. 'Spitting', our brutal English equivalent of this word, does not convey its sound or sense. Potsupotsu is a tentative tattoo, as of sparse fat drops upon an umbrella or a lotus leaf, which could come to nothing or could portend a deluge.

Similarly, each of the three words for 'lake' in widespread use indicates something distinctive. *Ike* is a pool or a pond. That seems clear enough; but ike can be a small sump or a vast expanse of water, a millpond or a moat. Bashō's frog leaps into a *furuike*, an ancient pond, which one imagines as a jewel of a pool, edged with moss and rocks, half hidden by ferns in some secret garden. At the same time, Lady Masako's lotus lakes in Kamakura are *hasuike* – large, open, prominent but still ike. The defining characteristic of ike is not their size or use, but that they are deliberately created or, if natural in origin, maintained in an artificial setting such as a garden. *Ko*, by contrast, are natural phenomena, immense, deep and often steep-sided bodies of water. The lakes of the English Lake District, North

America's Great Lakes and Scottish lochs are all ko, as, of course, is Japan's Lake Biwa, *Biwako*.

In the lake stakes, however, neither ko nor ike is quite the equal of *numa* in antiquity, precision and resonance. A numa is a large and shallow body of water, usually fresh, sometimes brackish, with a muddy bottom and gently sloping margins. It arises, or used to arise, within a wider area of wetland. Although 'ike' appears in its name, Japan's most famous lotus lake, Shinobazu-no-ike in central Tokyo, began its long life in this way. Typically, the vegetation of the surrounding marsh runs into the numa and may, depending on the season, fill it. The word is sometimes translated as 'swamp', but this is to confuse mire with mere. The essential quality of a numa is that it is a watery clearing within a swamp. It is a space, an absence, another instance of that pre-eminent Japanese non-entity Ma.

It is also the water-filled crucible of Japanese civilisation. The Jōmon lived among and in association with numa. Before the arrival of intensive rice cultivation and extensive population concentrations, numa were one of Japan's principal human habitats – equable, easily navigated and richly stocked. They were a respite from the mountains that covered the interior and from the adjacent ocean, both of which teemed with implacable gods and terrible unknowns.

From the third century BC onwards, rice cultivation became one of the main activities of Japan's Yayoi people. Not only were the numa's Jōmon inhabitants overtaken by the advent of agriculture, so were the numa themselves. With their wild *Oryza* component and pattern of seasonal flooding, such pools had provided the inspiration and materials for the rice revolution. But they also happened to sit exactly where one would want to grow the new crop – on wet and richly fertile lowland plains. Little by little, the numa were drained and dug. As the population grew, this process accelerated, propelled by the fact that their low-lying and level environs were also admirably suited to urbanisation. By modern times, numa, Japan's most important aboriginal habitat, had all but vanished. But not quite – and nor quite their most important plant inhabitant, the lotus.

Naganuma is the largest and southernmost of a trio of numa that sit close together on the Senpoku Plain in Miyagi Prefecture, some 50 kilometres north-east of Sendai and halfway between the city and our final destination, Hiraizumi. They are immense bodies of water. Naganuma is around 400 hectares; Izunuma some 300 hectares; at just 100 hectares Uchinuma still seems vast, an aquatic prairie. The figures are necessarily imprecise, for the breadth of these sheets of water alters according to season. Sometimes it is augmented by snow melt from nearby mountains, monsoon rains and a veritable vascular system of rivers and streams. At other times it shrinks as water is drained away to irrigate paddy-fields. Ever-present and always an influence is the surrounding marshland, some 50 square kilometres of bog, reedbed and willow mangrove, which expands and contracts, retreats and advances, adding to or subtracting from the numa's breadth. The depth of two of these lakes, by contrast, remains stable. Izunuma and Uchinuma are astonishingly shallow, often little more than a metre deep. Naganuma is much deeper in parts, especially where it is used as a reservoir. In many places, however, its original, waist-deep condition endures. These three magnificent survivors are fragile films of water that have lain for millennia, with mystifying tenacity, over a very great depth of mud.

Many of the surviving numa are now protected wildlife sanctuaries, and the most significant of them are listed under the Ramsar Convention, the international treaty on the conservation and sustainable use of wetlands. Izunuma and Uchinuma are among them, designated habitats of world import-ance and subject at home to the protection of Japanese law and of their own environmental foundation established by Miyagi Prefecture in 1988. Strangely Naganuma, our destination that summer afternoon, is not subject to such protection, although it struck me as seeming far wilder in places than either of its sisters. Conservation with its necessary adjuncts of communication and interpretation can have a curiously taming effect on landscapes. I began to suspect that Yoko's mother had wanted me to see a numa without the gloss, with lakeside life (or desolation) carrying on as it always has, and with a hair or two out of place.

The rubric of the Ramsar Convention refers to 'wetlands of international importance, especially as wildfowl habitat'. The numa of the Senpoku Plain are ideal candidates: they are a critical stopover on the great East Asian flyway for migratory birds. Summer visitors flock there to breed before heading off to winter in South-east Asia and Australia. In autumn, clouds of roosting sand martins plunge the reedbeds into shadow. Winter sees the arrival of thousands of white-fronted and bean geese whose melancholy calls have become a cherished seasonal event and marker, the auditory and hibernal equivalent of cherry blossom. With them come pintail ducks, mallards and mergansers. This is to name only a very few. There are 556 species of birds found in Japan; each year some 200 species are recorded in or around these three marshy lakes. Most striking of all the winter visitors are the whooper swans. Each February, as they sail across the numa, the swans negotiate a memory of summer which makes their spectral transit the epitome of *sabi*. Breasting the ice, they drift, white among sere, through the remnants of the lake's other giant denizen, the parchment leaves, fractured stalks and stranded seed heads of the lotus.

I had qualms as we arrived at the southern end of Naganuma. There is always a risk in finding a treasured rarity in such superabundance. I need not have worried. A dragonfly, faience blue and newly fledged, swerved to avoid us as we stepped onto a jetty.

'Tombo,' said Yoko with delight, 'the emblem of victory in battle. Or shall we say, for our purposes, a successful mission?'

Following its flight path, we found ourselves penetrating an area of some 50 hectares, thick with aquamarine leaves and deep pink flowerbuds. It was a sea of lotuses navigated by narrow wooden walkways that stood on stilts. Wandering along them we were soon engulfed, lost amid the sacred flower and unable to see the shore. Moored alongside these walkways were flat-bottomed boats that would be used in a few weeks' time for lotus-viewing parties, culminating in a hasu festival in the build-up to Obon. They brought to mind the prints of lotus spectators made by Hokusai in the early nineteenth century – women of the floating world, some of them trailing a hand in the water, others with kimono sleeves rolled back as they bent over the prow to take a deep breath of perfume.

The day had been long and very hot. We sat on the planking, overshadowed by lotus leaves. The cool air beneath them smelt not of stagnation but growth. The intense green odour of fresh lotus leaves was close to the fragrance of dried seaweed, *nori*, and *macha*, powdered green tea. The coincidence seemed only proper: after all, this vegetable trio lay at the heart of life here. Theirs was the stored-up essence of vernal vitality made perennially available as if to balance the other pervasive Japanese scent, the year-round autumnal wood smoke that I first noticed in Fukushima: beginnings and endings ever present. The leaf undersides danced with fractured reflections. Caused by bubbles that broke the surface every few minutes, these were reflections of the lotuses themselves – not mephitic exhalations but the calling cards of advancing rhizomes. Every stream of bubbles heralded another metre of subaquatic mud infiltrated and conquered, and the emergence, a day or so later, of a new leaf or flower. It was easy to see why poets and print-makers should have expended so much ink on this intoxicating idyll; why one could talk of lacustral in the East as one talks of pastoral in the West. For a while there was no world beyond the numa.

This idyll has not always been so undisturbed. In modern times areas of the Senpoku lotus-lands were drained, developed, polluted, and the hasu went into retreat, sometimes coming perilously close to disappearing. In recent decades, however, the dereliction has ended and the damage has been reversed. The water has grown cleaner and cleaner until it has arrived at a peak of muddy viability, much assisted by the purifying action of healthy colonies of Nelumbo. The unique numa biotope has been actively rehabilitated in some places, and in others left to recover by itself. In this resurgence, the lotus is not only a key ecological player; it is also an important crop and a major visitor attraction. For these reasons the numa lotuses have been propagated and reintroduced to areas of the lakes where they had declined or vanished. It is essential to restore the status ante quo for the sake of all the species that inhabit the numa, and the surest way to do that is to ensure the lotus prospers. Humankind has long played a hand in the husbandry of these lotuses. Even when it was simply a matter of a Jōmon gatherer paddling among the leaves, harvesting some rhizomes and leaving others, the hasu colony was already being shaped, influenced by man. The new plantings are not so much an artificial intervention as the resumption of an age-old symbiosis.

More than two species are bound by this relationship. Eventually I managed to rouse myself from the strange distraction, the Homeric forgetfulness induced by seeing so many wild lotuses, and began to notice the wildfowl that lived among them. Much as I loved the phrase, I had always suspected 'heron priested shore' was yet another of Dylan Thomas's euphonious nonsenses. No end of wandering in South Wales had failed to turn up any such clerical coastline. Now, thousands of miles from Laugharne, I realised I had done him wrong: the heron population of the shores of Naganuma was decidedly hieratic. In denominational terms, it was the classic Japanese split. Far out among the lotuses stood grey herons, or as they are known there ao-sagi, 'blue herons'. The ashy garb of these ascetic-looking figures had a distinctly Zen quality, as did their liking for life amid the hasu and, of course, their talent for remaining motionless until the moment of illumination comes and with it the darting neck and skewered fish. Nearer the shore were their Shinto counterparts, dressed in gauzy white and a deal more sociable. These were the little egret or *ko-sagi* (*Egretta garzetta*), one of Japan's most iconic birds.

I do, for once, mean iconic. Ko-sagi is a common subject in art and literature. It gave its name to one of Japan's loveliest marshland orchids, *sagi-sō* (*Pecteilis radiata*), a plant whose white flowers exactly resemble the little egret, even down to the floral lip which has two outstretched and incised lobes like the wings of ko-sagi in flight. The Japanese like to grow sagi-sō in pots decorated with the image of the bird itself. Bashō was more of a crane man, a devotee of *tsuru* as an avian emblem of the transcendent spirit. But even he was not immune to ko-sagi's charms. In 1690, he wrote a poem that conjures his ideal monochrome landscape:

> *Lake Biwa is under snow as are Mount Hira to the west and Mount Mikami to the east. If only a flight of sagi would make a bridge of white between the two.*

The bird seems to symbolise unadulterated beauty and natural purity – it would be too moralistic to call it innocence – and the uncluttered happiness those states can evoke. Looking at the egrets at Naganuma, it was easy to imagine some atavistic link between them and the rites of Shinto, in which purity is all. There seemed to be no breeze on the lake that afternoon, only tumultuous stillness, heat and humidity. Nonetheless, some zephyr played with the fringed breast feathers of the sagi around us. It was impossible not to connect their dancing plumage with the 'shide', the white paper strips that fluttered around the entrance of the Shinto shrine on the nearby shore. As I watched these blemishless birds wading delicately among the carmine buds and sea-green leaves, I felt that was it – that would do for an icon, an emblem for my entire journey.

As the sunset turned the lotus lake dark rose, we encountered the last and most mysterious of these plumed priests, the true heron-hierophant. It was a member of a closed order, although emphatically not one sworn to silence. He only revealed himself by his unearthly chant with which the reedbeds began to reverberate at four-second intervals. No bird was seen and it was not until later that I worked out his identity. For the moment I froze on the gangway, imagining we must have been stalked by an asthmatic bassoonist.

'What the hell is that?' I said to Yoko.

'Sankanogoi, I think,' came the answer, as if it were an everyday occurrence.

Sankanogoi, I discovered, is that reclusive exhibitionist the bittern. Geoffrey Chaucer used the lovely verb *bomblen* to describe its cry: 'And as a bitore bombleth in the myre.' I had always trusted him to have got it right, not having encountered the thing myself even during long watches on the Norfolk Broads. As I heard its voice that summer evening, I was no longer so sure. Perhaps it was because this was a Japanese and not a British bittern (although both are *Botaurus stellaris*), but I thought it less like a bombler and more like a melancholy note played on the ryūteki, the bamboo flute whose sound was thought to resemble the windrush of a dragon in flight, which I had heard at the wedding in Kamakura.

Rice farmers around the numa transcribe the bittern's cry as 'Buō-Buō', which is not bad, but still does not convey the eerie disembodiment of the call. At an inn later that night our host told us that these farmers, being for the most part early and light sleepers, regard sankanogoi with grumpy resignation for keeping them awake at one of their busiest times. The sight of thousands upon thousands of lotuses growing just as they have for thousands upon thousands of years had already driven home the message of the breath-takingly unspoilt abundance of the numa. But the inn-keeper's tale of the bittern and the sleepless farmers seemed even more eloquent. Something which for us is so famously rare and secretive was for them merely one of life's more wearying facts.

As we set out the next day, I caught a snatch of some human chorus accompanied by drumming. At once lilting and triumphant, the music seemed as strangely disembodied as the bittern's as it drifted over the paddy-fields.

'They're late,' said Yoko crisply.

'Late for what?' I asked. Our start that morning, as with all our excursions, had seemed indecently early to me. She explained the sound emanated from a rice-planting festival at one of the nearby shrines. These were the songs that Bashō thought were poetry's beginning.

29

The Deep North

I called her Cio-Cio-san because she was always available, always compliant, the personification of self-sacrificing submission. Our relationship had its ups and downs. At first I was enchanted by the musicality of her tone, her unfailing courtesy and ever-present sense of duty. Later I could find myself feeling irritated or even burdened by her. Despite which, and unlike Pinkerton's, my Cio-Cio-san could do perfectly well without her gaijin swain, whereas I came to depend on her. I am sure she must have belonged to somebody somewhere and to that person I apologise unreservedly for any unintended slight. I am equally sure that I have never met a real Japanese woman who was anything like as docile as my sweet soprano seemed, and I thank heavens for that. Cio-Cio-san was the name I gave to our canary-voiced car satellite navigation system.

'That's enough of her,' said Yoko, killing the satnav and flooring the accelerator. 'Listen up – it's time for your briefing.'

It was hard to obey. Apart from delighting in my virtual sweetheart's talent for making pillow talk out of phrases that probably meant 'bear right' or 'junction ahead', I was absorbing a new Japan. Travelling along a large but isolated temperate landmass that runs more or less north–south provides endless distractions for botanists, even in the fast lane. The darkly forested peaks and luxuriant plains of Miyagi Prefecture were giving way to woodland that was more mixed and less subtropical-seeming, and to great sweeps of hilly grassland. It was a landscape that grew more strangely familiar with every mile, at times more suggestive of the Lake District than the Furthest East.

Yet it was another type of familiarity that made this terrain like no other. Its flora seemed entirely composed of the untamed originals of plants that could be found in every garden centre, if not quite every garden, in the Western world. Those bulky broad-crowned trees which might at a glance be taken for oaks were, in fact, magnolias. Their boughs were draped with the dinner-plate-sized leaves of *Vitis coignetiae*, and with tresses of *Parthenocissus tricuspidata*, that commonest of garden climbers, Boston ivy, which, despite its name, is a Japanese interloper among the Brahmins of Beacon Hill. The billows of apple-blossom pink and white that flashed past us were not mayflower or blackthorn but wild *Weigela* and the snowy cascades of *Rosa wichurana* and *Spiraea nipponica*. On the rare occasions that Yoko slowed down a little, the grassland would come into focus and reveal itself as a spring garden painted on a silk screen – a matrix of silver-striped *Miscanthus*, golden day lilies and lilac-flowered hostas with, here and there, vivid magenta flares of *Rosa rugosa* and chinchilla plumes of *Macleaya cordata*. The roadside woods were festooned with wild *Wisteria floribunda*, still in full flower and some-times making a 100-foot mauve-clad geisha of a normally sombre sugi tree.

But I had to put this million-hectare garden behind me and concentrate. We were heading into the Deep North, Ōshū, or Oku as poets prefer it. The Deep North is as much an idea as a geographical reality. Yes, it is physically the northern region of Japan's main island of Honshu, but our destination, the town of Hiraizumi, lies on the same latitude as Washington DC. Heavy snowfall is common there in winter, but the summers are marked by tumul-tuous heat and humidity and the vegetation is correspondingly lush. Do not imagine windswept steppe: for much of the year, the Deep North is an equable and fertile paradise. Its fabled depth and northness are, rather, tropes to do with the region's ancient reputation for inaccessibility and its remote-ness from the old capital of Kyoto. In the tenth and eleventh centuries, the Deep North was the isolated stronghold of the Emishi, the 'northern barbar-ians', many of whom were of Jōmon descent and few of whom felt allegiance to the southern Japanese or their emperor. At that time, Oku was effect-ively another country populated by another race, a race whose forebears had controlled Japan long before Yayoi immigrants arrived from the Asian mainland.

Today Hiraizumi is a quiet rural town of some 9,000 souls. In the mid-twelfth century, however, its population peaked at around 150,000, a figure that compares favourably with the 160,000 to 300,000 inhabitants of Heian Period Kyoto. It was not just in its population that mediaeval Hiraizumi gave the lie to the Deep North's image as a wilderness. The city was once a centre of the highest culture, of profound scholarship and spirituality, architectural splendour and flourishing fine arts. Most significantly, this Kyoto of the north was the hub of Japan's and, for a while, the Far East's largest gold-mining region. Kyoto may have had the mandate of heaven, but Hiraizumi had all the loot. It belongs beside Ophir, Golconda and El Dorado in the thesaurus of treasure towns. This pre-eminence was achieved and lost in less than a century. In the summer of 1189 the implacable Deep North reasserted itself. The city was swept by events that left it the epitome of *mono no aware*, the pathos of passing things. From its brief flowering, Hiraizumi became a byword for desolation, transience and fallen glory, a quasi-mythic place that would trigger much the same emotions in the Japanese as tales of Avalon or Troy would in the Western mind. Somewhere in this saga, I had been promised, was a lotus, one that would provide a resolution for my entire quest.

'I am afraid I'm going to trouble you with a long story,' said Yoko, 'many names, some of them very similar-sounding to your ears, and a lot of dates. It will appear to have nothing at all to do with lotuses. You must be patient. Unless you know this tale with all its ins and outs, you can't really hope to understand the place we're making for, or the real significance of what's growing there. In fact, I'd go so far as to say that the 200 years that I have to cram into the next hour explain a great deal not just about Hiraizumi and the role of the lotus, but about the character of Japan itself. I think it will strike you as rather familiar in some ways. It certainly has Shakespearean undertones. One more thing – if you ever repeat what I am about to tell you, please smooth out the wrinkles and let me add a detail here and there. I think it was Raymond Chandler who said that when a woman drives well she is almost perfect. He said nothing about her lecturing on Japanese history at the same time.' I had already learnt that mediaeval Japan was her forte, was in her blood, and so I stopped staring at the fly-past flora and listened. She began.

Early in the eleventh century, Ōshū, the Deep North, was every bit as wild as legend has it – an area of impassably dense forests, peaks without paths and unfordable rivers. Its natural resources were believed to be poor. Its population included those remnants of the Emishi aboriginals who had not been driven even further north to the island of Hokkaido. These people were considered savages and the places they inhabited were, likewise, thought savage, beyond the realm and indeed the comprehension of 'real' Japan. If control is not too masterful a word, one northern clan of Japanese controlled the region of Ōshū where Hiraizumi would develop. They were the Abe family and they managed to scratch a living while policing what was in effect a vast and wild open ghetto. Skirmishes between these Japanese overlords and the native barbarians were common, but so too were instances of cooperation and even of intermarriage.

At court in Kyoto, it was suspected that the Abe clan might need assistance in their role as guardians of the north. This suspicion may have arisen because of conflicts with Emishi or because of rumours of Abe integration, a going native which would have been taboo. The clan's own records, and anatomical studies, provide strong evidence that they interbred with the aboriginals. When they described themselves as 'barbarian rulers', they were not just saying 'rulers of barbarians' – they had become at least part Emishi. In addition to these concerns, something else had attracted the interest of the imperial court. Around the first half of the eleventh century, gold was discovered in Ōshū: the waste land was beginning to look like the promised land.

Scions of the Fujiwara clan were duly sent from Kyoto to act as imperial governors and revenue-takers for the region, ostensibly in collaboration with the Abe family. Since the eighth century, the Fujiwara had built, and inhabited, many of the palaces and ministries of the capital Kyoto. Through intermarriage with the imperial line, they had become Japan's de facto rulers, implementing systems of government that included general taxation, a more or less equitable allotment of rice fields for householders, and codes of civil and criminal law. Besides ruling, they fostered a flowering of poetry, calligraphy and gardening.

When these courtly figures, now known as the Ōshū – North – Fujiwara, arrived in their rugged new domain, they found it far from easy to perform their duties. The region's existing incumbents, the Abe clan, feared for their prerogative and property, so they embarked on a programme of resistance which culminated in the outbreak of Zen-kunen-no-eki, 'the Nine Year War'. To settle this conflict, Kyoto called on another imperial clan, the Minamoto or Genji, known to be loyal servants of the emperor and ferocious fighters. The Genji leader, General Yoriyoshi Minamoto, and his army of samurai marched north in 1051. Before long he and his son Yoshi'ie had engineered a truce between the Abe and Fujiwara clans – indeed Tsunekiyo, head of the Ōshū Fujiwara, married the sister of Sadatō, chief of the Abe clan. Then an Abe retainer attacked one of the Genji household. Assault became skirmish which in turn became battle: the Nine Year War was on again. This time the Fujiwara joined forces with their new in-laws, the Abe, *against* the Genji. Meanwhile the Genji looked to another northern clan, the Kiyohara, for help.

The Genji triumphed in this second and final phase of the war. 'To understand what they did next,' said Yoko, 'you must grasp the importance of the Japanese concept of *On*, of a debt of gratitude incurred and, if not exactly repaid in kind, then at least honoured in friendship and service. As I've told you before and as you've probably worked out for yourself, Genji are very strong on *On*.' Yoriyoshi, leader of the Genji militia in the north, had protected the Fujiwara from the Abe. He had, moreover, striven to ensure that both clans emerged from their clash as harmoniously as could be hoped, with names and lands intact and even linked by marriage. This meant that the Abe and Fujiwara owed a huge debt of *On* to Yoriyoshi. It was a debt that they had chosen to repay by joining forces against him. To a Genji general this was an unconscionable insult. In 1062 Yoriyoshi, now acting governor of Ōshū, had the prisoner Tsunekiyo Fujiwara brought before him. The contemporary account *Mutsu-waki* ('The Chronicle of the North') reports what happened next:

'Your people,' the seventy-four-year-old Yoriyoshi roared, 'have been in the service and debt of my clan, so tell me how it is that you could so easily forget the authority of the imperial court and turn against your old masters the Genji? You are a mutinous outlaw. Worse than that, you are corrupt. Tell me, what use are those white papers to you now?'

The white papers in question were official bills that allowed the bearer to collect taxes for the court. Tsunekiyo, it seems, had fallen into the habit of manufacturing his own fraudulent bills and pocketing the income they secured.

'Tell me,' Yoriyoshi demanded, 'now that you have lost the war, will you continue with this graft right under my nose? Or will you have the grace to apologise and to work for your salvation?'

Tsunekiyo had been given his chance but chose to say nothing. So the general ordered him to be beheaded with a blunt sword.

'Yoriyoshi's vengefulness and cruelty,' the chronicler bravely noted, 'are sometimes beyond all describing.' If further proof were needed, the general also had Tsunekiyo's brother-in-law Sadatō Abe decapitated and his head nailed to the gate of Genji headquarters.

So the Nine Year War ended with the Abe and northern Fujiwara clans all but wiped out and the Genji nominally in charge of Ōshū. Day-to-day running of the Deep North was now given to their allies, the Kiyohara clan. Of the Abe clan, however, there remained one very significant survivor, Sadatō's sister, and of the Fujiwara there remained her seven-year-old son by Tsunekiyo.

'Yoriyoshi Minamoto was not altogether heartless, you see,' said Yoko, leaving me altogether unconvinced, 'but as events turned out, it might have been better had mother and son been killed off too. On the other hand, that would have left you with nothing to see at Hiraizumi today.'

Tsunekiyo's widow swiftly remarried, this time into the governing Kiyohara clan which also adopted her son. This boy, confusingly named Kiyohira, grew to manhood alongside his Kiyohara half-brothers. At this point versions of the story differ. Romantics like to believe that Kiyohira endured two decades of living with the enemy, waiting patiently until 1083 to make good his vow to avenge his fallen father and to recover his lost domains. Contemporary records offer a more plausible account, to do with fraternal jealousy and, surprisingly, Genji goodwill. In early maturity Kiyohira and his Kiyohara half-brothers were given various areas of Ōshū to rule. The division was undertaken by Yoriyoshi's son, Yoshi'ie Minamoto, on behalf of the imperial court in Kyoto. Kiyohira received what was thought to be the best territory, much to the disgust of his Kiyohara siblings who rose up against him. Aged twenty-eight, Kiyohira rejected his adopted clan and reverted to his father's family name of Fujiwara. He rallied his retainers and promptly joined battle against his half-brothers.

So began Go-san'nen-no-eki, 'the Three Year War', and there was really only one thing to do – call once again for those most warlike of peace-keepers, the Genji. This time they smiled upon young Kiyohira rather than the Kiyohara clan, as this would achieve the imperial court's aim of ensuring Fujiwara hegemony in the north. With Genji assistance, by the conclusion of the Three Year War, Kiyohira Fujiwara had control of his own lands, the old Fujiwara and Abe territories *and* the possessions of the now vanquished Kiyohara clan.

'This,' said Yoko, 'is what I believe my old English teacher would have called "the jackpot".'

With peace and the Ōshū Fujiwara ascendancy secured, it was time for the Genji to go home. They were perfectly prepared to believe that virtue is its own reward – that would be very much in the spirit of bushidō. But what the Genji were not prepared to accept was that they should actually lose out on the deal. They had marched north and fought bravely for a second time and they had done so on the orders of the court. Now, unexpectedly, Kyoto distanced itself from their actions: the Genji were informed that they had helped the Ōshū Fujiwara for personal gain and glory and without an imperial mandate. Not only would they receive no reward for imposing a peace, but the Genji themselves would have to meet the vast financial cost of having done so.

So it was that Kyoto managed to keep its coffers closed.

'This is, of course, an even greater offence against *On*,' said Yoko, returning to a favourite theme and suddenly driving rather too fast, 'but it is also much more than that. In fact, I can't overemphasise the importance of this act of imperial tightfistedness. It changed the course of Japanese history. The Genji paid the bill for the conflict, looking after their men out of their own pockets. This meant that their warriors and retainers felt an immense bond of loyalty not to the emperor and the court but to their Minamoto masters – and don't forget the Genji warriors and retainers were the most powerful in the land.' In time that bond became indissoluble, indeed it became a code and a way of life. So a simple act of meanness might be said to have resulted in the rapid diminution of imperial might and to have led to the age of the samurai and the founding, a century later, of the Kamakura Bakufu, the military 'tent government' of the Shogun Yoritomo Minamoto.

Kiyohira was now the first undisputed Fujiwara lord of the Deep North and the emperor's richest subject. He took up residence in Hiraizumi, a humble settlement that would not remain so for long. As his refurbishment of the town proceeded, Kiyohira turned his attention to a derelict temple high on the peak that overlooked Hiraizumi. Its site was originally called Kanzan, meaning 'border post', which gives some sense of the mediaeval belief that this really was the outer limit. The building Kiyohira discovered dated from 859; the temple itself had been founded in 850 by Ennin (Jikaku Daishi), the great master of the Tendai Sect. The sect had called this new temple Chūson-ji, a name that Kōryū Tada, one of its recent high priests, interprets as signifying 'value [son] in the human world [jinchū]'. That value was both numinous and physical, for Chūson-ji was an attempt to create the Pure Land and the paradise of the *Lotus Sutra* on earth.

In 1105 Kiyohira, now aged fifty, sent a petition to the Emperor Horikawa and the Tendai Sect, seeking leave to rededicate Chūson-ji – He owes all his good fortune to His Imperial Majesty. To repay this debt of *On*, he wants to create a temple complex that will spread the civilising influence of Buddhism and honour the gods of Shinto. Excluding the taxes that he pays to Kyoto, he will dedicate all his wealth to this goal. He will not only spend his gold to make Chūson-ji happen, he will use gold as a raw material, plating and gilding the temples and towers with it and melting it to illuminate a new library of sutras.

As he stated them, Kiyohira's aims in refurbishing Chūson-ji were three-fold – to bring peace to his dead family, soldiers and (in a flourish typical of the all-nature-is-equal spirit of the *Lotus Sutra*) 'the injured animals, plants and rocks of this place'; to elevate the Deep North, making it a centre of Buddhist civilisation; to prevent the region from ever becoming a war zone again. His petition was granted and Kiyohira threw his vast resources into the restoration. Within a few years, Chūson-ji had risen, lotus-like, from the bloody mud of the battlefield. A thousand monks were required to serve the new complex of 40 halls, temples and shrines. Craftsmen from across Japan and materials from across Asia were deployed in its making. The result was a sacred citadel wrought in gold and pearl. Perched upon a mountain and reached via a winding ascent through dark forest, it revealed itself like the rising sun. This was the holy heart of Kiyohira's territory. He signified as much by lining all roads to it with golden figures of the Amida Buddha, stationed 109 metres apart, extending from Ōshū's more civilised southern borders to the untamed ultima Thule of the Deep North.

Chūson-ji's gilded sancta, library of sutras and gardened precincts were sublimely incongruous in this northern wilderness: it was a dazzling satellite of the highest Fujiwara culture. After Kiyohira's death in 1128, each of his aims in rebuilding Chūson-ji – propitiation, prosperity and peace – was furthered by his son and grandson, Motohira and Hidehira, the three of them becoming known as the great Ōshū Fujiwara lords. Meanwhile, the town of Hiraizumi became a thriving city. Where there had been flood plain and forest, there were now red-lacquered palaces and landscape gardens that were the equal of anything in Kyoto. In many instances these new creations outshone their models, and sometimes literally so for Hiraizumi was a city of gold. Then, after less than a century of this spectacular growth, the Genji clan re-entered the lives of the northern Fujiwara.

In 1185, the thirty-eight-year-old Genji chief Yoritomo Minamoto assumed control of Japan. As I had learnt on the Hill of Cranes, Yoritomo was the great-great-great-nephew of Yoriyoshi, hammer of the north and founder, in 1063, of the first Hachiman shrine at Kamakura, which he built to commemorate his triumph in the Nine Year War. Emulous of his ancestor, Yoritomo rebuilt this shrine as Tsurugaoka Hachiman-gū and established the Bakufu, his 'tent government', in its precincts. In 1192, the imperial court recognised its authority, naming him shogun. But before he could claim this accolade, Yoritomo had to attend to some family business. Yoshitsune, his half-brother and junior by twelve years, was becoming a nuisance.

Remarkably few Japanese would see Yoshitsune in that light. In the eight centuries since his death, the youthful and rather diminutive Genji commander has grown in stature to mythic proportions. If the fall of Hiraizumi is reminiscent of Troy, then Yoshitsune Minamoto manages to conjure Achilles tinged with shades of Sir Philip Sidney and Bonnie Prince Charlie. He is Japan's tragic courtly warrior hero. A brilliant and brave fighter, Yoshitsune served the Genji cause well in the clan's bid to recover from the dispersal and exile that followed its earlier adventures in the north and the long years of Kyoto intrigue. Under his command the Minamoto finally seized control of Kyoto, and he ended the protracted war with the rival Heike clan in 1185 by routing them at the naval battle of Dan-no-Ura.

Yoshitsune was, however, rather too successful in his campaigns, and he was also, unlike his elder sibling, flamboyantly chivalrous, charismatic and well-loved in the capital. While Yoritomo and Lady Masako masterminded the Minamoto resurgence in distant Kamakura and shunned Kyoto as a place of decadence, faction and corruption, Yoshitsune cut a dash at the imperial court. There he caught the fancy of that ruthless puppeteer, the cloistered emperor Go-Shirakawa, still alive after all the backbiting and bloodshed and still taking a very active approach to retirement.

At first Go-Shirakawa had reluctantly sided with Yoritomo, seeing no option but to back this most dangerous strategist and warrior. But early in the Genji chief's campaigns, he noticed that Yoritomo was not quite as pliable as he would have wished – not to mention Lady Masako. Now

Go-Shirakawa believed he had found himself a more personable and biddable Genji in Yoritomo's half-brother Yoshitsune. He showered the glamorous victor of Dan-no-Ura with favours while pointedly denying the distant Yoritomo the one honour he strove for, the title of shogun. He appointed Yoshitsune protector of the imperial capital. He gave posts and prizes to his retainers and none to Yoritomo's. All of which went to Yoshitsune's head. He began to prefix his given name with 'Minamoto no', a style that was the prerogative of the chief of the Genji clan, his half-brother Yoritomo. He began rewriting recent history: the great victories of the Genpei War had been won not by the massed Genji forces, let alone by Yoritomo and his cunning wife, but by his brilliance and heroism alone. Finally, in October 1185, Yoshitsune accepted an order from Go-Shirakawa to assassinate Yoritomo.

The ink on this order was scarcely dry when Yoritomo and Masako learnt of it in Kamakura. They responded with a demand that places them in the view of some people on a par with the Macbeths and Richard III. They called for Yoshitsune's head. With his half-brother gearing for battle, Yoshitsune was suddenly less popular at court. His popularity declined still more sharply when, on 29 October 1185, Yoritomo and his troops set out for the capital to kill him. Yoshitsune looked for a place of refuge, eventually settling on Hiraizumi, the glittering city far to the north that had been gifted to the Fujiwara by his forefathers.

His flight to Hiraizumi has generated a popular mythology of its own, inspiring Kabuki plays, poetic sagas and television dramas. One reason for the attraction is the cast the doomed young star took north with him. There was his mistress who was ditched, pregnant and with only a servant and a bag of coins for comfort, on the snowy slopes of Mount Yoshino. There were his long-suffering wife and baby daughter. There was the handful of retainers, among them Kanefusa, his elderly but indefatigable warrior-liegeman. Above all, there was Benkei.

Saito Musashibo Benkei was born in 1155 – it is said, the product of the rape of a blacksmith's daughter by a priest. In infancy, he exhibited superhuman strength, canine teeth and a leonine mane and so he was declared *onikawa*, 'a demon child'. By his late teens he stood over 6 feet tall, which would mark him out as something strange even in Japan today, let alone in the Middle Ages. Notwithstanding his fast-growing demonic reputation, Benkei was a devout Buddhist and became a *Sohei*, a warrior-monk. His weapon of choice was the *naginata*, the sickle-bladed lance. One day Benkei made a stand on Kyoto's Gojo Bridge, determined to deprive every passing samurai of his sword. He had successfully challenged 999 of them and acquired as many swords when he faced his thousandth opponent. This was, of course, the youthful Yoshitsune, and of course Yoshitsune beat him. Benkei the giant, the most feared fighter in Japan, swore lifelong loyalty to him and was at his side throughout the Genpei War. Many felt the Genji owed much of their success in battle to this monk who was half-man half-monster.

Yoshitsune and his party arrived in Hiraizumi between late 1185 and early 1186. Hidehira, the third Ōshū Fujiwara lord and grandson of Chūson-ji's restorer, welcomed them and ensured their exile was as princely as possible. From their new residence, Koromogawa-no-tachi, a mansion on a small bluff beside the Koromo River, they climbed the hill to worship at Chūson-ji; they ventured along the valley to the complex of gilt and cinnabar palaces to dine with their Fujiwara hosts. They began to feel secure. Then, in October 1187, Hidehira Fujiwara died aged sixty-five. His last will and testament makes clear his wish for Yoshitsune's continued safekeeping:

'Treat the general,' he tells his two sons, 'as if he were your master. Govern our region under his authority.'

One of them, Tadahira, was happy to obey. The other, Yasuhira, was not.

Soon after Hidehira's death, Yoritomo learnt that his half-brother was hiding at Hiraizumi. When Yoshitsune was in his pomp, the court had conferred high rank on him at the cloistered emperor's insistence. Because of this rank, Yoritomo, a stickler for protocol, could not simply kill the fugitive: he had to receive an imperial mandate first. He petitioned Go-Shirakawa for permission to capture Yoshitsune. Permission was refused. Then one of Yoritomo's advisors came up with a solution that obeyed the samurai pecking order and offered no explicit offence to the court:

'Sir, these northern Fujiwara owe our clan everything. They are, in effect, your vassals. Never mind the Emperor – this is family business. Order Yasuhira to execute Yoshitsune for you.'

Yasuhira, Hidehira's elder son and successor, wasted no time in carrying out the order. On 30 April 1189, Yoshitsune, his family and servants were run to ground inside Koromogawa-no-tachi. One of the original party of refugees was missing, however – Benkei, who had stayed outside the mansion to face Yasuhira's men. Benkei's last stand is one of the most potent images of mediaeval Japanese history. He is often imagined raging upon the bridge of a castle which, in the Western-influenced imagination, sometimes morphs into a drawbridge. The likely reality has far greater pathos, and a brutal incongruity. The Fujiwara mansions were exquisite buildings, scarcely conceived with defence in mind. Many of them were approached via rainbow bridges, arcs of painted wood that spanned landscaped streams or lakes. In a poignant echo of Benkei's first meeting with Yoshitsune on the Gojo Bridge in Kyoto, it was upon just such an acme of refinement that the gargantuan warrior met his end.

He fought single-handedly, killing many of Yasuhira's men and terrifying many more into retreat. Eventually, his assailants noticed that Benkei had stopped fighting, that he was simply standing motionless between them and the mansion gates. Still they did not dare to approach until, covered in arrows and sword cuts, the giant finally fell like a tree. He had been dead for some time. *Benkei no tachi ōjō*, 'the standing death of Benkei', is one of the great symbols of Japanese stoicism and adherence to duty. And what, in this case, was Benkei's duty? Well, it was not the continued survival of his master but something far more important. When Yasuhira's troops swarmed into Koromogawa-no-tachi they found that the thirty-one-year-old exiled darling of feudal Japan had committed seppuku in the mansion's inner hall. Beside his dead body was his elderly retainer Kanefusa who had just helped Yoshitsune to kill his wife and four-year-old daughter, thus saving them from disgrace and cheating the enemy of trophies. Benkei had succeeded in fending off the enemy long enough for his master to perform these terrible duties. This is the point, and the tragic glory, of his standing death.

By obeying Yoritomo's order, Yasuhira had flouted his father's dying wishes. Worse still, he had miscalculated. Always a champion of Yoshitsune, his younger brother Tadahira now split from him, causing internecine strife in the northern Fujiwara family for the first time in four generations. Two months later, in June 1189, Yasuhira killed him. Although, with Tadahira out of the way, he believed the conflict had been resolved, the city of gold was beginning to look tarnished. Yasuhira had given Yoritomo a licence to do the very thing he had hoped to avert. On 19 July 1189, the Genji chief led his forces out of Kamakura. Their mission was the same as it had been for their ancestors, to bring peace to the troubled Deep North.

Yoritomo arrived in Hiraizumi on 22 August. He set up his headquarters exactly where his forebear Yoriyoshi had over a century before and he surrounded himself with the descendants of the earlier general's retainers.

Azuma Kagami, the official chronicle of the Bakufu, paints a remarkable picture of Yoritomo's troops rallied by night: 'Thousands upon thousands of soldiers stood before the general's hall, each holding a pure white Genji banner, with plumes of *Miscanthus* massed around them and the moon shining brightly overhead.' The city was soon under his control as, not long after, was the entire region of Ōshū. But what of Yasuhira? You might think the fourth Fujiwara lord gained favour with the Genji commander by killing Yoshitsune. Not so.

'I keep mentioning,' said Yoko, 'the key concept you need to grasp if you are to understand Yoritomo's thinking – On, the continuing debt of gratitude and service. Yoritomo's ancestors had cleared the way for the Fujiwara in the north; they had made Hiraizumi possible. In protecting Yoshitsune, the Fujiwara had done far worse than disobey Yoritomo: they had offended against On. It was not the first time the family had done so and this later offence was enough to condemn them all and for ever. No matter what Yasuhira did to make amends, his life was forfeit. But there was something else. Yasuhira had betrayed Yoshitsune and gone against the will of his own father, Hidehira. It didn't matter that Yoritomo actually wanted his half-brother dead and had ordered as much. In flouting duty and his father's principled stand, Yasuhira had disgraced himself. In Yoritomo's eyes, trust, family ties and the sanctity of pledges were the basis not just of clan life but of society as a whole. Yasuhira had made a mockery of them. He didn't have a hope.'

Rather than fight or commit suicide, Yasuhira fled north. *Azuma Kagami* reported:

> *Faced with several thousand soldiers, Yasuhira, scurrying like a rat and diving like a cormorant, headed for Tsugaru* [in Aomori Prefecture], *his plan being to cross to Hokkaido. He arrived in Nienosaku, hoping to win the support of his retainer Jirō Kawada whose family had served the Fujiwara clan for generations. Like master, like servant: Kawada took Yasuhira in, but has since had him beheaded. It is believed that Kawada is now travelling to Hiraizumi to make Yoritomo a present of Yasuhira's head.*

So on 3 September 1189 Yasuhira died, thirty-five years old and the last of the Fujiwara line in the north. Kawada duly delivered his late lord's head to Yoritomo. The Genji chief thanked him for his trouble and then had him decapitated for betraying his master. The samurai code is nothing if not punctilious.

On 6 September, Yoritomo assembled the descendants of the soldiers who had removed and exhibited the head of Sadatō Abe 127 years before. In an exact re-enactment of those events, he had them hammer Yasuhira's head to the gateposts of his camp with a nail 24 centimetres long. Soon afterwards he gave the running of the region to a loyal retainer. The Genji chief had to wait a few years more for his own reward. In July 1192, five months after the death of his old adversary Emperor Go-Shirakawa, Yoritomo was finally appointed shogun. Meanwhile, the Deep North was harrowed by war once more. The Ōshū Fujiwara clan was dishonoured and dismembered. In less than a century, they had made Hiraizumi shine and had seen it extinguished.

Cio-Cio-san stirred into life to announce our arrival. She sounded like a young mother promising to kiss it better.

'I do wish she wouldn't interrupt,' said Yoko. 'I seem to have depressed you. Don't worry: there's a happy ending of sorts. You see that small mountain over there? All you have to do is climb it to find out how the lotus fits into this story.'

30

Bamboo Autumn

It was bamboo autumn when I first saw Chūson-ji. No real autumn, *take no aki* falls at the beginning of summer. It starts in the south and travels northwards in a golden wave, washing over the landscape in the interval between the two other seasonal waves that sweep the archipelago – the pink of cherry blossom and the scarlet of maple. It is the time when Japan's larger bamboos lose last year's leaves in readiness for the midsummer rainy season and the violent flush of new growth that it brings. On the hills around Hiraizumi, their groves intersperse dark stands of firs and become, for the brief duration of *take no aki*, glittering backlit fountains. Deceptively gentle, soon drifting and banking to form thick carpets beneath polished canes, their leaves drop in a rain of Nankeen yellow. In this strange pseudo-season, an interlude of unearthly luminosity and regeneration foretold, I set out on the pilgrim's path to the citadel of gold.

It is a demanding path, beginning on the flat with Benkei's grave, an enclosure that contains a small stupa and a huddle of stones engraved with calligraphy. Beside them soars a single black pine. Mingled with its roots are the remains of the monster-warrior who single-handedly enabled Yoshitsune's last stand. Soon afterwards, the way begins to climb, ascending the flank of Kanzan, the peak which, a thousand years ago, was the northernmost outpost of Japanese civilisation and on whose summit Chūson-ji sits. The path's appearance owes much to Masamune Date, the seventeenth-century daimyō of the north and inveterate plantsman. He and his successors lined the route to Chūson-ji with retaining walls of grey granite sets. The procession of lantern-lit, gilded statues that marked the way in Fujiwara times had long since gone. In their place, the Date clan planted colonnades of sugi (*Cryptomeria japonica*). Three or four centuries later, these conifers tower like redwoods, their cinnamon boles and black-green boughs forming vast sentry lines, unperturbed unless by a sudden shower of bamboo leaves or the passage of some low-flying cloud.

'It will be,' said this horticultural warlord, 'a tunnel to lead you through time to the age of glory.'

Time is not the only dimension through which Date's tunnel transports pilgrims. As one climbs, a chill asserts itself and the air becomes pine-scented. Gone are the miasmas of Hiraizumi's humid flood plain: the magic mountain is an alpine peak. The flattened crowns and parchment-edged leaves of sasa (the smaller, shrubbier bamboos) attested to the fact that, not long before, these slopes had lain under snow. I found it hard to imagine anything so exotic as a lotus growing there. And yet prodigies are nurtured in the kind embrace of bamboo autumn. All around us, wild and unbidden, a Western gardener's wish list erupted from the leaf litter– fiddleheads of reawakened ferns, python-mouthed pitchers of *Arisaema*, and arching stems of *Lilium auratum*, the celebrated golden-rayed lily of Japan. It was just conceivable that the lotus might be sheltering here in some favoured hollow. Step away from the trees and the temperature soared, which is what *Nelumbo* needs in summer.

Some Japanese landscapes are designed purely to be seen under snow. The route to Chūson-ji was planned with a slightly wider window of opportunity in mind. It is called Tsukimi-zaka, 'the moon view approach'. The idea was twofold: by night the path itself would be rendered sublime by the vast shadows of Date's legion of guardian conifers; meanwhile, a platform cut midway up the mountain's eastern side would give a moonlit vista of plain beneath and hills beyond. In daylight the prospect from this eyrie was less dramatic, more Arcadian. Below us, the Kitakami and Koromo Rivers met and idled through a patchwork of *Miscanthus* grassland and newly planted paddy-fields. Like the multicoloured, transecting layers of a Heian Period kimono, the slopes of faraway hills overlapped, each assuming a different tone according to its vegetation, mistiness and distance. The plain's utter emptiness and tranquillity made it all the more poignant that this had been the theatre of two centuries of conflict, conflict whose crises now revealed themselves as if in a three-dimensional map – this curve in the river was where Yoriyoshi and Yoritomo made their headquarters; that gentle slope was where an army fell in a day; on a nearby hill once stood Koromogawa-no-tachi, the mansion where Yoshitsune and his family met their end, protected to the last by implacable Benkei. In 1689, 500 years after these events unfolded, Bashō surveyed this same scene:

> *Countless acts of valour took place here in the span of just three genera-*
> *tions, but the protagonists are long since dead. They and their deeds have*
> *passed into oblivion, lost in a wilderness of grass. In a land laid waste by*
> *war, rivers and mountains endure: in spring only weeds flourish on a ruined*
> *castle. My bamboo hat beneath me, I sat weeping at this sight, so grief-*
> *stricken that I lost all sense of time.*
>
> *Wildflowers are the legacy of the dreams of fallen warriors.*

As I took in this prospect, I had a strange sense of all the dramatis personae in my lotus quest gathering in this one place as if for some final act – the refined Fujiwara, the austere Genji, Bashō the poet. Even the Jōmon with whom the saga began survived longer here than they did further south. Such was this sense of convergence, of figures in a landscape, that for a moment I felt almost as if it was they who had led me there. Perhaps they had – woefully little planning had gone into my journey after all; or perhaps I was simply lucky in my choice of the living.

Eventually the moon view approach arrived at a plateau about 130 metres above the plain, navigated by cobbled lanes and screened by forest. This was Chūson-ji, now a complex of some 20 religious buildings constructed and reconstructed over the past millennium. At first sight, there was little indi-cation of the gilded splendour of the Fujiwara settlement, much of which had been lost either to time or to a fire that engulfed the peak in 1337. What remained, however, was perhaps more moving – an aura of profound simplicity and antiquity engendered by the weather-worn grain and sere tones of the surviving wooden structures as they sat, each within its own close and glade, in this sacred village.

Into muted pared-down scenes such as this the Japanese have a genius for introducing small but transforming accents of colour. Like the red seal that lifts and finishes a work of calligraphy, flashes of scarlet could be glimpsed among the sombre verticals of bamboo and standing stones. These were the brilliant bibs and mobcaps with which petitioning pilgrims – worried or mourning parents mostly – had dressed beaming figures of O-Jizō-sama or Jizō-Bosatsu, the winsome guardian deity of children. These smiling statuettes congregated about a small moat filled with brilliant yellow irises. Beyond it, and reached via a bleached-wood rainbow bridge, was the hall of Benzaiten, the watery goddess to whom the centrepiece of Tokyo's Secret Lake and Lady Masako's shrine at Kamakura are also dedicated. Before addressing the sacred image in her shadowy sanctuary, supplicants would observe the ritual of hand-washing, but not – I noticed – in the usual rough-hewn basin. Before Benzaiten's shrine stood the massive granite likeness of a lotus, strangely reminiscent of a Romanesque font as it shot skywards, brimming with water, on its stout stone stalk.

Comforted by having encountered at least one lotus on this northern peak, I wandered on. I found myself questioning the idea that Chūson-ji had reached its climax in the twelfth century and since become a synonym for sadness. Surely the real wonder of the place was not that it was once clad in gold but that the bones of the buildings had survived and with them their spiritual essence? In 1126, for example, Kiyohira wrote to the emperor describing the library that he had constructed. It was a two-tiered structure vividly painted, gilded and lacquered and containing thousands of illuminated sutras. Astonishingly, the lower storey of this library remained, seemingly immune to warfare and conflagration, earthquake and extreme weather. Its scented cypress shelves were now devoid of sutras, but it had found a new purpose. The bone-white wooden beams had become a pilgrims' palimpsest, plastered in a myriad paper prayer stickers that identified generations of worshippers who had made the journey to Chūson-ji. The contents of Kiyohira's library, I learnt, were long ago rehoused elsewhere. As sacred texts go, however, the centuries of godly graffiti that had supplanted them seemed no less venerable.

The buildings are not all of such ruinous perfection. Hondō, the main hall and ceremonial centre of the temple complex, has been rebuilt at intervals since its founding in the ninth century when the eternal flame was first carried to the Deep North from the Tendai Sect in Kyoto. The same fire flickers in Hondō's sanctuary to this day. The hall's last substantial re-incarnation was in 1909 and this was effectively what I now saw. A massive structure with a shimmering, low-skirted roof and gold-trimmed beams and walls, it radiated power and polish. Even at this early hour, the forecourt was busy with worshippers, their devotions announced by the repeated ringing of coins thrown into the offertory chest. Their number was noticeably strong on two classes – dewy young couples full of anxious hope, and corvine-suited businessmen. Yet while Hondō exuded none of the melancholy of the old sutra library, it too was a palimpsest: 'When we rebuild,' I was later told, 'we do not erase.' In addition to a flame that had burned since the Dark Ages, the hall possessed artefacts that antedated our Norman Conquest, a bell that was first heard around the time of the Battle of Agincourt, and a timber gateway that was contemporary with the English Civil War.

None of these miracles of endurance was quite a match for Hondō's gardens. Here grew *ume*, Japanese plum trees, whose blossom had heralded the arrival of a thousand springs. Hollowed and blackened, their trunks were nothing more than enfolded robes of bark, looming from the gravelled precincts. From their upper volutes, however, sprang fresh green rods which just a few weeks earlier had borne a mass of white, rose and crimson – flowers whose scent solaced the first Fujiwara lord of the Deep North when, battle-bloodied, he climbed Kanzan and resolved to restore the temple he found on its summit. Dancing from branch to branch was an olive-brown bird that wolf-whistled with a fruitiness and volume out of all proportion to its size. This, Yoko told me, was *uguisu* (*Cettia diphone*). Beloved of poets as a harbinger of summer, it is often called the Japanese nightingale, although it sings by day and in impudent four-syllable bursts that are far from the Rāg-like descanting of its Western namesake.

'It has another name which might amuse you,' she said. 'We call it *Kyō-yomi-dori*, "sutra-chanting bird".' The nightingale sang again, deafeningly, bobbing on the twig to get its wind up and staring me out with jet bead eyes. 'Don't you hear it? The cry is exactly the same as *Hō-Hoke-kyō*.'

'I certainly hear it,' I told her, 'but what does *Hō-Hoke-kyō* mean?'

Hoke-Kyō, she explained, is the *Lotus Sutra*; 'Hō-Hoke-Kyō' a way of invoking it. Kiyohira had founded Chūson-ji with a request that the sutra should be said endlessly for the injured creatures of his war-torn domain. Here they were, 900 years later, not only in rude health but reciting it back at him. Because of the Lord of Hiraizumi's request, I was able to compare the bird's call with the real thing, a comparison from which the nightingale emerged the worse. From the hall of Hondō and the buildings behind it, there emanated 'Nam myō hō Renge-Kyō', the formal invocation of the *Lotus Sutra*. Ceaselessly chanted by Chūson-ji's monks, it provided a haunting basso-continuo for our investigations. At intervals the officiating priest would strike the *rin*, the bronze standing bell or singing bowl. Its chime would wander with the chants from the shadows of the sanctum to find us in sunlight, often coinciding with some small discovery of our own, and reinforcing the sense that everything at Chūson-ji was choreographed.

Just within the gate of Hondō there thrived another survivor, still more surprising than the aged plum trees. It was a sketch of Kiyohira's later endeavours, a small and perfect sample of the Jōdo-tei'en, the paradisiacal Pure Land gardens that he and his sons would go on to create on such a vast scale around Hiraizumi. Jewelled with violets and trimmed with irises, turf ran down to the sinuous outlines of an ancient pond. In its centre was a heart-shaped islet, a 'mystic island' of the kind pioneered by Fujiwara garden-makers in Heian Period Kyoto. But this was a paradise of the Deep North, not the suave south, and so the islet was fringed with *mizu bashō*, 'water banana'. Japanese folk botany classified this denizen of cold watery places as a banana on account of its large and lolling leaves. It was not an unreasonable identification: as summer advances, its foliage does come to resemble that of *bashō*, Japan's true banana. *Mizu bashō*, however, is a member of the arum family, *Lysichiton camtschatcensis*, and it is most remarkable for its inflorescences which appear in low-borne clumps before the leaves – sometimes so long before them that they have to break ice to flower. Each comprises a large waxy white cowl that envelops a golden club-shaped spadix. I pictured their pale hooded forms on the mystic island, a preternatural-seeming sight amid the receding snows of Chūson-ji, like a raft of ghosts adrift on the Pure Land pond.

At that moment, something disturbed the pool. It was not *mizu no oto*, Bashō's famous frog splash. This was subtler, a swiftly advancing arc-shaped tremor. A split second later, I realised it was the pre-shock of Hondō's huge hanging bell which now filled the air with an immense and lingering sound midway between the boom of a gong and the shimmer of a cymbal. Its impact could be described as neither knell nor peal. It seemed, rather, to drench the entire landscape or perhaps even to emanate from it like a seismic pulse. Later I found a description of this root-numbing resonance, in a letter that Kiyohira wrote to the Emperor in 1126, as he neared death and after two decades of rebuilding Chūson-ji:

> The sound of the temple bell will be heard all over the world, removing pain and bringing pleasure. It will resonate with all living creatures alike. Here

in the Deep North many warriors, both friend and foe, have surrendered their lives down the years of strife. Moreover, countless beasts, birds and fish have been killed in the course of these conflicts. Their spirits now have all gone to another world; their bones have decayed and become the very soil of the Deep North. I pray that the sound of the great temple bell at Chūson-ji may heal the souls of all these creatures who have died without blame and lead them towards the Pure Land.

I made for the source of the sound in the hope of discovering what it proclaimed. Once beside the great bronze bell in its wooden frame, I noticed that my fellow visitors were staring and bowing in my direction. This caused me some puzzlement, not to say discomfort, until, on a nod from Yoko, I turned to find the real object of their attention standing behind me. He was a well-built man, perhaps fifty or older, but impossible to age more precisely such was the bloom of well-being that marked, or rather had not marked, his face. He was wearing traditional robes and plain wooden geta, the whole costume brilliant white save for a wide-sleeved coat of black silk gauze. Around his wrist was a loop of lacquered prayer beads. He bowed and then, as his close-cropped head rose, fixed me with the smiling, searching stillness that is sometimes ascribed to the first diagnostic glance of great physicians. Finally he spoke:

'My name is Haseki. I believe you have come to see me.'

31

The Golden Hall

Chūson-ji has a collegiate structure that recalls Oxford University, or perhaps Mount Athos, given its terrain and purpose. Although autonomous, its various temples and shrines are bound within a confederation served by common facilities that include libraries, museums and a Noh theatre. Haseki-Jūshoku, to give him his title, is the chief priest of one such temple, Kongō-in. To judge by the reception he was accorded by the crowd around us, his writ goes far wider than that. Like his ancestors before him, he was born and raised at Hiraizumi and has spent his life on the sacred mountain, apart from periods of study in Tokyo and overseas. Somehow the bush or lotus telegraph had reached his northern fastness: just as I was beginning to wonder why my journey should have brought me there, Haseki-Jūshoku materialised to explain.

He began by leading us to Sankōzō. Opened in 2000, the 'treasure house' is one of several modern buildings at Chūson-ji that mark a new flowering for the temple complex. I was relieved to see that it made no attempt to parody its antique neighbours. Although imbued with a distinctly Japanese aesthetic and constructed in part from local materials, Sankōzō was, rather, monumental, minimalist, all sharp lines and sleek surfaces. Into this immaculate case, the priests had placed a thousand years' worth of treasures, anything that could no longer be safely housed in its original setting or which deserved to be drawn from the secrecy of temple sanctuaries and placed on public display.

'You will see,' said Haseki-Jūshoku, 'that this is not just a museum and a library. It is also a place of worship.' The first chamber of the treasure house left no room for doubt. A lofty, sugi-wood-coffered hall, it was a working temple. On a broad dais sat a trinity of great gilded Buddhas; before them stood the traditional permanent offerings of vases containing sinuous bouquets of lotus flowers and leaves sculpted in bronze-gilt, and altars bearing more transient tributes of cut flowers and daily gifts of food. 'The building is new, but these statues date from the founding of Chūson-ji and were moved here to consecrate the treasure house. In the centre is the Amida Buddha, the originator of the Pure Land and the principal Buddha of our faith. To either side of him are statues of Yakushi-nyorai, the Buddha of medicine. He is important for us because he embodies the two aims with which Chūson-ji was founded and then restored – physical healing, as in making good the actual damage done here by decades of warfare; and spiritual healing, as in coming to terms with the grief and loss inflicted by all those years of conflict. You have doubtless noticed the most potent emblem of this process of recon-ciliation and regeneration.' Behind the head of the right-hand figure was a halo some 6 feet wide and fashioned in the image of a massive lotus flower, its outspread petals lit with the deep honeyed lustre of thousand-year-old gold leaf. 'That is the largest lotus I will show you,' said the Chief Priest, 'but not the most important.'

We continued through the treasure house, the other visitors standing aside and bowing to Haseki-Jūshoku in a way that elicited a beguiling expression from him, somewhere between unspoken benediction and apology. There followed a cascade of lotuses: the sacred flower bloomed everywhere among Sankōzō's accessions, engraved, sculpted, painted and described in every object, on every text, in gold, wood, stone and ink. Finally he paused before a 6-foot statue of a standing figure. It was carved in wood and lacquered with obsidian black save for its bare torso, unreadably beautiful face and a halo from whose centre a lotus cast spoke-like sunbeams. All of these were brightly gilded, as were most of the objects that it held in 24 of its 32 hands. I found myself transfixed by the lifelike suppleness of its serried arms: they appeared to move, a disturbing effect echoed in other features of the figure such as the big toe of his left foot which was upturned as if tapping time upon its golden lotus pedestal. The appearance of these notes of naturalism in so unearthly a chimaera inspired a curious mixture of awe and sympathy, of distance and identification. This, I would soon discover, was the general intention.

'Don't you think he looks like a superhuman Swiss Army pocket knife?' whispered Yoko. When I expressed shock at her impiety, she countered, 'If you think that was sacrilegious, you'll find it hard to understand what this god is for.'

'Meet Senju Kannon Bosatsu,' said the Chief Priest, revealing a better grasp of English than either of us had reckoned on; and then, reverting to Japanese: 'You might translate his name as "The Thousand-Handed Bodhisattva of Mercy", although ours actually has only a symbolic 32 hands. He is a *bosatsu*, an enlightened being who exists to guide us along the path to enlightenment, to protect and to heal us, and to show us compassion, the quality of which he is the divine embodiment. You should know him anyway; but, for your immediate purposes, Kannon is also the subject of the twenty-fifth chapter of the *Lotus Sutra*, a chapter so well-known that it is sometimes recited as if it were a sutra in its own right. It ends with an invocation to him as the deity who hears and understands all the sounds of the world, the great sage who answers the pleas of those who are suffering or in peril, and who views all living things with sympathy. His multiple arms indicate two things – the extent of his reaching out to life on earth, and his mastery of countless different disciplines. In other words these many hands, each holding a useful tool or some precious object, symbolise his sheer helpfulness, or the fathomless ocean of his blessings as the *Lotus Sutra* puts it.'

The Chief Priest stepped away to let my gaze range over Kannon's heavenly battery. The deity was holding, *inter alia*, a horsehair flywhisk, a medicine pot, a pen, a miniature pagoda that might have been a model of Chūson-ji's original sutra library, a cloisonné dagger, an ormolu garland of herbs, and a wheel like a gilded ship's wheel or perhaps like the Genji Guruma, the family crest that Yoko had hidden from me for so long. Interspersed among these objects were small gilt sculptures of the lotus at various stages of growth, delicately proffered by Senju Kannon's pitch-black, perfectly poised fingers. From somewhere behind me Haseki-Jūshoku's gentle baritone interrupted my reverie:

'When Kannon holds them, these lotuses symbolise purification, the expiation of what in your world are termed sins. That process of cleansing and redemption is an important part of the story here at Hiraizumi as I will show you. But these flowers are not the objects on which you should focus if you really wish to understand the lotus and its role in our lives. You need instead to look at Senju Kannon's fourth hand from the top on the left.

You see he is holding a golden wheel. This is known as *Hōrin* which you might translate as the wheel of dharma, or the wheel of becoming. It represents the different phases of being through which we must progress if we are ever to become enlightened. The key feature of Hōrin is that it is circular: it symbolises the cyclical nature of our progress through birth, life, death and rebirth, in a rotation that can only be broken, a spinning that can only be stopped by achieving true enlightenment. This cycle is called Samsara. It is sometimes misrepresented as a process of suffering and waiting, as if it were some earth-bound equivalent of the Christian Purgatory; but it is much more positive than that. Samsara is the great flow of life in which all creatures must engage. It has been said that the wheel of becoming was originally suggested by the lotus with its circular leaves and flowers. That may be so. Certainly Hōrin has spokes, as you see, which might be reminiscent of either leaf veins or petals. The important thing to hang on to, however, is the idea of the cycle, Samsara. Before our meeting has finished, I will show you how this idea relates equally to lotuses and humans.'

A modest pavilion stood at the crest of a forested slope, unadorned and unannounced, a quietly enigmatic building that challenged one to ascend and enter. At the foot of the long flight of steps that led to it, the Chief Priest began: 'Shogun Yoritomo's widow, Lady Masako, was a great one for dreams. One night in 1213 she received a visitor as she lay sleeping in Kamakura. It was the spirit of Hidehira, the last of the three great lords of Hiraizumi, father of the treacherous Yasuhira, and protector of Yoshitsune, Lady Masako's outlawed brother-in-law. In a dream, Hidehira suggested to her that Chūson-ji should be repaired. *Suggested* is what the chronicler says – not pleaded or demanded. In death as in life, it appears the gentle lord of the Ōshū Fujiwara managed exactly the right tone to mollify a Genji. Although officially retired and in religious seclusion, Lady Masako was now the Nun Shogun and even more powerful than she had been during her husband's lifetime. So it was with a troubled conscience but no practical difficulty that, on waking, she called for the Bakufu's property manager and ordered him to attend to her ghostly visitor's wishes.

No sooner had he taken Hiraizumi than Yoritomo assembled the monks. The general assured them that Chūson-ji would be safe and asked them to pray for those who had died in the assault. Thereafter, the Genji were careful not to desecrate the temple complex. But they had, perhaps, neglected it. Finally, a quarter-century after the battle, Yoritomo's widow began its restoration. Work culminated some 60 years after her own death, in the construction of what appeared to be a very large and well-made but otherwise completely plain wooden shed. This was ō'i-dō, 'the sheath house', of 1288. For the past seven centuries the shed and its modern successor, which you see now, have contained and protected our greatest treasure, Konjiki-dō, the Golden Hall.'

As I climbed the steps, my first impression of Konjiki-dō was olfactory. Fingers of incense coiled from the open doors of the sheath house. Haseki-Jūshoku explained it was called Kanzan-kō, 'border post scent', from the original name of Chūson-ji's remote site, and that it was made from the same plants and in the same way as it had been 1,000 years ago. In its complexity Kanzan-kō was quite unlike any other incense I had smelt. In one draught it seemed to contain a progress from riches and sensuality to austerity and sanctity, the progress of Chūson-ji itself. Its first hit was heavy and exotic, warmed with sandalwood and spices more redolent of India than Japan. Yet there soon followed something mellower and more mesmeric, conjuring camphor and star anise, gardenia and bergamot. This finished on a long ghostly note, vetiver perhaps, a recondite and tranquillising perfume suggestive of hallowed dust.

The journey so far had been into darkness, away from sunny precincts, up shadowy steps with woodland surrounds, through shrouds of incense and into the twilight of the sheath house. Then, as I went further, all became brilliance. Before me stood a pavilion with an up-curved roof and a solidly built sanctuary. Such was the wonder of this structure that all sense of scale was banished. Konjiki-dō exerts monumentality out of all proportion with its actual size of just a little over 5 metres square and 8 metres tall. This pavilion was what the shed had been designed to protect – hardly surprising, for every inch of its surface was gold. Howard Carter would have been hard pressed to describe the awe of discovering such a shining artefact within the sepulchral gloom of its humble shelter.

For all its brilliance, sepulchral is essentially what Konjiki-dō is. The golden hall is tomb as well as temple. Beneath its three-part altar lie the coffined remains of the great lords of the Deep North. They include the dynasty's founding father, Kiyohira, who began building his final resting place in August 1124, four years before he died, and Hidehira whose own death in 1187 marked the beginning of the end for the Ōshū Fujiwara. Over their mummies there soars an ecstatic vision in sculpture and inlay of the paradise of the

Tendai Sect. On the central dais, the Amida Buddha sits enthroned amid a crowd of statues consisting of irenic bodhisattvas and ferocious guardian deities. Recessed to either side of him, two further daises repeat this tableau with different attendant divinities and protectors: Guardian of the East and one of the four fearsome Heavenly Kings, Jikokuten, for example, is shown like some 24-carat superhero, trampling a swine-snouted demon to dust. Every contour of these figures is covered in gold leaf. Other features are solid gold, among them the fretwork bo-leaf screens behind the Buddhas, the sanctuary's spangled veils, and the giant lotus blossom lantern that hangs like a sunburst in the temple vault.

The altars and railings of Konjiki-dō are gilded to such a depth that it would be fairer to talk of plating. On the front panel of the main altar three paradisiacal peacocks preen themselves in fields of gleaming peonies. The woodwork that surrounds them is inlaid with stylised floral motifs in mother-of-pearl. It is a pattern that reaches its climax on the pillars of the sanctuary in great discs of nacreous arabesque that shimmer in the half-light of the sheath house.

'This inlay,' said Haseki-Jūshoku, 'was probably more important to the Fujiwara than the gold. You see it was a product from mainland Asia. Similarly, the designs, which strike one as so stylised and symmetrical, so seemingly un-Japanese, were heavily influenced by the arts of the Middle East. In their day they were the acme of modernity, of imported chic. But they were readily assimilated by Buddhism: the Pure Land paradise of the Tendai Sect lies to the symbolic west, so motifs and materials from the geographical west were thought to be of special spiritual value. And you have doubtless noticed that what might in Persia have been a tulip or a poppy flower motif has sometimes evolved here into the buds and seed heads of the lotus.

'Where the flowers are so idealised that they can no longer be identified, they are known as *Hōsōge*, and the pattern of swirling leaves in which they bloom is called *Hōsōge-karakusa-moyo*. It is a design that is closely associated with the mediaeval Japanese arts of Pure Land Buddhism. It was brought to perfection here at Chūson-ji. I see you are attempting to identify just what exactly Hōsōge flowers might be. It is like watching an ornithologist trying to anatomise a phoenix. You shouldn't try. Hōsōge is an imaginary portmanteau plant, an impossible hybrid: acanthus, peonies, roses, lilies, ivy, grape vines, date palms, poppies and lotuses are all in its make-up. In terms of lineage, it is the harvest of Ancient Egypt, Greece, Mesopotamia, India,

China *and* Japan. This may be the most fascinating thing that Hōsōge flowers proclaim. They reveal the extent to which the Ōshū Fujiwara penetrated the Asian continent and beyond via trade, by might of gold and through connoisseurship. What these flowers of paradise tell us is that this building, Konjiki-dō, was the eastern terminus of the Silk Road.'

The impression created by all this artistry is of energy and plenitude, of the bad put down and the good life embraced. It is the most brilliant of all the attempts made at Chūson-ji to realise the Pure Land in this life, and the ultimate attempt because it is believed to be the threshold of the next life. It strives to embody the profusion of the *Lotus Sutra*, the surreal opulence that erupts time after time in passages such as this one from chapter 24, 'The Bodhisattva Wonderful Sound':

> *Thereupon the Bodhisattva Wonderful Sound, without rising from his seat or swaying his body, entered into a samadhi [meditative state], and through the power of the samadhi, in a place not far removed from the Dharma seat on Mount Gridhrakuta, created a jewelled mass of eighty-four thousand lotus blossoms. Their stems were made of Jambunada gold, their leaves were of silver, their stamens of diamond, and their calyxes of kimshuka jewels.*

But the ornate dynamism of the altar is pacified by the smiling countenance of the Amida Buddha. As one steps as far away from Konjiki-dō as the walls of the sheath house permit, only this central figure remains in view, shining within his aureate sanctum. At this little distance, the temple's superstructure is revealed to be entirely and dazzlingly gold from its roof to its flooring, and gold that is not yellow and meretricious but of a lambent autumnal cast that seems to emit a light of its own. I noticed that my companions' faces had become amber in its radiance, as if admiring a sunset.

Unlike many of Japan's wooden temples and shrines, the golden hall has never been rebuilt, only restored and re-covered with its protective shed, and then just once or twice in its nine-century history. It is, perhaps, poetic justice that the finest achievement and final resting place of the Ōshū Fujiwara should have endured thanks to the troubled dream-life of Lady Masako, the widow of that clan's nemesis. The persistence of so precious an artefact in so wild a place struck Bashō when he visited Konjiki-dō in the bamboo autumn of 1689:

. . . At last I saw inside the temple itself, whose marvels I had often heard described . . . In the Golden Hall were coffins that contained the bodies of the three lords who once ruled this region, and the trinity of sacred images. Like the mansions of Hiraizumi, this holy building would also have vanished under a choking blanket of grass, its treasures dispersed, its glittering doors broken in and golden columns shattered, were it not for the temple's stout outer housing and waterproof tiles. Only in this way does it survive, a monument for a millennium and longer.

Even spring's long rains cannot reach the Golden Hall to douse its shining.

Apart from the miracle of its survival, the real wonder of Konjiki-dō is that this small structure, so secret in its sylvan shelter, so little known outside Japan, should have spawned mysteries and quests that in turn made history and spanned the globe. Japan's most familiar gilded buildings, such as Kinkakuji, Kyoto's Golden Pavilion, were erected long after Konjiki-dō. In their day, Chūson-ji's golden hall, and Hiraizumi, the Fujiwara Shangri-la, were without rivals. So it seems safe to assume, as several historians have, that it was these marvels that lay behind the mediaeval Western legend of Chipangu, Zipang, Japan the island of gold.

According to Marco Polo:

The palace of the lord of that island is entirely roofed with fine gold, just as our churches are roofed with lead, insomuch as it would scarcely be possible to estimate its value. Moreover, all the pavements of the palace, and the floors of its chambers, are entirely in gold, in plates like slabs of stone, a good two fingers thick; and the windows are also of gold, so that altogether the richness of this palace is past all bounds and all belief.

Although this is a confabulation which the traveller probably picked up in China, we should not discount it. The Ōshū Fujiwara had been vigorously trading with mainland Asia just a century before Marco Polo heard these Chinese whispers, and in the Middle Ages 'Chipangu' – Japan – had no other city of gold, or gold-producing region, to equal Hiraizumi. If we allow that distance lends enlargement was well as enchantment, Marco Polo's 'palace' could easily have been Konjiki-dō. His descriptions of the thickness and extent of the gold plating are by no means exaggerated. Even his impossible-sounding gold windows can be explained. The sanctuary of Konjiki-dō is effectively a giant box. Its heavenly contents can be exposed, glimpsed or sealed in their own effulgence, through a sequence of stout golden shutters.

Consequences flowed from the rumour that Japan was so rich in gold that the metal was used there for building. In Polo's own lifetime, it provoked his hero, Khubilai Khan, China's Mongol ruler, to attempt two invasions of Japan. The second of these, in 1281, was then the largest foreign campaign ever mounted. Although the forces of the Kamakura Bakufu had managed to hold the first wave of invaders at bay, there was little hope for Japan the second time, faced with such monstrous odds. The Mighty Khan, however, had not reckoned on the weather. Just as all seemed lost for the samurai, a typhoon destroyed the greater part of the Mongol fleet and forced the rump to flee. This typhoon was, of course, the original *kamikaze* – 'divine wind', heaven-sent protection for the land of the gods. Just over two centuries later, another expedition inspired by Polo's swooning over auric Chipangu produced still more sensational results – namely, Christopher Columbus's 'discovery' of the Americas. Columbus had believed himself headed for Japan's mythical mother lode when he ran into the Bahamas.

Great events had proceeded from this sublime incongruity hidden on its remote and wooded hilltop. But as Haseki-Jūshoku led us away, I found myself pondering something more trivial-seeming, a whodunnit sort of question that it would have been sacrilege to ask within the incandescent sanctity of Konjiki-dō. If the golden hall contained the remains of three Fujiwara lords, what had become of Yasuhira, the headless fourth and final lord?

32

Samsara

'I think this may be what you really came to see,' said Haseki-Jūshoku. Before us was a circular wooden box, 35 centimetres across by 22 centimetres deep, and with a close-fitting lid. After the galleries of gilded statues and the gold and pearl sanctum of Konjiki-dō, this tub was a strikingly simple object, somewhat scuffed and thinly lacquered in plain black – rather a comedown, in short. The Chief Priest explained:

'The year was 1950 and in the course of restoring Konjiki-dō, it was decided that we should examine the coffins of the three great Ōshū Fujiwara lords who lay beneath the altar. To the right-hand side, you will remember, there is the Buddha surrounded by guardian deities. Underneath them we found the coffin of Hidehira who had died in 1187. It was Hidehira who welcomed Yoshitsune and his retinue to Hiraizumi and gave them asylum here. He was also, of course, the father of Yasuhira, the last of the northern Fujiwara lords who notoriously betrayed the exiled Yoshitsune before losing his own head in 1189.

'These coffins had remained unopened for more than seven centuries and so the anticipation in lifting their lids was intense. Hidehira's was a long narrow casket made from the wood of hiba [the conifer *Thujopsis dolabrata*] and unadorned save for a coating of gilt. Within it we found his body and various objects – small jewelled ornaments that were wrapped in his shroud together with various seeds. When you consider the great wealth of the Ōshū Fujiwara and the splendour of Konjiki-dō, the inclusion of these seeds rather than more ostentatious grave goods is fascinating. They represent – in embryo, shall we say? – the ideal flora of the Pure Land, and wealth not in this life but the next.

'Consider these seeds that were found in the coffin. The reason for including rice and millet is obvious enough. With *momo* [peach, *Prunus persica*] and *ume* [the Japanese plum, *Prunus mume*], it is a little more complex. Both fruits are edible and the first is a symbol of longevity while the second is medicinal. But they are also important emblems of a kind of paradise. Our equivalent of your Classical Elysian Fields is filled with the blossom of peach and plum, which is why you will find specimens of ume still flowering in the precincts of Chūson-ji that date from Kiyohira's time. Also in the coffin were stones of *uamizu-zakura* [*Prunus grayana*], a small cherry. We used to pickle its young flower sprays and fruit, believing that the resulting liqueur was an elixir. But this cherry was thought able to tell the future too: long ago, carving a groove on a branch of it was an important part of Shinto divination ceremonies. So an ecumenical note enters this Buddhist burial – quite typical of Japanese religion.

'Now to more practical matters. Next we found seeds of *aburachan* [*Lindera praecox*], a shrub whose oil was used for lamps. *Urushi* [*Rhus verniciflua*] is the source of lacquer. A medicine for chest and skin complaints was derived from seeds of *oni-gurumi* [the walnut, *Juglans mandschurica* var. *sieboldiana*]. *Kuri* [the chestnut *Castanea crenata*] has edible nuts, but it is also a tree of great spiritual resonance, as I shall explain to you later. Good heavy-duty timber came from *kaya* [*Torreya nucifera*, the same softwood from which the Kemigawa Jōmon canoes were hewn], and lesser wood from *shira-kashi* [the evergreen oak, *Quercus myrsinaefolia*]. Both these trees were equally useful alive, as sources of shelter and windbreaks. Both were entombed with Hidehira. So you see, the coffin contained a vegetable economy, the seeds of most things that the late lord would need to recreate Hiraizumi in the afterlife. Most things except the gold that had made him so powerful in this life, and all plants but one.

'Where, you must be asking, does this plain black box come into the story? Well, it too was found inside Hidehira's coffin. It is a tub for keeping and serving cooked rice, and you will see containers like it all over Japan to this day – nothing special, just honest, everyday domestic ware. But this is a tub with a difference. We call it Kubi-oke, "the head box", for the very good reason that, when we opened it, we found it contained a human head, the well-preserved head of an aristocratic man probably in his thirties. Because it had been severed with a diagonal stroke that ran from the occipital bulge to just below the jaw bone, the head fitted into the rice box very neatly. Although I was very young at the time, I remember it clearly: when the lid was taken off and the cotton covering removed, the head was sitting there on its cut surface, as if he was looking up at me. Our first thought was that it must belong to Tadahira, Hidehira's younger son whom Yasuhira killed in 1189. It seemed likely that Yasuhira might have added to fratricide the insult of burying his brother's remains in something as ignominious as a rice box.

'Once we examined this find more closely, we knew we had to question our assumption. In the centre of the forehead we found a hole; this corresponded to another hole, like an exit wound, at the back of the skull. It dawned on us that here was the head not of Tadahira but of his brother and killer, the treacherous Yasuhira, unhappy last chief of the Ōshū Fujiwara. We knew this because Yoritomo had Yasuhira's head attached to the gates of his headquarters with an iron nail of 8 *sun* – that is, 24 centimetres long. Such a nail would produce exactly the wounds inflicted on the rice-box head.

'Although the chronicle *Azuma Kagami* tells us what happened to Yasuhira's head up to the point of its being mounted as a trophy, there is no record of what happened to it afterwards. For centuries, anyone who thought about such matters assumed the head was left on the gatepost until it had delivered its message and was then discarded as carrion. What we found suggested a different fate. Yasuhira's head was in good condition, and had been cleaned and anointed not long after death. It seems to have been spirited away from Genji headquarters soon after it was displayed. It then received the ministrations of priests at Chūson-ji. The stealth required to cheat Yoritomo of his trophy would explain the rice box, a singularly humdrum resting place for one of the wealthiest nobles in Japan. What you are looking at is a fine example of make-do camouflage, one that went undetected for over 700 years.

'So it was that, for the northern Fujiwara, the line ended in desperate improvisation, and a rice box. Not only was it strategically impossible to bury Yasuhira in anything more obviously like a casket, it was practically impossible too: Yoritomo was there to ensure that, in future, Hiraizumi's craftsmen worked only for him. But those who performed Yasuhira's secret obsequies did have one act still in their power, an act whose significance far outstripped any quantity of gold or pearls. As you have seen, the coffin of his father, Lord

Hidehira, contained seeds of plants that would be useful to him in the life to come. Importantly, one plant was missing from this cache – the lotus.

'The rice box that we found in the coffin compensated for that, or by its inclusion made the paradisiacal Fujiwara flora complete. For inside, all around Yasuhira's head, we found the seeds of the lotus. They had been sealed into the box just before it was laid to rest, 108 of them in total. This number intrigues me as the bells of Japanese temples toll that many times at the end of the year. With each tolling we are meant to free ourselves of *bonnō*, toxic emotions, amounting to 108 sloughings-off of harmful desires and malign traits. I feel there may be some correspondence between this ritual and the placing of that many seeds around the severed head of a man who had committed shameful acts and whose line, once great, had died with him. So the lotus seeds were there as a form of expiation. But they were also a form of spiritual time capsule. They contained a promise that Yasuhira and his entire lost family, the Ōshū Fujiwara, would achieve some sort of rebirth and, eventually, rehabilitation in the Pure Land.'

This plain box, it seemed to me, was the true treasure of Konjiki-dō. Had Christopher Columbus turned left instead of right, missed the Americas and found his golden hall in the north-east of Zipangu, he might just have lived long enough to fill his gaze, if not his boots, with gold galore. But he would never have known that the real booty was a stash of seeds beneath all the gilded glory and alongside a severed head in the humblest of boxes; let alone that these dull dry beans were thought to hold the secret of everlasting life. I took a tentative stab at doctrine:

'And this cycle of birth and death, transcendence and transfiguration, is that what you mean by Samsara? Were the seeds thought to ensure resurrection?'

'You could say that; but remember Samsara is a cycle. You must not confuse our idea of resurrection with the Christian one. Ours is a continuing process, a journey. If I understand correctly, the Christian's is an arrival at the ultimate destination. In much the same way, the Pure Land of the Amida Buddha is not the same as the Christian Paradise. It is something we can strive to realise in the here and now, the quest being the same thing as attainment. So these seeds also have an important practical message for us.'

'Which is?'

'*Plant me.*'

*　　*　　*

Haseki-Jūshoku led us out of the temple, his geta ringing down a steep cobbled lane. Soon screens of verdigris-stemmed bamboo surrounded us and cobbles became leaf litter. With each step we travelled deeper into the vaults of forest and further from the halls of gold and immaculate gardens that had grown up so incongruously in their midst almost a thousand years before. The Japanese nightingale had fallen silent, but the *Lotus Sutra* was still audible in the monks' chanting, now entirely disembodied. A strange mist-iness began to pervade the grove's under-canopy, and, before long, a dense hush broken only by the whisper of bamboo leaves and the rubbery creak of their fast-shooting canes. Just as this aura began to thicken into claustro-phobic darkness, the grove disgorged us upon a plain. It was a large area of terraces fringed by cherry trees and set like an emerald amid the forested slopes. Here and there, strips of turf had been cleared and bright spikes of newly planted rice punctuated the pools that had replaced the sod. This Far Eastern giveaway aside, at first sight the plain had every appearance of a meadow of the kind that one encounters in the mountains of Central Europe – fir-tree-girt, lush with grasses and wildflowers, not long ago released by snow and bracingly northern in feeling. Then I looked more closely.

The terracing was odd, not easily explained by rice cultivation alone. Below lay a sunken, broadly triangular area far too large to be a paddy-field. Above it was a mezzanine-like rampart and above that a further series of stepped levels which were perhaps the footprint of a lost building. In the centre of the larger expanse a small mound supported a clump of trees, mixed trees of great antiquity and value including hinoki cypress and chestnut – in other words, no forest relic but an ancient planting. As a feature this mound recalled the inland islands, hillocks isolated amid the sea of paddy and preserved as sites for sacred groves and Shinto shrines, which are one of Japan's greatest beauties. Next my eye was caught by a glittering indigo that stippled the margins of this pseudo-pasture. It was the blooms of kakit-subata, *Iris laevigata*, fast unfurling in the early-summer sun. In the Heian Period, this water iris was beloved of the Fujiwara clan, its flowers echoing the deep purple livery that was the prerogative of the imperial aristocracy. Now they danced before me, a haunting reminder of that clan's quietus in the mummified head of Yasuhira.

'You are searching for the story in these fields,' said Haseki-Jūshoku. 'Since the late 1960s, we have been excavating the areas around Chūson-ji, little by little, without wanting to destroy the harmony of the landscape. Not far from here, for example, we have found the remains of the main residences of the Fujiwara lords and the great red-lacquered palace known as Yanagi-no Gosho, "Willow Mansion". This was once the administrative centre of Hiraizumi. At the time of his downfall, Yasuhira set fire to Willow Mansion before fleeing north, rather than let it fall into Yoritomo's hands. Buried at sites like this one we have found various twelfth-century artefacts, including ceramics that were imported from Song Dynasty China. To the Ōshū Fujiwara, these would have been enormously valuable objects, far more precious than the gold that they had in such abundance. I am always amazed that such translucently thin porcelain should have survived the sacking of Hiraizumi, let alone the passage of 800 years.

'So you must picture a vista of massive and highly ornate buildings unfolding before you, intersected by rivers and streams and centred on gardens and lakes. We are standing on the footings of just such a building – in fact, one of the oldest and most beautiful. It dates from the time of Kiyohira, the first Fujiwara lord of Hiraizumi. The landforms you are trying to decipher are the remains of Jōdo-tei'en, "the Pure Land Garden". It was intended to represent the Buddhist Pure Land, the blessed future state of rebirth and redemption. On these terraces we believe Kiyohira created a series of small temples and pavilions. The large sunken area below them was an ornamental lake. In its centre was an island planted with trees – the mound you see today rising from the grasses. Among these trees are some whose seeds were included in the burials of the Fujiwara on account of their spiritual significance. In Hidehira's coffin, for example, we found seeds of the same kind of kuri [the chestnut *Castanea crenata*] that grows on the stranded island. Another of our visitors, the poet Bashō, explains its significance in *The Narrow Road to the Deep North*: "The written character for kuri is composed of two parts which mean *west* and *tree*. This betokens its association with the Amida Buddha's western paradise." Away from the island and around the lake itself there was a pebbled shore, perhaps fringed with irises. Within the shallows of the lake grew something else, to which I shall return. So what you see here is the ghost of a garden, a splendid garden in the true Fujiwara style made almost a millennium ago. But what you need to see is the garden we are making now.'

Planks lay across the marshy surface of what was once the Pure Land Garden. Between them, I could see rows of sunken buckets. As we came closer, their contents came into focus – the sovereign-sized leaves of juvenile lotuses bobbing on turbid water.

'These are Yasuhira's legacy,' said Haseki-Jūshoku. 'After the coffins and the head box were opened in 1950, Dr Ichirō Ōga was invited to study the plant remains. We allowed him to take some of the lotus seeds in the hope that he would germinate them. As you probably know, not long afterwards he made his sensational discovery at Kemigawa, the ancient lotus now known as Ōga-hasu. I am afraid that in the excitement he seems to have forgotten all about our seeds. When the doctor died in 1965, they were returned to Chūson-ji as hard and dry as they were when they left us. In the end Lord Yasuhira would have to wait another four decades until his lotus sprang into life again.

'By the early 1990s I had begun to take a close interest in these seeds and it was decided that two of them should be sent to Professor Tokiko Nagashima, a lotus expert who had studied under Ōga-sensei. In respect of what happened to Yasuhira's head post-mortem, her examination of the seeds was illuminating. Their shells indicated that very little putrefaction had taken place inside the rice tub – an initial spike of bacterial activity and then centuries of stasis. So the monks had done their job of mummifying well, as we had long suspected from the state of the head. But what we really wanted to hear was that the seeds were viable and that the last lord's lotus would flower again at Chūson-ji. Nagashima-sensei did not disappoint us. In May 1993, she succeeded in germinating one of them. This seedling she guarded and tended, dividing its rhizomes each year until finally, on 14 July 1998, the first flower bud appeared. Two weeks later it opened, a bloom 23 centimetres across. What you see around you are the offspring of that plant, the lotus that blossomed after 800 years of limbo in the tomb.'

It is difficult to press the Japanese on reincarnation, impertinent not just in the sense of rude, but also, and more significantly, in the sense of irrelevant. A literal belief in the transmigration of souls has long been a comfort of some schools of Buddhism. It always seems, however, to have run parallel with a more metaphorical view, nourished perhaps by the animism of Shinto, which underpinned Japanese attitudes to life as a whole and to living organisms in particular. It was in this spirit that Kiyohira, the first Fujiwara lord of the north, sought permission to restore Chūson-ji: he wished to memorialise all of the humans, creatures, plants and even the rocks of his war-torn domain. In so doing, he was aiming to ensure their rehabilitation and continuity.

Seen this way, reincarnation has a practical dimension in acts of veneration, restoration and conservation. This seemed to be Haseki-Jūshoku's attitude to Yasuhira's resurgence in the germination of the head-box lotus. To ask if anyone believed these plants were Yasuhira reborn would be to miss the point. If I understood correctly, that point was reincarnation's value as a prompt for empathy with fellow organisms. Metamorphoses represented phases in an infinite stream of variation whose components were linked in a vast web of symbiosis, all living things connected and driven by a single formative dynamic. This idea is as compelling for a twenty-first-century biologist as it was for a twelfth-century Buddhist. Yasuhira's lotus is an ideal beacon for this empathising spirit. If it helps to talk of it in terms of reincarnation, so be it.

One of the most attractive characteristics of the Japanese in conversation is their reluctance to rush into silences. Having led us through the long history of Chūson-ji and shared its secrets, the Chief Priest allowed complete calm to settle as we observed the lotuses, thriving but improbably exotic in their regained paradise of alpine meadow and pine-scented air. It fell to me to spoil the moment, to fill this special space or *Ma* with another impertinent query: 'These plants mostly appear to be the same, as you would expect if they were all clones of Yasuhira's one seedling; but what about those four tubs? Their leaves are larger and bluer. I hate to ask, but could there have been a mix-up?'

Haseki-Jūshoku smiled: 'We talked about the excavations that have been going on here. I told you that between 900 and 800 years ago this site was the shore of a large ornamental pool. But there has been no lake here since the fall of the Fujiwara, and no record of lotuses. In 2001 in the course of a dig, eight lotus seeds were discovered a metre beneath the soil surface just a little way from where you are standing. They were the remnants of the lotuses that once filled the margins of the Pure Land Garden lake, seeds dropped by their parents into the muddy darkness and consigned to potentially eternal sleep. Five of these seeds were given to Professor Nagashima who succeeded in germinating them. The first flowered only last summer in early August 2006. So your visit is well-timed.

'As you noticed, our Pure Land Garden lotus is quite unlike the head-box lotus. We have called it Ōike-hasu, "big pool lotus", whereas plants that come from the seeds buried with Yasuhira's head are known as Chūson-ji-hasu. Both bear some resemblance to other ancient lotuses such as Ōga-hasu, and they have been identified as selections of Wa-hasu, meaning wild Japanese lotus rather than varieties imported from China. Yet both these plants are unique in their shape, scent and colour. Centuries ago they may have been abundant here in Hiraizumi and possibly elsewhere, but there is nothing exactly like them anywhere else today – apart, that is, from the offspring of Yasuhira's lotus which Chūson-ji has donated to other temples belonging to our sect in the past few years.'

Opposite the Pure Land Garden site, a cultivated plot ran down from Kongō-in, the temple where Haseki-Jūshoku presides. In spirit it was far from the clipped and raked perfection, the masterly minimalism of the inner temple gardens. All around were the rank regeneration of grasses and the remains of last summer's mowing in the form of piles of straw which, not long ago, had protected the crowns of more tender specimens. Here all was profusion and productivity, and a hectic mixture of plants. Some were decorous niwaki, artfully trained and pruned evergreen shrubs and small trees. Others were informal incomers from the surrounding forest, curtains of golden bamboo, the massive-leaved *Magnolia obovata* and the delicate snow-white bells of *Styrax japonicus*. Others again were Japanese kitchen garden favourites, among them *Zingiber mioga*, the ginger whose young inflorescences, chopped and soused in soy sauce, are such an adornment to rice. Grandest of all of these domestic plants was the non-edible banana, *Musa basjoo*, sprouting with visible speed in the soaring heat.

In 1830, shortly after he was banished from Japan for espionage, the botanist and physician Philipp Franz von Siebold coined the scientific epithet for this tree-like herbaceous perennial – *basjoo* – from its Japanese vernacular name *bashō*. The world's botanists and gardeners have known it by this name ever since. Around 150 years earlier, Japan's greatest poet had adopted his nom de plume from this same plant. It happened, he relates, sometime after 1680, the year in which one of his students presented him with an offset of the banana as a gift. Planted in the garden of his cottage in Fukagawa, it grew apace and stole the poet's heart:

> *The leaves of bashō are big enough to cover a koto [Japanese harp]. When gales thrash them, they conjure in my imagination the injured tail of a phoenix, and when they are torn they resemble a green fan frayed by the wind. Although bashō does produce flowers, they are unlike other flowers in that they are not in the least attractive. Its stout trunk is immune to the axe for the simple reason that it is of no value as timber. Despite all of which, I love this plant. No – I love it precisely because it is so useless. I love to sit beneath it and to listen to the wind and rain battering its great big leaves.*

313

Such was his fondness for the banana that the poet gave its name first to his cottage, Bashō-an, and then to himself, Matsuo Bashō. Amid the boreal slopes of Chūson-ji, dark with the silhouettes of sentry-like sugi trees, its giant green paddles were a curious sight. They recalled Pierre Loti's comment that Japan's greenery and landscapes suggest a tropical country that has been pushed north yet has somehow retained its essential exoticism. Bashō, whose spirit pervades Hiraizumi nearly as much as those of the vanquished Fujiwara, would have been delighted to see his signature plant now flourishing at the remotest point of his northern journey, a place of desolation no longer.

But the garden of Kongō-in contained plants that were even more exotic and suggestive of rebirth than Bashō's banana. It was here that the full-grown specimens of Chūson-ji's two famous revenants resided. In large tubs sat Ōike-hasu, the Pure Land Garden lotus that flowered in 2006 after 800 years of subterranean slumber following the fall of Hiraizumi and the decline of gilded capital and paradise gardens into ruin and rough grassland. The 'big pool lotus' was a big plant with celadon leaves over 50 centimetres across. Hovering above them, its flowers were of a lilac-pink so pale as to be luminous save for a carmine trim. At a distance they had an aura that recalled the ancient pan-Asiatic legend of the blue lotus. This opalescent glow revealed to me why many lotuses depicted in illuminated manuscripts of the Heian Period were lavender, a curious colour explained by neither the lack nor the fading of proper pink pigment. It was perhaps plants like these and not some mythical figment that those mediaeval artists strove to paint.

Nearby, a small pond brimmed with the broad blushing leaves of Chūson-ji-hasu. Among them arose torch-like blooms of a deep crimson faintly combed with pale rose. As the morning progressed and the flowers pulsed, peaked and perished, so their perfume became heavier and more complex, transporting us from fresh-scented Pure Land to incense-clouded temple. Anthropomorphism is hard to avoid with an organism that has been so intimately associated with human themes and questions for so long. Chūson-ji-hasu is a botanical and horticultural prodigy, a thriving colony of a plant that sprang to life from seeds stored for 804 years in conditions that modern science would scarcely consider optimal. This should be marvel enough, and yet the temptation to remember Yasuhira, whose severed head the seeds accompanied for most of that time, proved irresistible. This was his lotus, the last lord's bid for posthumous rehabilitation, and the plant somehow summoned him forth – more sensuous and less sublime than Ōike-hasu and more than a little sanguinary, but standing proud and now with neck intact. The priests who salvaged and salved Yasuhira's head chose well when they picked this patrician plant with which to bury it. But then for the last of the line, for the man who had greatest need of redemption, what could they have chosen apart from a lotus?

Despite the brilliance of the morning, thunder echoed through the hills of Hiraizumi, reminding us that the rainy season was at hand. The spell of Chūson-ji-hasu, its hypnotically beautiful flowers and head-spinning scent, was broken only by the first fat raindrops as they drummed and danced upon its leaves like quicksilver. Moments later the deluge was upon us and our audience was at an end. Before we parted, I had one last question for the Chief Priest, something so bathetic as to be indecent, but which I had to ask nonetheless.

'What happened to Yasuhira afterwards?'

'If you mean his head, we reburied it with all due ceremony alongside his father and forefathers. If you mean Yasuhira himself, just look at the flowers around you. They are evidence of his, or anybody's, or any living thing's engagement in the great cycle of being and becoming. These, you might say, are Samsara.'

With a final smile and courtly bow, Haseki-Jūshoku returned to his temple. We lingered to watch lotuses through the downpour, taking shelter with the shade of the poet beneath the rattling bashō tree.

Notes on Sources and Further Reading

The Lotus Quest is rife with quotations from non-English sources. Unless stated otherwise, these translations have been made by me, or by Yoko Otsuki in the case of Japanese texts. Where they exist, I refer to published English-language editions of these works in the bibliographical notes that follow.

Prologue: In the Strong Room

Chapter 1. The life of Carl Linnaeus and his achievements as a reformer of biological nomenclature are vividly described in *Linnaeus – The Compleat Naturalist* by Wilfrid Blunt with an introduction by William T. Stearn (Frances Lincoln, new edition 2001). I discuss the role De Hartekamp played in his development in *Clifford's Banana: How Natural History was made in a Garden*, in *The Linnaean Collections* (*The Linnean*, special issue number 7, Wiley-Blackwell, 2007).

Astonishingly, there is no one comprehensive English-language study of the sacred lotus in both its botanical and cultural incarnations. Among many Japanese works on *Nelumbo*, my favourite remains *Hasu* (Hōsei University Press, fifth printing 2002), a compact but wonderfully rich book by the great lotus expert Yūji Sakamoto.

I. A Celestial Plant

Chapter 2. The peculiar attributes of *Nelumbo* and its newly allotted position in the scheme of life are summarised by David Mabberley in *The Plant Book* (Cambridge University Press, new edition 2008). The details of the lotus's anatomy and life cycle form the basis of over a half-century's worth of research articles in Japanese and English by 'Dr Lotus', Ichirō Ōga. In 1979, Saishū to Shiiku no Kai, 'The Collecting and Breeding Association', reprinted these in a single volume titled *Rigaku Hakase Ōga Ichirō Kanaku Ronbun Senshū* ('Collected Scientific Papers of Dr Ichirō Ōga'). I have drawn on this collection in describing the biology of *Nelumbo* and in my account of Ōga's career and the Kemigawa discovery. The present-day pioneer of *Nelumbo* studies is Dr Jane Shen-Miller. She and her colleagues at the University of California, Los Angeles, have unlocked the lotus seed's secrets in a series of ground-breaking publications. See Shen-Miller et al., *Exceptional Seed Longevity and Robust Growth: Ancient Sacred Lotus from China* (*American Journal of Botany*, vol. 82, no. 11, November 1995).

Medicinal Plants of the World by Ben-Erik van Wyk and Michael Wink (Timber Press, 2004) contains a useful digest of the biochemical properties and therapeutic uses of *Nelumbo*. The Rajasthan lotus contraceptive study I cite is Anju Mutreja et al., *Effect of* Nelumbo nucifera *seeds on the reproductive organs of female rats* (*Iranian Journal of Reproductive Medicine*, vol. 6, no. 1, 2008). The lotus's impact on the human nervous system is discussed by S. K. Bhattacharya et al. in *Psychopharmacological Studies on Nuciferine and its Hofmann degradation product Atherosperminine* (*Psychopharmacology*, 59 (1), 1978). Although I do not agree with his diagnosis, the link between the lotus and Soma, the magical plant of Hindu scripture, is fascinatingly made by Andrew McDonald in *A Botanical Perspective on the Identity of Soma* (Nelumbo nucifera Gaertn.) *Based on Scriptural and Iconographic Records* (*Economic Botany*, vol. 58, December 2004). For a less controversial, but still startling, record of the uses humans have found for lotuses, see the entry for *Nelumbo lutea* in *Native American Ethnobotany* by Daniel E. Moerman (Timber Press, 1998).

Chapters 3–4. Alexander the Great's identification of *Nelumbo* on the banks of the River Acesines and the consequences that flowed from it are described by Strabo (*Geography* XV, i, 25), and by Arrian (*Anabasis of Alexander* VI, i, 2–6). For both the primary source was Nearchus who became admiral of the very fleet that resulted from this episode. The famous description of the Egyptian bean or kyamos (*Nelumbo nucifera*) by Theophrastus is at Book IV, viii, 7–8 of his *Enquiry into Plants* – volume 1, pp. 350–353 in Sir Arthur Hort's Loeb Classical Library edition. The description is immediately followed by Theophrastus's account of the Nile waterlilies (*Nymphaea*) then commonly known as 'lōtos'. For the derivations of kyamos and lōtos, see *Dictionnaire Étymologique de la Langue Grecque* by Pierre Chantraine (Paris, 1999).

The myth of Lotis/Lotus appears in Book Nine of Ovid's *Metamorphoses* (ix, lines 346 to 377 in the 1998 Oxford World's Classics translation by A. D. Melville). Homer's Lotophagoi appear in Book Nine of *The Odyssey* (ix, lines 92 to 117 in the 2004 Penguin Classics translation by Robert Fagles). Pliny's discussions of *Nelumbo* under its various Greek and Roman names, and of the many plants masquerading as lotuses, can be found in books XIII, chapter 32; XVIII, chapter 30; XXI, chapter 51, chapter 102; XXII, chapter 27 of his *Natural History*, translated by H. Rackham, W. H. S. Jones and D. E. Eichholz (Loeb Classical Library, Harvard University Press and William Heinemann Ltd). Columella's tips on creating lotus ponds appear at VIII, xv, 4 of his *De Re Rustica*, translated as *On Agriculture* by E. S. Forster and Edward H. Heffner in the Loeb Classical Library. For *Nelumbo* in Roman gardens and decorative arts see *The Natural History of Pompeii*, edited by Wilhelmina Feemster Jashemski and Frederick G. Meyer (Cambridge University Press, 2002).

Herodotus describes *Nelumbo nucifera* in the Nile, and Egypt's native *Nymphaea* species, in *Histories*, II, 92, in A. D. Godley's translation for the Loeb Classical Library. Strabo's description of the Alexandrian lotus-land of Lake Mareotis is at XVII, i, 14–15 of his *Geography*, translated by Horace Leonard Jones for the Loeb Classical Library. Horace refers to the ciborium, the lotus receptacle beaker, in his poem on the return of Pompeius (*Odes* II, 7). The historian Phylarchus's account of the miraculous appearance of *Nelumbo* in the kingdom of Alexander II of Epirus is in Book 1 of *Deipnosophistae* by Athenaeus – volume I, page 317 of *The Deipnosophists*, the translation by C. B. Gulick for the Loeb Classical Library. A general discussion of lotuses precedes it, mentioning their various names and uses.

For more on the Praeneste mosaic, see *The Nile Mosaic of Palestrina: Early Evidence of Egyptian Religion in Italy* by P. G. P. Meyboom (Brill, 1994), and *Mosaics of the Greek and Roman World* by Katherine M. D. Dunbabin (Cambridge University Press, 1999). The apotheosis of Antinous, Emperor Hadrian's lover, in the lotus Antinoeios is described in Book 7 of *Deipnosophistae* by Athenaeus – volume III, p. 127 of *The Deipnosophists*, the translation by C. B. Gulick for the Loeb Classical Library. The rebuke to Socrates is in Plato's *Phaedrus* (275.B).

Chapter 5. The source for the story of the persecution of Pythagoreans by Dionysius II, as for so many other aspects of the first philosopher's teachings and disciples, is Iamblichus. In her translation of Iamblichus's *On the Pythagorean Life* (Liverpool University Press, 1989), Gillian Clark comments on the various interpretations placed on Pythagoras's bean taboo. I favour the idea that the philosopher's kyamos was the lotus; but the case for its having been the fava bean and for the prohibition's arising from a fear of the blood disorder Favism is well put by John Meletis and Kostas Konstantopoulos in *Favism – from the 'avoid fava beans' of Pythagoras to the present* (*Haema* 7(1): 17–21, 2004). Many Croton (Kroton) coins from the Pythagorean period are in private hands. The easiest way to see and compare them is at http://www.wildwinds.com/coins/greece/bruttium/kroton/t.html. A good example of the lotus receptacle-like lebes with dropping seed is illustrated on this website under the catalogue number SNGANS 259ff.

Along with numerous ideas adopted from the Pythagoreans, Plato's description of man as 'a celestial plant' appears in his *Timaeus* (at 90.A or page 245 of R. G. Bury's edition for the Loeb Classical Library). Plutarch focuses on the lotus (sometimes *melilōtos*, 'honey lotus') in *Isis and Osiris* (at 355.11, 356.14, 366.38, and 377.66, or pages 29, 39, 93 and 153 of volume 5 of the 1986 Loeb edition of Plutarch's *Moralia* translated by Frank Cole Babbitt). He returns to the lotus, debunking the religious superstitions around it but elevating the plant as a Plato-style symbol of human transcendence in *The Oracles at Delphi* (pp. 289–291 of volume 5 of Babbitt's translation of *Moralia* for the Loeb Classical Library). For Iamblichus on the lotus, see *Iamblique: Les Mystères d'Égypte*, the original Greek text with parallel French translation by Édouard des Places (Paris, Société d'Éditions 'Les Belles Lettres', 1966). For a curious contrast, see Thomas Taylor's 1821 translation (*Iamblichus on the Mysteries of the Egyptians, Chaldeans and Assyrians*), a fascinating instance of the Georgian period's new interest in antiquities converging with a romantic striving for the pantheistic, or polytheistic, sublime.

Chapter 6. Although William H. Goodyear's analysis is questionable today, his 1891 work, *The Grammar of the Lotus: a New History of Classic Ornament as a Development of Sun Worship* (New York, Dodd, Mead & Co.), is unsurpassed as a treasury of lotus iconography from the Ancient Middle East and Classical World. For the lotus as a symbol of kingship in Mesopotamia and the etymology of the name Hammurabi, see L. Austine Waddell, *Makers of Civilization in Race and History* (1929, reissued by Kessinger Publishing, 2004). Now in the University of Pennsylvania Museum, plaques from Palestine depicting the Phoenician goddess Astarte holding lotuses can be seen on Dr John Abercrombie's website on the material culture of the Ancient Canaanites, Israelites and Related Peoples – http://www.bu.edu/anep/LB.html#Figurines. The St Just Bull now resides at the Royal Cornwall Museum, Truro.

Chapter 7. First published in 1931, and reissued as a facsimile by Asian Educational Services, India, in 1996, John Marshall's *Mohenjo-Daro and the Indus Civilization* remains the richest resource for the remarkable culture revealed by his excavations between 1922 and 1927. Similarities or continuities between the eight-petalled lotus iconography of Mesopotamia and that of the Indus Valley and later Indian civilisations are discussed by Thomas McEvilley in *The Shape of Ancient Thought: Comparative Studies in Greek and Indian Philosophies* (Allworth Communications Inc., 2002). The evolution of Lakshmi, the Hindu lotus goddess, is lovingly described by Heinrich Robert Zimmer in *Myths and Symbols in Indian Art and Civilization* (ed. Joseph Campbell, Princeton University Press, 1972). For the Vedic scriptures see *Upanisads* translated by Patrick Olivelle (Oxford World's Classics, Oxford University Press, 1996).

II. Western Dreamers

Chapter 8. A description of St Mary's, Iffley, can be found in *Oxfordshire* by Jennifer Sherwood and Nikolaus Pevsner (Yale University Press, 1974). My Masonic source was *The Encyclopedia of Freemasonry and its Kindred Sciences* by Albert G. Mackey

(The Masonic History Co., London and New York, 1918). His Holiness the Dalai Lama's reflections on the mantra *Om mani padme hum* can be found at http://www.tibet.com/Buddhism/om-mantra.html.

Chapters 9–10. Herbert Ponting's *In Lotus-Land Japan* was published by Macmillan in 1910. The two works by Pierre Loti, *Madame Chrysanthème* (1887) and *Japoneries d'Automne* (1889), were recently republished side by side in a facsimile of the collected edition of 1893 – *Oeuvres Complètes de Pierre Loti: Tome 4* (Elibron Classics Series, Adamant Media Corporation, 2005). Kegan Paul published Laura Ensor's English translation *Japan: Madame Chrysanthemum* in 1985 and again in 2002. Manet's borrowing of Hokusai's drawing for Mallarmé's 'lotus' is discussed and illustrated by Anne Coffin Hanson in her review of *The Drawings of Édouard Manet* by Alain De Leiris. This appears in *The Art Bulletin*, volume LIII, number 4, December 1971. Lafcadio Hearn's 1894 essay 'In a Japanese Garden' can be found in *Lafcadio Hearn's Japan*, selected writings edited by Donald Richie (Charles E. Tuttle Publishing, 1997). Alfred Parsons's articles and paintings for *Harper's Magazine* were published in book form as *Notes in Japan* by Osgood, McIlvaine & Co. in 1896.

For a general introduction to nineteenth-century British travels in Japan see Hugh Cortazzi's excellent *Victorians in Japan: In and Around the Treaty Ports* (Athlone Press, 1987). Josiah Conder illustrates the elaborate, time past and time present lotus flower arrangement in his *The Flowers of Japan and the Art of Floral Arrangement* (Tokyo, 1891). Francis Piggott's Shirakawa lotus epiphany is described in his *The Garden of Japan: a year's diary of its flowers* (George Allen, 1892). Two recent publications give a pulpit to two of the most important voices among these Victorian visitors. The first is *Kipling's Japan: Collected Writings* edited by Hugh Cortazzi and George Webb (Athlone Press, 1988). The second is *The Diary of Charles Holme's 1889 Visit to Japan and North America* with Mrs Lasenby Liberty's *Japan: A Pictorial Record* edited by Toni Huberman, Sonia Ashmore and Yasuko Suga (Global Oriental, 2008). Both these texts were of value to me in forming a picture of nineteenth-century Kamakura as well as in providing background to British Japonisme. Ella and Florence Du Cane's *The Flowers and Gardens of Japan* was published by Adam & Charles Black in 1908.

The extraordinary frogs-and-lotuses Christmas card that Yamakawa Rinpo designed for Arthur Silver in 1890 is reproduced as item 210 of the catalogue *Japan and Britain: An Aesthetic Dialogue 1850–1930* (Lund Humphries, London, in association with Barbican Art Gallery and Setagaya Art Museum, 1991). Other Anglo-Japanese lotus designs appear in this publication, such as the trade card for the art materials supplier Rottmann & Co. Ayako Ono's *Japonisme in Britain* (RoutledgeCurzon, 2003) is invaluable – not least for its discussion of E. A. Hornel's 1894 painting *The Lotus Flower*. I have also used *Japonisme in Art: An International Symposium* (Kodansha International, 2001), Gabriel and Yvonne Weisberg's *Japonisme – An Annotated Bibliography* (Garland Publishing, 1990), and Toshio Watanabe's *High Victorian Japonisme* (Peter Lang, 1991).

Chapter 11. The two fullest accounts of the life and immediate impact of Ernest Fenollosa are *Fenollosa and His Circle* by Van Wyck Brooks (E. P. Dutton & Co., 1962), and *Fenollosa: The Far East and American Culture* by Lawrence W. Chisolm (Yale University Press, 1963). The poem *Legend of the Lotos* is in *Out of the Nest – A Flight of Verses* by Mary McNeil Fenollosa (Gay and Bird, 1899).

III. Seeds of Eternity

Chapters 12–14. Researchers at Tokyo University have shown that Ōga's lotus is genetically close but not identical to other ancient lotus seeds excavated in Japan and North-east China and that these plants form a group that diverges from *Nelumbo nucifera* populations elsewhere in Asia and the Pacific. In other words, these ancient lotuses are distinctive and confined to the Far East, and comparison between them and other strains of *Nelumbo nucifera* appears to reveal a species in the process of evolutionary diversification. See Akira Kanazawa et al., *Phylogenetic relationships in the genus* Nelumbo *based on polymorphism and quantitative variations in mitochondrial DNA* (*Genes and Genetic Systems*, vol. 73, number 1, 1998).

The Sound of the Mountain, Edward G. Seidensticker's beautiful translation of Yasunari Kawabata's novel *Yama no Oto*, is published by Vintage International (Vintage Books, Random House Inc., 1996). The honorary or ersatz Japanese lotuses to which Taeko-san refers are illustrated in the two-volume *Makino's Illustrated Flora in Colour* by Tomitaro Makino, edited by Masaji Honda (Hokuryukan Co., 1986), and in *Endangered Plants of Japan: A Florilegium* by Hideaki Ohba with Yoko Otsuki and Mark Griffiths (Aboc-sha Publishing, 2004).

Chapter 15. *Ancient Jomon of Japan* by Junko Habu (Cambridge University Press, 2004) is an ideal guide to this remote and fascinating culture. The Jōmon contribution to Japan's present-day population is discussed by Luigi Luca Cavalli-Sforza, Paolo Menozzi and Alberto Piazza in *The History and Geography of Human Genes* (Princeton University Press, 1994). *Ethnogenesis and craniofacial change in Japan from the perspective of nonmetric traits*, by Nancy Ossenberg, Yukio Dodo, Tomoko Maeda and Yoshinori Kawakubo (*Anthropological Science*, vol. 114, 2006), likewise supports the dual ancestry hypothesis of the modern Japanese (Jōmon plus Yayoi) – important in the context of *The Lotus Quest* in that it implies a continuation and adaptation of aboriginal culture.

Chapter 16. The best-known English translation of *Nihon Shoki*, the annals of ancient Japan, is *Nihongi: Chronicles of Japan from the Earliest Times to AD 697* by W. G. Aston (Tuttle Publishing, new edition, 2005). The excitement surrounding the discovery of what was thought to be Queen Himiko's tomb is described by Walter Edwards in *Mirrors to Japanese History* (*Archaeology – Journal of the Archaeological Institute of America*, vol. 51, iii, 1998). In the journal of the Japanese Archaeological Association, *Nihon*

Kōkogaku (no. 8, October 1999), Toshikatsu Nishikawa concludes that these bronze mirrors are unlike Chinese models and therefore Japanese or Japan-influenced.

Kojiki, the seventh-century annals in which Emperor Yūryaku's exploits appear, was translated as *Kojiki: Records of Ancient Matters* by Basil Hall Chamberlain (Tuttle Publishing, new edition, 2005). There are two popular translations of the great anthology *Man'yōshū: 1000 Poems from the Man'yōshū: The Complete Nippon Gakujutsu Shinkokai Translation* (Dover Publications, 2005), and *Ten Thousand Leaves: Love Poems from the Manyoshu* translated by Harold Wright (Overlook Press, 1991).

Chapters 17–18. My English *Lotus Sutra* of choice is the translation by Burton Watson (Columbia University Press, 1993). Its introduction is outstanding, as is the opulence of its style. More important for the purposes of *The Lotus Quest*, it was produced in collaboration with Japanese Buddhists and accords with their conception of this scripture. The best general introduction to Buddhism and its cultural impact is *The World of Buddhism* edited by Heinz Bechert and Richard Gombrich (Thames & Hudson, 1984, reprinted 2002). Chapter 9, by Robert K. Heinemann on Buddhism in Japan, is a marvel of cogency and compression.

Technical details of the making of Empress Shōtoku's Million Towers can be found in *Papermaking – The History and Technique of an Ancient Craft* by Dard Hunter (Courier Dover Publications, second edition 1978). The translation of Murasaki Shikibu's *Tale of Genji* is by Edward G. Seidensticker (Everyman's Library, 1992). Ivan Morris's translation of *The Pillow Book of Sei Shōnagon* perfectly captures her strange blend of seductiveness and fastidiousness (Penguin Classics, 1971).

Chapters 19–22. Ōgai Mori's novel *Gan* was translated as *The Wild Geese* by Ochiai Kingo and Sanford Goldstein (Tuttle Publishing 1959, reprinted 2000). The finest and, indeed, only comprehensive English-language work on *Nihon no dento engei* ('Traditional Japanese Horticulture') is *Illustrated History and Principle of the Traditional Floriculture in Japan* by Seizo Kashioka and Mikinori Ogisu (Aboc-sha Publishing, 1997). For the political structure of the Tokugawa Shogunate, see Conrad Totman's *Politics in the Tokugawa Bakufu, 1600–1843* (Harvard University Press, 1967). For Edo Period Neo-Confucianism, see *The Motivation of Confucian Orthodoxy in Tokugawa Japan* by Robert L. Backus in *Harvard Journal of Asiatic Studies*, vol. 39, no. 2 (1979).

Sadanobu Matsudaira lampooned himself and his peers in a sketch of a daimyō's life. See *Portrait of a Daimyo: Comical Fiction by Matsudaira Sadanobu* by Iwasaki Haruko in *Monumenta Nipponica*, vol. 38, no. 1 (1983). An English translation of Matsudaira's satire *Daimyō Katagi* is in the same volume. For a more sedate portrait of the Edo Period's lotus king, see *Charismatic Bureaucrat: A political biography of Matsudaira Sadanobu, 1758–1829* by Herman Ooms (University of Chicago Press, 1975).

IV. Tales of Genji

Chapters 23–25. The statuary of the Hall of the Lotus King and other mediaeval Japanese kannon are discussed in *Kannon – Divine Compassion: Early Buddhist Art from Japan*, a magnificent catalogue published by the Museum Rietberg Zürich in 2007. In addition to court and temple records and other primary documents, our knowledge of the struggle between the Heike (Taira) and Genji (Minamoto) clans has been shaped by *Heike Monogatari*, a multi-authored and essentially anonymous bardic epic that was transmitted orally at first, starting soon after these conflicts occurred, and then gradually refined and committed to paper in the thirteenth and fourteenth centuries. There are now two excellent English translations of this heroic narrative – Helen Craig McCullough's *The Tale of the Heike* (Stanford University Press, 1988); and *The Tale of the Heike* abridged and translated by Burton Watson and Haruo Shirane (Columbia University Press, 2006).

Another mediaeval epic is *Soga Monogatari*, the tale of a family feud that took place during Yoritomo's shogunate. Like *The Tale of the Heike*, it originated in oral tradition and was based on real events. It is rich in episodes and details which are borne out by official records of the time, even though they appear to have all the colour of fiction. In one such episode Masako trades a kimono for her sister's unwelcome dream of Yoritomo. A modern Japanese edition of *Soga Monogatari* by Shūhei Hayama was published by Bensei Shuppan in 2005.

Yoritomo and Masako left nothing to the vicissitudes of spoken word and quasi-fiction. At their command, the Bakufu kept detailed and frank records covering the period from the Genji uprising to the fall of the Kamakura Shogunate. From the thirteenth century onwards, these reports, diaries and accounts were consolidated as a single sequence of dated bulletins, known as *Azuma Kagami*, 'The Mirror of the East'. Although this document took shape decades after Yoritomo's death, those parts of it that deal with him can be regarded as contemporary with him since they were first set down in his lifetime and on his instructions. This is the principal source for my chapters on the rise of the Kamakura Bakufu, the marriage of Yoritomo and Masako, the creation of the Tsurugaoka Hachiman Shrine and of the Genpei lotus ponds, Emperor Go-Shirakawa's machinations, and the fall of the Northern Fujiwara. I have drawn on various versions of *Azuma Kagami*. Among them are two recent renderings into modern Japanese – *Kokushi Taikei Azumakagami*, vols 1–4, edited by Katsumi Kuroita and Kokushi Taikei (Henshū Kai: Yoshikawa Kōbunkan, 1972, 1974); and *Gendaigoyaku Azumakagami*, vols 1–5 with another 11 in preparation, edited by Humihiko Gomi and Kazuto Hongō (Yoshikawa Kōbunkan, 2007 onwards).

Chapter 27. Among many translations of Matsuo Bashō's *Oku no Hosomichi*, the two I keep by me are *The Narrow Road to the Deep North and other travel sketches*, translated by Nobuyuki Yuasa (Penguin Classics, 1966), and *The Narrow Road to Oku*, translated by Donald Keene (Kodansha International, 1996). They are markedly different – the first low-key and simple, the second polished and with parallel Japanese text and illustrations by Miyata Masayuki. Each, however, comes close to Bashō's original text where *sabi* and sophistication coexist. The lotus poems I cite do not occur in *Oku no Hosomichi*. Their Japanese originals can be found online in a collected works and concordance created by the Bashō Memorial Museum in the poet's birthplace Iga City in Mi'e Prefecture: http://www.ict.ne.jp/~basho/index.html.

Chapters 29–31. My main sources here were *Azuma Kagami* (see chapters 23–25 above), *Mutsu Waki*, the early mediaeval 'Chronicle of the North' (most recently issued in 2006 by the publishers Gendai Shichō Shinsha in a modern Japanese edition by Masa'aki Kajiwara), and twelfth-century records and correspondence held at Chūson-ji. The quotation from chapter 24 of the *Lotus Sutra* is from Burton Watson's translation (see notes to chapters 17–18). Marco Polo's observations on Chipangu – Japan – are in Volume II, Book 3, chapter 2 of *The Travels of Marco Polo – The Complete Yule–Cordier Edition* (Dover Publications, 1992).

Chapter 32. In *Mysticism: Christian and Buddhist* (1957, republished by Routledge 2002), the great Zen scholar D. T. Suzuki gives something of the flavour of the metaphorical attitude to reincarnation I encountered in Japan. What is striking is that this Creator-less, dynamic, empathising and almost evolutionary view of life has been a pattern of thought in Japan since soon after Buddhism's arrival there. Here Suzuki discusses *trisna*, the 'thirst' that compels beings into existence, and which he is careful to dissociate from any supernatural ordainer. Like so many in this nation of Nature-worshippers, he seizes on the lotus as a prompt for identification between *Homo sapiens* and other species:

> . . . *when we are restless, we have turned into the monkey; when we can imagine ourselves free from guilt, we bloom as the lotus or as the morning glory in the summer dawn, and so on. The whole universe depicts itself in human consciousness. That is to say, our daily life is an epitome of an indefinitely long career of transmigration . . .*
>
> *The stars are shining brightly, wistfully twinkling in a clear autumnal night; the lotus flowers bloom in the early summer morning even before the sun rises; when the spring comes, all the dead trees vie with one another to shoot out their fresh green leaves, waking up from a long winter sleep – do we not see here also some of our human trisna asserting itself?*
>
> *I do not know whether ultimate reality is one or two or three or many more, but I feel that one trisna, infinitely diversified and diversifiable, expresses itself making up this world of ours. As trisna is subject to infinite diversifications, it can take infinitely variable forms. It is trisna, therefore, that determines form and structure. This is what is given to our consciousness, and our consciousness is the last word, we cannot go any further.*

Index

Index

Index

Tang Dynasty 185–6, 186
Tankei 217
Tanuma, Okitsugu 198, 199
Tao Yuan-ming (or Tao Qian) 185
Taoism 185
Taratti 3
Tebtunis 43
Tendai Sect 103, 104, 281, 282, 292, 301
Tendai-Hokke sect 169–70
Tennyson, Alfred 32–3, 79, 80, 81, 84
Terra Nova 78, 79
Theophrastus (Tyrtamos) 25–8, 30, 35, 47, 62
Theosophy 105
Thesprotia 36
Thomas, Dylan 272
Thoreau, Henry David 103
Thrace 35
Three Kingdom Period (China) 155
Thujopsis dolabrata 305
Thyamis (or Kalamas) River 36
Tibet 11
T'ien-t'ai (see also Tendai Sect) 169
Tiffany, Louis Comfort 96–7
Tiffany Studios 83, 96
Tigris 52, 54
Timaeus (Plato) 49–50, 51
Time magazine 117, 126, 128
Timycha 47
Toba, Emperor 294
Tōdai Temple (Tōdai-ji) 164, 167
Tōhoku 244
Tōhoku Expressway 193–6
Tokihito, Prince *see* Antoku, Emperor
Tokimasa Hōjō 223–6
Tokugawa Shogunate 175, 179–83, 186–7, 198, 206, 231 (see also Ieyasu, Iemitsu, Hidetada and Ienari Tokugawa)
Tokuko, Dowager Empress 233
Tokyo 90, 91, 92, 97, 142, 174, 178, 179, 194, 237
Tokyo Fine Arts School 103, 107
Tokyo Imperial Museum 103
Tokyo National Museum 200
Tokyo University 100, 114, 120, 121, 177
Tokyo University Experimental Agricultural Station and Public Welfare Farm, Kemigawa 114, 120, 123, 125

Tōnen (Tokyo Metropolitan Fuel and Forestry Industrial Association) 114, 141
Torone 35
Torreya nucifera 141, 149, 306
Tournefort, Joseph Pitton de 3, 5
Toyoda, Kiyonobu 205–6
Tricyrtis 266
Trifolium fragiferum 30
Trigonella foenum-graecum 30
Tsukimi-zaka (The Moon View Approach) 290
Tsunekiyo Fujiwara 279–80
Tsunemoto *see* Minamoto no Tsunemoto
Tsurugaoka Hachiman Shrine, Kamakura (Tsurugaoka Hachiman-gū) 229, 230, 241–3, 283
Tsurugi Lake 163
Tunisia 32
Turkey 38, 61
Tyrtamos *see* Theophrastus

Uchinuma (lake, Miyagi Prefecture) 269–70
Udaipur 20
Ueno Park, Tokyo 174–9
Ukiyo-e 101
ume (*Prunus mume*, Japanese plum) 191, 293, 306
University of California, Berkeley 117
University of Chicago 117
unohana (*Spiraea nipponica*) 276
Upper Cretaceous Period 12
Ur 57, 58
Uruk 54
urushi (the lacquer tree *Rhus verniciflua*) 147, 306
Utsunomiya Castle 206
Utsunomiya Lotus Pond Revival Committee 208
Utsunomiya, Tochigi Prefecture 206–7, 208

Vairocana 163–4, 167
Varieties of Religious Experience: A Study in Human Nature, The (W. James) 105
Vespasian, Emperor 31
Vicia faba 28, 45, 46, 50
Vishnu 66–7
Vitis coignetiae 276

337